Erotic Citizens

ELIZABETH DILL

Erotic Citizens

SEX AND THE EMBODIED SUBJECT
IN THE ANTEBELLUM NOVEL

UNIVERSITY OF VIRGINIA PRESS
Charlottesville and London

University of Virginia Press
© 2019 by the Rector and Visitors of the University of Virginia
All rights reserved
Printed in the United States of America on acid-free paper

First published 2019

1 3 5 7 9 8 6 4 2

Library of Congress Cataloging-in-Publication Data
Names: Dill, Elizabeth, author.
Title: Erotic citizens : sex and the embodied subject in the antebellum novel / Elizabeth Dill.
Description: Charlottesville : University of Virginia Press, 2019. |
Includes bibliographical references and index.
Identifiers: LCCN 2019027079 (print) | LCCN 2019027080 (ebook) | ISBN 9780813943374 (hardback) | ISBN 9780813943398 (paperback) | ISBN 9780813943381 (ebook)
Subjects: LCSH: Sex in literature. | Sex customs in literature. | American fiction—18th century—History and criticism.
Classification: LCC PS374.S46 D55 2019 (print) | LCC PS 374.S46 (ebook) | DDC 818/.608—dc23
LC record available at https://lccn.loc.gov/2019027079
LC ebook record available at https://lccn.loc.gov/2019027080

Cover art: *St. Preux and Eloisa,* colored mezzotint after George Morland (1763–1804), c. 1790 (Private Collection, photo © Christie's Images/Bridgeman Images).

Contents

List of Illustrations   vii

Acknowledgments   ix

Introduction: Sexual Ruin and the Early American Novel   1

ONE   The Aesthetic Work of the Ruin Narrative   23

TWO   Ruin's Subject in Shaftesbury's *Characteristicks*   42

THREE   Incest and the Nature of Ruin in the Novels of William Hill Brown   77

FOUR   Seduction and the Patriotism of Ruin in Hannah Webster Foster's *The Coquette*   102

FIVE   Ruin, Martyrdom, and the Spectacle of Sympathy from *Clotel* to *The Scarlet Letter*   126

SIX   Ruin, Rape, and the Aesthetic Work of *Clarissa* in England and America   155

Conclusion: The Anatomy of Ruin   197

Notes   221

Bibliography   259

Index   273

Illustrations

1. *The Voyage of the Sable Venus, from Angola to the West Indies,* 1794   39
2. Frontispiece to *Leviathan,* 1651   49
3. Frontispiece to *The Power of Sympathy,* 1789   86
4. "Paper X" from *Clarissa,* 1748   171
5. Sketch for the frontispiece to *Leviathan,* 1651   201
6. Detail from the frontispiece to *Leviathan,* 1651   203
7. Detail from the frontispiece to *Leviathan,* 1651   204
8. The Wicker Man, *Britannia Antiqua Illustrata,* 1676   205
9. "The Doctrine of Two Persons," from *Characteristicks,* 1711   206
10. *Portrait Shaftesbury,* 1704   209
11. Frontispiece to *Characteristicks of Men, Manners, Opinions, Times,* 1711   210
12. "MAGNA *Britannia; her Colonies* REDUC'D," 1767   212
13. "JOIN, or DIE," 1754   213
14. Title page seal of *Journal of the Proceedings of the Congress,* 1774   214
15. "The Able Doctor; or, America Swallowing the Bitter Draught," 1774   217

Acknowledgments

Writers are, first, readers, and many of us find ourselves drawn to particular books that reveal our own relationship to the process. The volume I kept going back to as I continued to work on this project was Samuel Johnson's *Preface to a Dictionary of the English Language* (1755), which is not so much an introduction to the dictionary as it is a description of what it feels like to write a book. My favorite moment in this wonderful little read has to be when, after an encyclopedic recital of all that he tried to do and all that went wrong anyway, a beleaguered Johnson laments, "A large work is difficult because it is large." Indeed. Surely the only thing that makes writing a large work possible is the help of others, and I am happy to begin mine with an acknowledgment of that help.

My first and most resounding thanks must go to Libby Garland, for whose help and mentorship I will always be grateful. The blasphemous amount of time she spent reading and commenting on my work taught me how to be a better scholar. Certainly it is not an exaggeration to say that without her help, I would not have written this book. Next I must thank Kenneth Dauber, who, with what can only be described as the heart and selflessness of a Dickensian benefactor, read the rough, early draft of the manuscript and offered insights as kind as they were brilliant. I would also like to thank Stacy Hubbard, whose encouragement and advice about the publication process was of great value to me. And I must thank Robert Daly, under whose tutelage the earliest version of this project got started.

My experience at the University of Virginia Press has been exceptional, and I would like to express my gratitude to Eric Brandt for shepherding the manuscript through the publication process. I similarly appreciate the expertise and patience of Helen Chandler as well as all of the helpful members in the production team. And the collegiality of the anonymous peer reviewers, who offered such valuable comments, was one of the nicest surprises along the way.

I was aided by the knowledgeable advice of countless librarians and curators along the way toward publication. I would like to thank the fine experts at all of the following institutions for their time and expertise: the Library Company of Philadelphia, the Library of Congress, the New York Public Library, the Special Collections of St. John's College at Cambridge University, the British Museum, the British Library, the UK National Portrait Gallery, and the Department of Rare Books and Special Collections at Princeton University's Firestone Library. Lori Branch, whose scholarship on Shaftesbury is indispensable, was incredibly gracious about sharing contact information regarding permission to use the Closterman portrait. I would also like to issue a special thanks to the Twelfth Earl of Shaftesbury for permission to reproduce that image.

Several institutions provided me with the time, funds, and feedback necessary to complete this project. I could not have done this work without several PSC Grants from CUNY's Research Foundation. A seat reserved for a lone Americanist at an NEH Summer Seminar on the Reformation got me thinking about Atlantic frames for early US literature. Also critical was the ability to test out early drafts of chapters with such generous colleagues at conferences held by the American Literature Association, the Society for Early Americanists, and NeMLA. And I appreciate the permission, generously granted by *Eighteenth-Century Fiction* and the *Nathaniel Hawthorne Review*, to integrate material from two articles I published with them into chapters 4 and 5 of this book.

Of course it is the support of friends and family that makes such an endeavor thinkable. I am grateful to my family for their encouragement. I would also like to express my appreciation to Zsa Ho-Sang, Yolanda Dickerson, and Shelita Bradshaw, who kept assuring me that I could write a book; to my fearless Kingsborough colleagues, whose devotion to a life of ideas is a thing to behold; and to Sheri Weinstein, who read, or rather survived, a very early version of the introduction, and who offered unwavering support for me and for the project. Finally, my most profound gratitude goes to Steve, from whom I have learned all I ever really needed to know about the charms and attractions that draw people together.

Erotic Citizens

INTRODUCTION

Sexual Ruin and the Early American Novel

> Peoples once accustomed to masters are no longer in condition to do without them. If they try to shake off the yoke, they move still farther away from freedom, because they confuse it with an unbridled license that is opposed to it, and their revolutions nearly always deliver them into the hands of seducers who only make their chains heavier than before.
> —Jean-Jacques Rousseau, *Discourse on the Origin and Basis of Inequality among Men*, 1754

> You say, the awful spirit of democracy is in great progress. I believe it, and I know something of the nature of it. It is a young rake who thinks himself handsome and well made, and who has little faith in virtue. . . . Democracy is Lovelace, and the people are Clarissa. The artful villain will pursue the innocent lovely girl to her ruin and her death.
> —President John Adams, *Correspondence*, 1804

Erotic Citizens seeks to unfold the enigma of sex in the age of democratic beginnings. It demonstrates that in much of the Anglophone Atlantic world of letters during the eighteenth and nineteenth centuries, the body experiences intimacy as a peculiar kind of captivity, one that is often erotic and sometimes violent in nature and that is engendered by that act of sensate community so often featured in the antebellum US novel and its sources of influence: illicit sex. For as much as we might say about the sober republican ideals of the new American nation's rhetoric, its literature spoke of lust, of wayward desire, of the ways in which sex marks an occasion that is not just personal but also common, by which I mean that it creates a corporeal intimacy that is shared and therefore in some essential way political. *Erotic Citizens* explores the ubiquity of forbidden heterosexual encounters in the early US novel and its wider Atlantic context to show how these encounters regularly involve grappling with the inheritance of that most foundational Enlightenment ideal, self-possession. In place of this ideal, the illicitly sexed body featured in the ruin narrative projects a restive, uneasy presence that is rather *possessed by* the ungovernable desires of others. Such narratives reveal extramarital sex as an occasion of disintegrating autonomy, a moment in which nonjurisdictional embodiment does violence to traditional notions of sovereignty and self.

In the proliferation of narratives of sexual ruin during the antebellum period—a proliferation that justifies the term *genre*—the sexed body is captivating insofar as it confounds the premise that the democratic subject is a singular one. Sovereignty necessitates the independence of a nation, but a nation requires the interdependence of its citizenry. The democratic intimacy required to obtain such interdependence often registers as an intense, inappropriate, sexual expression of sodality that ruptures the Enlightenment body's promise of ontological containment—personhood. That is, democratic intimacy registers as sexual intimacy; the ruin of one's chastity is both personal and political, a condition not just of a body but of *bodies*. Ruin's subject is therefore an ontologically messy figure that enfolds more and often other than one's "self."

The antebellum ruin narrative regards the idealization of self-possession as, at best, a political blunder, at worst absolute villainy. One of the staples of the ruin narrative is invective against the individual, the outrage of self an unforgivable delinquency. One thinks of Susanna Rowson's bestselling tale of seduction *Charlotte Temple* (1791), whose villain, Belcour, receives the most damning insult of the novel: "Self, darling self, was the idol he worshipped, and to that he would have sacrificed the interest and happiness of all mankind." In Nathaniel Hawthorne's tale of utopian dreamers tangled in a skein of unrequited desire, *The Blithedale Romance* (1852), the ruined heroine Zenobia echoes that language all too clearly when to that novel's villain she launches a similar accusation: "'It is all self!'" she rages, "'Nothing else; nothing but self, self, self!'" In Samuel Richardson's meganovel about the rape of its eponymous heroine in *Clarissa* (1748), abridged and reprinted by popular demand for readers in late eighteenth-century America, the heroine administers this admonishment to herself, after the libertine has attempted to violate her through sexual violence: "Self, then, be banished from self."[1] In the stories discussed here, that is, characters often possess one another but rarely exhibit signs of self-containment, let alone self-possession. "Self" is something they cannot be said to *have*. It is, however, decidedly something they exchange. This kind of ontological sharing happens in the strange, and strangely beautiful, storylines that define the antebellum literary period—the incest romances and fatal seductions, the sordid tales of adultery, the tragic tales of miscegenation, the horrific tales of rape and concubinage. And it occurs in narratives and images of sexual ruin produced in the philosophical works and novels of the larger Atlantic Enlightenment. It happens when knowing bodies discover the frisson of community, when bodies enraptured by desire or ruptured by violence model an ascendance over self.

It is the distinctly sexual alchemy of sympathy that constitutes this ascendance and the shared community it affords. Sympathy, that vexed and yet also somehow charmed term that describes the joining of the many into one, defines an interosculatory (overlapping, so as to be mutually defining) ontological condition of the body that in the ruin narrative becomes the site of political feeling. Indeed, sympathy is a concept so central to Enlightenment thought that it can describe a relationship as intimate as two lovers and as widescale as the citizens of a nation. Eighteenth-century British philosophers persistently attempted to define the concept of sympathy as a condition that at once questioned the limits of self-containment and functioned as the linchpin of Enlightenment personhood. Building upon but also radicalizing the work of those philosophers, the antebellum ruin narrative represents sympathy as that which closes the gap between self and other, a gap that imperiled the American ideal of community. The most revolutionary claim of *Erotic Citizens* is, then, that in the ruin genre it is the body of the *other* that becomes the custodian of self.[2] The ordeals of the sexed body in the antebellum novel and the political works informing it make up a counternarrative to the individual and his arc through history. The stories and the images in this study enact the unraveling of self through the moment of illicit sexual encounter. Those encounters involve the fusion of self and other, and thus present an alternative to the ontologically isolating ideal of individual self-possession. In other words, the ruin narrative illustrates the heat of sympathy through the scene of extramarital sex, and it represents this scene as the point of entry into a democracy.

Identity and agency in the early American novel are unsteady, shifting phenomena. Who these characters *are* is a matter of confusion and doubt, and subjectivity—that enigmatic junction of power, identity, and agency—becomes one of the central problems posed by these texts. *Erotic Citizens* shows how the ruin narrative addresses the problem of subjectivity by proposing an alternative to the individual, an alternative that emerges from a decidedly Atlantic sphere of influence. Understood within this broader context, the novel of the sexual fall tells the story of the American Enlightenment in which the self is understood to be a dim and restless entity. It is within this shadowy and inconstant axis of identity that the Cartesian calculus of body and mind malfunctions. Thus the resolve of this book is to insist, above all else, that if we can learn anything from the ruin genre, it is that there can no longer be uncritical reference to the "individual" as such in this historical period. It is not a figure legible to all, or one we can safely assume constituted the cornerstone of the new republic.

The conventional understanding of a democracy suggests that its most basic operational need is an assembly of rational citizens invested in the principle of self-governance. This would mean that while the citizen—white, male, rights-bearing—might consult with his peers about the controversies of the day, he had to decide for himself what he believed according to his own principles—had, that is, to retreat to his own mind, understood to be an impenetrable intellectual reservoir, where he could form his thoughts, and then decide, sensibly and judiciously, whether to act on them. According to such a model, it is this solitary figure who makes a democracy possible. Yet at the core of the ruin narrative, a storyline central to the early US novel, is the dysfunction of the individual, and a consistent dismissal of the notion that human beings can rely on a separation from one another as an ontological given. For while readers might imagine the foundation of a republic to be an ideological investment in the rights-bearing individual, in so much early US fiction, the individual is a figure whose isolationist identity threatens to erode community bonds. He is not the cornerstone of democracy but its undoing. Indeed, the individual, these novels insist, is no mere scoundrel. He is a scourge to the republic, the epicenter of a political pathology, and he is unfit for democracy.

Alternatively, as it is characterized in the antebellum novel, the illicitly sexed body makes for a model of good citizenship. The erotic and violent extremes of the ruined body's sensate life present an ontological porousness that suits what the ruin narrative depicts as the deeply interactive, networked nature of democratic relations. Through the lens of the taboo, sexed body, then, *Erotic Citizens* locates the ontological confusion at the heart of the democratic subject, a figure marking the sovereignty-building project of the Enlightenment as always already unfinished. This book also traces the aesthetic work of the sensual body, and it shows how at the heart of the antebellum novel there is an operational lack of individual will that calls into question whether the rational, singular self can ever function as the centerpiece of a democratic polity.

Simply put: sex does the work of democracy in these texts, and it does so illicitly and at the expense of jurisdictional notions of embodiment. Indeed, these novels imagine the traffic of the sexed body—always, of course, a woman's—as a response to and a refutation of the isolated individual. *Erotic Citizens* thus unpacks the gendered nature of ruin as it addresses questions about the intersection between sex and democratic sovereignty. How does the compromised chastity of the female body speak to resistance against the political capital of the individual? What does it mean when the totality of a citizen's identity is vulnerable to the charms of sex and love? And why do so many early American novelists imagine the crisis of citizenship as an encounter ending in sexual ruin? What *is* the power of sex in this age of democratic beginnings? The answers to these questions lie in the ways in which these texts use the sensory life of the sexed body and its rupturing labors instead of cerebral acts of consent to define the agency of citizenship. From graphic images of political unions among sexed, ruined bodies in the early British Enlightenment, to stories of incest, rape, and seduction in eighteenth-century British and American novels and philosophical treatises, and finally to the miscegenation romances and slave narratives of pre–Civil War America, sexual ruin comes to stand in for a new kind of democratic identity, one based on episodes of illicit sexual intimacy and the sometimes erotic, sometimes violent nature of those episodes.

That identity moves well beyond the ideological range of the individual as the sole precinct of selfhood in the age of revolution and toward what we might think of as the polyontological subject, a figure that in the ruin narrative is defined by an identity with multiple valences. This figure performs a certain kind of aesthetic work—that is, the ontological labors of the sensate body—that makes distinguishing between sympathy and sex nearly impossible. In other words, the early American novel uses illicit sex to make radical claims about what a democracy might look like. Questions about sympathy, sovereignty, and the individual intersect in the trope of ruin and reveal the aesthetic work of the sexed, ruined body as the site of a uniquely democratic subjectivity. That is, the antebellum novel widens the scope of the erotic underlife of Enlightenment thought and culture to reveal the body as the custodian of democratic relations.

Erotic Citizens therefore uncovers how the bewitching relationality between sex and self can change a storyline from the individual's pursuit of happiness into something altogether murkier. In other words, the ruin narrative dramatizes the rise of community as, simultaneously, a sexual and moral fall, and it represents this fall as a political portal, a point of access for democratic relations. Such a descent into community occurs in direct opposition to the sober act of consent as the signature of democratic sovereignty. Depictions of ruin as a sexual fall into a social state thus offer a part of American mythology worth exploring, when the Atlantic world looked to this fledgling republic for new insights into the sovereign subjectivity of "Man" figured through the postlapsarian, sexed body of the ruined woman.

Sexual Ruin in the First American Novel

The first page of the first American novel, William Hill Brown's epistolary incest romance *The Power of Sympathy; or, The Triumph of Nature* (1789), illustrates this power of sex over the democratic subject. Brown introduces a plot to ruin a woman, when one seemingly upstanding citizen of the new republic corresponds with another about how to seduce a virgin of Boston's lower class. "I pursued my determination of discovering the dwelling of my charmer," says the protagonist Harrington, "and have at length obtained access."[3] On the one hand, as the quintessential Everyman of the nation's early years, Harrington speaks the language of the ideal citizen. Pursuit, determination, and discovery—his rhetoric appears to exemplify the spirit of Enlightenment personhood and its imagined subject, the sovereign individual. As I have suggested, in many respects, during the age of revolution, the individual may seem to be the foundational identity for democratic citizenship. The republican visions articulated by Jean-Jacques Rousseau and President John Adams in the epigraphs beginning this introduction rested on the liberal presumption that a democratic society was a voluntary association among free individuals exercising their political will toward the common good and cultivating the moral character of the citizen and the nation. Yet the ruin narrative—that tale of uncontrollable sexual passion and its disastrous consequences—called everything about this vision into question. Specifically, what these narratives suggest through remarks like Harrington's is that the "charmer" fundamentally threatens the assumptions of individual will upon which a particular vision of democratic society rests. Harrington is not able to be this kind of republican citizen—the morally upstanding one who makes good choices—because he is not able to exercise his own free political will. Increasingly consumed by a sensate romantic charm that holds him in thrall, Harrington finds himself in a state of erotic enchantment, a condition in which words like "determination" have very little to do with agency. And so it is that the first narrative task of the first American novel is to use the sexed body to sideswipe the narrative arc of the individual.

Novels like Brown's provide an account of how illicit lovers become strangers to themselves when they become entangled in one another's lives through acts of sexual ruin. And if Brown was the first American to articulate how the extramarital encounters of incest, seduction, and adultery caused such disintegration of the individual, he was certainly not the last. From *The Power of Sympathy* to the novels of the American Renaissance and the works of fiction and philosophy from the larger Atlantic world of the eighteenth and nineteenth centuries, what the ruin narrative demonstrates is that the "charm" that draws unmarried lovers to one another befuddles any ontological certainty they once assumed. In fact, the sexual encounters that ruin reputations, because they occur outside of the marriage contract, have a tendency to throw the lovers into chaos and confusion not just about what kind of people they are, but about what a "person" is in the first place. Ostensibly writing to his friend about the true love he feels for the girl he intends to seduce, Brown's hero Harrington is also in some ways preemptively addressing readers' ideas about his character as he follows his remark about the "charmer" with a characterization of himself that is quite revealing in this regard: "But you call me, with some degree of truth, a strange medley of contradiction—the moralist and the amoroso—the sentiment and the sensibility—are interwoven in my constitution, so that nature and grace are at continual fisticuffs" (9). The seducer refers to the "strange medley" of identity to explain the way that his desire to ruin a woman unravels his own sense of who, and what, he is. In the ruin narrative, characters often experience the sympathetic pulse of nature as an illicit desire that obscures a sense of self. It is the call of the body, the call of sex, and for citizens like Harrington, it is irresistible. For love, he later observes, "carries us away into captivity," and we are undone. Individuals in the throes of passion, it turns out, are not at liberty at all. They are everything the new republic protested it would not be: unfree, in chains, ensorcelled and enslaved.

In their depictions of extramarital sex, novels like *The Power of Sympathy* explore alternatives to the marriage contract and its ideological metonym, the social contract, as the model for democratic citizenship among rationally consenting individuals. Tales of sexual ruin portray the undoing of a woman's virtue to signal shifting paradigms of embodiment. To make sense of these paradigms, we can read the ruin narrative as a study of the corporeal power of sympathy. Most critics agree that sympathy was one of the central tenets of eighteenth-century Anglo-Atlantic philosophy and culture, and that it helped to shape the new American republic's egalitarian ethos by creating a citizenry who imagined themselves as emotionally bonded together. In other words, early Americanists agree that sympathy does the work of democracy. In *Erotic Citizens,* my point is that more often than not, in the antebellum novel, sex does the work of sympathy, and in doing so it produces a disunified subject that cannot be properly labeled as an "individual." Novels like *The Power of Sympathy* ask what it means to unify a people—what it means when their bodies issue calls and commands that cannot be refused—what it means, that is, to forge a republic based on "the power of sympathy."

To repeat: in contrast to that more familiar telling of the Enlightenment, through *Erotic Citizens* I hope to contribute to the current scholarly work that is trying to establish once and for all that there can no longer be any unproblematized reference to "the individual" as such in this literary period.[4] Though we may have once been accustomed to think of the principal subjectivity of the Enlightenment as the possessive individual, that Lockean figure of property in a personhood that is singular, contained, and volitional, in the ruin genre, the subjectivity of the illicit lover unravels as it possesses, and is possessed by, the other. In explaining these erotic and violent possessions, I examine how the ruin narrative rejects the modeling of democratic sovereign identity after the individual, and I show how the sexed, ruined body in stories of seduction, incest, adultery, and rape is central to that rejection. Indeed, if the scene of ruin in the antebellum novel teaches us anything, it is that we must resolutely give up on the individual as the foundational identity of the new republic.

In the age of democratic beginnings, the power of sex is radical indeed. For the ruin narrative questions whether community can occur among free people at all, among people, that is, who make choices and act on them, who are, or even believe they are, in control of themselves. In my focus on antebellum American literature and the Anglo-Atlantic writing informing it, especially the seventeenth- and eighteenth-century philosophies of sympathy and contract, I show that the ruin narrative is about the body's sublunary appetites and how these appetites express the power of corporeal union in a way that obfuscates Enlightenment configurations of agency. In other words, what a person is and why a person acts are thoroughly unclear in the ruin narrative, especially when what a person does is sexually taboo. And in the texts I discuss here, sex is never something characters *choose* to do. It is something they are drawn into by involuntary, uncontrollable (and often unwelcome[5]) desires, as well as by force. Sex happens *through* and *to* them. What is so interesting about this lack of choice is that in cases of both seduction and rape, desire and violence, the Enlightenment ideal of the consenting individual simply does not explain why illicit sex happens.

In particular, while rape-as-ruin narratives are often about the horror of sexual violation, they tend to interrogate the very ideal of female violability and its premise of embodied containment as a distinctly un-American Enlightenment fantasy. These novels continually demonstrate the limits of consent as an idea that explains agency. Consent and refusal, those definitive responses of self-sovereignty, are not always at work in the ruin narrative, where there appears to be something else entirely at the center of human volition. The rape-as-ruin narrative is distinct in this regard since it works against the idealization of the individual through a very different mode, defined as it is not by acts of desire but by acts of violence. Instead of engaging with the interosculatory pleasures of the illicitly sexed body, the rape-as-ruin narrative sets out to expose the insidious political agenda of racial and sexual violation as an agenda made possible in part by the ideological foundation of the individual. The rape-as-ruin novels considered in this book set out

Introduction

to resist patriarchal, supremacist ideas regarding embodiment that see the body of the other as a violable container of "self." It is important to understand that in these texts, novels about rape as a form of sexual ruin reveal the violence endured by real bodies, by people whose ability to refuse is limited or nullified. Rape is not just a metaphor for a political problem. Rape *is* the political problem. In scrutinizing this problem, these novels reveal that much Enlightenment thought about female consent exists within a discourse of personal rights that abets acts of patriarchal, supremacist violence. Indeed, these novels reveal how the rhetoric of consent figures into an idea of embodiment that endorses violence against women by endorsing certain notions about the female body as a violable container.

All of the texts I discuss in these pages are more interested in the ruined body as a site of the irrational, of nonvolitional agency, what we ought to think of as agency without personhood, namely a sense of identity outside the realm of the rights-bearing individual and its attendant notion of self-possession. And in ruin narratives that are not about violence but about desire, there exists a dynamic, sexed, sensate intermingling of self and other that points to a relational space between as a site of volition. Through relations with others, these novels argue, we develop multiple sympathies, multiple attractions, and these create multiple, simultaneous, intersecting arcs of embodied identity. The source of volition comes from interaction, not personal will, a polyontological quarter that the ruin narrative dramatizes with astonishing consistency.

An Alternative Story

What *Erotic Citizens* thus offers is an attempt to analyze another, concurrent ideal existing beside the figure of the individual within antebellum notions of self. The novel of the sexual fall, staging a powerful counternarrative to American Enlightenment discourse, points to a "something else" at the center of identity and occasions the moment at which sex and sympathy meet. What is this something else? The authors considered in this book offer an intriguing lexicon to define it: Susanna Rowson, for example, calls it the "impulse of inclination" and "thoughtless passion." For Nathaniel Hawthorne, it is "nervous sympathy" and "entanglement." William Hill Brown uses terms like "intoxicated" and "entranced." Hannah Webster

Foster identifies it as the condition of being "charmed," "besieged," and "possessed." Washington Irving calls it the "whole soul in the traffic of affection."[6] At stake in each of these sympathetic utterances is the attempt to define a different sort of agency. When it operates in the ruin narrative, sympathy, the sensibility of the period so prized as the wellspring of democratic feeling, is an erotic experience. When sympathy produces this democratic feeling, it occurs within the frisson of illicit sexual encounter, and it is this space of frisson that I explore in *Erotic Citizens* because it is an instance of where *else* agency exists. That is, I show how the ruin narrative allows for the ontological messiness of sympathy and its nonjurisdictional embodiments, a zone of volition that occurs between bodies and that disrupts the self/other binary.

That space between brings us to a new way of reading. Instead of looking at what Jane Tompkins so famously called the "cultural work" of the novel, in *Erotic Citizens*, I am proposing that we look to what I am calling the aesthetic work these texts produce.[7] For the purposes of this book, the *aesthetic* can be defined as the mutually generative, indivisible worlds of sensate and sentient experience.[8] The term *aesthetic* in fact comes from the Greek *aisthetikos*, which means perception by way of the senses. Though *aesthetics* is commonly understood to convey ideas about discernment and beauty emerging out of the mid-eighteenth-century study of art, another branch of Enlightenment thinkers saw it rather as the examination of the sensory life and its attendant emotional import.[9] These were philosophers who were interested in the political power of feeling and who began to consider the influence of that ultimate organ of perception, the body, and especially the influence of the body's pleasures within the realm of virtue. Indeed, they saw the body as predisposed by providential design to experience the good as the pleasurable. Our attractions, they argued, are moral things, and direct us toward not just the good but the *common* good: we form bonds with one another and do what is best for others because it gives us pleasure to do so. Pleasure works on and through the body to produce attractions, and our most fundamental attraction is toward one another, toward the formation of community. Thus aesthetic work is somatic work, and its inclination toward community inflects it with a fundamentally political valence. As the ruin narrative sees it, the pleasure experienced by the congress among extracontractual bodies is thus not an act of sin at all but a moral corrective, the body remedying the political error of yoking bodies together by contract.

The aesthetic sees the body as the arena of experience. For the ruined body, this experience is the site of an interdynamic impulse. The ruin narrative does not regard the body as that which secures a separation between self and other in a material finality. Instead, it sees the body as a site of connection, of sodality—a promise of fellowship, not evidence of an irrefutable individuating boundary. *Aesthetic work,* then, is what a text does to illuminate that experience and the subjectivities emerging out of it. In the ruin narrative, aesthetic work portrays the drama of shared somatic experience. Such work reveals identity and community as interdependent phenomena, a distinct addition to the period's investment in the individual. Ultimately, the aesthetic work of the ruin narrative reveals the ideas, feelings, and experiences made possible by the emotive, erotic, sexed body. That body registers the magnetic pull, the somatic tug, of other bodies; the experience of this body is the experience, fundamentally, of connectedness, not isolation. In this sense, the aesthetic work of the ruin narrative shows that marriage is a bad metaphor for community.[10] For if the body is fundamentally associative, a contract that purports to regulate sexual association through a legal utterance of consent is entirely unnecessary.

Sex outside of marriage becomes another way of representing the connection between human beings, and it is a connection untouched by the self-interest that defines contractual relations. In the novels under consideration here, sexual ruin accomplishes the aesthetic work of democracy by revealing identity to be a relational and dynamic ontological phenomenon. The kind of sympathy characters feel while they are entangled in taboo sexual relationships is so strong that their identities merge, sometimes even into the larger community. Sympathy is a force of sodality, a powerful and intimate association, as well as a source of corporeal instability. And in sexually ruinous unions, it forecloses on the possibility of the contract as that which brings (the) people together. Indeed, the ideological work of the contract—even, and perhaps especially, the marriage contract—is to imagine the barriers that separate us *by* calling the individual subject into being.

In the ruin narrative, sympathy is a force that reveals the individual as but one of the many models of identity. In the calamity of incest, in the tragedy of seduction, and in the depravity of adultery, readers find the potential for something *better* than marriage. If the marriage contract stands in for the social contract in the antebellum novel, then within the hardships created by extramarital sex lurks the promise of community without contract. When lovers abandon themselves to their desires, they find themselves again within one another. In other words, the abandonment of self, not its possession, defines the ideal of citizenship. The loss of chastity is both a sexual and an ontological matter, one that represents the formation of community as intimate and the bonds of community as unregulated. The aesthetic work of the ruin narrative offers a model of agency that looks to sympathy for an explanation of this other identity.

As my readings in the chapters that follow show, extramarital sex functions in part as a critique of the marriage contract. If the marriage contract in some ways represents the republic in miniature, and the ruin narrative reveals the problems of the marriage contract, then it follows that the merits of the social contract must also be in question.[11] The essence of contract culture is the value of consent. In some ways, consent embodies contract culture in the ceremonial utterance, "I do." Of course, such an utterance presupposes that there is already a rational "I" at work that consents or resists any given proposition based on the principle of self-interest. While I will go into much more detail in the following chapters about the ontological arguments that contract theory assumes, for now it is worth pointing out the links between the marriage contract and the social contract. For in the ruin narrative, sex and sympathy meet outside of the jurisdiction of contract culture. Sex is the joining of bodies; the body is the organ of sympathy; sympathy erases ontological boundaries. This syllogism, if a bit oversimplifying, represents how community can happen, and not just when the individual consents to a contract. Most scholarship on early American literature sees marriage as the ruling semiotic of civil life in the age of revolutions; marriage represents a contract, not a king, as that which rules the political relations among people. The early republic seemed to be seeking to place individual consent at the forefront of political agency by using marriage as the representation of consenting civil relations, by defining marriage as voluntary, egalitarian, and affectionate. Many historians of early US politics and culture have suggested that the contract was a founding principle of the new republic, promising that the new nation would be built upon the value of explicit, voluntary consent.[12] The nearly magical ontological properties associated with the monarch get translated into what Paul Downes has so effectively called "the spell of democracy."[13] If the king both represents and "is" the people, then that same magic (in which representation merges with being) applies to the maxim *e pluribus unum*. Yet as the founders saw it, in a republic, sympathy achieves the alchemy that forms the people into "one," and it is a powerful spell indeed, enacted in the ruin narrative through illicit sexual encounters.

The question remains: If marriage represents consent—if it represents the ideal of a voluntaristic society governed by a contract that allows the people to choose the company they keep, to choose to be represented rather than ruled—then why do so many antebellum novels instead tell stories about sexual ruin? Such a question prompts an extraordinary answer: that extramarital sex, not marriage, is the republic in miniature; that sexual ruin is a founding theme, perhaps *the* founding theme, used in the quest to define self and nation that is the hallmark of post-revolutionary American writing. To be sure, in the pages of the novels I discuss here, readers will not find many heroines pining for marriage. More typically, we find characters making claims like "Reader, my story ends with freedom; not in the usual way, with marriage," and "I am not married . . . I bless God, I am *not* married to this miscreant . . . I am no wife of this man. I am not his wife."[14]

The loss of chastity outside of the marriage contract illuminates intriguing political possibilities. When that loss is attended by powerful sexual desire, we witness the rise of the nation occurring as the result of a fall that is at once sexual and moral, attended by eros and ethos. Acts of sex with no contracts to institutionalize them enact, metonymically, a democracy without a social contract to hold it together. Illicit sex represents a democratic impulse, where the agency of human bonding is not consciously volitional. In ruin as in democracy, people do not choose one another or consent to one another, but find themselves drawn into one another by a force early American novelists were anxious to define. And in fact the early American canon offers a veritable lexicon for extracontractual desire. Words like "intoxicated," "possessed," and "entangled" occur with such ubiquity as to show how sex illustrates the impulsive tug of body to body that needs no contract to make it real. And in those moments when ruinous sex happens, authors portray this tug as the site of agency, the pull toward the other as the essence of volition. The gravitational draw of the lover's body, the very body that ought to repel because it is a sibling or a seducer, a reverend or a rogue, but never—*never*—a spouse, renders the ruined body as an ideal democratic subject, one of the People. In this context, chastity represents the isolated individual, whose fidelity to contract is a submission to the rules, not the feeling, of community. Scenes of ruin emphatically deny individual control over a singular, finite self and instead imagine a space in which the erotic body enacts interdependent, ontologically murky correspondences of action and reaction, the self and the other overlapping, always and ever orbiting about one another, the gravitational pull of the body at times determining in significant ways the narrative arc of this plural agent, decidedly not a self but a multitude: a nation.

The ruin narrative's stories of extramarital lust, libertine violence, and familial disintegration remind us that Hawthorne's scarlet letter, after all, represents both "America" and "Adultery," an emblem that represents the making of a nation as the breaking of a contract, locating the sexed, post-lapsarian body in a utopian landscape. In books about incest, seduction, or in the case of *The Scarlet Letter,* adultery, sexual ruin comes to signify not just the sexual practice of a body but the unchaste identity as the building block of the antebellum American nation. In the literary imaginings of that nation, that is, what is ruined is ipseity, that fidelity to self as a singular, contained experience.[15] The call for a theory that understands the ontological simultaneity of self and community formation exists in the manner by which these texts belie the individual self's ideological supremacy.

The debate concerning the role of sympathy in the new republic with which *Erotic Citizens* engages is in part about understanding the models of agency it offers. Critics are currently attempting to posit alternatives to the model of the Enlightenment individual, to offer other representations of selfhood in American letters.[16] The ruin narrative consistently presents one such alternative to consent, contract, and the individuals who agree to them, describing ruined women during an involuntary fall, driven by extrapersonal passions and persuasions that take the ontological reins. For at moments of sexual ruin there is an absence of decision, of will, of anything resembling self-possession. This is less a commentary on the absence of political power for women and more a claim that consent is a limiting model for all social relations. Indeed, the moment of sexual ruin is never written as a moment of individual will being exercised. The moment is always strangely vague, syntactically imprecise—at the sentence level, what is actually happening is often entirely unclear. When *Charlotte Temple*'s heroine faints as her seducer whisks her away in a carriage, when *The Coquette*'s heroine says that some "evil genius presided over my actions" when she has sex with a known libertine in her mother's kitchen, when the heroine of *Incidents in the Life of a Slave Girl* uses six different pronouns to refer to herself the moment she began a sexual relationship with a white man: whatever can these moments *mean*? What can they tell us about the agency that does not rely on the individual "I" to be articulated? Instead of "Reader, I married him," that romanticized, contractual utterance that constitutes the "I" as it deploys it, we have various warped adaptations of—or rather alternatives to—that utterance and the identity it implies. Thus we have either to resign ourselves to the explanation that, for lack of a better set of terms, the devil made them do it, or we must figure out what kind of identity makes the moment of volition without intent possible. If marriage is a state enacted by the words "I do," then what aesthetic work is accomplished by the fallen body's utterances, full of pronoun slippage and unaccountable volition as they are? In rupturing the political presumption that distinguishes self from community, stories of ruin ask a provocative question, remarkably appealing in its defiance of the obligatory "I" of the marriage contract: What would it mean to call agency and community into being *simultaneously,* as a doubled, disobedient response to the contract's hail?

The novel of ruin takes up the challenge of how a nation might conceive of itself, not as a person who grants or withholds consent, but as a social body that experiences the kinds of relations for which the concept of consent is not always relevant. The eighteenth-century philosophy of feeling that informs these novels helps us to understand the story of sexual ruin as a story of the body's moral affect, its capacity to alter agency and reconstruct an involuntarily sociable self defined by desire. Through a reading of desiring bodies, we see that the ruin narrative contests the value of the volitional self so often cast as a right or privilege of Enlightenment personhood. Scholars must study portrayals of sexuality in early American literature in such a way as to work against its pernicious association with Enlightenment configurations of identity, since, as Peter Coviello so wonderfully argues in *Tomorrow's Parties,* this literature "[provides] a fantastically rich resource for the articulation of sex away from its possessivist moorings, as something other than an accoutrement of the private self, and as something more like a mode of relation, a style of affiliation, even, for some, a blueprint for sociality."[17] Indeed, the early American novel theorizes the construction of postrevolutionary identity by finding the shift into social being through desire. Thus we must think about desire as a condition that, like the marriage narrative, represents a civic experience, and impacts traditional understandings of "the most famous and influential political story of modern times," namely the story of the social contract.[18]

A perhaps unlikely icon of American Revolutionary ideals, the figure of sexual ruin reveals that novels plotting the downfall of marriage and family employ an aesthetic that offers up to us an alternative operation of community to those with which we have busied ourselves in the past. Literary critics once understood the drama of the birth of the republic as a bloody clamoring toward a culture of contract—that is, toward becoming a nation built upon principles of free will, consent, and reason, a voluntary but binding obligation being the cornerstone of the rights-bearing individual. But the fall into community through more deviant bonds than those forged by principles of contract and consent seems to be the subject of so many early American novels. Indeed, what is most glorious about these stories is their unfailing insistence that at the center of all of life's plots is this messy and ambiguous business of what brings us together. Call it lust, desire, an impulse toward union, it is a force that ultimately challenges the contract as that which constitutes an ideal community.

What follows, then, is a study of Atlantic literature and iconography that connects the ideology of ruin to the struggles and vagaries of community-building bodies in America's nascent years. Writers as seemingly disparate as the Earl of Shaftesbury and Harriet Jacobs—a British aristocrat and an American slave—feature ruin as an operation of sympathy that locates the intersections among sex and self and characterizes these intersections as sharing the work of identity formation. Penned by a truly diverse collection of authors, ruin narratives establish that the sovereign individual was not the sole or even the ruling model of identity posited in this era; authors like Shaftesbury and Jacobs used sexual ruin to present the possibilities offered by an alternate model, the sympathetic subject. Each of my readings, then, constitutes an attempt to understand, define, and incorporate instances of how sympathy leads to a scene of ruined embodiment. My interpretations define sexual ruin as a central motif in early American literature; I show how this motif springs from the Atlantic world's need to reckon with the sexed body as a nation-building force. It is a motif that presents us with an alternative to definitions of community with which we are already familiar.

The first two chapters set up my discussion of texts that represent that alternative definition in full force. Chapter 1 presents the case for reading the ruin narrative as a genre, and it situates the story of sexual ruin within the larger literary landscape of sensationalism and sentimentalism. The first chapter also offers definitions for the key terms of this book like *sex* and *the body*, and considers how novels that for decades have been read for their "cultural work" might instead be read for their aesthetic work. Chapter 2 then investigates the philosophical underpinnings of ruin's aesthetic work. Beginning with a study of the Third Earl of Shaftesbury's remarkable fictional representation of rape, ruin, and the tyranny of desire in "The Story of an Amour," I then move to a broader analysis of seventeenth- and eighteenth-century Enlightenment philosophers and their ideas about the social roles that feelings and contracts play in the formation of community. I reframe the current conversation about antebellum literature's engagement with the eighteenth-century philosophy of feeling by putting it in the context of modern theories of subject-formation. From its discussion of Shaftesbury's *Characteristicks of Men, Manners, Opinions, Times* (1711) to Judith Butler's *Senses of the Subject* (2015), then, this chapter sets up a lexicon for subjectivity studies. The theory of the subject in this context is the theory of ruin; ruin narratives use sex as the site of passion, sympathy, tactility, intersubjectivity, and community—all key words of the aesthetic philosophy under consideration here that explain the human "nature" of sympathy.

Chapters 3 and 4 turn to American novels of ruin to see how such key words are dramatized. Chapter 3 offers a close reading of ruin in William Hill Brown's two novels, *The Power of Sympathy; or, The Triumph of Nature* (1789) and the lesser-known *Ira and Isabella; or, The Natural Children* (1807). In the third chapter, I unpack the connections among sympathy, agency, and desire that define ruin, placing these in the broader cultural context of a post-revolutionary nation that is struggling with the implications of radically new ideas about the meaning of social bonds. Chapter 3 examines the operations of "nature" as a code word for democratic sovereignty as well as illicit desire, a condition using ruin as a model for unwilled, nonindividualistic volition. In Brown's work, to be the subject not of a king but of the Declaration of Independence's "Laws of Nature and of Nature's God" means also to be subject *to* that nature. The contradictions Brown reveals within the rhetoric of nature help to explain why a bastard daughter of ruin in love with her half-brother becomes America's first novelistic heroine. Brown's generic play through his strange marginalization of the seduction story in favor of an incest romance mirrors his portrayal of identity as fractured and unstable. Chapter 4 continues my study of nature as Hannah Webster Foster represents it in her novel *The Coquette; or, The History of Eliza Wharton* (1797), a story that blurs the differences between sympathy and desire, two impulses that challenge the willed agency of the individual as the foundation for the sociability the new republic required its subjects to use as a nation-building tool. In *The Coquette,* the wayward desires of Eliza Wharton create a very different kind of social self whose seduction models Foster's interpretation of civic virtue, as Eliza's seduction confuses the question of individual moral agency.

Chapter 5 considers the spectacle of ruin as a catalyst for female martyrdom, specifically in Hawthorne's two novels *The Scarlet Letter* (1850) and *The Blithedale Romance* (1852), William Wells Brown's novel *Clotel; or, The President's Daughter* (1853), and one of Brown's source texts for *Clotel,* Washington Irving's lesser-known tale "The Broken Heart" from *The Sketch Book of Geoffrey Crayon, Gent.* (1819–20). When a loss of chastity occasions martyrdom, the ruin narrative goes further to question the merits of contractual communities in different ways. Though we might associate the ethic of self-denial with the vanilla domestic dramas of sentimental literature, such an ethic sometimes also presents a radicalized ontology. Martyrdom makes being an individual impossible as the ruin narrative characterizes it. The denial of self makes a space for the multitudes, for what theorist Jean-Luc Nancy calls "being-in-common."[19] As that which signals the ultimate denial of self, death signifies differently in the ruin narrative. Self-denial, even denial of life itself through suicide, does not create an absence. In the texts under consideration here, a denial of self *expands* identity rather than contracting it. Martyrs to ruin become larger than life, larger than any singularity, and, most radically, *more* than an individual. The fall out of self is a fall into a much grander ontological condition, one that takes on a representational—which is to say a national—value. These texts stage scenes of ruin as a defining element of the public sphere, a spectacle that occurs on the auction block as well as in the town square, and they explore the fallen woman as an eminently surveilled figure. In doing so, this collection of antebellum writers shows that to be a civic subject is to be a fallen one.

I return to the Atlantic framing of the ruin narrative in chapter 6, which studies the radical, ruined identity in stories of resistance to predatory power. Chapter 6 considers the darker question of rape as a form of ruin in four texts: Samuel Richardson's *Clarissa* (1748), *Clarissa*'s abridged colonial American edition (1773), Susanna Rowson's *Charlotte Temple* (1791), and Harriet Jacobs's *Incidents in the Life of a Slave Girl* (1861). Each text defines rape in part as a failed attempt to imagine a violable interiority—an individual—in the person of a woman. Novels of rape-as-ruin reveal that failure by highlighting their heroines' resistance to the double-sided coin of containment and violation that defines the rape wish. In other words, these texts consistently depict rape by the libertine or the slaver as, first and foremost, a wish to imagine female embodiment as a condition of containment that holds the promise of its violation. According to these novels, the purpose of rape is to break into the body to affirm its work of containment. In such cases, the "I" that for women spells but one political utterance, "I do," is reimagined as an unutterable "I do *not*." This is a move the rape-as-ruin narrative rejects when the imperiled heroine refuses to stay "inside" that body and instead forges sympathetic, subversive bonds that confuse the self/other binary. Resistance to rape, in other words, becomes resistance to the model of the individual as a subjectivity that for women would turn identity itself into a tormenting ordeal of containment and violence. In this chapter, I examine the semiotics of rape through the tropes of a larger Atlantic context, as sea crossings and the slave trade become sites of resistance to the master-as-rapist figure, who is the ultimate expression of individual self-possession.

Finally, in my conclusion, "The Anatomy of Ruin," I offer remarks about the troubled iconography of embodiment emerging out of the early Atlantic political philosophy that contextualizes the literature in my study. I show how the amputations, grotesqueries, and sexed "parts" of Enlightenment political bodies speak to this era's tendency to use intersections of sex and violence to illustrate sovereignty in the age of revolution. And I demonstrate the ways in which images designed by Thomas Hobbes, the Earl of Shaftesbury, and Benjamin Franklin depict the sharing of political power as a strangely erotic and violent moment of embodiment—as, that is, an experience of ruin.

If the personhood imagined by the Enlightenment involved an abstract, disembodied individual, the intellectual remnant of the Cartesian split, then in addition to that personhood, the stories of the democratic subject's sexual fall offer an escape from jurisdictional embodiment through a mode of evasion that is both networked and corporeal. The ruin narrative shows the generative energy in the space between the imprecise, intermingled margins of self and other. Indeed, its operation in early American fiction asks us to rethink the ways in which our discipline has formulated notions of public and private spaces. Literary criticism has become especially wary of making such clean-cut distinctions as that between the public and private spheres; as a general rule we distrust such tidy binaries because they oversimplify too much. Most critics have tended to agree that just about every work of literature in some way or another reveals the so-called separateness of the public and private spheres as a cultural illusion, or at the very least as an egregious reduction of the complex give-and-take between gendered sources of power in the operations of culture and in the formation of personal and national identities.[20] Yet in our effort to avoid these binaries we have missed an important point, namely that it is not only the separateness of the spheres that is the pretense of gendered culture, but also the understanding that they represent the only two categories. Instead, we might think of a profane sphere, an ideological space that shadows the culture of contract, to see what additional alternative models of identity and community exist alongside the private (ruled by the marriage contract) and public (ruled by the social contract) spheres.

Erotic Citizens thus establishes that the sexed, ruined body is used to interrogate the myth of individualism in America just as that myth was being written and just as the domestic realm was becoming the guardian and sponsor of that individual. Against the cult of the individual that once seemed to define the era, this fall into the social realm, represented by a fall from virtue, portrays the self as an unstable and nonsingular entity. That is, the illicit sexual encounter of the unmarried woman comes to represent a countermythology of the democratic subject as a deviant and sometimes illegible agent whose connections define the ethos of the new nation as embracing a social self whose boundaries are uncertain. The corporeal impetus that motivates extramarital erotic encounters dissociates the self from the ideological jurisdiction of the possessive individual. The illicitly sexed body does not choose a path so much as it is drawn toward it, and this lack of will functions as a powerful critique of the individual and his independent, conscious morality as the centerpiece of a working republic. What the fallen body demonstrates, in aberrant romances with seducers, half-siblings, and ultimately with the social sphere itself, is that the most radical aspect of the Revolution was not the invention of a self-governing body, but the recognition of a self whose body is ungovernable. It is the fall into, and not out of, community that the ruin narrative represents as part of the American mythology of identity.

· ONE ·
The Aesthetic Work of the Ruin Narrative

> There is one truth concerning novels, which is in our time pretty well established; none I presume will controvert the authenticity of my remark, that the foundation of these elegant fabrics is laid on the passion of love.
> —William Hill Brown, *Ira and Isabella; or, The Natural Children*, 1807

What defines the ruin narrative as a genre? The ruin plot is, of course, the story of extramarital sex, an unmarried woman's tragic loss of virginity and its cultural capital. The characters necessary to accomplish such a tragedy do not, however, always include a libertine and an innocent young maiden. They are sometimes brother and sister, master and slave, priest and parishioner. And they do not accomplish ruin alone. In the novels discussed in this book, they require multiple accomplices, characters whose base aims (the hoarding of a family fortune, the capture of a runaway slave) can be accomplished only through the sexual ruin of another person. In addition to involving all sorts of third-party intrigue, the ruin plot also involves sexual unions that are illicit on multiple fronts, presenting readers with lovers who cross racial and class divides as well as committing the ultimate offense of sex outside of marriage.

But more than anything else, what defines the ruin narrative as a genre is that its illicit unions never involve lovers who consciously choose to rebel against the custom of marriage in search of something more radical. These are no free-thinking lovers daring to defy convention. Rather, the most basic generic staple of the ruin novel is the idea that these New World bodies are not self-governing. Instead, sexual longing or sexual coercion—not conscious decisions, not choices—facilitates the characters' departure from the marriage plot.

In the ruin narrative, the characters' feelings, which involve both their physical and emotional sensations and which are not entirely their own, do the deciding for them. A history of the concepts driving the postrevolutionary novel is, above all else, a history of feelings. Reflective of the antebellum era's cultural and historical moment, feeling—its imperatives, its contagion—is the driving force of the ruin plot's momentum. During this age of revolution, as the storytellers of the Atlantic world sought ways of thinking about political bonds that might be forged without the controlling influence of an absolute monarch, they looked to the connections that human beings naturally form among themselves. The collective vision that emerged in their writing was a republican model of sovereignty based on the feelings that create those human ties.

Rooted in notions of feeling, the ruin narrative overlaps with two important genres in early American literature: the sensational novel and the sentimental novel. Indeed, the terms *sensation* and *sentiment*—terms that identify the human ties the ruin genre explores—dominate the rhetoric of feeling throughout the eighteenth and nineteenth centuries. What distinguishes the sensational novel from the sentimental novel is the subject of much scholarly work. At its most basic, however, scholars have generally defined the difference between the two literary forms according to the intensity and power of feeling in each.[1] While both genres take their narrative energy from an exploration of human feeling, the eighteenth-century sensational novel is often regarded as the strangely intense forerunner to the tamer nineteenth-century novel of sentiment. Though this divide merits some suspicions—suspicions I address below—it is worth outlining in order to establish where the ruin narrative fits into the larger historical and literary landscape.

For most of the twentieth century, critics regarded early American sensational novels as curious, and curiously ardent, artifacts of a postrevolutionary cultural instability. These novels were considered to be a bit too bizarre and heavy-handed to qualify as serious works of literature, in part because they were written in such fierce, urgent prose. Within the pages of the sensational novel, lovers are not mates so much as they are zealots, and the obstinacy of their passions leads to the kind of peril from which there is no hope of recovery. The plots of these stories are dominated by crimes like seduction, kidnapping, suicide, and murder; love is lost, tragically and ubiquitously, and through those losses these texts depict a world in which acute, overpowering feeling produces one catastrophe after another. The seduction subgenre, which *is* about libertines and innocent young maidens—maidens who often suffer an unwanted pregnancy, social shunning, and death—was a particularly popular form of the sensational novel in the antebellum era. Though it included moralizing lectures, always ostensibly in the name of preventing women from going down the same dark path of temptation, its stories were also full of illicit sexual liaisons. The world of the sensational novel is defined by unpredictable, volatile relationships, the kind in which a marginally injudicious amour can quickly lead to incest, bastardy, and death. And there is no domestic sanctuary in these stories. In them, the home is just as unstable as the marketplace, and the family is not a respite from such disasters but often their origin, the site of internecine injury.

Scholars long described the sentimental novel, meanwhile, as the steadier genre, one that seemed to temper such passions. In the stories told in these novels, feelings are not overpowering liabilities but agents of self-discipline. Certainly they are far less turbulent. The domestic dramas of the American Renaissance see the household as a wholesome refuge defined by kinship and virtue. But the same critics who saw the eighteenth-century novel as too dark and unrestrained to qualify as serious literature were equally dismissive of these later works, which they regarded as rather too mawkish and predictable. Orphans find mothers, chaotic households find order, and the rod is judiciously spared in the safeguarding of the home as an oasis of privacy that must be kept separate from the tumult of the public sphere. Sentimental feelings are gentle reminders of what should be: marriage, children, and fidelity to the home as a place where problems are resolved, not created. These stories are about preserving a domestic tranquility whose moral guide is almost always white, female, and Christian.

More recent scholarship has drawn our attention to the fact that such genre divisions do not always hold, and it has pushed readers to recognize that early American novels, long characterized as too overwrought or too tame to be of literary value, were in fact bursting with it. Late twentieth-century criticism rightly rejected the notion that the early American novel was a sub-literary form, more craft than art, and the new historicist project to place into the canon books neither by nor about white men helped expose readers to their merit.² Twenty-first-century criticism on the nation-building role of feeling in early American literature has, moreover, complicated the sensation/sentiment divide. Critics have established that the sensational novel often includes appeals to the virtues of marriage and domesticity, and they have noted that sex and violence pervade much domestic fiction, which is filled with all sorts of in-house villainy.³

Nevertheless, there are important differences between sensationalism and sentimentalism, and those differences have implications for decoding the political and social visions of the ruin narratives this book examines. The genre of sensation and the genre of sentiment, though they have much in common and often overlap, do present a shift in literary patterns between the revolutionary era and later decades of antebellum writing. One important difference between the sensational and the sentimental novel is the role of feeling and how much of a hold it has over human behavior. Sensation and sentiment pull at opposing poles of the spectrum of feeling that defined antebellum nation building. Sensational texts give free rein to feeling, while sentimental texts portray the work that feeling might accomplish when it is directed toward the good. Ruin narratives explore the tension between these two forces. Tales of sexual ruin are often both sensational and sentimental works, drawing on and radicalizing their representations of the body's feeling response to others; the ruin narrative uses the tropes of both sensationalism and sentimentalism as it takes each genre's representations of feeling to new extremes. Consequently, ruin is never simply an act of extramarital sex; rather, it is the moment when feeling obliterates the subject's ability to self-govern.⁴ For the ruin narrative, feeling is no simple love-thy-neighbor ethos, but a democratic hail, and the ruin genre explores the sexed body's experience of feeling as an imperative that cannot be refused.

The Citizen Drive

E pluribus unum—out of the many, one—if there was any question that the republic needed to answer, it was the question of how, beyond issuing declarations and accomplishing military victories, to form a nation. How *do* you form the one out of the many? The ruin narrative asserted that such a transformation could be achieved without interference from king or contract because of the power of feeling. That power makes the subject's purchase on identity uncertain. Yet according to the logic of the ruin narrative, this uncertainty is necessary for nation building. Why? For the novels published after the Revolution, it seemed there was no better model than illicit, extramarital sex—of bodies drawn together outside the boundaries of contractual obligation—to show what a nation without a monarch might look like. In tales of ruin, the republican ideal captured by the early nation's motto is enacted through a state of feeling intersubjectivity. The ruin genre points to a crucial parallel between the lover and the citizen, both of whom ascend over self to achieve that intersubjectivity. In other words, the ruin narrative portrays the ascendance over self through the medium of the other as a model for the *citizen's* ascendance over self through the medium of country.

Through this model, what becomes clear is that the distance between self and other obstructs nation building, and the ruin narrative represents the democratic imperative to close that distance through sexual desire. The sexed body—erotically charged to the point of obliterating self-mastery—is an effective portrait of citizenship because it involves contact with another that precludes the necessity for contractual obligation to sustain it. On the one hand, illicit sex stands in for that which transforms the self into a citizen, a transformation from belonging to one's self to belonging to someone else, to, we might say, a community, the essential catalyst for a nation-building ethos. On the other hand, as a contract, what marriage suggests is that we must make promises in order to bear one another's company for the long term, that human relationships must be enforced by the law because they do not flourish on their own and must therefore rely on acts of consent ritualized by the state to be legitimate. The marriage contract, *just like the social contract,* insists that nature does not already join people together in acceptable ways. The terms of contract require that one must assess the merits of a union and then consent to join it. In the ruin narrative, however, the rejection of the marriage contract models a rejection of the social contract, and this rejection is, in turn, a denial of consent as a necessary regulatory force managing human contact. For the one utterance we do not encounter in the scene of ruin is the word *yes.* Characters are rather swept up in a momentum that they cannot control. They are subject to the violence of others or the violence of their own passions, but they never say or do anything that we would describe as "consent." These characters do not weigh the consequences of illicit sex and then decide whether they will engage in it. There is in these texts something much more powerful at work than consent in the formation of human intimacies and the social—national—bonds they represent.

Ruin narratives use the metonym of illicit sex to portray citizenship as a state of perpetual longing. At a critical point in the nation's early history, these narratives made the political point that contract was unnecessary, that bodies did not need to be coerced into feeling a sense of national belonging. What they claimed existed in place of such coercion had to appear as something much more powerful precisely because it lacked the provisional shoddiness of that which is manmade. Indeed, to the reigning philosophers, artists, and novelists of the day, the artifice of contract spoke to a basic misperception of human nature as in need of help in this regard; on the contrary, they argued, human beings were designed for the good and for the social, not for a selfish or solitary life. To explain why that misperception was such a blunder, and to redirect Enlightenment thought toward a different understanding of the nation, they had to define that which draws human beings together over and beyond anything a contract might accomplish. Anything short of a *drive* would not do. Using sexual longing as the metonym for political longing, then, these novels show a citizen drive at work, a kind of absolute need to close the distance between self and other that precludes any call for the use of state power to legislate human affairs.

The ruin genre's contribution to the work of nation building is to show the merits of extracontractual relationships. Under the influence of the citizen drive, bodies simply cannot refuse one another's company, though they face calumny, banishment, and even death. The generic business of the ruin narrative is to explore the nation-building properties of such bodies, of lovers who do not consent to unions with one another but who are nevertheless compelled to be together in spite of such consequences. This absence of consent comes to take on the power of national allegory. America, it turns out, is a woman who does not *choose*, and whose chastity is lost in service of the drive to join.

The Subject of Sex

In order to understand the interactions among agency, sex, and identity in the eighteenth- and nineteenth-century novel of ruin that define such joinings, a few definitions are in order. First, a word about *sex*. None of the novels I discuss in this book offers what we would today regard as an explicit scene of sexual contact, and what their first readers actually imagined when they encountered the semiotics of illicit heterosexual congress must in some ways remain unknown to us. Through metaphor, imagery, and innuendo, from clandestine carriage rides to the blood that rises to a lover's cheek, the language used in these novels tells us that extramarital sex signified a taboo sensate pleasure of the body that overwhelms the characters' ability to judge whether that sex was a good idea. William Hill Brown, for example, mentions the "blush of wantonness" and uses the word "intoxication" several times to name this pleasure in his second incest romance *Ira and Isabella* (1807). Authors describe women on the precipice of sexual ruin as drunk with desire, nearly unconscious with it, even possessed by it. In novels of rape-as-ruin, the libertine or slave master weaponizes sex; for the heroines in tales of rape, sex is defined by the terror of violation and by resistance against the ideal of a self that is rational, contained, and therefore violable. And in novels in which the ruined body becomes a martyred one, authors often dramatize the afterlife of sex, when it functions as a passport into a current of circulation, in which an entire community becomes a part of the suffering, ruined body. No matter what else sex is or signifies in these stories, then, it is about body-to-body contact that means entrance into a new aesthetic condition. It means more than becoming a seducer, a villain, an adulterer, a whore. It means experiencing the body not as a container of self but as a site of contact, and in these stories, sexual contact is experienced as ontological traffic. For women, of course, this means carrying the punishing label of sexual immodesty. And in almost every scene of ruin, sex is something that is preceded by an act of overpowering. The ruined body is always a vanquished one, conquered by the brutality or the sensational pleasures of another body.

Sympathy and the Social Contract

The senses invoked by sex are most frequently identified by that vexed word, *sympathy*, which brings us to the next definition. For the seventeenth- and eighteenth-century Atlantic writers who engaged with the term, sympathy is an intimate, interosculatory ontological entanglement. It involves an intersubjectivity that is at times erotic, at other times violent. Sympathy makes a mess of identity, wrecking as it does the idea that bodies have materially uncrossable borders. It speaks of an innately sensate capacity to feel with and as another person, especially in scenes of suffering but also in illicit sexual encounters. To experience sympathy is to *be,* ever so ephemerally, someone else for a moment, to breathe through, for a heartbeat, the corporeal pains and pleasures of another person. This understanding of the body as an experience that can be shared, rather than as an isolated object, allows for an identity that is porous and fungible. For the philosophers who struggled so mightily with the term, men like Anthony Ashley Cooper, the Third Earl of Shaftesbury, Sir Francis Hutcheson, Adam Smith, and David Hume, sympathy is an ontologically uncontainable emotional pang originating, but not staying, in someone else. It is being someone else *in addition* to being oneself.

The seventeenth- and eighteenth-century philosophers discussed in this book were part of an intellectual movement interested in understanding what joins people together—what impels them to form and sustain human societies. The most prominent thinkers of this movement wrote about sympathy as a basic human trait, one that allows human beings to feel not just for but *as* another. This take on human nature was certainly not an isolated philosophical movement; alongside sympathy, philosophers of the day wrote animatedly about the powers of kings and contracts to forge political communities. In fact, the philosophy of sympathy exists in part in reaction to Thomas Hobbes's *Leviathan* (1651), which famously argues that without a social contract between the monarch and his people, life in a state of nature would be "solitary, poore, nasty, brutish, and short."[5] For Hobbes, the people consent to the rule of a monarch because his rule could provide the kind of discipline that prevents their lower natures from dominating the land; the people agree to this arrangement in order to be protected from the harm they would otherwise do to one another. A century after Hobbes, Jean-Jacques Rousseau's *Of the Social Contract* (1762) posits a similar need for discipline, though it comes from among people rather than from above them; for Rousseau, the social contract asks that the people of any society agree to sacrifice the advantages of radical freedom to each other rather than to a higher authority in order to protect themselves from the violence they might inflict upon one another without a mutually defensive arrangement in place.

In both cases, the social contract is that to which human beings agree only to safeguard their own persons and properties—it is a calculating and self-interested agreement made out of dark convictions about what people will do to each other when they are not forcibly stopped. The premise of each kind of contract is the notion that people are rational individuals who are inherently self-interested, who are separated from one another by the sinew and skin of a body that is mine and not yours, and who agree to the rules of community for personal profit and security. But in antebellum American literature, the idea that most often seems to take hold is the idea of sympathy as that which impels human beings toward one another without striking any rational, self-protecting bargains. The promise and the danger of sympathy to form human society without human beings willing it into existence became the subject of novels for decades after the Revolution.[6]

In more recent decades, scholarship on the eighteenth-century Anglo-Atlantic novel has rightly focused on sympathy to understand what models of self and community existed outside of the ideological jurisdiction of the contractual individual. Critics at the forefront of this trend in sympathy studies have produced important work about the relation between feeling and nation building. Sympathy, they have persuasively argued, operates as a democratizing force, prompting an emotional register that sustains a powerful human interest in the welfare of others.[7] This is a compelling reading of how sympathy fashions democratic relationships. Yet what is missing from that conversation is the role that illicit sex plays in enacting the democratic work of sympathy. As the ruin narrative shows, the role of sex in the operation of sympathy is a critical part of this political work. The triumph—and sometimes the burden—of the sexed body is that its capacity for sympathy brings communities together. For these novels, the sympathetic subject's architecture is scaffolded by the multitude, by the People, in an experience of embodied connectivity that the word "individual" simply does not come close to expressing. If out of the many, there emerges a unified one, these novels suggest, then that one springs from forces much more powerful than the self-interest that contract philosophy names as the origin of community.

Those forces are also less stable. Through their experience of sympathy, the characters in the ruin narrative often become confused about who they are to one another and to themselves. They express themselves with lines like "My husband, my brother," "I am no longer what I was in any one thing," and "[W]e are but mere machines. Let love once pervade our breasts; and its object may mould us into any form."[8] Moments like these, not at all uncommon in the ruin narrative, show how sympathy renders identity as decidedly unfixed. Indeed, such moments depict embodiment as hinging upon a mix of taboo desire and a romantic possession that questions the very foundations of human agency as emanating from anything even remotely resembling individual will.

The Individual

This brings up another definition central to the ruin genre: *the individual*. The ruin narrative presents the sympathetic subject as an alternative to, and as a reaction against, the politics of the individual. But what are the characteristics of this figure? Contract philosophers like Hobbes and Rousseau imagined the individual as, first and foremost, one who consents or rebels in enactments of a solitary and rational masculinity.[9] In starkly gendered and racial terms, the individual is a white man in full possession of himself. Where his body begins and ends is never in question. He assiduously (and often violently) seeks independence from oppressive monarchs and stifling domesticities by locating authority within the self. His whiteness signifies that he "owns" that self as an inalienable property, and this idea of self-ownership reifies the Cartesian split. The individual is a volitional, reasoning creature, a mind enclosed in a body, an agent that wills this material housing of the body into action. Dubbed the American Adam in decades past, he is "a self-reliant young man who does seem to have sprung from nowhere and whose characteristic pose, to employ Tocqueville's words, was the solitary stance in the presence of Nature and God."[10] Of course we must be careful not to oversimplify this figure.[11] The complex history surrounding the emergence of the Enlightenment's sovereign individual occurs within, at least in part, the ideologies informing slavery, sexual difference, and colonialism and is the result of the cultural work of centuries; literary critics today thus recognize the individual in multiple and layered forms.[12] Critics have over the last few years reimagined the American Adam and have questioned who, and what, an individual is. Yet what continues to be clear is that the individual *possesses* his individuating qualities, and this helps him to imagine for himself an identity that exists in a "marooned sort of self-enclosure."[13] As the ruin narrative portrays him, the individual imagines himself as inviolable in part through seeing his body as an isolating apparatus, and in part through the violation and subjugation of others. He imagines he owns himself by dispossessing others of that same "natural" right. Perhaps most importantly, the possessive individual must be himself *and no one else* to sustain a necessarily proprietary, objectifying gaze and the ontological distance that such always-potential ownership implies.

In the ruin narrative, the closing of that distance offers a critique of the individual and the principle of self-possession. The ruined body is not in possession of itself but of the other. Its nonjurisdictional corporeality enacts a sharing or circulation of identity that precludes self-possession. In this genre, the conditions of the body recall as they contradict the Lockean assessment of the self as a possession, a man's naturally occurring "property in his own person."[14] The drama of the ruin narrative thus comes to represent the conflict between belonging to oneself and belonging to another, a conflict that might also be said to define post-revolutionary America's struggle to define itself. The ruin narrative is of course about sex and desire, about violence and coercion—the dramas of eros and thanatos in full force—but it is also about what it might mean to experience a shared custody of self. In fact, these texts suggest that such a sharing is always already in practice inside a community, so that one *never* has the totality of one's entire self at all.

The Body

In the ruin narrative, extramarital sex marks the departure from a jurisdictional mode of embodiment into a corporeally networked one. Such a networking, according to the terms of the genre, is necessary for the enactment of democratic relations. At stake in that networking is the rejection of the self-possessed individual and the ontological chastity such a figure implies. Ruined bodies do the work of that rejection as a nation-building practice. Indeed, at the heart of the Atlantic Enlightenment's project of nation building is the way in which the sexed, ruined body becomes a site of political joining through "ontological slippage" and exchange.[15]

This brings us to our final definition, *the body*. In some ways, this is the most difficult term to define, for the ruin narrative asks us to rethink what a body is. And it asks us to do this in part by insisting on what the body is not. First and foremost, the story of sexual ruin is the story of the body failing to act as an uncrossable boundary. This genre sees the body as something other than a materialization of the isolated individual, an untraversable frontier of self. For these texts, embodiment is not a state of ontological quarantine.

That brings us to what the body *is*. For the ruin narrative, subjectivity and the flesh cannot be dissociated. Adulterers, coquettes, and the like consistently find that they *are* their bodies. And they are governed by lust, by violence, by anything but a willed, volitional self. The ruined body's relation to the other governs the terms of agency experienced through the intercorporeal—a shared, sensate experience. Ruined bodies, that is, are always subject *to* the corporeal network in which they find themselves. In opposition to the principle of mind/body dualism, the principle of the relational body is that there is no singular, willful, volitional agency motivating human thought and behavior. Instead, the ruined body is governed by the body of the other, whose attractions and assaults animate and arouse, subdue and occupy. Put another way, the relational body is not in control because it is not in sole possession of itself. Those who are ruined are simply not the sole occupants of the corporeal frame.[16] Thus the ruined body is, fundamentally, a relational body.

This ideal of relationality comes from what is known as the moral sense school, the eighteenth-century collection of philosophers grappling with sympathy as a source of ethical instincts issuing from the body's feeling response to others. For them, the body acts as a moral, sensate compass that is directed by the pains and pleasures of other bodies. It is a mechanism of community formation, and a site of relational promise. The body, according to this school, obscures any capacity for rational consent. Bodies are ruled, and ruled *well*, by other bodies. This is not apolitical work: in a perfect world, the state's investment in coerced bodies would be replaced by interpersonal, corporeal attraction and feeling, both of which are seen as fundamentally good. Recent scholarship has taken up and expanded upon the work of the moral sense school, exploring the possibilities of replacing the sole occupancy model of embodiment. In essence modern theorists are building upon the eighteenth-century ideal of the relational body with inspiring notions of "inter-embodiment" and calls for "rescrambling the dichotomy between objectified bodies or embodied subjects."[17] If there is anything that such terms have in common, it is that they show how the body is inseparable from subjectivity. And indeed such terms help us to understand the relational condition of embodiment in the ruin narrative. For the ruin genre, agency cannot be explained through an understanding of the body as a machine operated by a cerebral, rational, *singular* self's command. Rather, in the ruin narrative, the body is what Elizabeth Grosz calls "the very 'stuff' of subjectivity," that which does not "hide or reveal an otherwise unrepresented latency or depth but is a set of operational linkages and connections with other things, other bodies."[18] In other words, the body is not a material object with a self that is hidden "inside." There is no private, inaccessible interiority of self with a material body blocking access to it; bodies are bridges, not walls.

As Grosz argues, it is a distinctly patriarchal insistence on bodies as fundamentally separate from one another that abets the self/other dichotomy. The ruin narrative depicts this separation as an inherently undemocratic political relation among individuals. If the body *is* the subject, and the subject is always subject *to,* then a new term describing subjectivity is in order. This is what Lee Edelman and Lauren Berlant have recently named "negativity," or the notion of subjectivity that "unsettles the fantasy of sovereignty" and replaces it with a "scene of relationality." In other words, one's ontological capital becomes collective capital. And sex is central to building that relationality. As Berlant says, we need to consider "the subject as that which is structurally nonsovereign in a way that's intensified by sex."[19]

Indeed, we ought to think of the body as an ontological commons where political joinings occur. Certainly Enlightenment literature tends to locate its most powerful dramas within that commons. A full-scale struggle against mind/body dualism is at work in this historical period, an era that also saw the ascendance of the self-possessed individual as a fitting model for democratic political identity. Thus the rise of the ruined woman and the rise of the individual man are part of the same political debate, a debate about what kind of citizenship would be the most able servant of the democratic nation. At stake is the very essence of what it means to be a "man" or to be a "woman" in the nation and in the body. As Thomas Laqueur points out in his landmark study *Making Sex,* the Atlantic Enlightenment witnessed a radical change in understanding the relationship between gender and the body. The body, Laqueur notes, is not an immutable "fact" or an irrefutable matter of biological parts that are always and forever assembled according to a timeless, natural, and unchanging anatomy. The very notion of "opposite sexes" is a relatively new invention; Laqueur's work reveals how in fact the seventeenth century saw the "discovery" of two sexes where one used to be. This shift, from the one-sex model to the two-sex model, is a shift between seeing sex as part of a hierarchy (woman being the lesser version of man, rather than his opposite) to seeing two "incommensurate opposites" in the bodies of men and women.[20] The very history of such a "discovery" shows just how tenuous all this is, how fungible the body becomes, and how a retreat to biology as a point of certainty about the essential nature of bodies remains impossible.

Rape, Race, and Ruin

While many of the scenes of ruin considered in this book are scenes of desire, many are just the opposite, scenes of sexual and racial violence. A final discussion about these modes of violence is thus in order. Enlightenment thinking about the body produced many contradictions concerning race, sex, and consent. The ruin narrative as a genre engaged these contradictions through one trope in particular: the rape of a female slave by her master. Ruin narratives interrogated the political and philosophical paradox at the heart of such violent encounters, namely the master's attempt, through sexual violation, to obliterate a subjectivity that the logic of slavery presumed was already absent. Such rape scenes not only highlighted the horrors of slavery for women, then, but also threw into relief a profound inconsistency in the political notion of the integrity of the individual.

On one level, of course, depictions of the rape of slave women by their white masters reveal the emergent state's prurient and coercive investment in people who cannot withhold consent. Their very existence is meant to highlight the legitimacy and power of their opposite: the sovereign, consenting individual. Critics have made this point forcefully, noting that the political figure of the individual may define the age of revolution, but it also, equally and interconnectedly, defines the age of slavery.[21] Certainly ruin narratives about the particular plight of black women describe rape and enslavement as tools used to promote the individual's—the rapist's, the slaveholder's—political ascendancy. Scholars have noted that this ascendancy is born in part out of the slave trade, the semiotics of which, they have argued, figure Africa as the fallen woman; it is only through a violating and subjugating encounter with the other that the white male individual can imagine himself as inviolable.[22]

Such semiotics are, to be sure, at work in the texts examined in this book. But, at another level, scenes of the sexual subjugation of slaves by masters contained, in the pages of ruin narratives, the seeds of a profoundly subversive political question. Through these violent scenes, the ruin narrative asked: How does slavery's coerced divestiture of self relate to resistance against slavery through a radical, anti-individualist subjectivity? And how, in turn, does such subjectivity constitute an act of rebellion, one that threatens the essential legitimacy of notions of individuality, consent, and the foundations of the state and of the institution of slavery itself? In ruin narratives from throughout the Atlantic, the enslaved heroine's resistance to rape registers as an act of resistance to the ideology of the individual, the master who seeks reassurance of his own contained inviolability though acts of sexual, racial violence. In other words, in these narratives, instead of encountering the enslaved woman's pursuit of being recognized as an individual—along with all the security and power that status would seem to imply—we encounter scenes in which the slave woman rejects that pursuit. Thus one of the most radical claims of the ruin narrative as a genre is that the rape-as-ruin fantasy of slave violation can be contested by bodies that repudiate, as a tool of the master, the idealization of corporeal boundaries.

To understand that rejection more fully, we need to recognize that ruin narratives about slave rape emerged out of, and were written in reaction to, the complex history of racial and sexual violence in the Atlantic slave trade. The eighteenth century saw the production of a veritable epidemic of stories and images that romanticized slave rape. Works like John Gabriel Stedman's *Narrative of a Five Years Expedition against the Revolted Negroes of Surinam* (1790), William Pittis's *The Jamaica Lady; or, The Life of Bavia* (1720),[23] and Isaac Teale's poem "The Sable Venus: An Ode" (1765), to name but a few, were highly popular texts that represented slave rape and concubinage in the style of the adventure tale. Such texts eroticized and normalized slave rape by portraying it as part of a bawdy romp or as fodder for a naturalist's taxonomy. They presented the slave woman's suffering as a source of erotic pleasure or pseudo-scientific interest. And, as Marcus Wood notes, in a "hideous irony" they presented the female slave, not the slaver, as "the sexual aggressor" who had "enslaved white male hearts."[24]

These texts pretended to invert the racial and gendered power hierarchies that defined slavery. By doing so, they denied the sexual coercion at work in the subjugating unions they depicted while presenting what Wood calls a "mock celebration of the sexual desirability of black women."[25] In other words, as Wood points out, the irony of the inversions—the very idea that a female slave could hold any power, sexual or otherwise, over a white man—was meant to appear obviously, even humorously, false. These inversions and mockeries were designed to corroborate white male sexual dominance and inviolability. By insisting that his dominance was obvious, the inversion worked as a safeguard for the master's hold on his power as an individual.

An example illustrates this attempt at inversion quite dramatically. One of the era's most well-known images depicting the eroticized rape of a slave woman, Thomas Stothard's infamous painting (made into an engraving by William Grainger), *The Voyage of the Sable Venus, from Angola to the West Indies* (1794), serves as an instructive example of such portrayals—portrayals against which the ruin narrative about slave rape was reacting. (See figure 1.) Stothard was a prolific eighteenth-century artist who is best known for his illustrations of the popular literature of his time, and his engraving is a typical example of the eighteenth century's portrayals of slave rape.[26] (It is also a classic example of Enlightenment iconography in its representation of the damage done to subjugated bodies in service of the nation, a theme that adheres to the other images considered throughout this book.) Stothard's disturbing vision of the Middle Passage captive as the exoticized female slave is based on one of those popular tales eroticizing slave rape mentioned above, Teale's poem "The Sable Venus: An Ode." The poem recounts a story of the god Neptune transforming himself into the captain of a slave ship in order to have sex with a slave, an act that produces several mixed-race children ("Blest offspring of the warm embrace!").[27] Presented with a jaunty, rollicking tone, the poem's main theme is a celebration of sexual unions between slavers and their captives.

Stothard's engraving and texts like it reveal the white imperial slaver's attempt to romanticize the Middle Passage through what Marcus Wood identifies as a pornographic rendering of racial violence.[28] Indeed, what is most striking about *The Voyage of the Sable Venus* is the way in which its central figure appears as both an imperiled victim of sexual violence and a commanding, seductive siren. Venus looks pensively at Cupid, who hovers

Figure 1. Thomas Stothard, *The Voyage of the Sable Venus, from Angola to the West Indies,* 1794. Engraving by W. Grainger. (Miriam and Ira D. Wallach Division, The New York Public Library)

perpendicularly at the upper left portion of the engraving and whose arrow is aimed straight for Neptune, a god known for his sexual exploits and especially for his acts of rape. The presence of the cherubs of various racial shades implies that on the Atlantic, the "goddess of love" will be forced into acts of sexual reproduction with a slaver. Her majestic, muscular body exists in contradiction to the symbols of her sexual subjugation, the shackles and the lack of clothing. The symbolism of the image additionally manifests in the exposed folds within the opened clamshell that invoke the labial spread and depict the erotic invitation of putative black female lasciviousness. The reins held so loosely by Venus, along with the phallic sea monsters plowing the ocean in their trek toward the Americas, further the tension between the image's ironic exaltation of black female sexual dominance and the sexually violent intent of the imperial slaver. Neptune's genitals are barely covered by the most passive of the cherubs, whose coy mien meets the viewer's gaze, urging the viewer toward sexual conjectures; Neptune is waving the Union Jack in a gesture clearly designed to indicate that the Anglo-Atlantic investment in the African slave trade is an investment in the master's sexual access to the slave, the hideous production of human chattel rooted in the law of *partus sequitur ventrem*.

The Voyage of the Sable Venus is unrecoverably a celebration of slave rape, an eroticized phantasmagoria of threats to the female slave body, including sexual violation, captivity, forced migration, and compulsory sexual reproduction. In rendering her as a goddess with the irony of a predatory imperial gaze, Stothard presents the Sable Venus as an example of racially and sexually inverted power.[29] The engraving reveals the fantasy of inversion—the idea that it is she who holds sexual command of the moment, not the master-rapist, in order to divest the slaver of his violent intent. Such an ironic reversal of the captive/captor relation is, of course, an exculpatory fantasy. Violent sexual access to her body constitutes the essence of the Atlantic slave trade. In forcing her to embody the predatory sexual impulse of the master, Stothard's depiction demonstrates how representations of enslavement can signify the relationality of the subjugated body through violence. The engraving offers a scene of what Saidiya Hartman calls the master's "slipping into the captive body."[30] In this sense, the slave body becomes a "surrogate for the master's body" that is in a "perpetual state of ravishment," a state making "personhood coterminous with injury."[31] In other words, the violence must go further than skin and bone. Rape is not *enough*. Added to it is this act of inverting the power dynamics and inscribing the master's predatory desires onto the slave woman's body. Put another way, this is not just a sexual violation but also an ontological one.

What *The Voyage of the Sable Venus* presents, then, is an example of the ideologies of race and gender that the ruin narratives about slave rape set out to resist. They did so in what can only be called revolutionary ways, by exploring how such acts of surrogacy—acts of ontological violence—could be reclaimed, could, in fact, be used to contest the security of the individual's inviolability. These stories unmask the horrors of slavery's ontological violence. They reveal the ideological fraudulence of two linked ideas, mastery over another human being and self-mastery. And they reveal slavery for what it is, a scene of ontological exchange and instability. Slavery, they argue, does not secure the master's role as an inviolable individual. It unravels that role, one might even say *ruins* it.

Such arguments about ontological instability and its radical political potential are in abundant evidence throughout the ruin genre. In order to understand the genre's aesthetic work, both in tales of the ruin of slave women and in tales about the ruin of white women, a deeper look into the political operations of sympathy is in order. For while sympathy works through and against black and white bodies in greatly varied ways, as the texts we are about to examine show, its capacity to produce what we ought to think of as the commons body is surprisingly consistent. The text that illuminates Enlightenment understandings of sympathy perhaps better than any other, the Third Earl of Shaftesbury's *Characteristicks of Men, Manners, Opinions, Times* (1711), is the subject of the following chapter. For as Shaftesbury demonstrates, the power of sympathy disassembles the self as it works to assemble the nation, and it wields control in ways that mark human agency as entirely beyond human control.

· TWO ·

Ruin's Subject in Shaftesbury's *Characteristicks*

> One thought chases another, and draws after it a third, by which it is expelled in its turn. In this respect, I cannot compare the soul more properly to any thing than to a republic or commonwealth, in which the several members are united by the reciprocal ties of government and subordination, and give rise to other persons, who propagate the same republic in the incessant changes of its parts.
> —David Hume, *A Treatise of Human Nature*, 1739

> Nature hath implanted in our breasts a love of others, a sense of duty to them, a moral instinct, in short, which prompts us irresistibly to feel and to succor their distresses. . . . I sincerely, then, believe with you in the general existence of a moral instinct. I think it the brightest gem with which the human character is studded, and the want of it as more degrading than the most hideous of the bodily deformities.
> —Thomas Jefferson, *Letters*, 1814

We ought to understand ruin's subject as a democratic figure nevertheless ruled by a tyrant more fearsome than any other: the body itself. For the sexed body of the ruin narrative, acting under the sway of sympathy's interosculatory charms, is always subject *to*. Licentious, tragic, and always proscribed, the tales of extramarital sex so ubiquitous in the early American novel seek to dramatize the way in which sympathy operates to render intimacy into equality. In the imaginations of so many early US authors, the body was no mere house of flesh but a site of ethos, a fusion of the sensate and the sentimental; in their novels, the body is what constitutes democratic feeling, which is the same as saying it is what constitutes democratic equality.[1] As the philosophy of the day understood it, the body existed in a network of shared attractions and appetites, repulsions and mercies, and it was of great concern to the nation-building project of antebellum novelists because in its condition of sodality, the body does less to define what a person is than to suggest what a People might be.

The work of the philosophers discussed in this chapter offered a positive perspective on this power of the body, one that afforded the American founders the kind of utopian vision they needed to form a republic that could survive only if the people were united with each other rather than subordinate to a king. Thomas Jefferson, James Madison, John Adams, Benjamin Rush, Benjamin Franklin: all avidly read the works of the philosophers covered here, and the ideas about sympathy and the body that they represented informed the founders' ideas about what a republic could, and should, be.[2]

In the philosophical culture that gave rise to the ruin narrative, the body emerges as a civic authority. The most revered thinkers of the era regarded the body as an assembly of moral impulses and social appetites that form human society. According to the great philosophical works of the eighteenth century that in part made the age of revolution possible, what makes equality among men thinkable is the political power of sympathy. The aesthetic work of the ruin narrative emerges out of philosophical debates about whether sympathy could function as a kind of embodied political unity that would lend itself to the formation of a democracy. These debates defined what is called aesthetic or moral sense philosophy, which rejected social contract theory in favor of a more sentimental reading of human "nature." The moral sense philosophy so avidly read by the founders informed the post-revolutionary ruin narrative in extraordinary ways, especially through those philosophical works that insisted that sympathy was the social glue that would hold the new republic together.[3] Authors of the ruin narrative used illicit sexual encounters to explore how sympathy could recalibrate the monarchical subject into a figure whose appetites and instincts looked to the people rather than to the king for the power that community brings.

Only through a study of eighteenth-century British aesthetic philosophy can we properly understand the aesthetic work of sympathy experienced as sex in the antebellum ruin narrative. This chapter offers a reading of sympathy's place in the history of ideas and its role in understanding the body in Enlightenment terms. I begin with the seventeenth century's investment in the social contract and the eighteenth century's response to it, a response that gives rise to the ruin narrative. A close reading of one of the most overlooked of the moral sense philosophers offers an extremely helpful understanding of sympathy and its relation to the sexed body as a politically charged medium for civic intercourse. Such an understanding also, as we shall soon see, helps to reveal the limits of contract.

The Earl of Shaftesbury and the *Sensus Communis*

Perhaps nothing is more instructive of the aesthetic work performed by tales of sexual ruin than the book read more than almost any other during the eighteenth century, Anthony Ashley Cooper's *Characteristicks of Men, Manners, Opinions, Times* (1711).[4] Cooper, the Third Earl of Shaftesbury, considered the "father" of the moral sense philosophy normally associated with the Scottish Enlightenment, is a key figure among the eighteenth-century Atlantic philosophers who set out to define what exactly it is that binds human beings together. The more familiar works of philosophical giants like David Hume and Adam Smith rest squarely on the shoulders of *Characteristicks* and its inauguration of the moral sense school. This school holds that the body is a dependable moral compass that helps us navigate our way through ethical problems with the use of feeling—a sixth "sense"—that is both emotionally and physically *felt*. Throughout his work, Shaftesbury describes what he called the moral sense, or that sympathetic impulse that impels us toward the social good and that resides within the body, which is somewhere between calling it an instinct and an emotion. He returns to the ancient Greek concept of Κοινονοημοσύνη, or the *sensus communis,* to illuminate what he sees as the innate public spirit of humankind—the emotional glue that makes a commonwealth possible and that precludes the need for any social contract. The study of aesthetics became in *Characteristicks* a study of what Shaftesbury found to be the most beautiful and the most obvious attribute of human nature, namely that the body is the site of moral experience. The impulses toward the social and the good—the feelings that turn the body into a moral informant—that Shaftesbury writes about issue from what we might call the somatic spell. For within the pages of

Characteristicks we encounter a curious, unorthodox glossary of the body's powers—"secret charm," "force of nature," "impulse," "agitation," even, at one point, "moral Magick"—that witness the body entranced by the call to one another that constitutes a call to the good.[5]

Indeed, most of *Characteristicks* hardly reads like a sober work of philosophical argumentation at all. Today, its most widely read essay is the relatively short "An Inquiry Concerning Virtue and Merit," which argues that human beings are innately good and do good works because they are naturally inclined to (not because some selfish principle teaches them that what benefits their neighbors also benefits themselves), and which does not read anything like the rest of this three-volume work.[6] The bulk of Shaftesbury's treatise is as strange as it is eclectic. It is nearly impossible to convey to those unfamiliar with *Characteristicks* what an utter surprise and delight it is. Readers of the full text will find long passages in which Shaftesbury endorses the merits of talking to oneself, and others in which he tells stories about, for example, an imprisoned prophet who uses the time in his solitary cell to sound out the alphabet and see what letters are missing, an Ethiopian magically transported to a Paris carnival, the frenzied contagion of religious mobs, and the use of a good joke in political debates. There is a section on the mission of metaphysics and one on how to paint drapery. He peoples this multiform text with a sizable cast of imaginary characters, including clowns, travelers, hermits, and oracles. He uses fable, allegory, and countless hypotheticals to draw his readers in. And then he concludes by setting out on a "Miscellany" that leaps from one subject to another with what can be described only as a kind of gleeful postmodern abandon.

Throughout all of this, Shaftesbury offers what is clearly his own deeply felt advice on how to live honorably as the pawns we most certainly are in nature's theater of the passions. He urges us to recognize the "social Love" that "draws us out of our-selves" (46 II) and into the realm of sociability. This is a "natural affection" that he insists is "implanted in our Natures" (80 II). In other words, for Shaftesbury, nature is the body's own tyrant, but not the sort that one might wish to throw off. Nature impels us toward one another, instills within us an appetite for fellowship that is as salutary as it is irresistible.

Such a concept becomes a springboard for some of the strangest and most radical claims about identity to be found among the moral sense philosophers. Of especial interest in this study is Shaftesbury's use of a short allegorical tale about sexual ruin, a tale that he then uses as a vehicle for understanding a distinctly anti-individual portrait of human identity. As we shall soon see, his own doctrine dismisses the notion that human beings are devoted to what he calls "the narrow bottom of mere SELF" (74 I). For him, the idea that individuals are self-possessed, volitionally willful agents is a preposterous myth. Called "The Story of an Amour," this episode in *Characteristicks* helps explain how sympathy precludes the coldly rational social contract as that which binds us together, and the tale uses the sexed body to make a radical argument about the corporeal entanglements of civic life that, he insists, exist outside of the ideological jurisdiction of the social contract. Through these entanglements, Shaftesbury claims, what is ruined is a different sort of chastity, the imagined ontological boundary separating self from other.

Shaftesbury and the Monster of Malmesbury

Before we look at the way Shaftesbury uses sexual ruin in "The Story of an Amour" to illustrate the body's moral magic, we should understand that the primary objective of *Characteristicks* was to undermine the relatively recent emergence of social contract theory onto the Atlantic political scene. He designed his work as a refutation of a very different philosophical understanding of how civil bodies form. It's worth digging into this context a bit to get the full texture of Shaftesbury's purpose; his ideas about innate human sociability were his answer to a much, much darker vision of human nature. For the *sensus communis* refuted what was then the most popular, and for Shaftesbury, the most deeply disturbing, reigning political theory of the time: the people's surrender to a truly frightening figure, the monarch rendered as a polyontological monster. That monster is, of course, none other than the sovereign lurking within (or rather towering over) the pages of Thomas Hobbes's *Leviathan; or, The Matter, Forme, and Power of a Commonwealth Ecclesiasticall and Civill* (1651). The reception of Hobbes's work offers some insight into the import of its claims. It is no understatement to say that *Leviathan* was the most hated philosophical work of its century.[7] In it, Hobbes offered the first full-throated articulation of social contract theory, and for Shaftesbury, as for many of its readers, it represented the worst kind of cynicism. The idea of a "natural" moral sense—an innate, sympathetic register that assesses the moral qualities around us—thus really begins as Shaftesbury's fiery response to Hobbes's alarming claims about the necessary "art" of government.[8] By understanding why Shaftesbury so animatedly rejected Hobbes's social contract theory, we can begin to understand why the "art" of the marriage contract came to be rejected by so many early American authors.

First, a note on *Leviathan* and the misreading of it that sometimes leads to Hobbes's demonization as the "monster of Malmesbury." For well over three centuries, readers have been oversimplifying *Leviathan* as a defense of monarchy, which they then misconstrue as a defense of despotism.[9] This misinterpretation arises from Hobbes's depiction of the "state of nature," a philosophical exercise that assesses what it means to be human by imagining people surviving in a presocial, uncivilized environment, a project that for Hobbes ends in revealing what an awful menace we are to one another. *Leviathan* argues that human beings are naturally selfish and violent figures, unruly wrongdoers whose rampant egoism requires the absolute authority of a sovereign (*not* a lone monarch, a distinction that will make sense in a moment) to prevent a kind of barbaric chaos; without it, people live in state of nature, a bleak landscape that hosts a "warre of every man against every man" in which their lives are famously "solitary, poore, nasty, brutish, and short" (71, 70).[10] The story of the Enlightenment self as a possessive individual in some ways relies on the premise that without the social contract, all that would be left is this state of merciless anarchy governed by violent self-interest. In order to protect individual property and person, the story goes, we must engage in the social contract, a do-unto-others operation by which we all agree to be nicer than our nasty and brutish natures would otherwise permit. We conquer our natures so that each of us is rendered safe from the others. Thus the need for a "social" contract really comes from the need for preservation of self in a world peopled by distinctly antisocial beings who have no profound connection to one another. Other people are not allies but obstacles, worrisome rivals bent upon theft and violence. In other words, as Hobbes tells it, social contract theory assumes that we are—at least before we engage in the social contract—ontologically separate and therefore naturally antagonistic, in competition for resources and power.

The only hope is to form a covenant, which Hobbes defines as a "mutuall transferring of Right . . . which men call CONTRACT," in which everyone, *including* the monarch, agrees to submit to a mutually constituted sovereign power (74). What readers often miss about *Leviathan* is that Hobbes's description of the sovereign marks it as a *union*—one might even argue, a *marriage*—between the monarch and his subjects. Hobbes's "mutuall transferring of Right" fuses the inchoate political force of the masses into a single sovereign entity that is jointly constituted by a people and a king. The result is a superpolitical, superhuman figure of absolute might. As Hobbes puts it, "This is the Generation of that great LEVIATHAN, or rather (to speak more reverently) of that *Mortall God*, to which wee owe under the *Immortal God*, our peace and defence" (95). The power of the sovereign lies in the contract the parties make to form this political colossus; mixed in with all that mortal god business is the notion that because human beings are separate from one another, human selfishness is the motive for sovereign rule. It is the sublunary predilections of ordinary folk who make this power possible. This is a covenant and a representational amalgamation, born not of force, but choice, and the beast represents the monstrousness of a *consenting union*, an essentially conjugal joining of *all* members of civil society into one grotesque figure.[11]

Anyone looking at the original cover of Hobbes's work can get a clear picture of what this means. (See figure 2.) The head of the monarch is supported by a torso and limbs that are made of the masses, tiny little humans joining together to form, literally, a civil *body*. It is strange that echoes of *e pluribus unum* do not drown out the critical responses to Hobbes, which too often mistakenly denounce him as an apologist for tyranny.[12] Rather than a tyrant, Hobbes is careful to note, within such a sovereign "consisteth the Essence of the Commonwealth" and he is "*One Person, of whose Acts a great Multitude, by mutuall Covenants one with another, have made themselves every one the Author*" (96). In other words, the creation of a commonwealth requires more than a fair amount of ontological and political gerrymandering, but Hobbes thought men could do no better, since the only way a monarch can do well for himself is by serving the people (his people, who are in some way also himself) well. As Hobbes says, the agreement of animals "is Naturall; that of men, is by Covenant only, which is Artificiall" (95). As such a claim makes clear, for Hobbes, all we have is the art or artificiality of contract. Nature cannot save us from ourselves because it is too busy pitting us against one another.

How might a moral sense philosopher react to this insistence on artifice, on contract, as that which must bind us together in the face of our nasty

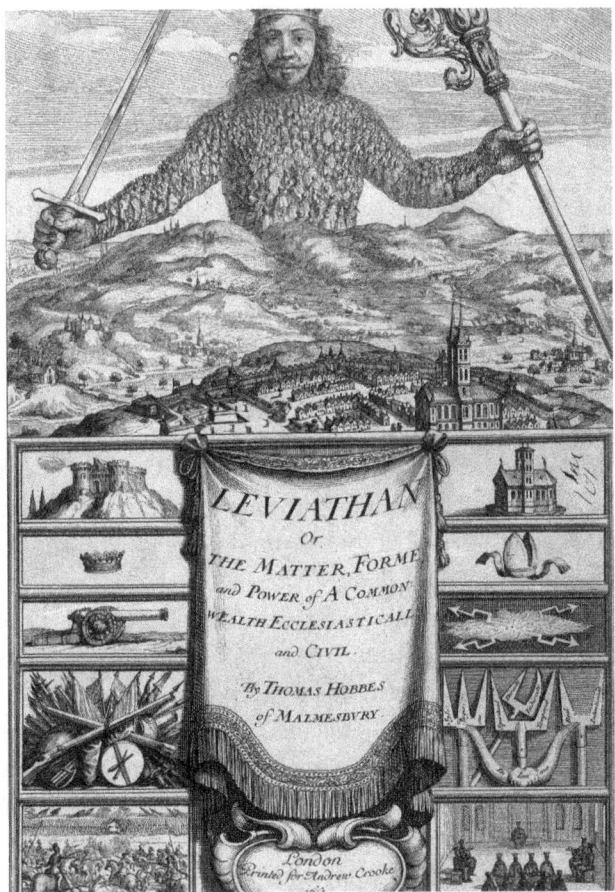

Figure 2. Abraham Bosse, frontispiece to Thomas Hobbes's *Leviathan,* 1651. (British Museum)

natures? Shaftesbury begins his response as a staged sort of bewilderment regarding Hobbes's personal role in issuing this warning to others about the state of nature being a state of war. It makes no sense, Shaftesbury argues, for one man to inform all the others of the natural selfishness of humankind, since it is presumably to his own selfish advantage to keep this knowledge to himself. The earl concludes that to "represent Men by Nature [as] *treacherous* and *wild,* 'tis out of care for Mankind" (59 I), a fact that proves his own point rather smugly.[13] A man who selflessly warns the world that all men are selfish is not logically possible. The warning emerges out of Hobbes's social conscience, and Shaftesbury characterizes *Leviathan* itself as an act of generosity that disproves the selfish principle Hobbes was trying to establish.[14]

Aside from this bit of sophistry about Hobbes's own selflessness as an author, Shaftesbury's response to *Leviathan* is largely about the *lack* of choice humankind has in the formation of civil society and about the horrors that lay behind the belief that an artificial, consciously designed covenant—or "art"—is the author of human society rather than "nature," which for him implies a divinely mandated physical response. The idea that we craft any of it is to Shaftesbury a sinister misreading of our natures. Instead, he insists, we must simply acknowledge our incapacity for choice—our lack of free will in the matter—which renders us sociable and in no need of contracts.[15] "How the Wit of Man shou'd so puzzle this Cause, as to make Civil Government and Society appear a kind of Invention, and Creature of Art, I know not" he muses (20 I). "'Tis ridiculous to say, there is any Obligation on Man to act sociably, or honestly, in a form'd Government; and not in that which is commonly call'd *the State of Nature*" (68–69 I). These are sensory perceptions at work, not moral choices, and for Shaftesbury, a feeling "demands its own . . . somatic space."[16] As Shaftesbury makes clear, not only does the "state of nature" prove us to be virtuous, but—and this is crucial—it proves us to be innately socially inclined and driven toward one another by sympathy. Fussing over how we came to *agree* to all of this is absurd; it springs from a useless fantasy that we decided to build what it was already in our nature to do.

It is from the notion of natural appetites that Shaftesbury's aesthetic theory takes its place in the history of ideas. As he says, the "NATURAL AFFECTION is predominant" and "it is inwardly join'd to us, and implanted in our Natures" (80 II). He identifies our "'inward Part' as a continuum of the sensorimotor system of the body," an "internal sense perception that feels the affections in much the same way that our external senses 'feel' sense impressions."[17] More specifically, he says that the feelings we have for one another are so obviously "*proper* and *natural*" as to be likened to "any Organ, Part or Member of an Animal-Body, or mere Vegetable, to work in its Known Course. . . . 'Tis not more *natural* for the Stomach to digest, the Lungs to breathe, the Glands to separate Juices, or other Intrails to perform their several Offices" (45 II). The organ that performs the work of assessing the affections is, of course, the heart. And it leaves us with no choice about the matter: "the Heart must approve in some measure of what is natural and honest, and disapprove of what is dishonest and corrupt" (17 II). Not only do we carry an innate impulse ("*must* approve") toward the common good, he argues, but as human beings we have the special capacity to reflect on such impulses, and judge for ourselves whether they are truly good: we have feelings (that tell us whether we are right) about our feelings (over which we have no control). Humans operate by an associative disposition that can be compared to a biological drive over which the moral sense performs a kind of sentimental audit. Says Shaftesbury, "If *Eating* and *Drinking* be natural, *Herding* is so too. If any *Appetite* or *Sense* be natural, the *Sense of Fellowship* is the same" (70 I). And "the *natural* and *just* Sense of Right and Wrong," combined with such an impulse to fellowship, compels us to be good to those we need to be with, to *feel* sociably. Here is the refutation of Hobbes: sympathy, not selfishness, is the first cause of human society. "The heart cannot possibly remain neutral," Shaftesbury insists (17 II), and "this *Sense* of Right and Wrong" becomes our moral compass (24 II), the gut check that no sophistry about "the state of nature" can supersede. Indeed, for Shaftesbury, there are powerful forces at work within the human constitution. Our feelings, and our feelings about our feelings, reward and punish—the body is a moral compass that always lets us know when we do right or wrong, and it does not let us *choose*.[18]

If this nature is the author of human agency, Shaftesbury nevertheless maintains an indefatigable faith in its merit over the artifice of contract; if any power is to rule us, it will be the power that mysteriously resides within our own hearts and that connects us to one another with an intimacy only nature—only the body—could produce. For the earl, the nearly magical properties of human nature result in a social alchemy of feeling, creating bonds that cannot be broken because we did not build them. They are, rather, constitutive of what we are, deeply *embodied* subjects. Subjectivity and embodiment are indivisible, together involving feeling as others feel, taking on their emotional lives as our own, or what scholars call "intersubjective access" via a "supplemental sense" or the "imperative of sociability."[19] "Men cannot live without the *Society* of others," Shaftesbury avers, adding that "we must feel the Sensations of *Joy* and *Sorrow*, from the State of others even in the strongest Degrees" (75 I). Words like "cannot" and "must" suggest an instinct at work, though for Shaftesbury, there is a bit more wonder in it than that. Indeed, his language practically waxes occult as he describes this impulse. There is a "secret *Charm*, or Force of Nature, by which everyone [is] made to operate willingly or unwillingly towards publick Good, and punish'd and tormented if he did otherwise" (58 I). The key is that word "unwillingly." We do not *permit* nature's rule; there is no "I do," no polite nod at one another that occurs at some moment imagined as the origin of civilization. We choose none of it; it chooses us. Like Hobbes, Shaftesbury sees humankind as driven by forces outside of our control. The difference is whether you think those forces are for the good. For moral sense philosophers like Shaftesbury, it is clear: we may have no choice in the matter, but it is all for the best. We are driven by a "social Feeling or *Sense of Partnership* with human Kind" (67 I). Elsewhere he calls this "the force of *the Confederating Charm*" and "that *social Love*, and *common Affection*, which is natural to Mankind" (71 I). It is ultimately what saves us from Hobbes's dark vision: because we are not solitary creatures, we need not fear that our lives will ever be nasty or brutish.

And here the role of the ruin narrative in relation to moral sense philosophy becomes clear. For what need of marriage can there be if contracts are unnecessary, if the body registers impulses that compel us to be together anyway? And what sort of utterances take the place of the contractual "I do" to represent this other way of imagining human sociability? We might use *Characteristicks* to find the answers to these questions, for tellingly, Shaftesbury never did, and never could, use marriage to represent the "common Affection" that sustains civilization. Marriage would surely make for an ineffective metaphor, since his work refutes the artifice of contracts and consent. To illustrate the community-building properties of human nature as he sees it, Shaftesbury instead presents readers with a remarkable example of sexual ruin. Through this example, he reveals the impact of that "confederating charm." For it is the business of how we are "made to operate unwillingly" in which Shaftesbury is interested, and the trope of sexual ruin most effectively illuminates the ontological machinery of the "unwilling" sympathetic subject. Indeed, he moves from a story of sexual ruin to one of ontological ruin quite overtly, when through an attempt to ruin a woman, a man is faced with his own lack of ontological chastity.

"The Story of an Amour"

That machinery has a surprising illustration in *Characteristicks*. It takes the shape of a sexually irresistible woman caught in the crossfire of a revolutionary war against a tyrant, and within it Shaftesbury links the sexual and the ontological directly. Called "The Story of an Amour," it depicts the charms of the moral as beguilingly erotic. This characterization quickly turns toward the violence of rape, a move that explores the need to contain a woman in order to violate her at the very moment when her charms call into question the inviolability of her would-be attacker. Shaftesbury's is an astonishingly instructive tale about what it means to lose one's self to desire, and what is at stake in instances of rape as ruin. Indeed, it offers one of the most extraordinary stories of ruin—or, rather, near-ruin—from the eighteenth-century Atlantic world. The role of appetite, the power of love, and what Shaftesbury identifies as a second self conspire to destabilize the presumed singularity of identity: such are the concerns of a philosopher interested in the *sensus communis*.

Told in an allegorical style, "The Story of an Amour" has three parts: a story that devolves into a doctrine that devolves into a practice. The story is about a good prince who has waged war on a tyrant and kidnapped the new bride of one of the tyrant's loyal subjects. The prince tasks a young nobleman with the guard and care of this captured princess, a woman of excellent virtue and refinement; the young nobleman is "charmed" by her despite the warning inherent in his prince's refusal to see her. Indeed, the prince will not go near her for fear, as he claims, that he will be bewitched by her graces. The nobleman fails to learn the lesson of his master's program, and predictably enough, he falls in love with her when she nurses him through an illness. When he confesses his adulterous passion for her, she rejects him, at which point he threatens to rape her. At the height of her peril she sends for help and is rescued by a magistrate. Ultimately, the young nobleman is forgiven, and the prince promises to see him through this challenge to his good name, sullied as it is by his seditious pursuit of the princess's ruin, she whom he was charged to protect from just such an injury. The crime is punishable by death, but the merciful prince instead sentences him to banishment. Before he leaves his homeland, the nobleman concludes the story with a moral: we "are often chang'd we know not how, without asking our consent," a transformation as unpredictable as it is uncontrollable

(115 I). It's not exactly that the devil made him do it. It's that the other version of himself, the one he didn't know existed, did it.

Shaftesbury's tale ends, if it can be said to end, in a strange passage about what he calls the "Doctrine of *Two Persons*," a Jekyll-and-Hyde arrangement that portrays identity as a changeable, fickle throng of competing agencies controlling human behavior. The doctrine allows the prince and his nobleman to conclude rather sharply, "*Independency* and *Freedom* were mere Glosses, and *Resolution* a Nose of wax" (115 I). To emphasize this final point, a story within "The Story of an Amour" occurs, in which Appetite and Reason are personified as bickering, embattled brothers at play, kicking about a toy that represents the "will" until the game grows too tiresome to pursue. Neither wins.

If it is a bit enthusiastic in its evolution from a plot of revolution and romance, to one of captivity and rape, and finally to one of sibling rivalry and ethical exhaustion, this chain of storytelling holds firm to the dominant theme of tyranny. In government and in captivity, controlled by lust and violence, the characters of "The Story of an Amour" are never masters of their own volition. As a final illustration of this lack of will, the plot is lost—brilliantly, by Shaftesbury himself, who slyly demonstrates that even our ideas have lives of their own; he himself cannot hold on to his principal tale and ends the first story with another; no one, including the young nobleman but also Shaftesbury himself, navigates the story in a clean arc of willed control. The main threat to the human will remains, however, the coercive nature of sexual attraction and its power of enchantment. In "The Story of an Amour," the prince who topples a despot nevertheless regards sexual "charm" as the most powerful tyrant of them all.

That Shaftesbury uses the threat of rape alongside this charm to demonstrate the tyranny of human "nature" should not surprise us. While this is no feminist telling of the body's story—what impels the nobleman to "talk of force" is not hate, but love, and the nobleman's wish to rape the princess is meant to prove how utterly in love with her he is, not how much he wants to hurt her—we can also see that the role of rape in the text is meant to represent the nobleman's ironic, repeating response to the force of her "charms." His own agency is thus the subject of a different kind of "violation." At the very core of *Characteristicks* is the idea that nature controls the body, that there are forces or charms at work in all the decisions we think we make, and that as a result of these charms, there is a sort of ontological traffic at work at the center of identity. The idea of a man wanting to invade what he wishes to perceive as a whole self (the rape wish that invents an interiority in order to violate it, to affirm the fantasy of the rapist's own inviolable interiority) is something I discuss at length in chapter 6. But that is not the aesthetic work of rape that is at stake in "The Story of an Amour." At the moment when the integrity of the nobleman's identity is most violated by impulses he said he didn't believe existed, he wishes to violate another. Shaftesbury uses the nobleman's threat of rape as an ironic replication of the force he himself is under. Indeed, immediately after referring to the rape threat as "talk of force," we learn that the nobleman was "forced" (Shaftesbury uses the same word) to act as he did. Unlike the terms of Hobbes's state of nature, the human condition in *Characteristicks* is one that leaves us with very few choices or freedoms. *Force* is the sine qua non of human interaction.

This theme of force is similarly at work in the prince's austere refusal to see his captive. Even after the nobleman tempts him to visit her with report of her unsurpassed beauty and virtue, the prince understands that he is not in command of himself and cannot risk the exposure to one so bewitching. He explains that fear to the nobleman by stating that people who "set the highest value upon *Liberty*" yet become servants to love. They turn "abject" and can be observed "finding themselves constrain'd and bound by a stronger chain than any Iron or Adamant" (115 I). The chains of tyranny are thus figured as the chains of sexual appetite and love; instead of the homosocial exchange readers might expect, the prince refuses an encounter with a beautiful woman to safeguard his revolutionary mojo against her allure.

The young nobleman scoffs at such caution. He believes that the will is triumphant, and anyone claiming otherwise is not to be trusted. Those who eschew their capacity for will, he bristles, are "'the very same Pretenders who thro' this Plea of *irresistible Necessity* make bold with what is another's, and attempt unlawful Beds.'" In other words, adulterers are liars whose feeble excuse is that they could not help themselves. No one, he continues, no power or force, compels them against their will. "'The Debauched compel themselves,'" he claims, and then they have the nerve to "'unjustly charge their Guilt on LOVE'" (112 I).

Thus poised to be knocked off his high horse, the young nobleman's belief about the power of individual free will is revealed as sheer hubris. Rejected by the princess, he finds that he cannot simply walk away, and soon "talk'd to her of *Force*," a direct disobedience of the prince's order and his own first step toward adultery (113 I). The language that the young nobleman had used just a page earlier to insist that the "Debauched compel themselves" finds direct contradiction when he admits of his own loss of self-control. He thus completely alters his beliefs about human nature. It is here that the text shifts into that strange allegory of the siblings kicking around a ball. Trying to explain the powers at work fueling his own actions, the nobleman claims, "For Appetite, which is the elder Brother of REASON, being the Lad of stronger growth, is sure, on every Contest, to take advantage of drawing all to his own side." It is absurd "Persecution" and "Pedantry," he concludes, "to be thus magisterial with our-selves; thus strict over our Imaginations, and with all the airs of a real Pedagogue to be solicitously taken up on the sour Care and Tutorage of so many boyish Fancys, unlucky Appetites and Desires, which are perpetually playing truant, and need Correction" (116 I). Morality is not, in other words, a frosty schoolmaster living inside your head, disciplining those mischievous appetites and desires into some semblance of order. Personally willed moral agency does not exist, and to believe it does is both harmful and absurd. "For let WILL be ever so free," he asserts, "*Humour* and *Fancy*, we see, govern it" (115 I). The fact that this lack of choice nearly leads the nobleman to rape—to impose himself on an unwilling victim who would be made to serve his purposes rather than her will—suggests that Shaftesbury knows what he is about. Again, this is no feminist project, but Shaftesbury's use of the phrase "talk of force" to indicate rape speaks to what for some are the horrors of *nature's* forces at work in what we erroneously call choices. At one point, Shaftesbury has the nobleman make this claim for him. "'Men, it seems, are unwilling to think they can be so outwitted, and impos'd on by Nature, as to be made to serve her Purposes, rather than their will,'" he says (73 I). It may seem like a gross misappropriation to modern readers, but Shaftesbury is using the threat of rape to reflect on men who, as he says above, are unwilling, imposed upon, and made to serve the purpose of a force greater than themselves. That force is nature, and it operates through the body.

Though as I explain in chapter 6, the threat of rape is often used as an attempt to render the female body a violable container, Shaftesbury uses it here to represent the idea of violence done not to the body of the princess but to *the identity* of the young nobleman. Says the nobleman, "I know the POWER of LOVE, and am no otherwise safe myself" since "no-one yet was ever strong enough" to beat this "unequal Adversary" (114 I). The idea that the most fearsome tyrant of this revolutionary world is not the despot, or even the would-be rapist intent on ruining the princess, but love itself, is a fascinating departure from traditional philosophical understandings of the will as a singular, volitional agency residing inside the person of each individual. The nobleman learns what the prince has already tried to tell him, that we are not in control of ourselves, and that "amour" is the most solid evidence we have to prove as much.

And so this tale of sexual ruin evolves into a story of ontology, and instead of the narrative trajectory we might expect, it leads Shaftesbury to describe the polyontological nature of self and the practice of soliloquy he recommends to cope with this condition. It turns out that all along, Shaftesbury's purpose in telling "The Story of an Amour" has been to use an illicit sexual impulse as the best way to locate the fault lines of identity.[20] This assessment is confirmed by the young nobleman's observation that his attempt to ruin the princess was caused by the principle that identity is not singular, that we are not our own persons, that the nobleman is "not himself," and, more to the point, he never really was, because no one ever is. Indeed, as he explains the lesson he has learned to the prince, he says, "''tis impossible to believe, that having one and the same Soul, it shou'd be actually both Good and Bad, passionate for Virtue and Vice, desirous of Contrarys. No. There must of necessity be *Two*.'" We are coming upon a portrait of identity that rejects the idea of a person as a singularity. We have the brothers Appetite and Reason, and then this business of what Shaftesbury names "the Doctrine of *Two Persons,* in one individual *Self*" (115 I). A story about desire leads to a theory of fragmented identity. Shaftesbury reveals that the integrity of the individual was never real, since it is not so much that the young nobleman breaks but that he discovers he has always been broken. The "boyish Fancys" have always governed him; he has never been "himself" but has always been a man of multiple selves.

E Unum, Pluribus

"The Story of an Amour" initiates Shaftesbury's interrogation of the workings of identity as a theater in which several actors have a say. This is where he proposes what he calls the practice of soliloquy. The only way to know one's selves, he argues, is through dialogue with them. But soliloquy does not exist between a self and a void—this is not solitary self-reflection, not a wondering aloud about life's big questions, but a kind of hail, a "Who's there?" issued from one vector of self to another, or rather to a multitude of others. And that multitude appears not as a sober parliament of thinkers reasoning through a problem but as a mob of seductive women. That's right: Shaftesbury imagines the many voices of the self as belonging to a group of alluring women. He calls them "temptresses," "enchantresses," and "sorceresses." They answer that inward hail with silky invitations, and there is something undeniably sexual, indeed ruinously sexual, about their influence.

It is difficult to explain just how weird this gets, when the story of Appetite and Reason devolves into the practice of talking to one's self in order to discover all the different voices at work in one's own head, voices that seem to belong to women whose epithets evoke qualities that are in equal parts supernatural and unchaste. As Shaftesbury puts it, "[T]he Mind *apostrophizes* its own FANCYS, raises 'em in their proper *Shapes* and *Personages*, and addresses 'em familiarly" (117 I). We move then from "The Story of an Amour" to these Althusserian apostrophes, inward hails to "*Lady-Fancys*, which present themselves as charmingly dress'd as possible to solicit their Cause" (193 I). These figures do not simply personify our feelings but take on much more powerful roles in the matrix of identity. The sexed figures of desire constituting our identities have agendas and the agency to make them happen. Shaftesbury depicts these "Phantoms" as female throughout, so that soliloquy resembles nothing so much as a seduction. Identity exists as this multitude; it is not self-possession but a self possessed.

If all this seems bizarre, then, that's because it is. Shaftesbury himself admits as much: "'What! Talk to my-self like some *Madman*, in different Persons, and under different Characters?'" His answer is that whether we will it or no, such fancies "must have their Field." All that is left to do is to listen and be directed. Yet he struggles to make sense of the cacophony once they all start talking:

> The Question is, Whether they shall have [the Field] wholly to themselves; or whether they shall acknowledge some *Controuler* or *Manager*. If none; 'tis this, I fear, which leads to *Madness*, or *Loss of Reason*. For if FANCY be left Judg of any thing, she must be Judg of all. Every-thing is right, if anything be so, because *I fansy it*. . . . The Question therefore is the same here, as in *a*

Family, or *Household,* when 'tis asked, *'Who rules?* or *Who is Master?'* Learn by the Voices. Observe who speaks aloud, in a commanding Tone: Who talks, who questions; or who is talk'd with, and who question'd. (198–99 I)

At first glance, this might appear to mark the rise of an individual, figured as the patriarch who leads a family, and while the passage does suggest that the "Field" of self might be gendered and hierarchical, the invocation of multiple agents does not portray a *singularity* but a sexed crush of women in need of discipline.[21] Indeed, this resembles nothing so much as Hobbes's state of nature, a jumbled horde of antagonistic figures fighting over command of territory.

In staging that battle, Shaftesbury offers a deeply ambivalent description of the "*Controuler* or *Manager*" (perhaps significantly a figure he cannot name only once). And of course the passage above invites the question: If the advice is to "observe who speaks aloud," then who is the observer? What are we to make of the confusion between "who questions" and "who [is] questioned"? The observer learns "who rules" or "who is master," but the observer is not identified *as* the ruler or master. The ruler is a figure who remains an unresolved ontological remainder. The practice of soliloquy thus evolves into mysterious and many-voiced theater. Among this confusing barrage of weird expostulations, there does emerge a "correctrice." "'Who tells me this?'" he asks, "'Who besides the CORRECTRICE, by whose means I am in my Wits, and without whom I am no longer my-self?'" (199 I). But the grammatical precision of this as another ("without whom I") bespeaks a supplementary figure whose aesthetic work it is to render the "I" wildly unstable, even untenable.

Like the novels of sexual ruin I discuss in the following chapters, Shaftesbury's portrait of identity depicts a possession of one's faculties by multiple and contending powers. And it turns out that these impulses are not always bad. Most of Shaftesbury's work is about the innate social virtue of man, the instinct to do good things for other people with no self-serving kickbacks. Yet in "The Story of an Amour," the charms of the princess compel the young nobleman to discover that he is himself *and* another man entirely from the one he thought he was, in the sense that he is not *one* man at all. His conclusion that there must be someone else, who is both himself and not himself, making him do what he knows to be wrong, is not about exculpating himself but about figuring out why "he" would do such a terrible thing, and the answer is that there is no "he," no single person calling the shots, but an ensemble of impulses.

"The Story of an Amour" is a story about love, rape, and tyranny. It belongs in the moral sense philosopher's response to *Leviathan* because it explains how that which draws us together involves the confused ontology of the sympathetic subject, and it illustrates the aesthetic work of sexually ruinous desire, which reveals identity to be multitudinous and somewhat anarchic. The illicit sexual desire the young nobleman feels for the captive princess segues into a discussion about why a man is not in sole possession of himself. "The Story of an Amour" thus demonstrates several principles of Enlightenment thought when it argues quite overtly that chastity is about identity, not just about sexual purity. Shaftesbury brilliantly moves from sexual charms and the threat of rape to the assertion that identity is not singular, contained, or self-governed. He moves from the tyranny of a despot and toward to the tyranny of the body. He begins with a revolution that sounds more like a fairy tale than a political war (a beautiful princess, a young nobleman), then shifts into an allegory. He takes us from a kidnapped princess to the brothers Appetite and Reason, from fiction to philosophy, as it were, to show that what is at stake in stories of charm, desire, and sexual ruin is identity. In other words, the nobleman's love for the princess and the violent urges to which it leads are the gateway to understanding the assembly of identity and the lack of singular will it implies. In "The Story of an Amour," Shaftesbury begins with sympathy as dangerous, something a political ruler knows to avoid but that an idealist does not. And the moral of the story? We are many out of one, and the body is the arena of these contending agencies.

Such a configuration of identity leaves no room for consent and contracts because it leaves no room for the individual. "The Doctrine of Two Persons" and the practice of soliloquy that Shaftesbury proposes give us a metaphor of Enlightenment identity as fragmented and overpopulated. They also offer a practical moral exercise for sorting it all out, a practice that itself erupts into yet more cacophony. To say that Shaftesbury simply recommends talking to oneself is to diminish how extraordinary his advice is. He offers the idea of a person who might "raise himself *a Companion.*" The language suggests an invocation, not a commonplace moment of self-reflection. Indeed, he goes on to suggest that a man can "multiply himself into *two Persons,* and be *his own Subject*" (99 I). This is a remarkable claim; to be one's own "subject" by calling yet another self into being is tantamount to a political conjuring that renders the self a kind of paranormal civic amphitheater. This fascinating version of sovereignty not only bypasses the monarch, but also identifies within the self something more powerful and more full of wonder. If Hobbes has his Leviathan, Shaftesbury has his own polycephalitic monster in the form of man himself, a hydra whose multiform agencies bring us close to a kind of ontological commonwealth.

Self as Republic

To make sense of this "commonwealth" of self, we might turn to a brief examination of the work of David Hume, who was born the year Shaftesbury published *Characteristicks* and who died the year the Declaration of Independence was written. Hume wrote *A Treatise on Human Nature* (1738–40) in his twenties, and in many ways it is a young writer's text. The intellectual sophistication of this three-volume gem is certainly unassailable, but its most remarkable quality may be Hume's ability to see beauty in the kind of ontological anarchy embraced by *Characteristicks*. For Hume, there is little to convince him of the existence of a single unified self—Shaftesbury's "Doctrine of Two Persons" hits much closer to the mark. Hume gives us a metaphor that dexterously expresses the intersections between the aesthetic and the political in identity formation. The matrix of alterable, fluid perceptions defining the human leads him to the astonishing claim that is set as the epigraph at the beginning of this chapter, one well worth repeating:

> One thought chases another, and draws after it a third, by which it is expelled in its turn. In this respect, I cannot compare the soul more properly to any thing than to a republic or commonwealth, in which the several members are united by the reciprocal ties of government and subordination, and give rise to other persons, who propagate the same republic in the incessant changes of its parts. And as the same individual republic may not only change its members, but also its laws and constitutions; in like manner the same person may vary his character and disposition, as well as his impressions and ideas, without losing his identity.[22]

We might consider this passage in the context of a startlingly similar claim made in Shaftesbury's *Characteristicks:*

> We must truly *know our*-selves, and in what this self of ours consists. . . . All is *Revolution* in us. We are no more the self-same Matter, or System of Matter, from one day to another. What Succession there may be *hereafter,* we know not; since even *now,* we live by Succession, and only perish and are renew'd. . . . What interested us *at first* in it, we know not; any more than have *since* held on, and continue *still* concern'd in such an Assemblage of fleeting Particles. (134 II)

Whether figured as a republic or an assembly, the point is the same. In neither *Characteristicks* nor *A Treatise on Human Nature* will readers find the self figured as a singular entity. They both figure identity as an unsettled collectivity. Importantly, Hume includes the idea of "reciprocal ties" that are changeable, and moves to the more ambiguous charms of impressions and disposition. Identity is fickle, populated, and variable. Its inconstant, unfixed impulses are formed by erratic, fungible perceptions—so while reason is a necessity to sanity and order, it is also subordinated by the unpredictable nature of identity.

Some of Hume's most beautiful prose comes precisely from the idea that like Shaftesbury's nobleman, we are not who or what we think ourselves to be. For Hume, the charm of existence is its mystery and its absolute refusal to remain static or contained. Echoes of Shaftesbury's sociable self are in abundance as Hume writes that a person is

> nothing but a bundle or collection of different perceptions, which succeed each other with an inconceivable rapidity, and are in a perpetual flux and movement . . . nor is there any single power of the soul, which remains unalterably the same, perhaps for one moment. The mind is a kind of theatre, where several perceptions successively make their appearance; pass, re-pass, glide away, and mingle in an infinite variety of postures and situations. There is properly no simplicity in it at one time, nor identity in different; whatever natural propension we may have to imagine that simplicity and identity. . . . What then gives us so great a propension to ascribe an identity to these successive perceptions, and to suppose ourselves possest of an invariable

and uninterrupted existence through the whole course of our lives? . . . We feign the continued existence of the perceptions of our senses, to remove the interruption: and run into the notion of a soul, and self, and substance, to disguise the variation. (229)

In the "theatre" of identity, instead of the one, we find the many, and the fiction of singularity is just a shoddy effort to impose a counterfeit stability onto the diversity of perceptions that constitute self and world. Words like *bundle, flux,* and *mingle* make up a vocabulary of "self" in which a multitude of identities occur. We command none of them; rather, they "make their appearance." Volition is defined by the fleeting moment, the gossamer, ephemeral arena of perception. The two philosophers would agree: no single or unalterable self hums at the center of this life, collecting and archiving experiences so as to assemble them into a static identity that, like a panopticon, would survey the world in order to fold it neatly into a schema of legibility. Thus it is that Hume is able to conclude with confidence, and perhaps a bit of relief, "The identity, which we ascribe to the mind of man, is only a fictitious one" (233).

Do Bodies Need Contracts?

What *does* marriage signify in a world in which, as the moral sense philosophers argue, we multiply ourselves, reproduce ourselves as our own subjects? If the self is a republic of ever-changing member states—if there is no stable individual—then whatever can the words "I do" mean? If we are driven by forces beyond our control, why do we mess about with utterances of promise, consent, and commitment—if human sympathy drives us to forge bonds with one another, ruinous, noncontractual bonds that are more aptly described as happening to us than by us, then what can the role of marriage be? In other words: Do bodies need contracts?

In order to understand the important work that the ruin narrative accomplishes by answering this question with a resounding *no*, we must understand how eighteenth-century philosophy about identity and sociability questions the validity of the marriage contract as a stand-in for the social contract. As the succeeding chapters will show, the ruin narrative challenges the social contract by revealing the marriage contract to be unnecessary. The logic of the social contract in a patriarchal culture is at the heart of that challenge. The social contract, or what Carole Pateman has called the "modern story of masculine political birth," secures patriarchal sexual right by creating a political reality out of the individual and his rational mind, which rule over the weaker minds and bodies of women.[23] The marriage contract is in some ways the legal enactment of this social order. Its misogynist appeal to biology justifies patriarchal right by assuming that hierarchy and heterosexuality are natural. A man must rule a woman and not the other way around because men are driven by synapses and not hormones; women are too sentimental and too sensate to be trusted with any ruling power.

Yet in the political climate of post-revolutionary America, some historians argue, the marriage contract took on a more radical cultural role. It seemed to have become a symbol for, as well as the practical application of, using contracts to secure equality. According to the logic of a contractual democracy, consenting citizens of the new republic could substitute contractual obligation for the subjugation of self to royal rule. Indeed, as historians like Anya Jabour have established, the new American republic's whole identity was bound up with ideas about marriage and family. Certainly the ideal of egalitarian marriage became symbolic of the larger move toward an egalitarian community.[24] According to this view, what marriage legally was, and what it meant culturally, was in essence a putting into practice of republican ideals, free will and consent being (theoretically at least) at the center of the marital contract. This perspective sees marriage as the republic writ small. It is democratic in nature, and, most importantly, a matter of individual choice rather than an arrangement made by one's elders.

Yet if this is so, then we must ask why it is that American fiction writers were more interested in the extramarital affairs of its citizens. These authors often penned dramas in which consent is irrelevant, since those involved almost universally claim to have been swept away by a force generally characterized as "nature," or what I referred to earlier as the citizen drive. The aesthetic arising from this operation of nature is thoroughly different from the state of nature as Hobbes represented it. It understands the sexed body as the source of an agency outside the influence of the contractual sphere. In place of contractual relationships are emotional and physical bonds formed by people who cannot be said to "consent" to them since what and who they are is neither stable nor singular. Shaftesbury's young nobleman is a case in point: he cannot resist his attraction to the princess, and as a result he discovers that his identity is operated by an agency that acts well outside the boundaries of individual personhood. Like Shaftesbury's "The Story of an Amour," the novels discussed in the chapters that follow spend the bulk of their pages mapping out the essence of this kind of radical relation. The ruin narrative that features the fallen woman as its protagonist looks to the body as nature's servant and then follows that premise where it leads.

Mostly it leads to sex. And that sex stands in for a different model of social relations, one less governable but also with less call for being governed. If the body forges social bonds through the laws of attraction, the idea that we need a social contract to do the same work is absurd. But to give up on the social contract is to surrender the notion of consent, which in essence is to admit that we are not free. As we saw earlier, Shaftesbury and others explain why that admission is difficult to procure.

In *The Social Contract; or, Principles of Political Right* (1762), Rousseau famously proposes that civilization costs the individual his freedom in a moment of mutual surrender. We must consent to this exchange in order to make society possible; such consent works from as it calls forth the subject-position of the individual (imagined, always, as a white man) who must be in possession of his "self" in order to bargain with it. That self comes with a collection of rights, the most important of which is the right to one's own body as the self's material possession. But of course to engage in such an ownership poses a strange ontological problem. Self-possession requires that one must be somehow within, but not exactly of, the flesh that one also already owns. It is this troubled hierarchy between mind and body that informs self-possession, and self-possession constitutes the ideological core of the contractual individual.[25] Social contract theory argues that in order to safeguard this possession of self as the essence of personhood, a man surrenders his primal desire to take possession of everything else (including that which other men have). In this way he ensures for himself the kind of rights that can be shared by giving up those that cannot. The social contract seems like a tidy exchange as it is theorized by Rousseau. As he puts it in *The Social Contract*, it is "sacred" yet "does not come from nature" and is rather "founded on agreement" (9). As with Hobbes, for Rousseau, the social contract necessitates the "art" of building peace through government to prevent anarchy and war. It thus requires, as Rousseau puts it, "the complete surrender of each associate, with all his rights, to the whole community" in its preservation of the individual (17).

The ruin narrative problematizes as it eroticizes this surrender of self by using sex as a metonym for civic relations. It sees the surrender of self as forming community through the preservation of intimacy, not of the individual. According to the logic of the ruin narrative, citizens surrender to each other much the same way that lovers do, insofar as they give of themselves—by ceding control of the boundary separating oneself from the other—in order to achieve a more powerful intimacy. The ruin narrative sees the moment of self-surrender as the origin of intimacy and community, which it understands as a nation-building moment. In other words, the citizen's social surrender to the community is dramatized through the scene of sexual surrender; the difference, of course, is that in the scene of ruin there is no moment of consent, no contract binding the union. The symbolism informing this sexual surrender does more than simply critique the social contract. If, as the ruin narrative would have it, the extracontractual relation involves an *ontological* surrender and not merely a simultaneous ceding and gaining of rights, the idea of a carefully wrought diplomacy between the individual and his associates in a contractual society quickly loses ground. Illicit sex models a powerful alternative because it shows how the traffic of self and other ruptures the idea of corporeally isolated containment. Further, the language of Rousseau's phrase "complete surrender" (the idea of giving oneself to someone else) is fraught with echoes of sexual ruin. As the author of several seduction novels himself, it seems unlikely that Rousseau could have been deaf to such echoes.[26] In drawing out what he means by such surrender, he writes in *The Social Contract* that "in giving himself to all, each man gives himself to no one" (17). Certainly early American authors found it difficult to resist the erotic undertow of such phrasing. The sexual implications of a seduction novelist's talk of "giving" oneself in a "complete surrender" are too obvious to ignore.

And then there is the matter of how the giving of oneself is rhetorically incongruous with self-possession, a dissonance that shows the fault lines in social contract theory. As the ruin narratives discussed in the following chapters will show, it is at these fault lines that sympathy does its aesthetic work. That "surrender" of oneself seems less like a trade (I'll give you this right if you assure me of the other) and more like an ontological shortfall that leaves one with less of one's *self* and more of something else. That something else is a sympathetic exchange that the ruin narrative stages as a sexual encounter. That is, the ruin narrative tends to reject this idea of contractual exchanges, and instead suggests a social and ontological traffic at work in the building of community. And the marriage contract does not make room for such traffic.

"I Do" and Resisting the Contractual Utterance

As some feminist historians of the period argue, the marriage contract failed to develop women's political power in several ways. Despite the claims that post-revolutionary Americans saw marriage as their political model for defining the "egalitarian" social relations of their new nation, no historian would deny that eighteenth-century marriage was a distinctly white supremacist and patriarchal architect of such relations. A slaveholding patriarchy relies on the exchange of free white women and the enslavement of nonwhite women and men, both groups separated from the model of identity formed by the contractual relations that rely on one's ability to possess oneself and to own property. For whites, "[n]o other contract contained a rule obliterating the identity and autonomy of one party to the contract" except marriage.[27] Thus white women "must be individuals capable of consenting to the marriage contract, even as the same contract effects a signing away of their subjectivity under the law of coverture."[28] Though later chapters will explore the ruin novel's treatment of slavery in much more depth, to understand fully the relationship between contract philosophy and the ruin genre, it is important to see how the ruin narrative resists both contract culture and slavery at once.

For while the rules of a slaveholding patriarchy may seem to doom all but white property-owning men to a grim political silence, in fact this expulsion from the sphere of the social contract ended up creating an animated political underlife in novels of ruin, in which those who do not traffic in the possession of others find that in order to navigate identity they do not have to be in possession of themselves. Of course, slavery reveals the most overt, and the most violent, practice of self-possession ideology; to belong to another by the terms of slavery is to not "have" a self at all.[29] The ruin narrative resists such gruesome politics by eschewing the principle of self-possession all together. These novels understand that identity, in Shaftesburian fashion, does not permit us to say categorically we *are* any one thing, and they depict the refusal of self-possession and its logic of individual identity as a refutation of slavery's logic.

We find Rousseau linking the contractual self to the language of self-enslavement and seduction when he writes that the advantage of the contract is also "moral freedom, which alone makes man truly his own master, for impulsion by appetite alone is slavery, and obedience to self-imposed law is freedom" (21). That achievement is marked by force, for the subject must coerce himself into the terms of contractual society. To be one's "own master" makes for a strange condition, one closer to Shaftesbury's idea of making a subject of one's self, and it suggests a dichotomized agency of slave/master within the self-possessed man, who must act as the cruel overseer to his own baser impulses. In other words, for the preeminent eighteenth-century Atlantic philosopher of the social contract, if self-possession is the precursor to freedom, then the precursor to freedom is making a slave of one's *self.*

In the abolitionist ruin narrative, the critique of slavery acts as both a critique of the supremacist doctrine of self-possession and as a rejection of the marriage contract. There is no "I do" available to the slave woman. The plots of abolitionist ruin narratives do not have access to marriage as the resolution to the problem of slavery. Instead, they offer a critique of the logic of individual self-possession that informs it. Such novels argue that the "I do" of marriage is the originary utterance of the social contract, the very ideological arena in which enslaved women are most imperiled. The slave narrative and the miscegenation romances of the ruin narrative thus offer the most scathing critique of the republic's interest in companionate marriage as a model for the nation. And like white ruin narratives, they posit that the intimacy of sympathy is the best refutation of contract culture and its calamitous logic of individual self-possession.

The marriage contract thus reveals the fault lines of the social contract. If the ties that bind a nation together are feeling ones—if sympathy is the great bond that holds a people together—then the idea of any contract as the symbol of that bond, or the bondage to which it leads, is deeply vexed. The ruin narrative suggests rather that the bond that unites a people is anything but rational or deliberate, and it looks nothing at all like a contract among consenting individuals. At the center of this problem is that the consent so fetishistically dramatized in the white romantic novel is the consent of a *woman*—she without political or property rights—she who in essence has but one instance of consent, and that one instance is selecting the man to whom she will subordinate her will for a lifetime. It is no wonder then that early American novelists sought a model other than marriage to represent the nation. Their stories ask: Ought a nation to see its citizenry as having given that kind of consent, a single "I do" that constitutes a forfeiture of all other choices in the political life of its people? The idealization of the home as that which represents the nation is fraught with the troubling matter of women not being actually free and certainly not sovereign within the contract that was supposed to define those very conditions. One reason coquetry, for example, was used as a popular expression of female power is that "the family home . . . was in no way a free space."[30] Laws of coverture meant that neither marriage nor its supposed signified, the nation, could consider itself free in identifying with the woman's "I do." Novels that deny the consenting self as the central role of a white woman therefore deny that marriage is an effective metaphor for nation building.

To understand this denial, we might begin with the premise that to have a contract, there must be an "I" to say "I do"; the contract and the "I" mutually construct one another, a construction to which the ruin narrative provided an alternative. In the ruin narrative, it is often the absence of the contractual utterance, the "I do," indeed of the first-person singular that defines its resistance to the marriage contract, and by association, the social contract. The "I" becomes a site of identity slippage, a troubled and troubling term that is a site of wordplay rather than an assertion of presence. Examples of such wordplay are ubiquitous. Attempting to make sense of her inability to resist the charms of a known libertine, for example, Eliza Wharton, the heroine of Hannah Webster Foster's great seduction novel *The Coquette,* refers to her heart (in a scene I will consider in greater depth in chapter 4) as if it were a strange sort of third party residing in her own breast: "The heart of your friend is again besieged," she writes, noting with peculiar grammatical precision that this heart is calling the shots as she adds, "Whether *it* will surrender to the assailants or not, I am unable at present to determine" (122, emphasis added). Such slippages exist prolifically in the ruin narrative. In its questioning of the self-possessed individual, the genre launches a powerful critique of the contractual society, in marriage as in the civic sphere, as the arena of agency. Scenes in which fallen women are unable to utter the word "I" define the genre, creating a pattern of the unstable reference to self.[31] Such pronoun play recalls Shaftesbury's grammatical ambiguity as he marks an observer who identifies a veritable throng of agents operating within a mind.

The refusal of marriage—the refusal to say "I do"—is, crucially, a refusal of the first-person singular. This refusal marks the exit from the consent narrative as it is represented by the marriage plot. And it is an exit from the ideological zone of individual personhood itself. In the early eighteenth century, moral sense philosophers like Shaftesbury and their ideas about sympathy suggest that what binds us together begins with something altogether more plural. Social contract theory's most fundamental tenet is that human beings can't count on the alchemy of sympathy to keep them in harmony. The marriage contract similarly suggests that love is not enough to secure a more intimate version of that harmony. We have seen how, as Hobbes argues, the social contract ostensibly saves us from one another. But in addition to saving the individual from others, the social contract calls him into being in the first place. My point is that the ruin narrative calls an alternative subjectivity into being, one more in line with Shaftesbury's moral sense theory, through the appetite for fellowship. It does so explicitly through the body. Because sympathy works among and within bodies, always plural, it constitutes a plurality that defines the republic and its philosophical origins. Figured through illicit sexual encounter because it denies the "I" and its co-originary power to forge contractual agreements, the alternative identity featured in the ruin narrative has little invested in chronicling individual inviolability. Sympathy *fuses* selves through a sensate impulse to feel as another feels, through a nonvolitional attraction, and calls into being a permeable, and often erotically charged, self. This charged self represents an agency outside the bounds of Lockean personhood. Unmarried sexual desire is a metaphor for and an expression of sympathy and its power. If marriage is the republic's stand-in for voluntarism and contract, then sexual ruin might be said to work through the republic's expression of other kinds of bonds, connections that are in equal parts involuntary and illicit. Indeed, the moral sense philosophy that the founding fathers read so avidly taught them that a volitional citizenry—a "people"—is the centerpiece of a republic that operates through sympathy. The body politic and the sexed body share that sympathetic impulse.

Philosophers interested in the power of the moral sense slipped, often, into idealizing the promise of the body as a mechanism of intersubjectivity. They saw acts of ontological substitution and transformation at the very heart of sodality. To understand the people, the ruin narrative thus suggests, one must understand the sympathetic workings of the body; in its aesthetic authority lies the stimulus for sodality. The aesthetic work of the ruin narrative—using sex to illustrate the sympathetic subject's sociability—occurs through its insistence that the body ought not to be understood as a container but as a conduit.

The notion of containment that attends the mind/body split is often treated as an empirically irrefutable material fact, so that one might simply point at the body and shrug as if it were too obvious: "But you're *in* there." Yet the philosophy of the body that refutes such an outlook has been thriving for hundreds of years. It begins in the eighteenth century's study of sympathy, and is picked up by more recent theoretical works that see the body as the instrument of a collective subjectivity. Most recently, Judith Butler's *Senses of the Subject* moves eighteenth-century aesthetics into the present tense, and offers a helpful frame for understanding where the moral sense philosophers' work puts us. Butler's book, perhaps more than any other of recent critical note, questions the premise of the individual—questions it as a political invention, and refutes it as a starting place in any discussion of the body. In other words, Butler moves well beyond the insistence that the body is a container with a mind "inside" it. Her work helps us to see how operations of sympathy question the individual as *having* a body.

For Butler, there is no such obvious *place*. The flesh works instead in "a relation of tactility that precedes and informs intersubjective relations, necessarily disorienting a subject-centered account."[32] In other words, the body is an intersection where identity is formed as a relational thing, and this intersection is not hampered by the body but possible because of it. In this sense, the body is not a container, not a Cartesian artifact. Sentience is always already sensate; sentience cannot be imagined in containment. Butler continues to explain that the body "is not something one has, but, rather the web in which one lives; it is not simply what I touch of the other, or of myself, but the condition of possibility of touch, a tactility that exceeds any given touch and that cannot be reducible to a unilateral action performed by a subject" (36). Tactility is the capacity for connection that precedes identity. The body is a *condition,* one marked by relationality, not containment. I am not "in here"—we are born and reborn, moment by moment, in encounter, not in isolation. The sensory life of touch and the emotional life of community are co-originary. Touch is not just what happens in an encounter.

Touch identifies existence *as* an encounter. It is what Terry Eagleton defines as the aesthetic—one's "biological insertion into the world"—rendered as intersubjectivity.[33]

Bodies do not need contracts because the body offers something more powerful, the promise of contact. As Butler's notion of the body shows, tactility constitutes intersubjectivity; in other words, the sensate body is always already enmeshed in a materially interrelational moment. Such thinking allows us to understand agency against the grain of the sovereign individual and to see instead that "the task is to think of being acted on and acting as simultaneous." This results in what Butler calls the "deconstitution of singularity" (76). Like Shaftesbury and Hume, Butler locates agency in a matrix of interactions defined by the experience of the body as interrelationally enmeshed. Butler sees agency existing at a give-and-take site of volitional exchange, or a sharing of the moment of volition. "I do" is an impossible utterance within this exchange. Butler offers an elegant summation of her critique of the contained individual when she writes, "Acted on, I act still, but it is hardly this 'I' that acts alone, and even though, or precisely because, it never quite gets done with being undone" (16). Butler's provocative use of the word "undone" speaks to the way in which the extramarital sexual encounter is called "ruin." The undoing of the contractual subject speaks to the undoing of singularity—to withdraw from the zone of contract is also to enunciate a noncontractual utterance, to refuse the "I" of "I do"; to resist the marriage contract and to locate intimacy outside of it is to enact this refusal, and the novels I look at in the following chapters argue that the body is the enunciator of this refusal.

Perhaps the best illustration of such a principle, however, exists in Adam Smith's *The Theory of Moral Sentiments,* in which he famously claims that there can be no true intersubjective experience. But then he uses turns of phrase that directly contradict that very notion. Most critics focus on his claim about the operation of sympathy as the incomplete sharing of the physical through the emotional: "Though our brother is upon the rack, as long as we ourselves are at our ease, our senses will never inform us of what he suffers. They never did, and never can, carry us beyond our own person." The agonies of the sufferer "are thus brought home to ourselves, when we have thus adopted and made them our own" so that "we tremble and shudder at the thought of what he feels."[34] Here Smith says that we need not be carried beyond our own person, as the sensate self invites the agonies of another *in*. But elsewhere his words seem to escape these limits, as when the ontological singularity of the sympathetic viewer is precluded by phrases like "we enter as it were into his body, and become in some measure the same person with him." And then there is this remarkable moment, when he says, "The passions, upon some occasions, may seem to be transfused from one man to another, instantaneously and antecedent to any knowledge of what excited them in the person principally concerned" (18). Echoes of Hume are clear, as when he similarly argues, "The passions are so contagious, that they pass with the greatest facility from one person to another, and produce correspondent movements in all human breasts" (332). Any fixed certainty about the singularity of self is lost in the shadowy matrix of transformative, fluid identity.

In their attempts to define sympathy, eighteenth-century philosophers edged ever closer to a language of eros. But what is both erotic and illicit about sympathy such that it shares in the lexicon of sexual ruin? We can find an answer to that question in the rhetorical links between eighteenth-century moral sense philosophy and the Atlantic novel of sexual ruin. For while these two genres may seem unlikely to share stylistic qualities, readers of both types of texts will soon discover otherwise. Books about sex and sympathy share a peculiar vernacular of self-surrender that describes a fall into the other's ontological sphere, a fall out of oneself, a moment in which the boundaries of self are at best uncertain. While we might expect as much in a romantic plotline, centuries-old treatises on contract theory, sense perception, and moral virtues hardly seem like the fertile grounds for sexual undercurrents. And yet such language abounds in these philosophical works.

To lose oneself in intimate association, whether sexual or sympathetic, amounts to the same thing—a catalyst into a non-individual moment in which the body functions as a bridge, not a boundary, between self and other. Sexual ruin is the most popular narrative to do so because it tells sympathy's story, which is the body's story. This merger figures neatly into eighteenth-century moral sense philosophy. Consider the glossary of sympathy: it is all about intermingling bodies and entangled selves. A quick review of the philosophical claims about sympathy that we have just seen reveals as much. Their vocabulary presents a troubled slippage between consent and impulse: people *enter into* one another, *agitate* one another; they *surrender, give themselves to* one another. *Contagion, transfusion, appetite, impulse, inclination.* These are the words philosophers like Rousseau, Hume, and

Smith use to describe human relations, and the erotic possibilities of this language are telling. In order to describe the way that one person's feelings can occupy another person's body, a condition that calls into question the inviolable individuality of identity, they used language that is tacitly sexual. The glossary of sympathy is a glossary of the sexually charged body.

It is easy to see why the language of such philosophical endeavors seems erotic. The intimacy of a shared ontological moment would require a language that bordered on the magical, a set of words that involved a romantic confusion of self-surrender and a sense that one's body was not one's own. Such terms are used by philosophers of feeling and early American novelists to tell what is in some ways exactly the same story. The rhetorical parallels are clear. One need only to look to the language to see them: "my heart catches the same passion" (Hume); "we enter as it were into his body," and "[t]he passions . . . may seem to be transfused from one man to another" (Smith);[35] the contractual subject "gives himself entirely" in a moment of "complete surrender" (Rousseau). The erotic underlife of Enlightenment belief pulses in each example. Let me be clear—this is not desire for phallic entry into the body but about the erotics of identification with the other, about the erotic charge of experiencing ontological *traffic*. When Smith uses the term "enter" or Rousseau speaks of "surrender," they signify such moments as ontological, and my claim here is that *ontological* entry—the transfusion of identity, the surrender of self—is erotic. This rhetoric of sympathy and shared feeling resonates with words that seem to be about sexual longing and confused corporeal boundaries because sympathy is a sensate sodality, and the shared ontology of such moments is inherently erotic. At stake is a nonjurisdictional embodiment, in which the senses are a portal into another person's body, that sphere of experience that we so often assume is isolated and unique but in these examples is exchangeable and shared. Indeed, each of these examples, from the "contagion" of feeling to the "entry" into another's body, observes the social power of the body as the appetitive, omnipotent epicenter of human "nature." And each sounds like it could describe a moment of sexual ruin. The theoretical enterprise that seeks to understand formulations of agency without personhood tells us quite a bit about why the ruin narrative uses a *sexual* fall into social relations. This understanding of social relations constitutes what Coviello astutely identifies as "a resistance . . . to the turning of sex into another of the liberal self's secured properties, into something that each of us, alone, is understood to *have*."³⁶ In opposition to this ideal of self-possession, the ruin narrative issues the call to the social as an erotic summons, beckoning the self into a communal merger.

The search for this "being-in-common" or "co-originary" identity is achieved by the deliberately awkward grammar of Jean-Luc Nancy's claim of subject-formation in *The Inoperative Community*, when he presents the beautiful phrase, "*you shares me.*" It is an utterance synonymous, as he claims, with the polysemous declaration: "you (are/and/is) (entirely other than) I."³⁷ The playful grammatical structure of this statement creates contradictions that are resolved through adaptation of rules that separate (like a set of parentheses) into rules that conjoin meanings. The *you* of Nancy's assertion at once "is I" and "is entirely other than I." Intriguingly, the various grammatical formations offer a message of community embedded in examples of separation and error. In Nancy's reading of community, the singularity of the *you* that "shares" *me* is a grammatical error—an error created by relation. There is, then, no alienated "other" in Nancy's reading of community. Singularity is a structural impossibility in any operation of community, a principle proven by the ruined woman's dalliances. Butler and Nancy address identity as a matter of sociability and interdependence, and selfhood as an experience of identification rather than of static identity, and such a radical shift into a "community of *others*" calls for further readings of that dynamic.

The romance of intermingling bodies, a shared sensate pulse: we tell stories about sex to tell ourselves the story of sympathy, of the very nature of human sociability. Eros is one way to explain that we are drawn to one another without choice or deliberation—to explain that, as Shaftesbury and his philosophical successors argue, there is no "I do," no contract, no act of consent at the origin of human society. If neither the monarchical subject nor the individual is the foundation of community, then what do human relations look like and what subjectivity is at their center? Shaftesbury's "The Story of an Amour" provides an answer as it engages with several key motifs of philosophical writing from the period. Yet the philosophical conversation is clearly not over. Indeed it is Butler who claims, "When we speak about subject formation, we invariably presume a threshold of susceptibility or impressionability that may be said to precede the formation of a conscious and deliberate 'I'" (1). Such claims continue to encourage major shifts in what we regard as the Enlightenment subject.

As a hallmark of such shifts, Shaftesbury's idea of the *sensus communis* marks the subrogation of subjectivity that operates as a moral seduction, a siren call to the good. It signifies a nonvolitional instinct toward being with, and being good to, one another. Its agency erupts outside of the boundaries of individual personhood. It is sympathy—the sensate, ontological exchange—rendered as civic kinship. Such an idea explains why the republic's first storytellers placed the sexed body at the political epicenter of the nation-building project. They recognized the political capital of the sympathetic subject. The appetite for fellowship that Shaftesbury marked as the key to civil society is a distinctly libidinal somatic impulse, and carries with it its own brand of tyranny.

Such is the case, to be sure, in the two works published by the first American novelist, William Hill Brown. The title of his more notable work, *The Power of Sympathy; or, The Triumph of Nature* (1789), advertises as much. Nature might authorize the rights outlined in the republic's founding documents, but in its founding literature, nature enacts its own absolute despotism through the body's appetites. In many ways, Brown puts Shaftesbury's most treasured principles to the test, investigating what he calls the *nature* of sympathy as he joins the attempt to define the sympathetic subject, this time in the post-revolutionary landscape of the new republic. And to Brown's new American audience, this matter of sympathy quickly leads to another question, namely how bodies—even, or perhaps especially, sexed, consanguineous bodies—form nations. In Brown's works, that is, the incestuous bed becomes the site of an illicit desire that abets a peculiarly American ontological confusion at the nexus of the body's "rule."

· THREE ·

Incest and the Nature of Ruin in the Novels of William Hill Brown

> Men, it seems, are unwilling to think they can be so outwitted, and impos'd on by Nature, as to be made to serve her Purposes, rather than their own. They are asham'd to be drawn thus out of *themselves,* and forc'd from what they esteem their *true Interest.*
> —Anthony Ashley Cooper, Third Earl of Shaftesbury, *Characteristicks of Men, Manners, Opinions, Times,* 1711

"Democracy," fumed John Adams in 1804, "is a young rake who thinks himself handsome and well made, and who has little faith in virtue."[1] This astonishing accusation, made by the second US president, appears to have several iterations in the writing of America's first novelist, William Hill Brown.[2] Like Shaftesbury, Brown had radical observations about the "nature" of the human will. The essential questions of democracy—which ideals of the intimate and the political ought to constitute human bonds, what defines the right to assume or dissolve those bonds—are of course the subject of what many deem to be the most famous document in the history of the Atlantic Enlightenment, the Declaration of Independence. It is here that Adams and his fellow founders make "the Laws of Nature and of Nature's God" the very axis of their justification for severance from the British monarchy and ascendance to the "separate and equal station" of an independent republic. Debated prolifically throughout the eighteenth century and ascribed a politically vital role in the nation-building rhetoric of America's founding, the "nature" that constitutes the people's sovereign authority is a power whose potency is outmatched only by its opacity. Perhaps not surprisingly, then, rather than revisiting the military success of the underdog revolutionaries or imagining the political power of the sovereign people, early American novelists tended to wonder: To what *else* might these laws of nature lead?

The answer, more often than not, is illicit sex, an encounter dictated by the laws of nature understood as the laws of the body. Atlantic sympathy studies has established feeling *for* and *as* the other as the hallmark of a democracy, so it is the very ontology of citizenship that is at stake in critical discussions of a sentimental, or as Adams would have it, a seducible citizenry.[3] Certainly a subjectivity imagined through the trope of sexual ruin is a remarkable starting point in any discussion of that ontology. When it manifests as desire in the ruined, incestuous body, the *nature* of democratic feeling illuminates the aesthetic work at play in the personification of democracy as a vicious rake.

As it turns out, in Brown's two novels at least, Adams's claim that America is a fallen woman is not so far off the mark. Brown expresses explicit concern about nature as the source of all the trouble in *The Power of Sympathy; or, The Triumph of Nature, Founded in Truth* (1789) and the lesser-known *Ira and Isabella; or, The Natural Children; A Novel, Founded in Fiction* (1807).[4] From the subtitles on, in both works, nature's laws are much more powerful than any others, even—or perhaps especially—those crafted by the founders, and the unsteady conditions of embodiment do nature's nation-building work. Indeed, the nature cited in the Declaration becomes, in Brown's hands, a Shaftesburian challenge to the central premise of contract culture discussed in chapter 1, namely that social bonds might be forged rationally as a means of protecting the possessive individual and his assets in person and property from the savagery of mobs and monarchs alike.[5] Contract culture assumes that human nature is a problem, that it must be tamed, and so it sets the terms by which human beings might associate with one another. But as it operates in *The Power of Sympathy* and *Ira and Isabella,* nature is not so much violent as it is carnal, and it cannot be subjugated, even by the sovereignty of the people. For, as Brown's novels tend to show, nature already rules *them.*

And it is not just the power of nature, which in Brown's works is really the power of the body, that becomes unruly. Both of his books have been characterized by critics as demonstrating a cacophonous heteroglossia that is extreme even for an epistolary novel, the texts presenting voices from a wide swath of cultural positions in the Anglophone Atlantic worlds of high and low culture.[6] These voices are informed by pulp sensation and by the pulpit, by gossip and by history, and they are expressed by characters from different generations, genders, races, and classes. Between the two books, we hear from a widow, a slave, a prostitute, a nanny, a madwoman, and a servant girl, and of course plenty of ruined women, as well as from propertied white men. Readers of *The Power of Sympathy* have come to appreciate its resulting disjointedness, for it is, as Cathy Davidson most notably observes in *Revolution and the Word*, "a novel divided against itself" that yet stands. It is not simply a matter of disentangling intersecting plot lines or even, as Davidson argues, making sense out of the multiple and sometimes "contradictory discourses" or conflicting, juxtaposed genres.[7] The "problem" of Brown's work, if it is a problem, is not just how the stories are told or who tells them, but more vitally the relationship between genres and bodies, the boundaries of which get disrupted and refigured throughout *The Power of Sympathy*. Similar peculiarities and disruptions mark *Ira and Isabella*, which at times reads more like an eccentric treatise than a polished novel and is written in a series of rhetorical extremes, though not through the epistolary style.[8]

In both books, characters espouse radical and opposing viewpoints on matters fundamental to the success of the republic, like what chaste American girls ought to be reading, how to find democratic solutions to the conflicts between the social classes, and the merits of a companionate marriage. These surface themes keep the plots humming along nicely for a while; pious characters try to counsel their unwise friends away from moral offenses like libertinism, prostitution, and suicide.[9] In *The Power of Sympathy*, friends Worthy and Myra try to keep Harrington and Harriot from a hasty marriage, as Ira's friends Lorenzo and Fidelio in *Ira and Isabella* try to keep him from taking himself and his moral codes too seriously. The novels explore some of the more nuanced debates surrounding the problems of seduction as well, like what happens when we keep one another's most terrible secrets, and how the tension between moral righteousness and boredom can wreck the minds of young people.

Likely to be of great interest to a contemporary readership, these themes nevertheless get relatively little play in either novel, as they become quickly overshadowed by the more sensational dominant plot of incest.[10] For *The Power of Sympathy* and *Ira and Isabella* are principally about how half-siblings "naturally" lust after one another.[11] In *The Power of Sympathy*, Harriot and Harrington discover their bodies are drawn together with the overpowering fervor of a blood tie after Harrington's father confesses that in his youth he seduced and abandoned Harriot's mother. Correspondingly, in *Ira and Isabella,* seduction and bastardy lead the lovers to believe that their strong physical attraction is due to what they are told too late is their sibling relation. In fact, they don't learn of it until the after they marry. Whereas Harriot and Harrington encounter only adversity after the revelation—Harriot falls ill and dies, and Harrington commits suicide, leaving the family devastated by tragedy—for Ira and Isabella, at least, there is a happy if convoluted ending. It turns out Isabella's father, initially suspected of having seduced Ira's mother, was taking the blame for Isabella's foster father.[12] In the last pages of the novel, then, the marriage assumes the sexual vigor temporarily denied to them.

What is most notable about all of this is that when the novels get to their most cherished plotlines, they wax positively romantic about incest, presumed *and* real.[13] Critics of the novel have suggested that Brown uses incest as a metaphor for all kinds of higher-order feelings, including "a particular way of relating to others, one that relies on likeness and familiarity as a precondition for sympathy."[14] Yet Philip Young perhaps said it best when he noted that *The Power of Sympathy* "generates a little heat peculiar to itself."[15] Long passages about the body's blushes and palpitations alongside speeches regarding the permissibility of incestuous love eclipse *The Power of Sympathy*'s halfhearted mourning and anemic moralizing. And *Ira and Isabella* contains several lengthy passages about the virtue of lust and the nonsense of prudery. In fact, throughout *Ira and Isabella,* instead of the preaching and pedantry of *The Power of Sympathy,* we find speeches about the virtue of "wanton" (yes, that's Brown's word) desire.[16] Even more important, though both works are often referred to as "seduction novels," the instances of sexual ruin through seduction occurring in them, though multitudinous, are brief, never lasting more than a few pages. They are relegated to subplot, seriously outranked by these much more compelling stories about incest.

And though ruin is a ubiquitous business in them, Brown's novels manifestly avoid generically stable tellings of it. The seduction tale typically requires the flawed virtue of a young, coquettish woman who abets her own fall by inviting, or at least not adequately discouraging, the attentions of a dissolute libertine who robs her of her virtue, and, through childbirth or suicide, often her life. However, if there is a thesis about ruin in either of Brown's works, it is centered upon ambivalence, the shifting of moral stances that attempt to identify who or what is to blame in a seduction, moments in the texts where the moral valence of the illicitly sexed body is robustly indeterminate. The vacillating and erratic ethical positions held by the novels' key characters operate to unsettle the moral landscape, such that the irregularity of moral codes becomes a central feature of the seduction tales framing, or at first seeming to frame, the incest plots. The anecdotal stories of seduction increasingly appear as disturbances. They become unwelcome interruptions of the main storyline, and seem, more and more, like generic, marginal intrusions.

What aesthetic work do these anecdotal passages about ruin produce at the periphery that they could not perhaps do elsewhere? In what follows, a closer look at those seemingly secondary accounts of seduction reveals how they inform through disrupting the ascendant narrative of incest. Indeed, seductions are "constantly displaced in a supplementary chain of announcements and cancellations" in *The Power of Sympathy*.[17] The aesthetic work achieved by these displacements, and the unexpected lacunae within them, argue for a new reading of the incestuous body in Brown's work. The novels stage a reimagining of the sexed, ruined body's admission into democratic relations. To do so, *The Power of Sympathy* and *Ira and Isabella* invest more rhetorical energy in the movement from seduction to incest as a shift inscribed by the variant models of agency occurring within them. The novels are more interested in the aesthetic space that opens up when such a radical genre change is featured as part of the text; the architecture of that stylistic alteration functions as a metonym for the unstable subjectivity at play in instances of nonjurisdictional embodiment. Two genres coexisting in one text abet the disruptions of self-possession and personhood that the novels stage. Further, those disruptions of subjectivity are conveyed with imagery suggesting a lack of volitional will or control. In the semiotics of troubled subjectivity within the marginal seduction stories offered by *The Power of Sympathy* and *Ira and Isabella,* we encounter women who are overcome by sleep, who are kidnapped, who are duped by magic and supernatural phenomena—women who *do* nothing at all. Their dreamlike agency informs Brown's characterization of the ungovernable desires of the incestuous body. They represent the agency without personhood in which the ruin narrative invests in its search for alternatives to the individual. In other words, the models of agency that emerge from these stories offer a much more complex understanding of the incestuous body's democratic valence. They also show

how the ruin narrative represents the self-possessed, self-governing subject as a political fantasy that cannot survive because the laws of nature must be obeyed.

Generic Bodies

There are a multitude of ruined women whose stories are told as marginal subplots in *Ira and Isabella,* including that of an oversexed matron who masquerades as an innocent country girl and nearly a dozen women of ill repute with names like Desire Goodale and Love Midnight. There are also several ruined women in *The Power of Sympathy,* including three who appear as the subjects of sometimes oblique, imprecise anecdotes that are mostly imparted by characters whose moralizings we have already been urged to distrust. But Brown's first fallen woman appears in a curious two-page footnote. She is not a fictional character at all, but Elizabeth Whitman (1752–1788), the real-life subject of Hannah Webster Foster's seduction novel *The Coquette* (1797). In 1788, Whitman gained notoriety as a victim of seduction who died soon after giving birth. The details of her story are played out in Brown's footnote, which occurs as a compact sentimental vignette followed by a sixty-line poem written by Whitman herself, "her own Elegy" ending the telling of her tale (23).[18] In his splendid analysis of the footnote, Winfried Fluck suggests that it represents a novelistic underlife: "In removing the transgressive impulse to the 'underground' of the text and thus creating a clear split (and graphic hierarchization) between its upper and nether world, the text dramatizes the difficulties it has in establishing an effective interaction between transgressive impulse and its narrative containment."[19] Indeed, this interpretation invites an anatomical reading of that "nether world" as the incestuous body's hidden lower half, tucked underneath layers of clothing (and lines of text) and perhaps also governed by a transgressive genital impulse. This understanding of the footnote as a site of illicit eros in the novel is suggestive of a taboo sexuality whose denial underwrites a sense of an incomplete or second, shadow body that gets resolved by the mirroring eroticism of incestuous siblings.

Lingering on the footnote also prompts a much less insightful if still necessary question. Put bluntly: With all of these materials available to him, why didn't Brown just write *The Coquette?* What might explain why

America's first ruined woman appears in a *footnote?* The notation shows that *The Power of Sympathy* could easily have been a very different book, the Elizabeth Whitman story written as a novel. Yet not only did he eschew writing that other book—one true to the dedication page's promise of a tale about "SEDUCTION" that is "founded in truth"—but he also made his novel's very first reference to sexual ruin so conspicuously *odd.* In fact, any one of the abridged sketches about seduction could have become the dominant storyline. A novel about Elizabeth Whitman or for that matter Fanny Apthorp (another true-life source for a later seduction anecdote in the text) certainly would have sold better. But written as compact fables, the stories of seduction in *The Power of Sympathy,* including and perhaps most noticeably the extraordinary footnote, stand out even in this book, a text chock-full of rhetorical instability and genre play. This is not evidence of Brown's weakness as a writer or of America's literary adolescence.[20] When Brown begins his first novel as a seduction tale, reforms the rake by the novel's sixth letter (only Harrington's third), and then turns to incest as the book's primary romantic coupling, the move is worth further consideration. Although it may be true that *The Power of Sympathy* and *Ira and Isabella* offer several moments when conflicting subject positions and incompatible storytelling devices hold the novels in the grip of a literary or generic tension, the theatrical switch from seduction to incest is not, or not only, one of those moments. It is something new. Appearing as a distinct turn, it is direct enough to indicate a deliberate and calculated jump from one story to another. Why did he do it?

The answer may lie in the power of narrative disruption. The text's spillage into that footnote evidences a curiosity about the carnal that dominates the novel. Read as a hidden, genital soffit, the footnote represents the disruptive power of the illicitly sexed body; it functions as an apparatus that disrupts any vision of a singular, unified text. Represented by the aptly named couples Harriot and Harrington and Ira and Isabella (names whose consonance craftily insinuates that they are differently gendered iterations of the same person), incest similarly insists on a disruption of identity through its doubling. While Shaftesbury sees embodiment as defined by multiple and competing agencies, then, Brown represents the democratic subject through a suggestion of doubled embodiment. The aesthetic work accomplished by the doubling effect of the incestuous body and the novel's insistence on textual replications and disruptions might then be said to signal a polyontological realignment of subjectivity. The doublings presented by these names abet incest's radicalization of embodiment, for incest refuses to identify the lover's body as either self or other, familiar or distinct; instead, it identifies the lover via what Brown insists is a "natural" appetite. Indeed, both novels quite explicitly feature the appetites of the body as definitive of agency. They do not depict the flesh as that which merely houses a humanizing capacity for reason, but show the body to be that which reconstitutes the very experience of "choosing," which for Brown's characters really amounts to an obedience to nature, not a conscious engagement with one's preferences. In these novels, exploring the boundaries of "the Laws of Nature and of Nature's God" means locating nature as the source of a corporeal volition. The incest plot therefore takes the body where nature will bring it, beyond all mores, to the taboo and the obscene.[21] These novels know the body as the arena of experience, in which characters encounter sympathy as an erotic attraction. They know it as nature's servant.[22]

In addition to the way in which the lovers' homophonic names in both books signal a disruption of corporeal limits, the marginal seduction stories of *The Power of Sympathy* mark the body as a site of ontological absence. The subplots about seduction in Brown's earlier novel almost always feature the slumber of the virgin at the point of sexual contact. Sleep, then, occurs rhetorically in lieu of a willful sexual act. It is a somatic velleity at work here, as Brown locates "the power of sympathy" in the body that lacks an animating subjectivity. Certainly in *The Power of Sympathy* bodies do not suffer from a lack of desire, defined within the context of the incest romance as the doubly intoxicating, sensate draw of sympathy and blood. Incest takes the disruptive corporeality of the sleeping maiden motif further and uses desire to reimagine the volitional. Connections both intimate and political come to be governed by something other than the ipseity of *self*. From the somnolent to the somatic, romantic couplings in *The Power of Sympathy* and *Ira and Isabella* occasion these strange lacunae featuring the absence of self just when a reader would expect its presence. The conundrum of agency without personhood gets resolved in Brown's work by figures animated by forces of nature that operate within the body but also between and among bodies. In the aesthetic work of incest—in the art beyond its outrage—is a move to resolve the Cartesian dilemma in a way that explores the modern subject within the complex underlife of Enlightenment culture.[23] The seduction stories within the two novels allegorize this absence of traditional concepts of agency, preparing the way for when nature's laws assert themselves and ascend to the "triumph" of the incestuous bed.

Abandoned Bodies

That triumph is possible only when we consider the role of the marginalized seduction narratives in Brown's work and how they expose that underlife. In part because what is at stake is no longer their morality but how they contribute to the texts' generic momentum, each of the ruined women in Brown's novels is properly exculpated.[24] A prime example occurs in *The Power of Sympathy* before the novel even properly begins, in the first edition's frontispiece. It illustrates the story of one of the novel's many brief subplots in which a young woman, Ophelia, poisons herself after being seduced by her brother-in-law. None of the main characters in *The Power of Sympathy* is connected to Ophelia in any significant way—they simply learn about her tragedy and discuss its import—and like the other short seduction subplots of minor characters, her story is an anecdote rather than part of the main story line. The frontispiece drawing in part may serve as a bait-and-switch device used by the publisher to entice buyers who were later disappointed to discover that they had not purchased a typical seduction novel.[25] Yet the image is worth pause, for the aesthetic work it accomplishes does in fact sketch for readers the key elements of the seduction stories peppered throughout *The Power of Sympathy*. (See figure 3.) First there is the strange matter of the open door in the background of the image. Overhung by tapestries, yet the only object left completely unshaded by the print, the open door suggests the possibility that someone has exited the scene of Ophelia's suicide; whether it is her seducer or more allegorically her virtue that has abandoned her is left for the reader to decide, though it is easy to imagine the open door at the back of the room representing the earlier enactments of extramarital sex that led to this moment. At the side of the room, the other open door features the father's entrance. He has followed Ophelia's mother into the room. He is gripping his arms together in horror, guilt, or perhaps in prayer. Ophelia's mother is clasping her daughter's hand, and their grasp becomes the intimate nucleus of a room disrupted by traffic, perhaps even sexual congress, and violence. Their hands form a solid grip that speaks to the centrality of the love between mother and daughter in the drama. The

Figure 3. Frontispiece to William Hill Brown's *The Power of Sympathy*, 1789. (Princeton University Library)

notion that the lover and the parents share this room as the scene of both sexual activity and familial tragedy anticipates the intersection of lust and bloodline that the novel's story of incest will soon introduce.

The other crucial object in the illustration is the large mirror hanging behind the three of them, empty of reflecting imagery. The mirror is at the visual center of the print, and if any face is reflected there, it would be the reader's; it does not reflect the drama ensuing beneath its ornate frame but the reader's reaction to it. Harriot's letter about Ophelia employs similar mirror imagery when she writes to Myra, "Whatever may be the other causes (if there were any besides her seduction) which drove the unhappy *Ophelia*, temerariously to end her existence, it certainly becomes us, my dear friend, to attend to them—and to draw such morals and lessons of instruction from each side of the question, as will be a mirror by which we may regulate our conduct and amend our lives" (42). At one level, then, the frontispiece mirror is designed to reflect the reader's judgment of the moral lesson offered by the novel; the tragic sentimental images suggest that the reader ought to find a sympathetic face reflected in that mirror. The "power of sympathy" ought to characterize the reader's sensibility as she forgives the characters their sexual trespasses. Of course, the mirror also represents the reader's ability to imagine what *else* happened in this room, filled with evidence not only of suicide but of the secret tryst that led to it; the reader must then face her own titillation. Readers would perhaps be reluctant to look into that mirror and then judge the stories of the ruined women within the book's covers too harshly.[26] Whatever else occurs in the reading of this book, judgment against Ophelia, and by extension the sorority of ruin to which she belongs, is strongly discouraged.

On another level, however, the mirror's emptiness creates an eerie and disorienting experience of disembodiment. It imposes on readers the experience of looking directly into a reflection that reports their absence. That kind of corporeal dissonance functions as the uncanny double at work in Brown's novel, living bodies with no animating agency, in part represented by the sleeping maidens of the seduction subplots. These two types of bodies, then, function together to disrupt dualism's promise, namely that the presence of one (a mind, a body) guarantees the presence of the other. Bodies are rather either in excess or absent altogether. The incestuous sibling acts as a body double that implies a kind of corporeal surplus ("Harriot" and "Harrington" occurring as but two versions of the same name echoes that surplus). Yet the mirror also manages a disembodied gaze. This opposition between presence and absence shows the novel's precincts of identity as unstable, defined by embodiment's disruptive properties.

Assisting that disruption is the detail Brown is careful to include in the subplot about Ophelia in *The Power of Sympathy*, that she was asleep when she was seduced. Somnambulant imagery will come into play later, when novels like Hannah Webster Foster's *The Coquette*, Samuel Richardson's *Clarissa* (1748), and Susanna Rowson's *Charlotte Temple* (1791) similarly depict women as unconscious during the moment of sexual ruin. For now, though, it is interesting to note that seduction victims often use language that exculpates by denying them the desire upon which their ruin is ostensibly predicated. An example occurs in yet another seduction subplot in *The Power of Sympathy*, this one involving Harriot's mother, Maria.

After Harrington Senior seduces her, she says she was "awakened . . . to the state of misery to which my imprudence had hurried me" (65). Ophelia goes even further, to suggest she was under a kind of gothic spell, when "deluded by an ignis fatuus" she "awoke from her dream of insensibility" (39). In the footnote, Brown includes Elizabeth Whitman's poem "Disappointment," in which she represents sex as "the sleep of innocence" and as "magick" in which she became "lost" (24). In part, this strange state of being, a kind of volition without ipseity, challenges the consent/resistance binary.[27] It is neither reluctance nor resistance to desire depicted here, nor is it the empowerment of deliberate radical choice. (Even Harrington Senior feels this usurpation of his control during his seduction of Maria, which he describes as "drifting upon a sea of inconsistency . . . like a ship without a rudder, buffeted on the bosom of the ocean, the sport of winds and waves" [71]).[28] Rather, Brown is redrawing the boundaries of the corporeal. These somewhat lobotomized figures seem to be living under a Shaftesburian somatic spell, and any sense they had of an individual will is gone. Nature, it seems, has a mind of its own.

The Aesthetic Work of Nature

We might wonder at Brown's use of nature as a commanding force, given that the era is often associated with a softening of the Atlantic world's understandings of nature.[29] Paul Downes's succinct and elegant appraisal of the "new" nature and its replacement of the "nasty, brutish, and short" nature Hobbes imagined, explains the context of this shift. In the late eighteenth-century world of radical philosophy, "Nature has been redeemed from the devil and Thomas Hobbes. . . . The settlement of America, and hence the Declaration that was its culmination, rejected the Hobbesian invocation of the state of nature as a state of emergency justifying the absolute power of sovereign authority."[30] In other words, as Downes notes, by the 1770s "nature" is no longer the source of original sin, which the Puritans tried to expunge spiritually, or the savagery Hobbes claimed required monarchical rule. But we ought to remember that in the philosophical works that redefined the era's relationship to nature, works like Shaftesbury's *Characteristicks of Men, Manners, Opinions, Times* (1711), nature is still that which governs human behavior. As the eighteenth-century philosophical world knew it, the new nature manifests as the condition of embodiment, reorienting the body as a moral compass. The "Laws of Nature and of Nature's God" endow the body with the sensate technology that, as Adam Smith's witness to his friend on the rack experiences it, eliminates a sense of self—he becomes in some measure the sufferer himself. But in Brown's novels, it is desire, not pain, that is transferable. There is an eros to the moral workings of the body. The body's registers can make us want to be *with* those whom the sympathetic body allows us to *be*.

When John Adams imagined democracy as a rake, was he also imagining the spell nature casts on human volition? Could desire do the aesthetic work of rendering the subject a democratic citizen, simply by taking away his choice to become one? For in both *The Power of Sympathy* and *Ira and Isabella*, it is "the power of sympathy" that fuels civic feeling. Critics have had much to say about sympathy's working parts in the last two decades or so.[31] From Harriet Beecher Stowe's nineteenth-century injunction to "feel right," back to philosophers of feeling from the seventeenth and eighteenth centuries discussed in chapter 2, sympathy signifies a heart *at work,* a cultural and aesthetic organ that allows us to feel not just *for* but *as* one another.[32] A republic was understood to be impossible without it. In his own observations of human beings, President Adams noted that "nature intended them for society."[33] All the philosophy of the Atlantic Enlightenment is embedded in Adams's concise remark. Sympathy is the engine of sociability, the feeling sixth sense that impels humans toward one another, and because it is the province of nature, it cannot be controlled.[34] Brown's novels thus retell seduction as a story for siblings whose commanding somatic bond ably represents nature as the author of human agency.

The republic, in other words, will abandon desire at its peril. For if we return to Adams's claim that democracy is a rake, the iteration of that claim in Brown's novels seems to be that the story of ruin readers are searching for is not Harriot's. It is not Isabella's. The ruined woman in Brown's novels is, as Adams argued, America itself. It's an ideal for which Harrington and Harriot become martyrs, and, significantly, an ideal for which no one must die in Brown's later work. The novels issue a call to the aesthetic, a heralding of the erotics of sympathy as a virtuous democratic impulse, a call that can—and eventually does, in *Ira and Isabella*—lead to a story with a happy ending.

Sexing the Political Body

A more in-depth look at the context of Adams's full remark about America and Samuel Richardson's famous victim of seduction, Clarissa Harlowe, may be useful here. Adams writes,

> You say, the awful spirit of democracy is in great progress. I believe it, and I know something of the nature of it. It is a young rake who thinks himself handsome and well made, and who has little faith in virtue.—When the people once admit his courtship, and permit him the least familiarity, they soon find themselves in the condition of the poor girl, who told her story in this affecting style.
>
>> The next day he grew a little bolder
>> But promised me marriage.
>> The next day—he began to be enterprising:
>> But the next day—O Sir! the next day he got me with child.
>
> Democracy is Lovelace, and the people are Clarissa. The artful villain will pursue the innocent lovely girl to her ruin and her death.[35]

It makes sense to ask: Why sex political bodies in this way? Such a characterization of the people as a sexually ruined body destabilizes the notion of political will. Adams's idea of "courtship," of what he describes as the "bolder" and "enterprising" moves of the seducer, signifies bodies agitated by extramarital desire that "find themselves" in circumspect positions, bodies that seem for all the world to have carried on the plot entirely on their own. We might say that Brown's novels act out the courtship Adams describes. Historians have tended to interpret Adams's claim to mean that the people are vulnerable to charismatic and corrupt leaders who would bend their will for personal gain.[36] But if the democratic subject is before all else a subject of nature, can the same nature invoked by the Declaration of Independence, the nature that authorized revolution, be that which animates deviant, extramarital sex?[37]

The Power of Sympathy and *Ira and Isabella* use an almost mystical language to describe the body as the site of that nature. Words like *charmer, bewitched,* and *impulse* are proof of the libidinal cathexis at stake in the incest plot. From the subtitles of his novels on, Brown's sustained invocation of the word "nature" will lead us to understand what it means to be free from tyranny but not from rule. Adams's remark suggests that ruin is a matter of democratic bodies being "ruled" by one another via a somatic civic agency that operates apart from individual will.[38] In *The Power of Sympathy* and *Ira and Isabella,* the strongest human bonds are formed by a passion erupting from an innate sensibility. These are the body's terms, and they defy the mores that try to govern desire. The body operates squarely inside nature's jurisdiction, and that leads to the profane imagining of incestuous ruin as the very pinnacle of human community.

When Ira and Isabella first declare their romantic love for one another, for example, Ira describes nature as the author of his actions. "Prompted to visit you by the irresistible force of Nature," he pines, "I have imperceptibly engaged my heart, and nothing shall wrest it from you" (13). Indeed, the language of love at times appears as the language of a nearly occult magic in *Ira and Isabella.* Ira is "entranced in [Isabella's] presence" and "charmed" by her; "the very sound" of her words in conversation "sunk into his unresisting heart" (10). Ira "had drank [*sic*] from the eyes of Isabella, those draughts of love which intoxicated his senses," a state which leads him to tell her, "'you overpower my senses'" (11, 13). Nature plays a similar role in the poem etched onto the graves of Harrington and Harriot in *The Power of Sympathy.* It is a verse that was written by Harrington before his suicide. "Unknown this union—Nature still presides," it reads, and certainly the nation-building language of a "union" is overt. When the incestuous connection is revealed, Mrs. Holmes says to Myra, "admire, O my friend! the operation of NATURE—and the power of SYMPATHY!—HARRIOT IS YOUR SISTER!" (63) Harrington refers to his passion for Harriot as the "dictates of nature" (14); his friend Worthy calls himself a "son of nature" (31); it is "THE TRIUMPH OF NATURE" that Harrington loves his sister; Harriot claims that it is impossible "to oppose the *link of nature* that draws us to each other" (87). Nature has seduced them through ruinous desires they cannot deny.

The republic had declared itself by naming nature as the author of its independence. Yet here nature is the author of the people's desires, desires that are not independent, liberated, or free. In *The Power of Sympathy,* this version of nature is more celebrated than feared.[39] Indeed, the disappearing possibility of one's capacity for choice is a source of comfort and even pleasure for the characters in both texts. To those who lecture them, however, a seducer, a lover, or even pleasure itself can mesmerize in dangerous ways. For example, in *The Power of Sympathy*, during a discussion of the evils of seduction, the family friend Mrs. Holmes describes her own take on the dark magic that desire practices on the human will. She says seduction is a "species of *American* serpent," though the metaphor breaks down into disturbing layers: "[The serpent] looks steadfastly on the bird—their eyes meet to separate no more—the charm begins to operate—the fascinated bird flutters and hops from limb to limb, till unable any longer to extend its wings, it falls into the voracious jaws of its enemy" (75). The whole point of the original biblical story of Eden is the tragic acquisition of free will. Why would Brown have revised it into a story about its tragic loss? Mrs. Holmes explains that women are especially vulnerable to the loss of will, because once "the charm begins to operate" they "have as little inclination to resist the temptation as our general parent to refuse the fatal apple." She goes on, "We . . . yield ourselves to a kind of voluntary slavery" in which "whim and caprice may chance to dictate" human behavior (74). Similar claims exist in *Ira and Isabella*. For example, Ira tells Isabella, "I have been led insensibly into the snares of love, and have attached myself to you without volition" (10). Both remarks paint a clear portrait of the claim desire has on agency and point out the irrelevance of the rights-bearing individual in the face of such power. It is easy to see how Ira's remark that he is "without volition" speaks to a "voluntary slavery," and Mrs. Holmes's off-mark metaphor about the serpent's business in the garden begins to make sense if it is meant to denote not a moral fall but the erosion of will. The main characters are without control over their actions and choices. If they fall they risk not their sexual chastity but something more foundational.

Full of references to Harrington's loss of self-governance, the first letter of *The Power of Sympathy* would have struck its contemporary readers as evidence of just such a loss of free will. In this letter, he describes his short-lived intent to seduce Harriot. But read in the context of early Enlightenment constructions of the possessive individual as the cornerstone of democratic citizenship, Harrington's letter exposes a larger and more urgent matter. Harrington reveals himself as lacking in those defining traits of white male citizenship, freedom and will, but more importantly, he is too besotted by Harriot to care much about it. After he meets her, no one could aptly describe him as existing in a state of isolated selfhood. In moments like the one below, Brown's novels offer special insight into nonvolitional agency and the questioning of Enlightenment personhood it represents. Here and elsewhere, the lover goes so far as to rejoice in the absence of freedom through a rhetorical deification of his oppressor:

> Hail gentle God of Love! While thou rivetest the chains of thy *slaves,* how dost thou make them leap for joy, as with delicious triumph. Happy enthusiasm! that while it carries us away into captivity, can make the heart to dance as in the bosom of content. Hail gentle God of Love! Encircled as thou art with darts, torments, and ensigns of cruelty, still do we hail thee. (10)

Rivets, chains, captives, and slaves: this passage offers a radical lexicon to describe the post-revolutionary American hero animated by an agency without personhood—without recourse to a singular identity or a sense of "self-possession." These references to enslavement, captivity, and "ensigns of cruelty" would have spoken to contemporary readers in a bewildering way. The figure of the happy slave ostensibly represents the absolute antithesis of the Enlightenment individual whose free will guarantees his pursuit of happiness through rational choice and virtuous decision making. Surely few post-revolutionary readers would have missed this, yet here the lover does not mourn but rather celebrates his loss of will. The beginning of the first American novel cheerfully commemorates a free man's transformation into a "slave." And make no mistake: *these* chains are not to be confused with the shackles of colonial rule. Whatever this "charm" is that draws one person to another in scenes of ruinous desire, it is not the kind of force one wishes to rebel against. These chains do not signify colonial oppression; they do not fasten around the body but issue from it; this isn't a Rousseauian problem but a Cartesian one. This first epistle relocates the problem of the times: it is the tyranny of the body, not the tyranny of the state, with which the new republic must deal. The American Revolution may have unshackled the people, but what can be done about the chains they carry within themselves, chains they do not *wish* to cast off?

Nature appears alternately as that which fuels an assertion of will and as that which facilitates its departure. It is the engine of self—the source of individual, isolated acts of volition—and the attraction between persons that makes that self disappear. Though it cannot be both, nevertheless nature defines ontology as an isolated *and* a shared phenomenon. What does it mean to appeal to nature in the Declaration of Independence and in a young citizen's declaration of love? Brown provides one answer to this question when he stages the revelation of the supposed incestuous relation in *Ira and Isabella*. When they first learn of their supposed blood relation, Ira's plan is to travel abroad. He thinks getting as far away from Isabella as possible will blunt the pain of not being able to be with her. "'To remain in your presence, my sister, my wife, is willingly to swim into the vortex of destruction,'" he insists, vowing, "'I have imposed upon myself a resolve, therefore, to see you no more'" (22). But Isabella scolds him for this plan. The revolutionary rhetoric she uses to do so tellingly aligns virtue with the operations of nature that have drawn them together. "'Give liberty to your sensations to act themselves,'" she counsels, adding that his tears are "'the characteristicks of Nature'" and not to be dammed up (22). The idea that he ought to "[g]ive liberty to [his] sensations to act themselves," however, does not exactly represent a "to thine own self be true" sentiment. A stronger paraphrase might emphasize the idea that desire nullifies the illusion of having choices. Distance cannot allay such a power.

The body is not just a collection of somatic appetites in this context. It is a moral compass, the site of sentiment. As we saw in chapter 2, eighteenth-century philosophers of feeling see nature as the source of humankind's innate ethical drive, the empathy that defines conscience. The concept of sympathy, closely linked with that of nature, offers several theories about the emotional essence of nature. We might usefully recall Hume's *A Treatise of Human Nature*, which argued that sympathy represents the contagion of the passions, about which Hume famously remarked, "I feel more from communication than from my own natural temper and disposition" (317). Also relevant is Shaftesbury's notion of the "inward eye" that "distinguishes and sees the fair and shapely, the amiable and admirable, apart from the foul, the odious, or the despicable" (134 II). The moral sense that this philosophical school describes allows for benevolent, intelligent, fellow feeling to direct human action. Instinct will map out the right thing to do.

We might consider the soapbox speech issued by Harriot and Harrington's father as an illustration of this moral sense. When the senior Harrington confesses his seduction and abandonment of Harriot's mother, he explains what he has learned from the incestuous attraction between his children and their tragic deaths. The language he uses is straight out of the moral sense philosophy we saw at work in Shaftesbury's writings: he says that if only a man will reflect upon his actions, his natural sense will tell him what it is that he should do. He goes on,

> From what innate principle does this arise, but from the *God within the mind!*—I assert it for the honour of human nature, that no man, however dissolute, but comes back to the hour of reflection and solemn thoughtfulness—when the actions that are passed return upon the mind, and this *internal monitor* sits in judgment upon them, and gives her verdict of approbation or dislike. (72)

At first, the passage might strike us as a condemnation of the love between Harriot and Harrington, the idea being that if only they listened to their "internal monitors," they would have known better. But it was their internal monitors that told them to seek one another out in the first place, and those monitors do not later impel a cessation of their desires after the sibling relation is revealed, in their case or in Ira and Isabella's. On the contrary, their impulse to be together commends their union in spite of the potent societal taboo of incest. In Brown's works, then, sympathy can be defined as the intersection of the sensate and the emotional that compels action. Incestuous desire dramatizes the struggle to define moral agency in the republic as the struggle to locate nature within a workable ideology of the state. When Ira tells Isabella he must leave her since his continued desire for her is his "pleasure" and his "perdition," her response is to call any such separation "forced" and "pretended" (22-23). They can never truly be separated in idea from one another. "'Personal presence is not necessary,'" she convinces him, for he will be "'[h]aunted'" by her wherever he goes (24). Isabella's argument that Ira cannot really ever leave her, and Harriot's claim that she and Harrington cannot "oppose the *link of nature*" that compels them toward one another, are the deciding arguments in each case. Incest becomes the unexpected ambassador of nature.

Their dialogue suggests that democracy points to the aesthetic condition of the modern subject as one who is networked into the social sphere by the material reality of the body, its appetites part of nature's interpellation of the human. Incestuous desire simply enacts the somatic throb of sensibility, the will of the body, that sensate tangle of longing and instinct. The loss of chastity in the tales of seduction-as-ruin that frame the larger incest narratives thus function to emphasize that sex, and the desires that lead to it, do the work of democratic joining. If all this seems a bit essentialist, that is because "nature" is characterized as an essentializing force. The aesthetic work of nature is to essentialize the body, to reduce it to its most animating business, the business of desire. Yet this essentializing also fails, in that it does not signify something whole, for the "natural" body is not a totality but a breaking away from such wholeness. For incestuous lovers as for a nation, nature is constitutive of democratic feeling, a regard not only for the rights but also for the appetites that draw a people together. If we read democracy as a metaphor for incest instead of the other way around, the aesthetic work of incest becomes the rendering of the body as a site of sovereignty. But this is the site of fracturing, multiple identities. As David Greven notes, "Using incest as a literary figure allowed nineteenth-century authors to register unrepresentable and unimaginable affiliations. Incest functions both allusively, signaling intersubjective dynamics among fictional characters that authors cannot explicitly name, and allegorically, suggesting other dynamics, such as the political and the social."[40] Thus it is that in one of his last letters before his suicide, Harrington subtly imagines himself to be his sister mourning his death. He calls himself a "hopeless maid" who "on the sea-beat shore . . . unmindful of the storm, bewails her drowned lover" (96–97).[41] These doublings, mirrored appetites, and strange transformations constitute a narrative that maps the self in an unstable, unfixed state.

"There Our Love Will Not Be a Crime"

Nature, then, is a fearsome matchmaker. The mapping of the body within nature's jurisdiction exerts yet more force in Harrington's early letters, as he unwittingly underscores the influence of physical attraction by mentioning Harriot's blush three times. His descriptive phrase, "a crimson drop," immediately forecasts the blood tie that compels their attraction (9). We find the half-siblings acquiescing to the power of this attraction after Harrington initiates his seduction plan. It is a notable instance of rebellion in the novel, though the fight is not a revolution against nature, but by it. If you take the democracy authorized by nature to the nth degree, Brown's work posits, nothing that nature authorizes is forbidden. It does not seem to be the "solitary, poore, nasty, brutish, and short" life with which Brown's novels are concerned. It is the desires that might be sated once custom is removed as an obstacle to them. Brown's point seems to be that in such a state of nature, you don't get Hobbes, you get Sade.

Yet nature is no villain. When Harrington asks Harriot about how they ought to respond to nature, he leaves his question unfinished. He asks, "Shall we obey the dictates of nature, rather than confine ourselves to the forced, unnatural rules of—" (14). Here, the unspeakable is not incest but the rejection of incest and the contractual world that rejection implies. Similarly, Ira rejects the concerns of elders who would prevent his marriage to Isabella, raging, "If we regulate our lives by the will of the world, we shall be governed by the caprice of one, the false delicacy of the other, and the injustice of the third" (21). What the "dictates of nature" are exactly is a matter of some question. For Harrington ultimately does not seduce Harriot; her beauty, that which drew him in and inspired his intention to seduce her, is the very antidote to his nefarious plan. The "all-conquering force of *Harriot's* eloquence" is how he describes her physical allure, and her influence is felt through "a language of the eye." The republic relies on women to discipline the passions, not evoke them, but Harriot seems to do both.[42] The blood in a cheek, the plea in a glance—such is the wordless, corporeal speech sexing the democratic subject.

For while their love accesses all the overwhelming emotions of romance, it is after all not in idea only that Brown's couples see each other as lovers. When, for example, Ira sees Isabella after the calamity of their relation is revealed, he is "agitated by a thousand sensations," and confesses to her, "'How are my senses bewildered in this meeting. I find, even now, that to meet your eye is at once my pleasure and my perdition'" (22). The same sort of scene occurs in *The Power of Sympathy*. Harriot's similar reaction to meeting Harrington post-revelation explains the impossibility of stifling the attraction:

> When you pressed my cheek with the kiss of love, of fraternal affection, what meant its conscious glow? What meant the ebullition of my veins, the disorder of my nerves, the intoxication of my brain, the blood that mantled in my heart? My hand trembled, and every object seemed to swim before my doubtful view—Amidst the struggle of passion, how could I pronounce the word—how could I call you by the title of brother. (87)

The vivid details of the passage—the pressing kisses and glowing cheeks, the "disordered nerves" and trembling hands—demonstrate how the body obeys the "dictates of nature" when the marriage contract would criminalize them. Harriot describes what must by anyone's standards be a powerful love scene, as the sensate eclipses the sibling relation, the possible enunciation of the word *brother* receding ever farther. The vocabulary of Harriot's speech explains their failure to resist.[43] Words like "ebullition" and "intoxication" suggest the intoxicating embodiment of the democratic subject, charmed by the somatic spell of the other. The attraction persists for quite a number of pages. Says Harriot, "I indulge, in idea, the recollection of his caresses . . . I cherish the dear idea of a lover—I see the danger and do not wish to shun it . . . I strive no longer to remember our present connexion. I endeavor to forget—I curse the idea of a brother" (87). The question now seems to be whether such a restoration of family ought to be pursued at all. To be ruined by an incestuous joining, a sexual union that no contract could ever ratify, might be the best possible outcome. The lovers consistently defend their attraction, complaining of the "unmerited criminality," as Harriot phrases it, of its origin. In his own heated defense of their love, Harrington asks Worthy, "'How am I guilty, my friend—How is this transport a crime? My love is the most pure, the most holy'" (80).[44]

The idea that their love is not just wholesome but "holy" is where things get especially interesting.[45] After Harriot dies, Harrington dreams of his own death, when, he outrageously insists, they will meet in Heaven where "there alone is happiness—there I shall meet her—there our love will not be a crime" (89). He even imagines Harriot practicing a kind of heavenly domesticity, claiming "she is preparing a place for me—a place of unutterable bliss" (91). A blunt paraphrase clarifies: If you can't have your sister in this life, have her in the next. Perhaps more than any traditional seduction plot, the story of incest represents the profanity of a passion utterly beyond the ideological reach of contract, existing as it does under the very guise of domestic shelter that it brings down. As Brown's novels see it, incest is the "triumph of nature"—the sensate call of desire that cannot countenance resistance—and there is something inherently sacrosanct in the call that Harrington imagines issuing from heaven itself and which "serves to idealize their attachment rather than critique it."[46] Incest holds the ultimate promise of ruin: a joining that must forever be dictated by nature, not by the laws of man that feebly reach to achieve nature's unsurpassable triumph. *The Power of Sympathy* wishes for a truly radical attachment in which the civic subject is constituted by passion and instinct, a moral sensibility, here depicted as the aesthetic work of incest.

In *Ira and Isabella*, this triumph is similarly told, as the novel uses some happy slave rhetoric of its own to describe how nature exchanges the lover's freedom for a kind of entrancement. But *Ira and Isabella* begins much differently than *The Power of Sympathy* does, with the aristocrat Harrington sharing his plan to ruin a young woman and then getting chastised for it by his pious friend named, appropriately enough, Worthy. Instead, we encounter Ira and his friend Lorenzo, two men debating about how to talk about sexual longing in the first place. Lorenzo is Worthy's polar opposite. He sets a tone of candor in the opening pages of *Ira and Isabella*, and he insists that Ira acknowledge, without shame, that his lust for Isabella is a great motivator, perhaps *the* great motivator. When Lorenzo asks Ira to admit his desires frankly, Ira demurs. Lorenzo scoffs and tells him to not be "'formal and proud'" but to declare openly his "'real passion.'" Though Ira protests that words like "'desire'" and "'possess'" are too explicit, too unguarded, Lorenzo presses on, insisting, "'You have heard with rapture her words, you have seen with desire'" her person and, whether Ira will admit it or not, "'you sigh to possess.'" Lorenzo drives his point further by mocking Ira, nicknaming him "'my dear Platonick,'" and asks, "'Why will you tie yourself to a foolish old system, unphilosophical, unnatural? To repeat to me your stupid notions of false delicacy, or rather untutored virtue, is ridiculous in the extreme; absolutely fighting against Nature herself, the informer of our hearts, the directress of our passions'" (11). In this sense, the condition of the democratic subject's freedom is obedience to a directress. In the Atlantic Enlightenment age that in some ways might be defined by its questioning of divine right, the omnipotence of nature operates in a murkier realm. The considerable aesthetic distance between the lover governed by a directress and the possessive individual governed by himself shows the advantage of using entranced sibling lovers as one's protagonists. When the novel idealizes the young republican who is "led insensibly into the snares of love," it looks to the ungovernable body as constitutive of the modern aesthetic subject.

Just as Harriot's blush was nature's informant in *The Power of Sympathy*, Isabella's blush signifies the many meanings of desire in *Ira and Isabella*. Only this time, Brown is on Lorenzo's side. In order that we see the blood rising to Isabella's cheek—the blood that would impel her to ruin—as a sign of natural desire, worthy of virtue and approbation, Brown turns to that prototypical disobedient lover, Shakespeare's Juliet. In one of his many authorial intrusions in the text, Brown seems to be turning directly to his readers as he asks if Isabella's coloring is "the blush of wantonness." He goes on to say, "why should Isabella be more *unnatural* in my hands than Juliet is in those of Shakespeare. When the ghostly father has proposed a scheme for her union with Romeo, 'Then hies the *wanton blood* up in her cheek'" (13).[47] The sexed body signals a kind of timeless civic virtue, and Brown warns that to repudiate such a figure is to "undertake to delineate Nature, and deviate into errour, by concealing the consequences of the passions" (13). In *Ira and Isabella,* that is, they really can trust nature as the custodian of human connections.

In *The Power of Sympathy,* Harriot acknowledges this principle when she notes that in a state of "warring passions," she cannot recategorize Harrington. In a particularly moving outburst in which she describes the inability to choose what he will be in her mind, she writes, "I vainly imagine I have my choice of a brother or———" (87–88). Unable to even use the word, she cannot entirely distinguish the brother from the lover. Instead, something perhaps even more profane happens, as the number of roles under which Harrington might be categorized expands instead of diminishing. "O *Harrington!* be a friend, a protector, a brother—be him, on whom I could never yet call by the tender, the endearing title of *parent.* . . . I will be dutiful and affectionate to you, and you shall be unto me as a father—I will bend on the knee of respect and love, and will receive your blessing" (87). In this scene, the multiplying of roles under the governance of nature obfuscates the boundaries of genre, gender, and generation, and the image of Harriot kneeling before Harrington as a wife, sister, and daughter offers a bewildering multitude of interpellating acts. The ruin narrative thus produces an Althusserian echo chamber that becomes a site of the individual's collapse. In a similar moment, when Isabella meets Ira after they have been told they are siblings, she says, "'My Husband, my brother,'" to which Ira replies, "'my sister, my wife'" (22). The utterance, "my sister, my wife" acts as a polyontological hail, which issues the possibility for multiple responses. Identity formation in scenes like these means not simply the permeability of "self" but an expansion of its periphery. The story of incest as ruin dismisses the notion that identity is singular and instead opens the possibility of the utterance, "my sister, my wife." It offers a place where interrelation renders the subject many times over. It is with great industry that *The Power of Sympathy* and *Ira and Isabella* participate in the opening of such a space. The fluid boundaries and ruptures of identity in Brown's works deny the rigid precincts of identity as finite spaces. For Brown, what is important are the occasions when all the space of community might be made legible as an unstable, interrelated *move* toward one another, a locating of identity that, as we shall soon see in *The Coquette,* one finds only under the spell of its pursuit.

· FOUR ·

Seduction and the Patriotism of Ruin in Hannah Webster Foster's *The Coquette*

> Men cannot live without the *Society* of others, and their *good Offices;* they must observe both the *Happiness* and *Misery,* the *Pleasures* and *Pains* of their Fellows. *Desire* and *Aversion* must arise in the Observer. Nay farther, as we cannot avoid more near Attachments of Love . . . we must feel the Sensations of *Joy* and *Sorrow,* from the State of others even in the strongest Degrees, and have the publick Desires in a greater Height.
> —Sir Francis Hutcheson, *An Essay on the Nature and Conduct of the Passions and Affections,* 1728

> For let will be ever so free, *Humour* and *Fancy,* we see, govern it. And these, as free as we suppose 'em, are often chang'd we know not how, without asking our consent, or giving us any account.
> —Anthony Ashley Cooper, Third Earl of Shaftesbury, *Characteristicks of Men, Manners, Opinions, Times,* 1711

Like the novels of William Hill Brown, Hannah Webster Foster's popular seduction tale, *The Coquette; or, The History of Eliza Wharton; A Novel; Founded on Fact* (1797) investigates the "nature" of attracted bodies. A story of how an aging flirt named Eliza Wharton escapes two unwanted marriages only to fall into the arms of the seducer Peter Sanford, *The Coquette* offers a fascinating look at how sexual attraction can sustain community when marriage fails to do so. In Foster's work, we encounter the same trancelike agency of the erotic encounter, though in this later and much more popular work, Foster links the sexed, ruined body not to the ties of a blood relation but to the gregarious impulse, what the founders referred to as the patriotic virtue of "sociability." Post-revolutionary Atlantic thinkers regarded this impulse, a politically enhanced version of Shaftesbury's *sensus communis*, as proof once and for all that the political ideas of Thomas Hobbes were wrong, as, left to rule themselves, the people of a republic would not turn against one another, but would in true Shaftesburian fashion seek one another out. According to the ideal of sociability, the innate human need for companionship, transferred into the public square to organize the people into a sovereign power, would propel the people forward into ever-loftier realms of civility and virtue.

The coquette figures into this political landscape in intriguing ways.[1] A ubiquitous stock character in the eighteenth-century Atlantic novel, the coquette is a particularly gendered figure in the sense that in spite of her wayward sexual practices, her promiscuity must serve a larger political narrative about social bonds. The body of the coquette acts as a site of traffic, of public joinings, of a nation building itself. Her virtue seems but a small price to pay in this larger narrative structure, mere collateral damage paid to the civic good. Resisting retirement to the private sphere through marriage, the coquette overstays her welcome in the social sphere so that she becomes isolated from its virtues while also defining its capacity for congress. Ultimately, in most novels she finds herself ensnared in a networked constellation of attractions, an overpowering series of connections to others that define her political purpose even as they become the source of her personal condemnation.

Published just eight years after *The Power of Sympathy*, *The Coquette* is in some ways an even darker novel than Brown's. Foster's story of seduction locates the powers of sociability in the gregarious body of a woman, which in *The Coquette* is governed by a kind of civic enchantment; it issues a somatic command that draws people together. In Foster's novel, moments of encounter rely on that same lexicon of involuntary impulses we saw operating in Shaftesbury's *Characteristicks*. Indeed, Foster's novel seems to take what Shaftesbury called the "moral Magick" of sociability further, as references to enchantment, witchcraft, and otherworldly forces explain the terms of embodiment throughout *The Coquette*. As a figure not of rebellion but of conformity, Foster's coquette Eliza Wharton is in some ways a model citizen because she is compelled to seek out human company, to exercise her sociable impulses, even as they become extramarital sexual encounters that ironically lead to her banishment. The aesthetic work of late eighteenth-century Atlantic novels of seduction is in part the exploration of the body's political valence. We might say that through the trope of coquetry read as sociability, *The Coquette* participates in that work by portraying the pleasure of company—in talk, in space, and in *bodies*—as having a certain power to enthrall. As such, it creates human bonds that need no contracts to enforce them. Instead, this power—this drive toward citizenship—relies on interdependence and the permeability of identity.

The Coquette presents an account of sociability that quickly spins out of control. In it, we find the novel Brown might have written, the artfully rendered story of the historical person Elizabeth Whitman and her attraction to a calculating libertine. Rather than a mere footnote, Foster presents the full, if fictionalized, story of Eliza Wharton, a character based on Whitman. Born in 1752, Whitman was an upper-class Bostonian whose illicit paramour was allegedly Pierpont Edwards (son of preacher Jonathan Edwards of Great Awakening fame); her death in 1788 after giving birth out of wedlock earned her story national notoriety.[2] Much has been written about the significance of Whitman's history. The question of *why* Whitman's story stands out, why it resonates so powerfully in the American imagination when it is not a particularly unusual one, is a more interesting question. One partial answer may be that the inn to which Whitman fled for her confinement was in Danvers, Massachusetts, which, as it turns out, was the new name for a much older and more familiar place in American history: Salem Village.

The semiotic power of Danvers as a site of American history is certainly noteworthy. Salem Village is of course the place where the infamous 1692 witch trials occurred.[3] (The newspaper that in 1788 first alerted Whitman's friends and family to her fate was called *The Salem Mercury*.) Rather than read *The Coquette* as it is nearly always read, as a generically typical seduction tale, I would suggest that we take the novel's history, and its frequent use of gothic imagery, more seriously. The darkly gendered history of colonial America can inform our reading of Hannah Webster Foster's tale, as a particularly republican revision of the public shaming and shunning of women whose bodies both wield and are subject to the moral magic of the social sphere. The change from Salem Village to Danvers serves as a compelling backdrop for the sorts of transformations occurring in and around this novel, where extroverted gentry turn into banished recluses, and rakes and reverends alike transform into besotted lovers. The electric current of sociability that binds the bodies of this novel's characters together operates through civic enchantment. Spending time with others may be a democratic virtue, but it ends up altering who they are and what they want, and in doing so it demonstrates the nearly occult power of sociability—of the body—in the Enlightenment age.

"Let not the magic arts of that worthless Sanford lead you, like an ignis fatuus, from the path of rectitude and virtue!" Though Eliza's friends issue this and other warnings, those "magic arts" are ultimately overpowering, and they do their work upon her, even as they turn against Sanford himself. Indeed, Eliza Wharton and Peter Sanford carry something of what Shaftesbury described as nature's somatic spell. *Charm* is a ubiquitously deployed word in both the works of William Hill Brown and in *The Coquette;* one can hardly get through a page without coming across a variation of it. Phrases like "charm my fancy," "my charmer," and "you are charmed" accomplish a particular aesthetic work in Foster's novel that engages with the ability of sexual desire to pilot bodies through their social encounters. Eliza notes that she does not quite know what to do with what she calls "these charms of mine." Her body is at times a delightful surprise to her, at times a frustratingly opaque director; experienced through the fugue state of desire, the sexed body enacts sociability as nature's province. The symbiosis between the powerful undertow of desire and the current of sociability is, then, key to understanding the agency of a woman who often talks of her freedom but rarely has access to it.

In *The Coquette,* Foster provides all the typical elements of a traditional seduction plot: the ruined charmer doomed to an early death, her stillborn babe, the reformed rake Major Sanford, the righteous, rejected suitor Reverend Boyer, the mother wrecked by grief, the friends who at first warn Eliza about her behavior and then scold her for it. Yet there are plenty of anomalies warping the arc of the genre. Released by the death of her first fiancé from what she calls the "shackles" of marriage and from her father's authority, Eliza garners approval but later concern from her circle of female friends as her return to what they regard as a properly sociable youthful gaiety lasts too long. Her closest friends, Lucy and Julia, worry, and rightly so, that her sociability will be read as coquetry, and that her coquetry will tarnish her marriageability. When the Reverend Boyer asks for her hand, her friends hastily advise her to take it. But Eliza insists she is not ready to make any promises, and instead forges with Boyer a "friendship" that he wrongly interprets as a prolonged engagement. Her increasing involvement with Sanford eventually prompts Boyer to rescind his offer and marry someone else. Eliza finds herself compelled to see more of Sanford, a married man, and eventually she and Sanford begin a physical affair. She appears to be in love with him. When Eliza discovers she is pregnant, she flees the community and dies after delivering the stillborn child. Among the mourners is Sanford himself, who, like many others in the novel, realizes in a moment of surprise his own feelings—he, too, is in love with Eliza.

Readers of *The Coquette* are perfectly familiar with this retelling of the story's plot. A second, much different summary of the novel, however, yields quite different results. The darker version tells of a woman and two men who are enchanted by one another beyond all scope of reason or accountability, three people who find themselves caught in an overpowering and terrible love triangle that ends in futility, desperation, and for one of them, an appalling death. Surrounding them is sadness and misfortune. Families are falling apart—dead infants, dead husbands, and dying fiancés encircle them—yet the three lovers cannot stop themselves. Bewitched by forces more powerful than they can understand, they almost relentlessly pursue one another, only to reproduce in that pursuit the unhappiness they observe all around them. Eliza, a young woman seemingly destined for a happy marriage, dies in love with two men yet unmarried and alone, a recluse mourning the death of her child and the abandonment by her two lovers. Sanford, a libertine of high fashion, falls desperately in love with the object of his machinations, and he loses everything—the girl, the money—all that he wanted is gone, and he is destroyed, exiled from the society that once gave him such power and such pleasure. And then there is the tragic clergyman, a young man who despite his strong judgment and religious convictions also falls in love with Eliza, and he finds himself loving her for all the wrong reasons. Her gregariousness and her coquetry (the two qualities he finds least morally permissible) are irresistible to him. When she wounds his pride by attending but briefly to the libertine, he runs off and marries someone else. Wretched and bitter, he insists at the novel's close that he is glad he escaped Eliza's spell while proving all the while that he will never truly be free from it.

Of course the novel tells both of these stories. But we should not read the magic or the eroticism out of *The Coquette.* Its brand of seduction as the sexual fall of immoderately sociable bodies—of sociability in excess—describes the disunified subjectivity invoked by involuntary attractions.[4] Rather than indicating simply the sexual ruin of a woman outside the bonds of marriage, seductions like this one also engage in the at once disruptive and generative affect of sociability. Perhaps more than anything else, *The Coquette* demonstrates that ruin is not always just about forming an extracontractual bond with someone but also about forming an extracontractual bond with *everyone*.

Sociability, then, involves the erosion not only of the body's boundaries but also those of the social body; that erosion provides the unifying properties of sociability that are the antidote to what Eliza bemoans in the novel as the isolation of marriage and the creep of self-interested individualism. The aesthetic work of this novel is to reframe seduction's power, presenting it as a model for the unifying exchange of the passions that form a community. The unifying intimacy of ruined bodies in *The Coquette* questions the political cost of the individual's limits. At the center of the novel's seduction plot is its investment in a diminishing individual agency; the "nature" at work in the novels of William Hill Brown is equally industrious in Foster's text. The move to defend the virtue of the seduced woman is typical of the genre, and *The Coquette* proves no exception. But at the heart of this defense is the fact that like Brown's couples, the lovers in *The Coquette*—Eliza, Sanford, and Boyer—are not in control of their sexual or emotional appetites.

Contesting the value of privacy and self-interest in post-revolutionary culture, the coquette's desire retheorizes the construction of self as a social shift into being. We might think about that shift as a condition of embodiment.[5] In the end, for *The Coquette*, seduction models the nation-building capacity of sexed, circulating bodies whose ruin marks their entrance into democratic relations. The closer we look at Eliza's claims about what propels her toward Sanford, the more it becomes clear that Eliza is not seduced by him, or only by him. It is the social realm around her, the bustle and encounter of human life. It is her reintroduction to society. It is, quite simply, other people who cause Eliza to feel this sensation of pleasure and the ruin to which it leads. If seduction is a sensate, emotional overpowering of one's volition, an occasion when desire either eclipses free will or reveals its false claims on agency and identity, then Eliza's first seducer is the people around her, or perhaps we might say the People, the interdynamic current of America itself.

The Citizen as Public Property

The novel begins with the term "possession" to define the pull of that current. "An unusual sensation possesses my breast," says Eliza, initiating her aesthetic journey (107).[6] That sensation is her "pleasure" on returning to "the gay world" (109). Eliza's first words offer a portrait of the body held in sociability's republican embrace. Foster uses the particular phrasing of a sensation *possessing* Eliza to invoke a Humean insistence that, as we saw in chapter 2, feelings take possession of persons, and this concept is crucial to understanding the aesthetic workings of the terms "seduction" and "ruin" in *The Coquette*. Eliza's comment specifically recalls Hume's claim that the passions possess the human heart, as when he describes that organ having sociable encounters: "my heart catches the passion, and is warm'd by those warm sentiments that display themselves before me" (254). The text begins with a body occupied by something or someone else, and in this sense feeling is a very public experience. As Hume would have it, "The passions are so contagious, that they pass with the greatest facility from one person to another, and produce correspondent movements in all human breasts" (254). Indeed, contagious passions are the controlling factor in Eliza's life; Foster begins her novel with a rejection of domesticity's gendered quarantine.[7]

Foster's work quickly becomes a catalog of what other people and their emotions *make* its characters feel.[8] Often Eliza refers to her feelings in a strangely personifying language, as if they are foreign to her will but also an intimate part of her—as if they are "possessing" her as spirits not quite her own. As she experiences them, these feelings are part of her, yet not quite herself, the agent of her actions operating outside of her control but within what we might call her ontological sphere, the intimate but not private geography of her identity. If, as we shall soon see, the founders would mark virtue as a civic matter—and if sociability is the virtue that will keep the republic sustained as a union—then the passion that possesses Eliza's breast in part defines an American moment of community formation. The aesthetic work of *The Coquette* is to resignify ruin, because, as is the case with *The Power of Sympathy* and *Ira and Isabella*, the sexed body's enactment of sociability does not operate through a source of volition that fits into the philosophical definition of the individual.

At the heart of constitutional debates over ideal models of civic relations are the even messier debates over human sociability. What really compels human beings to band together? Can a sovereign people be trusted as the custodian of those bonds? In letters published during the first year of his vice presidency, it is again John Adams who makes some energetic claims illuminating the matter. Human nature, he argues, makes social belonging a somewhat deterministic condition. Says Adams, "Men in their primitive conditions, however savage, were undoubtedly gregarious; and they continue to be social.... [N]ature has furnished them with passions, appetites, and propensities . . . to render them useful to each other in their social connections."[9] This condition is one that becomes quickly sexualized in Foster's seduction story. Used prolifically in *The Coquette*, words like "passion," "appetite," and "propensity" radicalize embodiment's relation to democracy, highlighting the unwilled volition of sensate encounter as the source of a more intense form of sodality.

Eighteenth-century Atlantic political philosophy was deeply invested in these nation-building properties of human nature. Certainly the founders saw the operation of sociability as a civic virtue. As Gordon S. Wood rightly notes, "[T]heir principal political problem was one of adhesion.... Republics were supposed to rely for cohesion on the moral qualities of their people—their virtue and their natural sociability."[10] Within this context, we might consider Thomas Jefferson's famous remark that "[t]he Creator would indeed have been a bungling artist, had he intended man for a social animal, without planting in him social dispositions."[11] For Shaftesbury, whose work was quite popular among the founders and avidly read by Jefferson in particular, the recluse is a political monster. "The bug which breeds with the butterfly is more properly a fly," he says, than the person who rejects society is a human being, since his "passions, appetites and organs must be wholly different. His whole inward make must be reversed to fit him for such a recluse economy and separate subsistence" (80 II).[12] In other words, other people make us human, and we abandon the aesthetic work accomplished by an inclination to be with them at our peril.

Jefferson was particularly eloquent on the connections among community and the moral fabric of the new republic:

Self-interest, or rather self-love, or egoism, has been more plausibly substituted as the basis of morality. But I consider our relations with others as constituting the boundaries of morality. With ourselves we stand on the ground of identity, not of relation, which last, requiring two subjects, excludes self-love confined to a single one. To ourselves, in strict language, we can owe no duties, obligation requiring also two parties. Self-love, therefore, is no part of morality. Indeed it is exactly its counterpart. It is the sole antagonist of virtue, leading us constantly by our propensities to self-gratification in violation of our moral duties to others.[13]

The idea of a nation standing on the ground of relation illustrates the civic ideal of sociability on a grand scale. Yet Jefferson immediately brings such airy philosophy down to the matter of two people who must love one another to achieve their moral duty. Of course, Jefferson is not talking of seduction or sex but of a human formation of community, of how the success of the nation rests on the fraternal love between "two subjects"; only the company of other people, he maintains, can incline us toward the moral.

A staunch supporter of a return to republican civic virtue, Benjamin Rush, a revolutionary era politician and one of the Declaration's signers, similarly pleads for the moral value of civic duty in his essay titled "Of the Mode of Education Proper in a Republic" (1798):

> Next to the duty which young men owe to their Creator, I wish to see a regard to their country, inculcated upon them. When the Duke of Sully became prime minister to Henry the IVth of France, the first thing he did, he tells us, "Was to subdue and forget his own heart." The same duty is incumbent upon every citizen of a republic. . . . Let our pupil be taught that he does not belong to himself, but that he is public property.[14]

As Rush would have it, each citizen of the republic must relinquish the benefits of individual identity, imagined here as peerage (that which sets one above and outside of the masses), now that his sovereignty constitutes a kind of public office. To become an American is in essence to give up one's heart to the people, which of course is to give one's heart back to oneself through the medium of country.[15] If this is a surrender, it is also an acquisition, a loss of the oneness of self exchanged for the expanse of "property" in a shared identity, in belonging itself. The citizen who does this is not contained but must erase the boundaries of containment; nation building requires the kind of sovereignty that dispossesses as it confers belonging. Indeed, in Jefferson's remark and throughout the more gothic episodes of *The Coquette,* sociability operates through the understanding of the self as public property insofar as belonging is a form of an almost mystical civic possession, not self-possession. Rush used his essays to promote the value of a social identity to a community perceiving itself in danger of a second revolution. Ontologically, the citizen who is "public property" disarticulates the idea of property in one's self from possessive individualism. Honoring citizenship above all else, then, presents identity as a flexible and shared ontological possibility. Unlike John Locke's notion of identity as singular self-possession, as when he most famously says, "Though the earth and all inferior creatures be common to all men, yet every man has a 'property' in his own 'person.' This nobody has any right to but himself," in *The Coquette* ruin means an ontological shift into public being as a moment of belonging, a communal self acting as a dismissal of Lockean self-rule.[16] Ruin is not only a fall into the arms of the libertine, then, but into the arms of the people.

Jean-Luc Nancy's *The Inoperative Community* gives us the vocabulary to understand the publicness of such property and the origin of the citizen drive leading to it. Applying the term *clinamen* to human behavior, he notes that community requires "an inclination or an inclining from one toward the other." Eliza illustrates the ontological import of this turn to the social, as she wishes to incline herself socially—to develop a sense of self mediated through the social that allows her to be herself without properly owning or containing that self. Nancy says, "Being *in* common means, to the contrary, no longer having . . . [a] substantial identity, and sharing this . . . lack of identity."[17] To be public property might be understood then as not belonging to oneself because a "self" belongs to everyone. This shared lack of identity is not to be seen as an absence but as "co-originary." In other words, it involves an ontological interdependence, *e pluribus unum* at its most material. The aesthetic work of the coquette arises from the construction of identity as something that is intimate but not private. It understands desire as the source of a sociable type of agency that inclines us out of the contained atmosphere of individual self. Physical attraction creates a climate of sociability wherein the bonds of sexual desire eclipse individual will.

But sociability in women can be misread as a different kind of traffic, sexual trade as well as homosocial exchange, commerce instead of congress. We can observe this phenomenon in the attitude of Boyer's friend, Thomas Selby, as he reports back to Boyer on Eliza's behavior when Boyer himself is away: "I am quite a convert to Pope's assertion, that 'Every woman is, at heart, a rake.' How else can we account for the pleasure which they evidently receive from the society, the flattery, the caresses of men of that character? Even the most virtuous of them seem naturally prone to gaiety and pleasure, and, I had almost said, to dissipation!" (146).[18] Nettled by Eliza's attractions, Thomas sticks to the periphery of the gathering, but in his watching of her, his gaze seems to be attracted by Eliza's magnetism; he witnesses that magnetism as he confers the male gaze on the surveilled, desired female body that is at once subject to that gaze and maneuvering to fall under it. Later noting his delivery of Eliza's letter to Boyer along with his own, he remarks, "I am almost tempted to break the seal of her letter to you" (141).[19] Rush's idea of the social self as "public property" takes on an ominous connotation in this case, as Thomas's casual remark indicates how easy it would be for him to ruin her himself. For women, that is, sociability can translate into a commodifying circulatability, either as property or as objects of homosocial exchange.[20]

But it is not at all clear that the patriarchal forces at work in the novel are ascendant. The scene of mourning over Eliza's dead fiancé with which the novel begins juxtaposes the costs of isolation with the moral pitfalls of social gatherings for the coquette. The isolation of mourning has been injurious for Eliza, so in her eyes the real sin is to cast a pall over a scene of gaiety, thus robbing community of its healing pleasures. For example, her reaction to a meddlesome woman intent on subtly chastising Eliza for her social nature suggests that to fall into the company of others is to cure the ills of seclusion, and to be removed from society is unhealthy and immoral. When the offender, Mrs. Laiton, pulls Eliza away from company to convey her condolences on the death of her fiancé, Eliza expresses disgust. She says "the laws of humanity forbid" what she calls mourning's "absurdity of custom" that interrupts the virtue of civic, sociable happiness. She notes that her "heart rose against the woman, so ignorant of human nature" (110). This invocation of nature is quite reminiscent of *The Power of Sympathy*'s portrayal of that force, a nature that, as Harrington puts it, "tyrant custom" tries to corrupt or even destroy (92). In their campaign for a sincere and happy world, the Elizas and Harringtons of the ruin genre would celebrate human nature in its rejection of the very customs that seem to keep the people "civil" but estrange them from their civic natures.

If, as the ruin narrative suggests, sex represents the sort of civic nature that is necessary for a democracy, then in *The Coquette* marriage is democracy's antithesis. Indeed, Eliza believes "[m]arriage is the tomb of friendship" (123). When her friends begin to marry, Eliza contends that through marriage a woman loses everything. Marriage, she says, "appears to me a very selfish state. Why do people, in general, as soon as they are married, center all their cares, their concerns, and pleasures in their own families?" The community of intimate friendships among women is torn apart by this isolationism, and Eliza wants no part of it. "The tenderest ties between friends are weakened, or dissolved; and benevolence itself moves in a very limited sphere" (123).[21] All of this occurs in direct contrast to Eliza's "nature," which instead reflects Rush's notion of identity as "public property." Eliza describes her "natural propensity for mixing in the busy scenes and active pleasures of life," and others know hers to be "a temper peculiarly formed for the enjoyments of social life" (109, 116). According to such a temperament, the marriage contract dims the corporeal zest of public life, and functions as a metonym for the social contract, returning the female citizen to the realm of private property.

Eliza's friends and family describe her sociable behavior as an unalterable trait rather than something she chooses to be, and this facet of her character creates a powerful tension in a novel ostensibly working the marriage plot, which, of course, is a story principally about choice. Recalling William Hill Brown's deployment of the word "nature," we find in *The Coquette* descriptions of Eliza in phrases like "naturally of a gay disposition," "the natural volatility of my temper," and "her natural disposition for gaiety" (111, 126, 116). She asks her friends to stop trying to interfere: "Let me . . . gratify my natural disposition," she pleads, and later her explanation for why she cannot marry a clergyman is that her "disposition is not calculated for that sphere" (113, 135).[22] The most important feature of Eliza's character seems to be the one that is designed by outside forces. Eliza has discovered she cannot marry herself off to a quiet life of domesticity because she is not *calculated* for it—it is not so much her refusal to choose as her discovery that she cannot choose. Just as the couples in Brown's novels cannot deny their natural feelings for one another, how this all plays out is not up to Eliza. The apparatus of choice linked to the institution of marriage isn't compatible with her nature.[23]

The Coquette's "Moral Magick"

The insistence that for Eliza, sex, which she herself calls a "dream of sensual gratification," occurs without pleasure or passion is one of the unaccountable but common critical misreadings of *The Coquette*.[24] Yet the sexual desire that Eliza experiences is extremely important to the novel, in part because in her descriptions of the sociability represented by the coquette's sexed body, Foster uses language that at times borders on the mystical. Indeed, the body of the coquette is subject to nearly occult powers of attraction, animated by an energy that Eliza herself demonstrates a struggle to define. Instead of denying the desire that Eliza experiences, we ought to see the illicitly sexed body animated by desire as a figure of sociability in Foster's novel.

If Eliza's sexed body is the site of democratic urges, then sex marks not just gratification but embodiment as a relational condition. The libertine may himself be subject to "passions originating in the 'mechanical' world of physiological determinism that render [him] an automaton."[25] Eliza reflects such automation, referring to herself as a "predestinarian" whose agency is a matter of whim and fancy more than rational reflection. Such deterministic forces assert the inevitability of Sanford and Eliza's sexual tryst, and sociability as the catalyst for such chemistry. The republic's reliance upon sociability as a nation-building force casts a new light on the novel's increasingly intense focus on Eliza's lack of autonomy as that which constitutes her sociability.

Importantly, Eliza describes the experience of sex as a cognitively overpowering one in which her actions are pleasurable but unintentional. She describes her desire with that phrase mentioned above, "the delusive dream of sensual gratification," and then says, "I soon awoke" (222). This claim establishes Eliza's desire quite unambiguously. She says, openly and often, that she desires Sanford for his similar disposition. Easy to talk to, handsome, clever, and (seemingly) rich, he strikes her as an "extraordinary man," adding, "His person, his manners, his situation, all combine to charm my fancy; and to my lively imagination, strew the path of life with flowers" (121). She constantly refers to her dispositional preference for him as if she has nothing to say in the matter, noting her "fancy" leans in his direction though she knows Boyer would make the smarter match. She is devastated when she discovers Sanford is married, and clearly her feelings for him run deep enough that when he returns as a married man, she begins a sexual relationship with him anyway. Whatever regrets she may feel for having adulterous sex with him, a failure to enjoy his company is not a reason for them.[26]

The idea that she "awoke" from the "dream" of her sexual experience is also important. Just as Brown's seduction passages include sleeping maidens, Foster's wording casts heavy ambiguity over the whole experience. Indeed, it is not a regular experience at all, but a "dream." The wording of her confession reveals that sexual desire has blurred the secure boundaries of self. This dreamlike subjectivity marks a politically potent transformation in which the parties of a seduction turn into nature's minions. Eliza makes constant reference to her inability to decide, to act willfully, and she often writes to her circle of female friends about that crisis of indecision. Wondering what to do about the advances of the Reverend Boyer after she finds herself so charmed by Sanford, for example, Eliza writes to her friend Lucy, "The heart of your friend is again besieged. Whether it will surrender to the assailants or not, I am unable at present to determine. Sometimes I think of becoming a predestinarian, and submitting implicitly to fate, without any exercise of free will; but, as mine seems to be a wayward one, I would counteract the operations of it, if possible" (122). The passage offers an extraordinary set of terms to define embodiment, conjuring a polyontological quorum of agencies. It relies on a vocabulary of what Gillian Brown calls "unaccountability" that problematizes Eliza's identity.[27] The language anatomizes volition in a way that precludes a contained, whole self, for it is "the heart" and "it" that evade the first-person singular just at the moment of identifying what controls her actions. There is also that grammatical confusion regarding the phrase "wayward one." Does she mean "wayward fate" or, more radically, "wayward free will," a troublingly oxymoronic claim? Eliza seems to be attempting to counteract her own wayward will with an unnamed alternative agency. A few lines later, she goes even further by citing a poet's line: "My feet were guilty, but my heart was free." The passage opposes the feet, as symbolic of wayward will, with the heart, that organ of sentiment, itself "besieged" by "assailants" whose wills comingle with her own in acts of persuasion and seduction. Her "will" has become a Shaftesburian throng of combatants, and she aptly concludes, "Well, be it what it may; either the impulse of my own passions, or some higher efficiency; sure

I am, that I pay dear for its operation" (192). The "I" at work here does not determine her impulses but instead experiences an equality with them—and with that entirely unclear "higher efficiency."

Eliza's letters chart the way in which her association with Sanford increasingly confuses the boundaries of agency. Her remark that her heart is "besieged" represents a condition she more fully defines just two letters later, when, responding to Lucy's plea that she reject Sanford, Eliza says, "My reason and judgment entirely coincide with your opinion; but my fancy claims some share in the decision: and I cannot yet tell which will preponderate" (125). Her use of "my" places reason and fancy in possession of the agent, but Eliza's remark that "I cannot tell which will preponderate" removes that sense. Later, the power of "fancy" takes on an even more dramatic effect, as when describing a conversation with Sanford, Eliza says, "My heart did not approve his sentiments, but my ear was charmed with his rhetoric, and my fancy captivated by his address" (132). This anatomy of identity recognizes many organs of volition, sometimes operating at cross-purposes, and such a rhetoric is distinctly anti-individualistic. Charmed and captivated, Eliza's agency is defined by influence and attraction, not moral choices. And as things progress between Eliza and Sanford, she claims that in direct spite of her will to remove herself from his company, she simply cannot help it. "I am sensible that the power is in my hands; but the disposition (shall I confess it) is wanting!" (174) Similarly, though Sanford vows not to seduce Eliza, just as Harrington vows not to seduce Harriot, he finds that it is not up to him. He says he will refrain "if I can help it" but obviously finds that he cannot help it (122). In these scenes of ontological confusion, the novel presents agency without personhood through the idea that one's "disposition" might be a separate organ of volition from one's own "power." In fact, Eliza uses language that suggests she is herself an observer of sorts, watching this multitude to see what will happen. Discussing whom she may prefer, Boyer or Sanford, she claims, "In regard to these men, it is impossible for me to decide what the operations of my mind may hereafter be," and then the distance grows as she says, "my fancy and my judgment are in scales. Sometimes one preponderates, sometimes the other. Which will finally outweigh, time alone can reveal" (126, 145).[28] There is no force of self-possession centering the self in observations like these, only a disunified subjectivity experiencing a determinism that issues from that which we might call identity but certainly not individuality.

Eliza is not the only one for whom this emotional determinism is a burden. Surprisingly, the Reverend Boyer experiences a period in which he loses control of his own actions. In a letter to his friend Thomas Selby, he confesses that while there may be reason to believe Eliza is seeing the known rake Sanford, he comes to realize (for a short spell) that it really doesn't matter. Yet another instance of that word "possession" helps him to explain: "I cannot refuse to believe her! I cannot cease to love her! My heart is in her possession. She has a perfect command of my passions. Persuasion dwells on her tongue. With all the boasted fortitude of our sex, we are but mere machines. Let love once pervade our breasts; and its object may mould us into any form that pleases her fancy, or even caprice" (165). This passage is especially surprising since anyone who reads the criticism of the novel will find characterizations of Boyer as a sanctimonious moralizer, full of reverence not for Eliza but for himself and the stolid mores of a mind-numbingly humdrum courtship. To be fair, at first he really does seem to be that dull, as when he says of his feelings for Eliza, "I am in no danger, however, of becoming an enthusiastic devotee. No, I mean to act upon just and rational principles" (111). But he later becomes a seriously romantic figure in the novel, once under the spell or "possession" of sociability's aesthetic work. Sanford follows in Boyer's footsteps, comparing himself not to a "mere machine" but to a woman. He says, "I cannot control my passions," and claims, "I never knew I had so much sensibility before! Why, I was as much a woman as the very weakest of the sex!" (205–6).[29] These renderings of emotional determinism as a machine and a woman characterize ruined bodies as automata willed by their own flesh, and mark the democratic work of illicit lovers as governed by what William Hill Brown calls the "triumph of nature."

It is difficult to overstate the degree to which the eighteenth-century ruin narrative is about these nonvolitional precincts of selfhood. What is important to remember is that the characters inhabiting these precincts are doing so as they are modeling the nation-building powers of what is alternately identified as nature or sociability. We saw, for example, Harrington's speech in *The Power of Sympathy* about how the "God of Love" takes the will into "captivity" and can "make the heart dance," thus rendering one a "slave" to that feeling, and other characters in Brown's novel refer to ideas like the "voluntary slavery" of a seduction in which "whim and caprice may chance to dictate" (74). In Brown's other novel *Ira and Isabella*, the hero likewise tells his lover, "I have been led insensibly into the snares of love, and have attached myself to you without volition" (13). Likening themselves to captives, slaves, and machines, these subjects of ruin move in a benighted world indeed, and they are ruled by a fugue state of desire they can neither understand nor control. The vocabulary of novels like *The Coquette*—*appetite, magic, possession,* and of course *charm*—interrupts a telos of willful volition. Through that vocabulary, the ruined body of the coquette materializes the civic model of sociability, as illicit sex stands in for, and enacts, its current of social attraction, the citizen drive.

A Social Death

Eliza's death forwards that drive. Her death occurs in two stages; the first is social and the second is biological. She experiences a mild sort of shunning through town gossip and the admonishment of her friends for attending to Sanford, quickly followed by a much more severe self-banishment, a sort of social suicide, when she runs away; soon after, that reclusiveness is revealed as a cover for her ruinous, clandestine affair with Sanford. Her biological death follows the ensuing pregnancy. After she dies, her community comes together and her gravestone acts as a kind of town square for her friends within and outside of the novel, readers gathering at both the representation of her grave and Elizabeth Whitman's actual one in Danvers. Through this engagement with reclusiveness and sexual congress, *The Coquette*'s aesthetic work is to explore this ambivalence about the female sociable body. In conflict with the republican moral imperative to create a civil society is the notion that women must do this work and yet are too delicate to do it.

When her close friend Lucy advises Eliza, "Avoid solitude," and entices her to return to her natural character by adding, "Your once favorite amusements court your attention. Refuse not their solicitations" (195), Eliza seems indeed to refuse, and continues to meet Sanford in secret. The novel comes to express a horror of reclusive behavior, which explains this flirtation between Eliza and the social body itself, its "courting" of her. This other romance requires the coquette's circulation, and explains the novel's concern over the loss of Eliza's sociability. Eliza's "fall" is marked first by her excessive need to be in the social sphere; in the seduction tale, the coquette eroticizes the social "self," thus representing an alternative to the moral authority of contractual individualism. But ultimately, her seduction forces her into secrecy and solitude. Eliza's "misanthropy" (her word) is perceived as an equally transgressive condition, and of great concern to her friends. So when Eliza proposes, "Having incurred so much censure by the indulgence of a gay disposition, I am now trying what a recluse and solitary mode of life will produce," she provokes their serious alarm (214).[30] Their worries over Eliza might be understood at the level of national politics whereby republican notions of civic culture understood that "[p]ersonal meaning and fulfillment are not matters of isolated experiments at self-discovery and self-expression. . . . Personal and social well-being are not antithetical."[31] Hence the panic-stricken tone of Eliza's companion Julia when she observes, "her vivacity has entirely forsaken her; and she has actually become, what she once dreaded above all things, a recluse! She flies from company, as eagerly as she formerly sought it!" (193). Julia's observation points to the threat "isolated experiments at self-discovery" pose to the common good, and suggests that the "meaning of virtue in the language of civic humanism is . . . the privileging of the public over the private."[32]

Eliza's self-banishment is even worse than any rejection she might experience with Boyer, Sanford, or her friends, and while Foster had historical reality to limit her literary imagination (readers knew Elizabeth Whitman died in Danvers after giving birth), the context she gives Eliza's death suggests that if the ruined woman merits punishment, it is for the crime of leaving her community. Shaftesbury's words on sociability and banishment describe the horror with which such solitude might be regarded: "Now if banishment from one's country, removal to a foreign place or anything which looks like solitude and desertion, be so heavy to endure, what must it be to feel this inward banishment, this real estrangement from human commerce, and to be after this manner in a desert and in the horridest of solitudes, even when in the midst of society?" (335). Eliza's feelings of self-loathing and her secrecy have exacted just this condition. In addition to her secret rendezvous with Sanford, Eliza bluntly states, "You will call me splenetic. I own it. I am pleased with nobody, still less with myself" (214).[33] Labeling her a "fugitive," the novel's conclusion places strong emphasis on Eliza's reclusive death, while making excessive reference to her postmortem social currency (236). "Nor do I doubt," writes Julia, "but you will join with me in execrating the measures by which *we* have been robbed of so valuable a friend; and *society*, of so ornamental a member" (237).

Her grave is a troubled site of both banishment and civic virtue through sociability. For her death signifies just how dangerous sociability can become for women; when they become "public property," they become merely property. Yet joining is the parting concept of the novel, one Eliza facilitates even in death, and the grave becomes the sexed artifact of the coquette's body still in circulation; as Cathy Davidson notes, people who visited Elizabeth Whitman's actual grave took pieces from it like lovers' mementos.[34] The act of joining together in mutual mourning offers a tribute to the more virtuous impact of Eliza's sociability. Her death functions as an event which brings people together, as a language of friendship and community overwhelms its meaning. "The grave of Eliza Wharton," insists Julia, "shall not be unbedewed by the tears of friendship" (241). As "the tears of strangers watered her grave," we witness Eliza's symbolic regeneration. The communal impact of desire creates a truly social being, as those tears carry a powerful social valence. For once they cry at her grave, they are no longer purely "strangers" at all, and the grave becomes something much more powerful.

Is the Vagina a Grave?

It may be that Eliza's grave is the image in the novel that most powerfully engages with the question of female power. It is the text's only illustration; appearing as Eliza's epitaph and bordered by a rectangular outline, it is a shocking textual rupture, a material reproduction of Eliza's gravestone, which might, of course, have simply been quoted or described. Why is it there? If, as Eliza insists, "Marriage is the tomb of friendship," then what aesthetic work is the grave pictured at the end of the novel doing? What is buried there, and what does that burial signify for the sexed, ruined body within it? And what do we make of the women watering that grave with their tears?

In a novel about women, sex, and democracy, readers are right to look for a redemptive, radical female homosociality at work among Foster's women. For the novel is, as critics have pointed out, a treatise on the power of female friendship, and the circle of friends that mourn Eliza's death at the novel's close constitute a kind of a richly protofeminist narration of female democratic relations.[35] Yet near its end, the novel does seem to be heading toward a pedantic condemnation of Eliza, and her story appears, until its very last page, to be closing with chaste female admonishments thinly veiled as loving forgiveness. In *The Coquette*'s penultimate letter, for example, Lucy writes, "Happy would it have been, had she exerted an equal degree of fortitude in repelling the first attacks upon her virtue! But she is no more; and heaven forbid that I should accuse or reproach her!" After a speech like that, readers might expect to find in the remaining few words of the novel a total abandonment of the homosocial desire that has been building up among the novel's women. Yet as we are about to see, the pictorial representation of Eliza's grave craftily denies that expectation. And so the sexed, democratic affect of female friendships in the novel is worth a deeper look—a look, that is, into the grave itself and the erotic pull issuing from it.

The homosocial desire of the novel is central to its conclusion. Certainly there is plenty of eros in *The Coquette*'s female bonds. The sexual semiotics of the circulated letter, with its fingered and broken seals, tell us as much. Benjamin Bateman's excellent reading of the novel adds a new depth to our understanding of that female homosocial desire in his discussion of the charged relationship between Eliza and her friend Julia. Eliza is a figure of queer sexual power, Bateman argues, because of the nonreproductive sexual pleasure she experiences while sustaining "her insistent difference from gender and sexual norms including the behavioral protocols" of marriage and childbearing. Such protocols are a "national fantasy" the early republic's investment in the figure of the coquette reveals.[36] As Bateman sees it, Julia's role as the virginal friend who is sent to guard Eliza's chastity only to experience her own queer, homosocial sexual pleasure through contact with Eliza challenges that fantasy. Bateman notes, for example, that near the end of the novel, when Julia and Eliza share the bed from which Eliza escapes to have secret sex with Sanford, Julia "waxes orgasmic" at signs of Eliza's illicit liaisons. Julia thus shares in the sexual pleasures of Eliza's ruin. Julia's pleasure reveals the novel's reliance on homosocial erotic exchange and desire when "Eliza's penetration becomes Julia's."[37]

The queering of the coquette's body goes even further. For the grave is the most female space in the novel, but also its queerest space and certainly the most semiotically intense object in the text—so intense, in fact, that Foster actually reproduces it pictorially. My understanding of the queer eros of this grave comes, of course, from Leo Bersani's well-known intervention into queer activism's right-leaning attempts at self-sanitizing, "Is the Rectum a Grave?" In this piece, Bersani asks if the penetrated rectum isn't where the "proud subjectivity" of the masculine is buried, a complex move against the "sacrosanct value of selfhood" that informs as it often misunderstands the signifying power of male homosexuality. As he says, "[I]f the rectum is the grave in which the masculine ideal (an ideal shared—differently—by men *and* women) of proud subjectivity is buried, then it should be celebrated for its very potential for death."[38] Bersani argues that homosexual male sex can counter, at the level of culture, the ascendant heterosexual narrative of futurity and reproduction, embracing the (feminine, penetrated) shattering of the orgasmic subject's integral self. Queer bodies, Bersani concludes, can signify the liberatory death of that self.

Is the vagina such a grave in *The Coquette?* Bersani's anti-individualistic ideal of the corporeal, penetrative phallic burial is part of a much more complex treatise on homosexuality, gender, power, and the nonreproductive queering of the body than I can do justice to here. But I would like to suggest that it can inform a recalculation of the ruined body's semiotic power in *The Coquette*. What sort of object *is* it that readers hold in their hands as the novel's "death" becomes co-incidental with Eliza's corporeal death, and as they gaze into a text that has become a kind of burial ground? To answer that question, we ought to consider Foster's pictorial representation of Eliza's tombstone, with its rectangular outline framing the epitaph, which again resembles not just her gravestone but an actual grave. It is a strange textual disruption, a literal block of text centered and squared just before the novel's final words. It offers a disorienting center of gravity for the novel, presenting readers with a material object and with a place for their own mourning. If we read the text's death as a stand-in for Eliza's buried corpse and readers' tears as a communal act of mourning morphing into an extratextual moment of nation-building sociability, we may get closer to understanding what the novel's last pages are up to. Perhaps because of its strange materiality, the text in some ways feels as though it holds Eliza's very corpse. Yet in readers' hands, this object, a book whose title after all is *The Coquette,* becomes not a space of individual containment or of finality but a place of joining, where readers enter into a community of mourning. Following the logic of the text's materiality, then, holding the book becomes a sort of shared, necrophilic handling of Eliza's sexed, ruined body.

These layers of the gravestone's materiality abet the queering of Eliza's body and of the text itself. The gravestone becomes a site of queer corporeal restoration among Eliza's mourners both inside and outside the world of the novel. In *The Coquette*'s final words, Julia describes for Eliza's grieving mother the trip her daughter's friends have made to visit her grave, a journey we might say gets reproduced by readers when they "arrive" at the book's conclusion. And the language in which the epitaph is written suggests a homosociality at work in this moment of textual rupture, which reads, in part, that it is "inscribed by her weeping friends" who ought to "throw a veil over her frailties." The text of the gravestone then famously ends with the line "And the tears of strangers watered her grave." Like an engraved stone tablet placed over a grave, the veil functions to cover the ruined body, and it seems that in their casting of that veil and in the shedding of their tears Eliza's friends have come, in essence, to restore her chastity. By the logic of redemption, this scrap of fabric becomes a metonymic stand-in for the vaginal seal of chastity, the hymen itself. The tears watering Eliza's grave are an important component of that restoration. As I have argued elsewhere, the water imagery that represents Eliza's ruin—Sanford's narration of adulterous sex as "stolen waters"—is here water that restores virtue rather than taking it away. "The tears of strangers watered her grave" comes to mean that the tears' sociability contraindicates the very notion of strangers; their tears transform strangers into a community modeled as female homosocial mourning. The restorative tears of friends, strangers, and even readers, along with the "veil" they cast over Eliza's ruin, thus mark as they replace the ruptured hymen and the ruptured text, enacting a queering of the ruined body impossibly restored to prelapsarian corporeality. The semiotic chain of the coquette's body, the hymen, the text, and the grave, all gendered spaces of rupture that are both penetrated and contained, signify the democratic work of ruin in *The Coquette*.

The grave semiotically supersedes marriage. In this sense, female homosociality does the work of ruinous sex, the democratic work whose logic insists that no one is a stranger. Eliza's sociability forms community even, or perhaps especially, after death, as if in holding a copy of *The Coquette*, all of America might water this grave.

Love and Nation

As critics of this novel, and perhaps of the seduction novel more generally, we can tell ourselves that these stories are about other things, about a loveless match or an unconsenting girl or even about a liberty-loving protofeminist. We can tell *The Coquette* back to ourselves in all of these ways and learn quite a bit from those tellings. What we ought not to do is ignore the fact that most of the action of the novel occurs under a sort of enchantment, a dark sphere of volition in which the nation-building work of the novel is in the hands of a throng of lovers driven outside of themselves through acts of "possession." It is understandable why critics wish to see this novel as a drama of consent and manipulation, but it is more than that. Eliza is hardly in control of herself, and Sanford's attraction to her has him equally incapacitated. Consent is a powerful feminist concern, but it is not Eliza's problem.[39]

When we view novels like *The Power of Sympathy* and *The Coquette* through the lens of a Shaftesburian sensibility, they read like political treatises that depict romantic love and sexual desire as the engines of a disunified subjectivity that unifies the nation. When in *The Power of Sympathy*, Harrington asks, "What is love?" his is in fact a question many philosophers of the day tried earnestly to answer. In Mary Wollstonecraft's feminist treatise *A Vindication of the Rights of Woman* (1792), for example, she acerbically observes, "Love is, in a great degree, an arbitrary passion, and will reign like some other stalking mischiefs, by its own authority."[40] In his typically dramatic style, Rousseau writes, "Among the passions that stir the human heart, there is an ardent, impetuous one that makes one sex necessary to the other, a terrible passion that braves all dangers, overcomes all obstacles, and, in its fury, seems calculated to destroy the human race that it is destined to preserve. The physical element [of love] is the general desire that impels one sex to unite with the other."[41] Shaftesbury himself offers his own observations about lovers. Ironically comparing them to distracted philosophers, he describes love as a dreamlike trance. "You might perceive it by their Looks, their Admiration, their profound Thoughtfulness, their waking ever and anon as out of a Dream, their talking still of one thing, and scarce minding what they said on any other Subject. Sad indications!" (104 II). It is in this context, among these voices, that we ought to understand Eliza's remark about feelings of love: "The events in my life have always been unaccountably wayward. In many instances I have been ready to suppose that some evil genius presided over my actions, which has directed them contrary to the sober dictates of my own judgment" (192). Indeed, in the hands of the most eloquent and astute philosophers of the age, "the devil made me do it" is what it pretty much comes down to. Foster's novel thus speaks directly to this philosophical problem, namely that love and the sexual appetites it engenders are uncontrollable, amorphous devils that possess bodies, which, once in motion, accomplish the aesthetic work of making human connections.

The question of bodies in motion so central to *The Coquette* and its iteration of the seduction story takes on new significance in the ruin narrative as a story of martyrdom. As we will see in chapter 5, the circulation of self as public property carries an ambivalence of extremes for women. In their efforts to celebrate acts of self-dispossession, novels invested in the sacrificed, suffering body of the sexually ruined martyr resignify that circulation, and the valence of ruined, surveilled bodies facilitates an exit from a culture of self-possession as it points to a much more radical corporeal economy.

· FIVE ·

Ruin, Martyrdom, and the Spectacle of Sympathy from *Clotel* to *The Scarlet Letter*

> Chuse a day on which to represent the most sublime and affecting tragedy we have . . . and when you have collected your audience, just at the moment when their minds are erect with expectation, let it be reported that a state criminal of high rank is on the point of being executed in the adjoining square, in a moment the emptiness of the theatre would demonstrate the comparative weakness of the imitative arts, and proclaim the triumph of real sympathy.
> —Edmund Burke, *Philosophical Enquiry into the Origin of Our Ideas of the Sublime and the Beautiful*, 1757

In novels that present ruin as an occasion for martyrdom, it is the capacity of illicit sex to render the body a shared, circulating spectacle that accomplishes the aesthetic work of ruin. The fallen woman is featured as a corporeally networked martyr in Nathaniel Hawthorne's two novels of sexual ruin, *The Scarlet Letter* (1850) and *The Blithedale Romance* (1852), as well as in William Wells Brown's embattled miscegenation romance *Clotel; or, The President's Daughter* (1853) and one of its source texts, Washington Irving's lesser-known tale about rebellion and loss, "The Broken Heart," from *The Sketch Book of Geoffrey Crayon, Gent.* (1819–20). All four stories explore the aesthetic work of ruin through a study of the sexed, martyred body of the woman who suffers terribly and publicly for her unchaste ways. In their constructions of martyred ruin, these texts present a radical alternative to the individual as the building block for the nation. The martyred body takes on a different sort of life in a constellation of social relations and becomes, in essence, uncontainable by the material limits of the flesh. In this sense, the sexually ruined martyr's body presents the most forceful radicalization yet of the trope of ruin. For in these stories, to be a martyr is not only to die punitively for an idea or to die for the welfare of other people, though it is both of these things. To die as a ruined martyr is to die *as* other people. The body at once becomes more insistently physical in death, a corpse acting as the undeniable material residue of the fleshly life, *and* becomes less materially tangible, as the spectacle of death continues to circulate, making erotic and sentimentally necrophilic contact with the public sphere.

The ruin narrative thus takes on the principle of self-denial, that definitive trait of the martyr, and makes room for something else. That something else arrives in the form of the martyred body, the public spectacle of the ruined woman's suffering. In these tales, that body is a carnal spectacle that invites erotically charged ontological traffic. Sexed martyrdom creates an ontological opening, a space within the suffering body that might be inhabited by the multitudes, and so while self-denial may be the central ethic of martyrdom, it does not leave an absence. In the texts under consideration here, a denial of self *expands* the peripheries of identity rather than contracting it. The watched and interpellated body adds a communal dimension to the aesthetic work of ruin; under such a gaze, and indeed constituted by it, the sexed, suffering body of the ruined woman participates in an alternative agency to that represented by the individual, who, after all, is universally regarded in the ruin narrative as the worst kind of villain. The body cannot be contained through this aesthetic work. In the novels of Brown and Hawthorne, a networked connectivity forms the sympathetic subject's architecture, what we might think of as an extracontractual precinct of selfhood. It is the "electric chain," as Hawthorne puts it, that animates identity through connection. If in the Shaftesburian sense, out of many, there is one, then these books suggest that within that one, there are also many.

The metatextual architecture of *Clotel* abets this configuration of identity. *Clotel* is itself a ruined, textual body that cannot be contained; its publication history is as troubled as the ruined daughters of miscegenation, rape, and concubinage that it depicts. First published in 1853 and long considered the first African American novel, Brown's story worked with what was then deemed a rumor, but which was ultimately proven to be true nearly one hundred fifty years later, about the children of slave Sally Hemings and President Thomas Jefferson. Brown's novel characterizes the nation's third president as the father of the "tragic mulatta" figure Clotel, who is one among many martyrs to slavery and ruin; the plot of *Clotel* traces the lives of Clotel's family line, full of mixed-race daughters who like herself bravely meet death to avoid rape by the master. Such acts of preservation through self-sacrifice speak to the sentimental novel's contribution to radically anti-individualistic rhetoric. In such sacrifice, identity circulates by becoming an idea, not only through death but also through what Jean-Luc Nancy identifies as the experience of "being-in-common" that precludes the possibility of the individual as a construct.[1] *Clotel* also speaks to the dangers of using the language of the master to evade his oppressive rule. For like the identity it describes, Brown's novel is itself as much an anthology as it is an act of authorship. Much of what is included within the pages of *Clotel* is what we might now call "plagiarism" but which is clearly something else, a text in active relation to the rhetoric it re-presents.[2] Thus the compromised chastity of Clotel and of *Clotel* represent parallel symbols of ruin in the mixed-race body and the mixed-source text. In presenting a hybrid, multivocal text, Brown offers a meta-discourse at the heart of the miscegenation story—a narrative that seeks to redeem the ruined woman by locating her virtue in her lack of ontological "purity."

The stories of Brown, Irving, and Hawthorne all include this relocation of virtue through spectacle, and in addition to the striking similarities in plotline, these texts include some of the most famous spectacles in antebellum literature. *Clotel*'s most famous moment arrives when its eponymous heroine flees the grasp of slavers by jumping off a bridge to her death. Clotel finds herself on that bridge after she is abandoned by Horatio, the white man who had purchased her and fathered her child, a man who had promised to be a "husband" to her, though not legally. Driven by odious political ambition, he instead marries a white woman who eventually sees to it that Clotel is sold and her daughter kept as a servant. It is in her attempt to save that daughter, Mary, from slavery that Clotel dies. Ultimately Mary ends up in Europe, finally reunited with her lost love, one of the Nat Turner rebels whom Brown compares to the hero of "The BJ134roken Heart," Washington Irving's tale of romantic loss set against the backdrop of the 1803 Irish rebellion.

The Scarlet Letter and *The Blithedale Romance*, like *Clotel*, are stories of surveilled, ruined bodies. Hawthorne's famous novel about a colonial Puritan immigrant's sexual ruin with a minister, *The Scarlet Letter*, presents us with Hester Prynne's defiance against a community whose hypocrisy is embodied most perfectly by the Reverend Dimmesdale, the man who leads the inquest against her though he is the father of the child, Pearl, she bears out of wedlock; their ability to keep their liaison a secret crumbles when Hester's shrewdly observant husband Chillingworth, long presumed dead, arrives to torment them. *The Scarlet Letter* in some ways anticipates Hawthorne's later novel, *The Blithedale Romance,* a story about a group of utopian dreamers who build their ideal community only to disband after their resident feminist, Zenobia, drowns herself, long since ruined and abandoned by a vicious man named Westervelt. Hester Prynne's public square shaming and Zenobia's drowned corpse become key spectacles around which each novel orbits. Clotel, Hester, and Zenobia are connected to very public men—a politician, a minister, and a mesmerist—to whom they are not married. Clotel and Horatio, Hester and Dimmesdale, Zenobia and Westervelt: these are all ruinous couplings with men who pretend to serve the public, and they all end in spectacles of martyrdom hungrily consumed by that same public. And Hawthorne's novels, like Brown's, present characters who become more than merely or solely themselves, who through their martyrdom take on a kind of representational quality.

The trajectory in literary history from stories of ruin centered around incest and seduction to those of martyrdom may seem to reveal a conservative and even misogynist move in antebellum America, a move toward the ruined woman's shaming and public destruction. However, these later ruin narratives model some of the most powerfully subversive moments in the genre. Martyrdom and redemption fashion an ethic of self-circulation that contests the primacy of an individual in possession of himself. Perhaps more importantly, such circulation suggests that chastity no longer functions as the patriarchal imagining of a woman in possession of her body (a possession read as virtue). Indeed, in the narrative that features martyrdom as the fate of the ruined woman, chastity no longer signifies individual self-possession, the self protecting the "property" of her own person. The ruined, circulating body, rather than the possessive self, comes to signify a celebrated identity shared by the community, and it offers its own unique critique of the individual as the centerpiece of a republic. In the novels under consideration here, then, the logic of community is organized around the gift of self, not its possession.

It is worth reconsidering the basic contradictions between martyrdom and self-possession in this context. Among classic contractarian formulations of the self as property is Rousseau's assessment of natural man in his

Discourse on the Origin and Basis of Inequality among Men (1754). Admiring man in his primal state, a creature whose most important resource is his own body, Rousseau notes the defining condition "of always carrying one's entire self, so to speak, with one."[3] Such a condition recalls too Locke's assessment of the self as a natural possession, the "property in his own person."[4] Yet in the novels considered in this chapter, the notion of agency without personhood finds purchase in the self-sacrifice of the ruined woman. The conflict between belonging to oneself and belonging to a community is still often about sex and desire in the martyrdom-as-ruin novel, but it is also about what it might mean to *deliver* one's self to others, not only in an act of erotic coupling but in an act of communal circulation that produces a shared embodiment. These novels move from extramarital sex, a giving of one's self to the other outside the bounds of marriage, to what it might mean to give one's self away entirely to a community. This act of giving opens up the body's democratic valence as it suggests that such a deliverance of self is always already in practice inside a community. In these novels, that is, one never *has* the totality of one's entire self.

In this way, sentimentalism has something to say about ruin. The sexed, martyred body, figuring identity as an act of giving rather than a property one carries with one's self, represents a volatile, unstable ontology. Indeed, some of the most infamous ruined women in American literature earn their reputations through acts of redemption as much as through any acts of illicit desire. The loss of the body's chastity allows it to take on a kind of currency—allows it to feel for and as other people in decidedly *democratic* ways. In the works of Hawthorne and Brown, the ruined woman joins people together by becoming a shared spectacle of suffering that circulates among the multitudes while also embodying them.

In all three novels of ruin, the zone of the spectacle, what Hawthorne's Zenobia calls being subject to "eyeshot," is where the circulating self begins its communal aesthetic work. The most powerful scenes of spectacle and martyrdom occur in places that are architecturally raised, places where to be seen is the point of the design. The town scaffold, the auction block, the bridge over the Potomac: all are rendered as simulacra of the city upon a hill. In other words, when narrated as a cause for martyrdom, ruin requires an audience. In *Clotel* it is the auction block and the bridge over the Potomac; in *The Scarlet Letter* it is the town square's scaffold; in *The Blithedale Romance* it is a meeting spot called Eliot's pulpit. These are spaces for a particular kind of performance, that of the disassembly of individual self into a gift that can circulate. All three, Clotel, Hester, and Zenobia, occupy architecturally public spaces of spectacle before they can complete the ontological shift into a circulating agent. Identity cannot stay contained when it is rendered so visibly, and these novels question whether the ruined woman can give herself away or whether, in being watched, she will be taken. Brown's depiction of female enslavement in particular problematizes any notion today's readers might mistakenly have about the division between private and public spaces in a world of what Aliyyah I. Abdur-Rahman calls "scopic terror," the constant watch of the master being an attempt to degrade the human into that which he can dominate and brutalize by *seeing*.[5] In *Clotel*, Brown most radically represents this site as occupied by the female slave—and in his telling of it, he shows how to be watched is not always to be taken. Watching can sometimes facilitate the martyr's radicalization of identity as a ruinous act of dis-containment, when she is *seen* giving herself away not only to death but also to the ideals shared by other people.

It might seem a gross misjudgment to connect Brown's enslaved black martyrs to Hawthorne's free white ones. The unstable because representational aspect of the slave body, and its radical critique of the master's fantasy of containment and control over the slave's agency, is well documented by major critics in the field. Such critics have shown how the master's gaze attempts to erase the slave body in order to serve white supremacist racial, sexual, and economic appetites.[6] When the master's gaze fantasizes the slave body as vacant, when that gaze interpellates the body as property rather than a person, critics have also shown how the body's agency takes on a potentially emancipatory aspect.[7] But because Brown and Hawthorne both use the language of sentimental martyrdom to radicalize agency, it is important to see that as different as they are, these texts deploy that rhetoric toward a similar end, a construction of identity that combats the violence enacted by the rhetoric of self-possession. Both authors contest the rendering of identity as that which might be possessed and purchased, by one's "self" or—through enslavement or mesmerism—by anyone else, through a language of martyrdom. Hawthorne's work develops ruin as a matter of radicalizing identity into a representational life; Brown's work in *Clotel* suggests that to be rendered as representational is to be stolen, and that the only way to combat the stealing of one's property in one's person is to give it away. Clotel, Hester, and Zenobia all manage that gift of self by becoming living exhibitions as well as the curators of their own ruin. They treat themselves as public works of art, which, it turns out, is a distinction their sexual ruin affords them.

The Plagiarized Heart

The complexity of *Clotel* as a text mimics this kind of curatorship. In its overt duplication of source materials, *Clotel* reads as either plagiarized or postmodern to today's readers, though certainly Brown was up to something much more extraordinary. As many critics have noted, much of *Clotel* is in fact an assembly, word for word, of other writers' work.[8] Through this novelized enjambment of replicas, *Clotel* turns its source material into a text that is much more radical than a bricolage.[9] *Clotel* isn't only a text that challenges white voices by appropriating them. Here is no Bakhtinian dialogic speech but something else. In reproducing the published materials of other writers, *Clotel* does not offer multivocality so much as it metanarratively layers each voice within the context of its being reproduced. *Clotel*'s "thefts" certainly offer a telling indictment of slavery. It is difficult to read sections of the novel without a fragmented awareness, once you know that what you're reading is really a copy of someone else's work. But Brown's terms of reproduction in the Bhabhaist sense mean precisely that you are *not* reading those sources, since the subversive nature of mimicry is, of course, that it is almost the same, but *not quite*.[10] So in part *Clotel* is a rendering of white voices that are *not quite* themselves, a move that, through black textual reproduction, questions the relations among race, property, authorship, and embodiment, and marks Brown's role in the text is as a metanarrative power, one that can neither be identified nor denied, a present absence that pushes *Clotel* to the absolute limits of what it means to be a story.

Suggesting that there is never any *one* story to tell, any *one* voice to do the telling, Brown disperses stories of sexual ruin in *Clotel* among a panoply of public texts, including passages of oratory, newspaper reporting, and the like. The texts woven into *Clotel* include Lydia Maria Child's short story "The Quadroons," used almost word for word; English abolitionist John Reilly Beard's *The Life of Touissaint L'Ouverture;* and American bishop William Meade's supremacist screed *Sermons Addressed to Masters and*

Servants. Clotel's story is then told between the pages of these other texts. The short installments of her "private" story become more and more the property of *Clotel* itself. Clotel's story is one among many in these archives, whose structure as an anthology fragments any whole narrative and itself models a radical embodiment. Indeed, this genre play offers an elegant metaphor for the mixed-race, mixed-narrative heroine Clotel, who dies not only because she is ruined by America but also because she represents it.

For if *Clotel* does anything, it denies its own singularity on multiple fronts. The novel signifies that, like the mixed-race body of the almost, but *not quite,* white woman, the "tragic mulatta" narrative as such does not and cannot come from a single origin. *Clotel* reveals the lie behind the 1662 *partus sequitur ventrem* law that says the child born of an enslaved woman must "follow the condition of the mother." Instead, like its heroine who has both a mother and a father, *Clotel* shows evidence of being a text with more than one source. For Brown, any abolitionist stance must admit the patrilineal line, which is to expose the master-rapist as a sexual predator and as the father of the mixed-race slave family. In its plagiarisms, then, *Clotel* refutes the parthenogenetic fantasy of the master who denies his rape of the female slave and his paternity of the mixed-race slave child. In fact, Brown's novel begins by lashing out against the outrage of the master's rape; the first sentences of his novel are about the predatory sexual violence of slavers. Out of the collection of all of Brown's source materials, however, one text does emerge, if not a *whole* text—out of many, one, *but not quite*—an ironic echoing of the republic's motto *e pluribus unum. Clotel* shows that while the aesthetic work of sympathy is to produce a feeling of oneness, sympathy must also find, in the story of the sexually ruined slave woman, a feeling not *for* the many but *as* the many. And in doing so, *Clotel* "rejects the kind of self-sovereignty that authorizes black writers like Douglass or Equiano," a move that allows Brown to attend to more radical, anti-individual subjectivities.[11]

The beginning of *Clotel* is particularly telling in this regard. The novel starts off by addressing the fact that the master's rape has made the slaves black *and* white rather than either black or white. "[T]here is a fearful increase of half whites," Brown says, "most of whose fathers are slave owners and their mothers slaves," and then he notes that only one in four of slaves is "a real Negro or clear black." Indeed, he concludes, "This fact is, of itself, the best evidence of the degraded and immoral condition of the relation of master and slave in the United States of America." Brown often names the country with the full appellation, "the United States of America," which has the doubling effect of naming the united "states" of blackness and whiteness. His mention of the father is an especially important part of this hybridity, the legacy of whiteness in the body of the tragic mulatta being the evidence of concubinage and rape.

For Brown, this constitutes a scene of culturally underwritten ruin, as there is "no inducement held out to slave women to be chaste" in the slaveholding South. "Indeed," he charges, "most of the slave women have no higher aspiration than that of becoming the finely-dressed mistress of some white man." Brown's use of the word "chaste" in this context carries manifold meanings. On the one hand, he is offering a clear satire of the idealized white woman as a bastion of sexual purity—for the black women of *Clotel* guard their virginity and what it signifies with as much vigilance as the novel's white women. On the other hand, Brown exposes the slave woman's sexual brutalization and absolute lack of access to such terms, a vulnerability he makes clear through subplots in which female slaves use death and suicide to escape the master's rape. Finally, *Clotel* suggests that romanticizing a slave woman's "choice" of a partner, white or black, dangerously obscures the enforced ruin of the woman who cannot legally marry.[12]

The ultimate configuration of such a case of ruin is through the union of Sally Hemings and Thomas Jefferson, a founding father cast as the father of two slave daughters, Clotel and her sister Althesa. From its subtitle *The President's Daughter* on, the novel insists on the parents, plural, of the daughters' lineage and indeed of their misery, since as mixed-race females their doom is inscribed on their very bodies. The obscenity of Jefferson's fatherhood, of his keeping Hemings a slave during all the years of his sexually defined relation to her, compromises any ideal of him as a representative of freedom's cause while insisting that the black woman and white man, the *parents* of mixed-race slaves, figure into a new iconography of the American family. At first, Brown's treatment of the relation between Currer (the fictional Hemings) and Jefferson seems opaque in the extreme. Only one sentence addresses the matter: "The gentleman for whom she had kept house was Thomas Jefferson, by whom she had two daughters." The rest of the passage is about the tragic lack of chastity among mixed-race slave daughters and the ironically denoted "democratic" nature of their social circle, represented as "Negro balls" where white gentlemen of any economic class might comfortably mingle and then select a mistress.

What does it mean that the first specific scene of ruin imagined in *Clotel* occurs at a "democratic gathering" of white and black guests at a "ball" designed for interracial sexual unions, and that the ruin of the president's daughter occurs as a result of such a ball? Brown mentions that Currer had a single ambition for her daughters, which was "[t]o bring up Clotel and Althesa to attract attention, and especially at balls and parties." For Currer, her daughters' survival depends on managing the moment of appraisal as much as possible. The question is how to arrange the circumstances of the white gaze, since to elude it is impossible. A ball places her daughters Clotel and Althesa under the kind of surveillance that a slave mother might hope to use in order to rescue her daughters from the horrors of the auction.

But as Brown's novel quickly demonstrates, the horrors of white surveillance prevail. The spectacle of Clotel dressed in all her finery at the ball quickly transfers to the spectacle of Althesa and Clotel sold as sexual chattel on the auction block. Clotel's beau, the white Horatio, who meets her at the ball and becomes enamored of her, cannot simply begin to see her socially; he must buy Clotel at an auction to make possible their romantic union. But the auction scene is where the meanings of her ruin (and by extension of all young female slaves) erupt into a supremacist phantasmagoria. This is because the auction is where the promise of virgin rape is overt. Brown's use of language is perfectly transparent as the auctioneer pushes the price higher by explaining that Clotel is a virgin, at which point the bidding intensifies:

> "The chastity of this girl is pure; she has never been from under her mother's care, she is a virtuous creature." "Thirteen." "Fourteen." "Fifteen." "Fifteen hundred dollars," cried the auctioneer, and the maiden was struck for that sum. This was a Southern auction, at which the bones, muscles, sinews, blood, and nerves of a young lady of sixteen were sold for five hundred dollars; her moral character for two hundred; her improved intellect for one hundred; her Christianity for three hundred; and her chastity and virtue for four hundred dollars more. . . . Thus closed a negro sale, at which two daughters of Thomas Jefferson, the writer of the Declaration of American Independence, and one of the presidents of the great republic, were disposed of to the highest bidder!

The disassembly of Clotel in this passage suggests not just the obscenity of the auction block, though it does that as well. It also distinguishes between enforced representation and being-in-common—between, that is, the gaze that denies the humanity of the other and the gaze that shares in the humanity of the other. Brown is careful to include "the bones, muscles, sinews, blood, and nerves," a list of any body's anatomy. The implied cataloging of the auction commodifies her merits and renders Clotel a collection of generic, anonymous qualities; in doing so, the auction anthologizes a set of reproducible "parts" that *Clotel*'s plagiarisms emphasize. Thus reproducibility constitutes one of the many forms of violence that slavery commits. Clotel's sale, like the sale of the other slaves in the scene, "constructs them as representatives."[13] Indeed, the auction block becomes "as a type of stage" in which the slave body "is a multiplicitous subject, a vessel onto which is projected the anxieties and contradictions of those living in a historically white-supremacist nation."[14] Brown sets up the "various types of embodiment and disembodiment at auction sites" in the scene of Clotel's sale so that her martyrdom, a completely different spectacle, can combat this enforced representationality and recover the being-in-commonness that constitutes Clotel's humanity.[15]

Brown's novel also explores what ruin might mean under the rubric of the word he uses to describe the scene, "atrocity." To do so, the narrative follows, for the rest of their story, several possible outcomes through the characters of Clotel and Althesa as well as Clotel's daughter Mary and Althesa's daughters Ellen and Jane. Althesa and Mary experience romantic love with white men, though they are never manumitted by their lovers. The others suffer everything from captivity and the threat of rape to mortal heartbreak and suicide. All of their stories are defined by ruin in one form or another, for even Althesa, who wrongly believes she is legally married to her white husband, turns out to be legally a slave, so that after her death her daughters face the threat of rape from the white men who purchase them. No matter what the plot of their ruin or its threat involves, it becomes increasingly clear that for Brown, these instances of ruin point to the calamitous absence of sympathy in the crowd. In the sexually predatory gaze of the white man, sex fails to intersect with sympathy. The selling of the body for the purpose of sexual violation is in obvious contrast both to the body's sentimental circulation and to the way in which eros figures as the site of commingling identity in novels like *The Power of Sympathy* and *Ira and Isabella*. Instead, *Clotel* represents ruin as the mutually enforcing violence of rape and enslavement. In both, the master uses his power to *see* as the way to initiate such violence.

After the violating display of the auction, Clotel's ruin becomes a private matter. Once her virginity is sold to Horatio for fifteen hundred dollars, he removes her to "a beautiful cottage surrounded by trees so as scarcely to be seen," a place that is "far retired from the public roads, and almost hidden." Despite the seclusion, appearances are all Clotel has. Brown makes it clear that Clotel demands at least "an outward marriage" since miscegenation laws make a legal one unavailable. Yet that outwardness is a private matter, since it is possible only by "[living] secluded from the world." Brown reveals the irony of this ostensible privacy and its dark reality, which is that Clotel is a secret, enslaved concubine; in hiding her, Horatio ensures that she is *seen*, rendered his own scopic subject through the violating gaze of white supremacy. Horatio's quick legal marriage to Gertrude, a white woman, reveals his true intentions, and when he suggests that Clotel "would ever be his real wife," his despicable denial that he is himself the agent of Clotel's ruin enacts it more surely than any sexual encounter with her ever could.

But perhaps the most intriguing rhetoric of ruin and sacrifice occurs through Brown's management of one of his more obscure source texts. The story of Clotel's daughter Mary follows the plotline from Washington Irving's "The Broken Heart," a tale from *The Sketch Book of Geoffrey Crayon, Gent.* (The fact that Brown borrows from an author using a narrative persona adds yet more textual layers to Brown's veritable palimpsest of source material.) "The Broken Heart" is based on what was then a fairly well-known historical romance. A young woman, Sarah Curran, fell in love with Robert Emmet, an Irish political dissident who led a rebellion against British rule in 1803. It was a match Curran's wealthy father attempted to prevent. Arrested with Sarah's secret love letters hidden inside his clothing, Emmet refused to name her as their author. He was hanged and then beheaded for his part in the rebellion; Curran ultimately married someone else and left Ireland.[16] The parallels between Sarah Curran (whose name sounds quite like *Currer*, the name of Clotel's mother) and Mary are several. Mary loves a political dissident named George who was a fighter in the Nat Turner rebellion. Due to their entanglements in the cruel institution of slavery, they are separated, and Mary never expects to see George again (though she does, unexpectedly, years later). She ultimately marries a Frenchman who secures her freedom and takes her to Europe where she might heal the broken heart she suffers after slavery wrenches her away from her one true love.

These parallels help us to understand Brown's use of a passage copied from "The Broken Heart" in *Clotel*. The popular story of Robert Emmet would surely have resonated with early Americans, who after all had just had their own rebellion against British colonial rule. The speech Emmet gave before his death was well known throughout the Anglo-Atlantic world, and Brown's use of the story as one of his sources speaks to the convergence of ruin, rebellion, and political justice in *Clotel*.[17] Here is the passage out of "The Broken Heart" that Brown uses to describe Mary's feelings when she agrees to marry the Frenchman, M. Devenant, though she loves George still: "A woman's whole life is a history of the affections. The heart is her world; it is there her ambition strives for empire; it is there her avarice seeks for hidden treasures. She sends forth her sympathies on adventure; she embarks her whole soul in the traffic of affection; and, if shipwrecked, her case is hopeless, for it is a bankruptcy of the heart." The passage reflects a Humean idea of sympathy as a contagious emotional current that is the emissary of the feeling subject. It represents sympathy's affectionate interaction as "traffic." At the metanarrative level, Brown's use of Irving's story signifies a sort of traffic through the interaction of the two texts, and the lost chastity of *Clotel* as a text echoes the ruin of its heroines in such moments. Yet Brown's use of this passage does more, since Irving's story, though the text is not absolutely explicit, uses some fairly transparent imagery to suggest that the character based on Sarah Curran has been sexually ruined in her tryst with the character based on Robert Emmet. In "The Broken Heart," the narrator notes that in Sarah's case "her heart is like some fortress that has been captured, and sacked, and abandoned, and left desolate." Irving uses the loaded word "ruin" to describe her, referring to "the ruins of her peace" and describing her with phallic, penetrative imagery, comparing her to a young tree "with the worm preying at its heart," what he describes as a "beautiful ruin." The language of domination and rape is woven within Irving's story, words like "ruin" used alongside imagery of a "sacked" body, conquered in a wartime attack. It is clear why Brown found Irving's heroine to be an apt symbol in his novel. Sarah Curran represents both the conquered, embattled body of the slave woman and the romanticized ruin of a political hero's lover.

The parallels run deeper, for both Clotel and the Irish rebel die publicly as martyrs. The scaffolds of Clotel and of Robert Emmet—their very public deaths inciting support for resistance against tyranny—are sites of spectacle that engage with themes of political rebellion and representation, the terms of martyrdom that the ruined woman experiences in the works of Brown and, as we are about to see, the works of Hawthorne. Hawthorne's presentation of the spectacle of the ruined martyr in both *The Scarlet Letter* and *The Blithedale Romance* illuminates the significance of the scopic, public death. Hester Prynne's martyrdom speaks to the kind of spectacle in *Clotel* that establishes the ruin of self through its circulation.

The Adulterous Letter A

If *Clotel* is a ruined, unchaste text, then the notorious "A" of *The Scarlet Letter* is an unchaste letter whose polysemy circulates among the community's interpretations of its meaning. Hester's infamous embroidery of the letter she must wear as a punishment signifying her adultery with the Reverend Dimmesdale certainly inscribes her identity as both a sexually deviant woman and as a community member who has a special kind of public currency. Hawthorne writes, "On the breast of her gown, in fine red cloth, surrounded with an elaborate embroidery and fantastic flourishes of gold-thread, appeared the letter A."[18] Hester's entrance into the novel and into the community is the letter's entrance as well, the emergence of the symbol that has eclipsed the particular, the "A" that has eclipsed the "I." There is something overtly promiscuous about the novel's eponymous "character"—the letter as the figure of ruin—dressed in harlot red with all the "fertility and gorgeous luxuriance of fancy" (50). The pun on *character* that the letter conveys signifies the ruin of chastity as a metonym for the ruin of self.

Hawthorne is hardly subtle about this connection, as he points, again and again, to Hester's sexual ruin as the origin of her transformation into a relational self that can no longer be identified as an individual: "Through them all, giving up her individuality, she would become the general symbol at which the preacher and moralist might point, and in which they might vivify and embody their images of woman's frailty and sinful passion . . . as the figure, the body, the reality of sin" (73). Here we see what Hawthorne makes of an embodied, representational ontology, of a woman who becomes, like a letter, always busy at the task of representation. That phrase, "the figure, the body, the reality" renders Hester a representational abstraction that signals a loss of self. The ontology of this embodiment is selflessness of a kind, a new but equally radical departure from the individual. Hester is not simply a ruined woman. Whatever we might say about the material limits of the body, of the life of the symbol as outside the life of the human—indeed, whatever we might say about biological life existing in opposition to the sphere of abstract ideas—Hester is not simply the town's adulteress. Hester is *adultery*.

This representational ontology radically reconfigures the community that creates it. Hester reenters her community as an idea that goes into circulation the second she emerges from the prison door. The entanglement that ensues between Hester and her community constitutes a radical power. As the narrator notes, "the letter was the symbol of her calling" and held "so much power to do, and power to sympathize" (148). That power to sympathize draws upon eighteenth-century ideas of sympathy as an erasure of the self/other divide, an ontological interdependence that Hawthorne explicitly makes a condition of Hester's losing her individuality.[19] And though she has lost her chastity, Hawthorne's narrator suggests that she has not lost her "purity." He says that "the torture of her daily shame would at length purge her soul, and work out another purity than that which she had lost; more saint-like, because the result of martyrdom" (74). Crucially, Hester's adultery is the catalyst for her newfound sense of sympathy; her representation of illicit sex is that which facilitates her democratizing sensibility, turning her into what, as we saw in chapter 4, Benjamin Rush called "public property." This other purity ironically turns Hester into a site of traffic with the entire community, as the letter's "power to sympathize" transforms her into one who is both Hester and more than Hester.

In other words, in *The Scarlet Letter,* the adulterous body as a site of traffic has the capacity to feel communally. The letter does the aesthetic work of ruin for Hester as it links self to other in a Shaftesburian sensory chain of sympathy. Hester discovers that her identification not just with but *as* illicit sex has transformed her, investing in her a supernatural capacity to sympathize with the sins of others. "[S]he felt or fancied, then, that the scarlet letter had endowed her with a new sense . . . a sympathetic knowledge of the hidden sin in other hearts" that induces "a sympathetic throb"

(80). The differences among sex, suffering, and sympathy become obscured in the "throbs" of the ruined body, its martyrdom defined as the social feeling of others' pain. Adultery is the perfect stand-in for the kind of "lexus of interdependence" created by "complex networks of sympathy aroused by the plights of suffering individuals in the courtroom or on the scaffold."[20] In other words, Hawthorne's language evokes a Shaftesburian mode of feeling. Hester's "new sense" is none other than the *sensus communis*.

In feeling this sense, Hester might seem to be disappearing into the anonymity of abstraction. But her embodiment of an idea is a spectacle that ensures a different kind of presence, one always representing the body rather than merely "inhabiting" it. Because Hester's ruin is of course her actual adultery with Dimmesdale, her body becomes, synecdochally, an organ of public feeling that points to the role of desire in community formation. Hawthorne writes, "She who has once been woman, and ceased to be so, might at any moment become a woman again if there were only the magic touch to effect the transfiguration" (150). Rather than read this as a reference to Dimmesdale's touch exclusively, we might think of him as an instrument of and minister to the communal body. The idea that she might "become a woman again" should not necessarily imply that she will return to the sphere of the merely materially human. And indeed it is this most public man's connection to Hester that animates him. We see this animation at work when he joins hands with Hester and their illegitimate daughter Pearl at their nighttime visit to the scaffold: "The moment that he did so, there came what seemed a tumultuous rush of new life, other life than his own, pouring like a torrent into his heart, and hurrying through all his veins, as if the mother and the child were communicating their vital warmth to his half-torpid system. The three formed an electric chain" (140). Sex does the work of democracy through this "electric chain" fairly explicitly, especially through that sexual "torrent" curing Dimmesdale of his phallic "torpor." As we saw in chapter 2, this erotic, animating sympathy is very much in keeping with Enlightenment ideas about sympathy as a "magnetic-mechanistic" power and a "binding force or an emotional chain that brings communities together."[21] And it implies that with his touch, though Hester may have become a "woman again," it is not an atomizing, individuating transformation but a drive toward citizenship.

If Hester's spectacular social body adulterates as it embodies the community, it is through such acts of sympathetic joining that rely on the union of spectacle and spectator. As the scarlet letter transforms Hester's into a social body, it also becomes, as Hawthorne insists, "her passport into regions where other women dared not tread" (183). Just as her role as martyr has endowed Hester with a secret sympathy, so that no one in the community is every really alone, so too has Dimmesdale's moral isolation been replaced by a sympathetic "chain" with Hester in a way that at least partially erases the ontological boundaries between them. Indeed, the characters in *The Scarlet Letter* often function as ontological scaffolding for one another, and Hawthorne uses erotically charged imagery to illustrate it, as when Hester is with Dimmesdale, she is "instinctively exercising a magnetic power over a spirit so shattered and subdued that it could hardly hold itself erect" (180). Tellingly, Hester herself uses the word "'ruin'" to identify what Chillingworth has done to Dimmesdale in his attempt to avenge the cuckoldry by controlling, almost like a mesmerist, Dimmesdale's will (180). The stigmata of adultery that mark their ruined bodies (Dimmesdale's is literally the letter A etched into his skin) become that passport. And it is this notion of the body as a passport to community that Hawthorne's novel *The Blithedale Romance* will pursue to its absolute limits.

The Ruin of Blithedale

The Blithedale Romance introduces us to one of American literature's earliest examples of a love triangle: the actress and feminist Zenobia, her abused half-sister Priscilla, and the monomaniac Hollingsworth vie for one another's affections with varying degrees of failure as they pursue "the reformation of the world" in a "blessed state of brotherhood and sisterhood."[22] Blithedale is an experimental society populated by strangers to one another, utopian-building dreamers who will test the "electric chain" of sympathy and its power to forge a community. The story is told from the perspective of narrator Miles Coverdale, whose role seems to be to observe just about everything, and he becomes known by the others for his watchful observations of them, seemingly always from the margins of the drama. As Miles tells it, this group has decided to reject the materialism of their old urban lives and run a farm outside of the city (they retain the services of an old resident, Silas, to help them do it). But everything goes terribly wrong: soon after settling in to their new environs, Priscilla shows up at their doorstep in need of help, and they take her in, only to discover that she is Zenobia's long-lost half-sister who has been used by others for profit as the star of a seedy spiritualist performance; a man from Zenobia's past, Westervelt, and possibly their father Moody, have been forcing Priscilla to perform. Both Miles and Blithedale's magnetic personality, Hollingsworth, fall in love with Priscilla, though this is Zenobia's loss, since she too is in love with Hollingsworth. Yet Hollingsworth is in some ways the least likely candidate for their love, since his goal is to completely change what Blithedale is—he wants to turn it into a reformed prison. When it becomes the backdrop to lost love, Blithedale's bucolic experiment becomes increasingly radicalized. With Hollingsworth as the brawny, brooding philosopher, Priscilla as the waif fleeing a villainous charlatan, and Zenobia as the theatrical brunette with a secret, the amorous dealings of these three lovers end in the apparent ruin not only of Zenobia but also of Blithedale itself.

The instability of identity's boundaries within the "electric chain" of ontological traffic becomes all powerful in Hawthorne's later novel. The tragedy of *Blithedale,* Zenobia's suicide, is predicated in part on oblique references to her sexual ruin.[23] Though Miles wryly uses the word "wife" to describe her as a woman who seems to have had sexual experience, with no declared attachment or marriage to her name, he indicates something else. From what he hears from Zenobia's father Moody, and from scenes he observes himself, Miles learns that her connection with the repellent mesmerist Westervelt is one based on a former liaison that becomes a source of great anxiety for Zenobia. Westervelt's continued presence in her life despite her clear hatred for him suggests blackmail or worse. Zenobia is clearly a woman in search of a place where her ruinous past cannot follow her, a place where sympathy and not the sordid facts of her past might define her bonds with other people. And at first, Blithedale seems to offer that kind of sanctuary. Thus Miles's comment, "Zenobia is a wife!" ironically signifies not only Zenobia's ruin, but also her reason for seeking asylum among utopian-minded freethinkers. Zenobia is anything *but* a wife, and indeed her self-sacrifice through suicide acts out a martyrdom to the very principles at Blithedale she sought as her only possible refuge from a world that judges a woman's extramarital sexual history with unjust scrutiny.

The spectacle of Zenobia's suffering turns the whole of Blithedale into a stage in Hawthorne's novel. Zenobia's first role on that stage is as the ultimate ruined woman of Christendom, Eve herself. For Miles, Zenobia is as overdetermined as Hawthorne's "A," her body the site of an Edenic ruin, and the first encounter between Miles and Zenobia is fraught with postlapsarian erotic tension.[24] Zenobia alludes to wearing the "'garb of Eden'" and their banter gives Miles an image of Zenobia's unashamed nakedness, after which he reflects, "One felt an influence breathing out of her, such as we might suppose to come from Eve, when she was just made, and her Creator brought her to Adam, saying—'Behold, here is a woman!'" (17) Zenobia's immediate and powerful association with the first fallen woman indicates that her ruin has work to do among them yet, especially regarding their attempt to build their own Eden.

Indeed, Zenobia's fallenness is of great interest in *Blithedale*. For not only is she the Eve to Miles's Adam, but she belongs on stage, what Miles says "would have been her proper sphere" (44). Full of sin and eminently watchable, "beheld" by Miles from treetops and bedside perches, Zenobia's spectacular, representational aspect pervades Blithedale. Zenobia generates a spectacular economy of self similar to that which operates in *The Scarlet Letter* and *Clotel*, such that Zenobia is perpetually seeking to sacrifice herself by turning herself into a display in which her interlocutors can invest. Such behavior engages others as it draws in their gazes and thus their sympathies. She invites them into Blithedale by inviting them to look.

When it comes to Zenobia's watchability, Miles makes for an ideal audience, since of course his tendency is already to observe everything. Many critics assess that tendency as voyeurism. But it is more that Zenobia's mesmeric quality draws him into a sympathy so powerful that they both lose themselves in the mix. An early scene between Miles and Zenobia is a perfect example of how she initiates such a spectacular community. Miles is the captive audience, trapped in his sickbed, awaiting visits from his caretakers. He reports that at one point Zenobia "bent her head towards me, and let me look into her eyes, as if challenging me to drop a plummet-line down into the depths of her consciousness" (47–48). His is a gaze that ought to have secured a distance between them, but instead it ushers in an unmanageable sympathy. Miles refers to the moment resentfully, claiming she has "defrauded" him by having "given herself away" (48). But in doing so, she has clearly also taken him in.

These troubled exchanges of self are typical at Blithedale. The "plummet" that Miles mentions is certainly vaginal at a metaphorical level, and points to the idea of a physical, sexual exchange that stands for an ontological one.

But Zenobia's invitations to look also constitute gifts of self, offerings that issue a hail to *join*. Many critics miss these offerings, and interpret Zenobia as either scheming, pathetic, or both. They read her as a woman whose feminism has failed her and whose encounters with men nearly always mark her desperation to be, or to be with, someone else.[25] But the novel reads more like a tribute to Zenobia than anything else. Miles may love Priscilla enough to say so with four dashes and an exclamation point ("I—I myself—was in love—with—Priscilla!") but he admires Zenobia enough to explain why for three hundred pages or so. This is not to suggest, as some have done, that Miles is really in love with Zenobia. Rather, the novel becomes in some ways a sentimental homage to her ruin and the martyrdom to which it leads. He also characterizes Zenobia as a sentimental martyr. In his telling of her story, Zenobia arrives at Blithedale a ruined woman, estranged from her nefarious lover, yet perhaps through her death she leaves Blithedale, like Hester, with "another purity" intact. Ultimately, Zenobia is a martyr to Blithedale, when the philanthropist Hollingsworth lacked the heart, and the gentleman Miles lacked the valor, to fight for Blithedale themselves.

Omitting a discussion of the sentimental qualities that Miles admires in Zenobia, and reading her as either a selfish contestant for the affections of a man or a madwoman driven to suicide because Hollingsworth does not return her affections, misses her crucial role as Blithedale's martyr.[26] In fact, there is plenty of evidence to suggest that her ruin gives Zenobia a space to inhabit the role of the sentimental woman who becomes a martyr to the ideal of an interdependent community.[27] The aesthetic work of her sexual ruin is thus to link sentiment to a radicalization of embodiment as an experience of sympathetic connection rather than individual existence. Remarkably, most readers overlook Zenobia's sentimental entrance into *Blithedale*. She politely confesses to Miles, "'I have long wished to know you, Mr. Coverdale, and to thank you for your beautiful poetry, some of which I have learned by heart;—or, rather, it has stolen into my memory without my exercising any choice or volition about the matter,'" adding, "'you will certainly hear me singing them, sometimes, in the summer evenings'" (14-15). In addition to the exotic flowers she wears in her hair and the feminist politics for which she is known, her initiation into the novel reads like a stock scene out of a work by Harriet Beecher Stowe or Susan Warner.

Indeed, Miles offers multiple sentimental characterizations of Zenobia in *Blithedale:* her voice is "mellow"; her hand is "soft and warm" (14); she is described as the "hostess" of Blithedale when members of the new community begin to arrive (16); Miles notes that "her smile beamed warmth upon us all" (16); she brings food "hither in a basket" to the hungry newcomers "with the instinct of a housewife" (18); Miles sees in her a "certain warm and rich characteristic, which seems, for the most part, to have been refined away out of the feminine system" (17); she gives "a little bit of embroidered muslin" to one of Blithedale's handmaidens who wants to sew a frock "for her Sunday wear" (32). Zenobia's suggestion for the new name of Blithedale is "Sunny Glimpse," which the others deem "to be rather too fine and sentimental a name" (37). She reads and then lends to Miles the romances of George Sand, whose work is classically sentimental (52). Indeed, Hawthorne subtly chastises readers who would later make the error of overlooking or misreading Zenobia's sentimentality, aligning them with the loathsome Westervelt, who, it turns out, makes this very mistake at Zenobia's funeral. When Westervelt refers to Zenobia's heart as "'that troublesome organ,'" Miles reacts—never mind his reputation as a voyeuristic Hamlet—and reacts with uncharacteristic gusto. "'You seem to intend a eulogy,'" he fumes, "'yet leave out whatever was noblest in her, and blacken, while you mean to praise'" (240).

As will soon become clear, Zenobia's death as a martyr does not undermine but rather complicates those soft-spoken angels of the house who have come, a bit unfairly, to represent the sentimental woman. As a figure of sexual ruin, Zenobia nevertheless follows the pattern of self-sacrifice so emblematic of the type. The final spectacle of her dead body works as a representation of Blithedale and as a vehicle for its most radical ideal of sympathy, and her sexed corpse circulates as a haunting necrophilic image that haunts *Blithedale* as well as Blithedale. Indeed, she does not renounce her feminism and destroy herself because a man does not love her. Zenobia does not die for Hollingsworth. She dies for Blithedale.

The Meaning of Blithedale

It is worth pausing to define the principles of the community for which Zenobia gives her life. In many ways, Blithedale is a sentimental reformist community.[28] Its residents have chosen intimacy and communal labor over individuality and personal property, to be sure a major reformist move, and these people who feel their emotions so intensely and work so hard together in the fields define an intriguing demographic. The nineteenth-century American reformer's experience is centered on the emotional life of the community, one that "invokes a domestic model of human relations" and is governed by values like a "common sense of purpose, increased intimacy, and mutual respect."[29] Though Hawthorne may successfully satirize the aristocrat who would wear his finery out into the cornfields, he also makes approving observations when the threads begin to fray in the solidarity of shared labor, and Zenobia's death signifies the community's ultimate triumph of sympathy. Blithedale is not an absurdity or a failure. Their progress toward utopia is wobbly but not unreliable: they hardly know how to begin and they must rely on the old resident farmer Silas for direction, but sure enough, their crops do grow and their community thrives. And sympathy is the most powerful contributor to this endeavor.

Hawthorne establishes a Shaftesburian community in Blithedale, in part defined by the novel's terminology. The word "heart" is used ubiquitously in *Blithedale*. As a sympathetic community, Blithedale is a hub of feeling, and Hawthorne does not let us forget it: there are 131 occurrences of the word "heart" in the novel.[30] Though Hawthorne's use of the word is surely polysemous, its sentimental meaning implies an epistemology of feeling that Miles experiences as anti-individualist. For him, feeling obscures the self/other boundary one might expect from a self-described "frosty bachelor." Indeed, like many of his fellow reformers, Miles *feels* his way into Blithedale. The business of Miles keeping his distance to preserve his sense of self is not necessarily the commitment-phobic rhetoric of a man who prefers surveillance over participation. Miles's acts of what may be read on one level as voyeurism also constitute sentimental moments in which he emotionally closes, rather than expands, the distance between himself and the others around him. It is true that in one scene Miles climbs a tree when he could be knee-deep in earthy labor with his fellow utopians, but he does so to cultivate (not repel) a powerful sympathy with his community. When he accidentally sees the pantomimed drama between Westervelt and Zenobia from his arboreal vantage, he walks away more deeply connected to Zenobia. When he sees her suffer in her dealings with Westervelt, Miles says, "it seemed to me that the self-same pang, with hardly mitigated torment, leaped thrilling from her heart-strings to my own" (222). Miles is explicit about what might be the most important aspect of Blithedale's philosophy, that which helps to define its sympathetic bonds, namely the "blessed state of brotherhood and sisterhood" that he describes early on in his narrative to explain what these reformers are all about (13). Miles's language echoes the philosophical rhetoric of the Atlantic Enlightenment about the power of sympathy to create a merger between self and other, as when he notes that he feels "too much sympathy" with the others at Blithedale (154). His sympathetic need "to look on, as it seemed my part to do" would ultimately mean for him a life "now attenuated of much of its proper substance, and diffused among many alien interests," giving him what he calls a "kind of heart-sickness" (157). At once a throwback to the eighteenth-century philosophy of feeling and a figure of nineteenth-century romanticism, Miles is eager to explain that he feels the pangs of others' suffering so fully as "to live in other lives, against my own will, and to the detriment of my own comfort" (160). As a character bound by the gravity of sympathy, he is willing to accept self-sacrifice ("the detriment of my own comfort") to enhance fellow-feeling, an interconnectedness that constitutes that "blessed state of brotherhood and sisterhood" Blithedale was created to forge.

Miles does not tell us a great deal about the time he spends with the other residents of the commune besides his three main interests, but when he does, he reveals much about the role of sympathetic connectedness at Blithedale. He experiences that brotherhood and sisterhood as a bone-deep sympathy that is both enervating and buoying. As Miles says, the general inhabitants of the place share a very eighteenth-century "nervous sympathy." He goes on to describe it as "a pretty characteristic enough, sentimentally considered, and apparently betokening an actual bond of love among us" though, he adds, it "was yet found rather inconvenient"—so inconvenient that, as his well-known comparison goes, if one member boxes the other in the ear, "the tingle was immediately felt, on the same side of everybody's head" (139). They are in possession of one another's sensate experience—even if he means it as a metaphor, the comparison suggests that these are not self-possessed individuals but people so attuned to one another that they cannot separate the pain one of them feels from the hearts of the rest. Later in the novel, Miles returns from a stint in the city to a strange masquerade scene, where all the members of Blithedale are wearing bacchanalian costumes. One would think that their masquerade would render them strangers to him. Instead, though, he notes, "Not a voice spoke, but I knew it better than my own; not a laugh, but its cadences were familiar" (209). Whatever else one might say about Blithedale, the sympathy that brings people together seems to be working.³¹

Ruin's Death Pose

Just as Blithedale seems to be on the verge of collapse, the discovery of Zenobia's corpse at once allows the founders of Blithedale to reenact her sexual ruin and causes Miles to rediscover his commitment to Blithedale's principle of communal sympathy. Blithedale is in trouble when Zenobia takes her life. Hollingsworth is in pursuit of Priscilla, whose weakness and general need to please make her a tempting match for his authoritative tastes. He is gathering disciples from the ranks of those who came to build a commune and trying to convince them to build a reformed prison there instead. If he succeeds, Blithedale will be destroyed. Hollingsworth's rejection of Zenobia is, then, less an instance of unrequited love than a rejection of Blithedale itself, an attack on its promise to seek out what sympathy can accomplish in the building of community. That is, Hollingsworth is attempting to destroy Blithedale, and Zenobia's suicide is an attempt to honor it.

Zenobia's death is a scene of sexual ruin like no other. Its violence can help us to gain deeper insight into the role of erotic sympathy as a counterforce to Hollingsworth's monomaniacal patriarchal authority; it also helps explain Miles's own emotional revolutions at Blithedale. Zenobia's sinewy, grotesque corpse represents an occasion of sexed embodiment responding to a community in peril. It is a defense against the attack on the sympathetic bonds of equality Zenobia sought at Blithedale. As we shall see, Miles's reaction to her corpse reveals her posthumous impact as the "ghost" of the commune.³² Miles has earlier claimed that their utopia will truly commence for him only after someone dies. "'And I shall never feel,'" he says to Hollingsworth, "'as if this were a real, practical, as well as a poetical, system of human life, until somebody has sanctified it by death'" (130). Zenobia's death may thus be easily read as that which sanctifies Blithedale. Death's labor, as it turns out, is not a thing of beauty. But the cause of Blithedale is. Once Zenobia's beauty, that "touch of Arcadia," is removed, Miles's grief allows him to see what Zenobia died for. Her sexually ruined corpse acts as a passport for him, transforming him into the feeling subject whose joining with that body represents his point of entry into Blithedale and thus into an ideal democracy.

Indeed, reading the deaths of all three martyrs to ruin, Clotel, Hester, and Zenobia, shows how the spectacle of the ruined woman's death, real or metaphorical, initiates a mutually unchaste, sympathetic embodiment among the spectators. The conditions in which these martyrs meet their deaths have disturbed readers of Brown and Hawthorne for good reasons. The corpses and scenes of suicide are profoundly unsettling. After death, the three characters continue the work of ruin through spectacle, as the dead or dying body reveals a strictly symbolic identity at play. Each novel shows how within a community of spectators, the amplified semiotic power of the female corpse circulates as it produces that "electric chain." The dead body of the martyr is in this way the artifact of one having (as Miles put it) "given oneself away," the rhetoric of ruin as a gift of self that pervades Brown's and Hawthorne's texts.

The graphic images of martyrdom in the works of Brown and Hawthorne are well known to their readers: Clotel's suicide pose, Zenobia's terrible rigor mortis, and Hester's metaphorical death mask all contribute to the aesthetic work of ruin in tales of martyrdom. In each novel, the spectacle of the ruined woman's death enacts the social contact that figures identity as a shared experience rather than an isolated or individual one. Thus the passages in which those deaths occur are worth quoting at length and considering together, for these deaths actualize the "giving away" of a woman's chastity, literally and metaphorically.

We encounter Zenobia's drowned body, punctured by the hooked pole they drag under the water's surface in search of it, as a spectacle of horrific death witnessed by Miles, Hollingsworth, and their guide Silas:

> Her arms had grown rigid in the act of struggling, and were bent before her, with clenched hands; her knees, too, were bent, and—thank God for it!—in the attitude of a prayer. Ah, that rigidity! . . . She knelt, as if in prayer. With the last, choking consciousness, her soul, bubbling out through her lips, it may be, had given itself up to the Father, reconciled and penitent. But her arms! They were bent before her, as if she struggled against Providence in never-ending hostility. Her hands! They were clenched in immitigable defiance. (235)

Then there is Clotel, who makes her suicidal leap into the Potomac to evade the slave traders grasping at her:

> She clasped her hands convulsively, and raised them, as she at the same time raised her eyes towards heaven, and begged for that mercy and compassion there, which had been denied her on earth; and then, with a single bound, she vaulted over the railings of the bridge, and sunk for ever beneath the waves of the river!

And finally there is the figurative death of Hester, the "A" obscuring her to the point of death. Though alive, Hester's drab clothes

> had the effect of making her fade personally out of sight and outline; while, again, the scarlet letter brought her back from this twilight indistinctness, and revealed her under the moral aspect of its own illuminations. . . . [Her face] was like a mask; or, rather, like the frozen calmness of a dead woman's features; owing this dreary resemblance to the fact that Hester was actually dead, in respect to any claim of sympathy, and had departed out of the world, with which she still seemed to mingle. (206)

For Zenobia and Clotel, prayer in death signals not only a redemption but a dual movement, an upward, heaven-bound move and a (literal and metaphorical) fall. Clotel is both "vaulted" and "sunk." Zenobia's body is similarly both defiant and penitent. Brown writes, "The body of Clotel was picked up from the bank of the river, where it had been washed by the strong current, a hole dug in the sand, and there deposited." The power of these images of the body in suicidal action lies in part in their work as spectacles. A conservative reading of these scenes would suggest that the unchaste female must meet her death, and that the plots of their stories punish Clotel and Zenobia for their moral weakness. But the emphasis each text places on the visual spectacle of these moments suggests that even after death, the work of sympathy is not finished. In these incidents, there is a Smithian sympathy informing the viewer's gaze. For in "[entering] into" the body of the other, in "[becoming] in some measure the same person" as the dead or dying figure, the viewers' interiority must vanish in relationality, in a necrophilic scene of shared sympathy.

In that shared spectacle, these novels offer a new kind of circulation of the ruined body. Ivy G. Wilson describes Clotel's leap "less as a jump into the Potomac River than a hovering above it, making her presence as much ethereal as material, as much spectral as social."[33] If Clotel hovers, Zenobia sinks, her literal fall representing an insistence of the materiality of the sacrificed body. On the other hand, Clotel's heavenly pose suggests an attempt at disembodiment, a move to release the slave woman from the horrors of material suffering.[34] "In identifying the body of the slave as 'both singular and collective'" it has no access to individuality and the rights associated with it; thus slave bodies like Clotel's "almost always function as representative bodies."[35]

Hester's death mask marks an additional kind of social death, so that she is all the more alive as a representative figure than as a singular person. In a brilliant study of the gothic aspects of *The Scarlet Letter,* Siân Silyn Roberts notes that Hester's presence on the scaffold signals "nothing less than the social death of the slave, a category of nonbeing to which Hawthorne metaphorically alludes each time he likens Hester to a dead woman, a corpse, or a ghost. . . . Like the slave on the block, the martyr in the arena . . . Hester represents those whom civil society has set outside the pale."[36] In her flamboyant adornment of the letter, Hester has given her self away—has given herself over to a kind of relational existence that obliterates the ipseity of self. Her martyrdom means that she might be reborn ("the scarlet letter brought her back") as a moral character, and here the pun on "character" nicely fits into Hester's transfiguration from person to allegorical "figure." The notion that there is a dead Hester Prynne at the center of *The Scarlet Letter* is distressing only if that death is understood as a finality to her existence. The reborn *character* of the A—the adulteress—shows that there is a different kind of life left. Hester may no longer be a person, but she is undoubtedly an active agent of community.

Resting over her heart, the letter that has metaphorically killed Hester recalls the puncturing of Zenobia's corpse at the heart. Earlier in *The Blithedale Romance,* Zenobia claims Hollingsworth has killed her with his heartlessness, and when Miles, Silas, and Hollingsworth end up searching the river for Zenobia's body with a "hooked-pole," the scene could not be a more viscerally gruesome enactment of that idea. The postmortem "deathblow" occurs as a "plunge," a "thrust," and a "strike" into her lifeless chest and "looks cruelly" (233). Often used to symbolize the labial spread, in this instance, the heart, punctured by the phallic pole, re-creates the scene of Zenobia's sexual ruin.[37] Thus the three men's search for her corpse represents at least on one level a search for the violable female body. But martyrdom means death has provided an evasion, and the pursuit of that violability ends in failure.

The heroine of the ruin narrative never insulates her heart from injury because to do so would mean insulating it from all emotional connections. This means that chastity is a bad metaphor for community. Indeed, the wounded chest of Zenobia's corpse works as a carefully crafted metaphor for both the ruined female body and the aesthetic work of that body in imagining a communal identity. It is thus appropriate that Hollingsworth's stroke with the hooked pole is aimed first figuratively and then literally at her heart. For before her death, Zenobia says that if there is a moral to her story, it is this:

> "[T]hat in the battlefield of life, the downright stroke, that would fall only on a man's steel head-piece, is sure to light on a woman's heart, over which she wears no breastplate, and whose wisdom it is, therefore, to keep out of the conflict. Or this:—that the whole universe, her own sex and yours, and Providence, or Destiny, to boot, make common cause against the woman who swerves one hair's breadth out of the beaten track. Yes; and add (for I may as well own it, now) that, with that one hair's breadth she goes all astray, and never sees the world in its true aspect, afterwards!" (224)

On one level, the passage may be read as Zenobia's final admission of her past sexual ruin (she herself is the woman who, with Westervelt, "has [swerved] one hair's breadth," and as a result she has gone "all astray"). The passage also intriguingly evokes the description of Hester's grave, which has an "escutcheon" or breastplate on which is etched the famously ambiguous epitaph, "'ON A FIELD, SABLE; THE LETTER A, GULES'" (240–41). It is the letter (worn by Hester like nothing so much as that missing breastplate, since it represents a lack of insulation from the world and its suffering) that is honored by this burial. It is a grave for a *symbol*, honoring that A for adultery. A symbol is what a ruined martyr becomes before her second, biological death. When Zenobia martyrs herself to Blithedale, the missing breastplate ensures the representation of her sexual ruin. The stabbings of the corpse thus show that the breastplate which Zenobia so ardently

Ruin, Martyrdom, and Sympathy from Clotel *to* The Scarlet Letter refuses to wear would protect only an uncirculated—one might say virginal—heart. That which is unprotected is also uncontained, and when Miles concludes that Zenobia "haunts" Blithedale, her ghostly omnipresence is an apt appointment for a figure now larger than life in more ways than one.

Finally, it is the sexually fallen martyr's association with circulation and her resistance to containment that show the power of the ruin narrative to construct a valid alternative to the individual. That alternative allows community to flourish in its battle against the monomaniacal individual and his pursuit of happiness. As we are about to see, such resistance finds strength in novels about rape as ruin. Stories about seduction and enslavement that turn into stories about rape present a unique kind of resistance to the violating aims of the predatory individual. Indeed, the radicalization of embodiment in the rape-as-ruin narrative reveals that the patriarchal forces at work in the construction of the sexed female body do not always triumph, even when rape becomes the central plotline.

· SIX ·

Ruin, Rape, and the Aesthetic Work of *Clarissa* in England and America

Force, and Fraud, are in warre the two Cardinall vertues, Justice, and Injustice are none of the Faculties neither of the Body, nor Mind.
—Thomas Hobbes, *Leviathan*, 1651

"I am not married—ruined, as I am, by your assistance, I bless God, I am *not* married to this miscreant."
—*The History in Miniature of Clarissa Harlowe*, US edition, 1773

Authors from William Hill Brown to William Wells Brown portray sexual ruin through the heat of impulsive, erotic encounters that posit an alternative to the marriage contract and the consenting individual as fitting emblems of democracy. But of course the ruin narrative is not always set outside the ideological boundaries of consent rhetoric. Instead, its staging within those boundaries allows it to explore the punitively gendered features of jurisdictional embodiment. The ruin genre's most radical work may in fact be its interrogation of consent as a political ideal that enforces those boundaries. Certainly Atlantic Enlightenment theorists of contract are no stranger to the politics of consent and their ideal of violation through rape.[1] Author of *The Social Contract* (1762), Jean-Jacques Rousseau is a key figure among such theorists. Yet he was as well known for his romantic fiction as for his political theories.[2] And, perhaps not surprisingly, his fictional works are notable for featuring sexual ruin. His 1761 epistolary novel *Julie; or, The New Heloise*, for example, was a European best-seller about the kind of passion found in the seductions of the post-revolutionary American novel. *Julie* is in part about a love that, existing outside of marriage, includes an illicit sexual encounter between a married woman and the man she still loves but could never wed. Rousseau's work also invests in what he characterizes as the erotics of force. Tellingly, in order to illustrate the political role consent ought to play in the nation-building enterprise of Enlightenment thought, Rousseau uses rape, and in his notorious "silent consent" passage, he belies the logic of consent by defining it as that which one gains by force:

> To win this silent consent is to make use of all the violence permitted in love. To read it in the eyes, to see it in the ways in spite of the mouth's denial, that is the art of he who knows how to love. If he then completes his happiness, he is not brutal, he is decent. He does not insult chasteness; he respects it; he serves it. He leaves it the honor of still defending what it would have perhaps abandoned.[3]

The language that celebrates violence as a form of chivalry points not only to misogynist sexual practice but also to the political paradox of bodies subject to such violence: the denial of consent is the only respectable means of its assertion. This is of course also to say that the presence of consent is determined by the promise of its violation.[4] It is that promise that the rape-as-ruin novel resists. And it is a resistance that requires an absolute rejection of the principles readers might expect the rape-as-ruin novel to embrace: personhood, self-possession, even consent itself. The novel that rhetorically manages the rape scene to reveal its political failures thus addresses an entirely different facet of the aesthetic work of ruin. That work, especially as it relates to a novel about an enslaved woman, interrogates the relationship between sexed bodies and consent in astonishing ways. Rather than insisting that their heroines should have access to the power of consent, the voice to accept or to refuse, novels about rape as a form of sexual ruin repudiate the politics of consent altogether. Why?

Black and White Plots

In order to answer that question, it is necessary to understand the plots—including their missing pieces—of three of the most notable rape-as-ruin stories in the Atlantic world: Samuel Richardson's *Clarissa; or, The*

History of a Young Lady (1747–48), Susanna Rowson's *Charlotte Temple* (1794),[5] and Harriet Jacobs's *Incidents in the Life of a Slave Girl* (1861). Rowson and Richardson, two eighteenth-century white authors born in England who wrote what would become immensely popular books in America, produced texts that have a privileged generic access to figuring seduction as rape, a privilege upon which *Incidents* signifies. Despite the differences among these three texts, they adhere to some of the same key tropes, including captivity, rape, and Atlantic crossings. And all three manage a theatrical omission of the rape scene that is crucial to their portrayal of how ruin radicalizes the body.

The crossing of the Atlantic and the aesthetic work it represents are central to what was perhaps the most influential story of rape-as-ruin in the eighteenth century, *Clarissa*. Richardson's epistolary beast, originally published in 1747–48 but abridged and revised for an American audience in 1773, is devoted to a single event: the libertine Lovelace's rape of Clarissa.[6] Leading up to that event are the distinctly patriarchal machinations of her brother and father, who attempt to hold her captive until she consents to wed the man of their choosing. Lovelace capitalizes on their oppressive influence, presenting himself as a charitable hero who arranges to arrive by carriage to help her escape, only to kidnap her himself. Unable to seduce her through conventional means, he eventually drugs and rapes her, and she has but a vague and incoherent memory of the event that serves as the novel's mechanism for omitting the rape scene; the novel then turns into a protracted study of her martyrdom and death. The epistles that constitute the bulk of the novel make way in the book's final pages to paratextual matter in which Richardson makes a case for the story's historical authenticity. Revised for an American audience, *Clarissa* crossed the Atlantic to become, in a breathtaking example of New World transformation, in some ways exactly the same, in some ways unrecognizable. The US edition of 1773 was loyal to the basic plot but told through the voice of an omniscient narrator rather than through the letters of its characters; it was also published decades later and about fourteen hundred pages shorter.[7]

Novels in some way retelling *Clarissa*'s story became quite popular in the decades after the abridged edition was published in colonial America. The influence of *Clarissa* on the early US novel is in abundant evidence in what was America's first best seller, *Charlotte Temple*, which is about a girl who is ruined by rape when she leaves England for the American colonies.

Rowson's novel describes the tribulations of a young English rose duped by her French schoolmistress Mademoiselle La Rue into involving herself in a romance with Montraville, a British soldier about to leave England to fight in the Revolutionary War in America. After fainting during a moment of melodramatic indecision, Charlotte is kidnapped by Montraville, who puts her in a carriage that takes her to a ship headed to the colonies. There is unresolvable ambiguity about what happens next. It is clear that *Charlotte Temple* relies on the archaic definition of rape—to carry off by force—as a metonym for sexual assault. But confusing the matter is Charlotte's continued emotional fidelity to Montraville until her death, when she dies in America after giving birth to their daughter. Charlotte's unconscious state in the carriage acts as the novel's chief tool of omission. The absence of information about what happens in that carriage ride is central to the rape story, a rhetorical device *Charlotte Temple* overtly borrows from *Clarissa*.

But the most remarkable of all of the American retellings of *Clarissa* may occur in Harriet Jacobs's novel *Incidents in the Life of a Slave Girl*, a tale about the terrorizing use of slave rape that signifies on the seduction genre, in part through Jacobs's artistic treatment of the Middle Passage. Published serially in the *New York Tribune* under the pseudonym Linda Brent, its subject matter was regarded as so incendiary that it was dropped by that newspaper and later published in its entirety by another press, and then only after the white sentimentalist Lydia Maria Child agreed to write a preface for it. *Incidents* tells the story of its narrator's flight from her master Dr. Flint, a sadistic predator intent on both sexual and psychological dominance. The master's rape fantasy and its consequences dictate most of the novel's action. He is so fixated on her ruin that she can design no conventional means of escape. Yet unlike Clarissa and Charlotte, Linda Brent *does* escape the rape, first by involving herself with a different white man, Mr. Sands, and later by concealing herself in her grandmother's tiny crawl space—the size, one might say, of a carriage—for seven long years. The omission of the rape scene occurs not through the unconsciousness of the heroine, then, but through the text's overt refusal to present it, despite the fact that readers must have expected rape to be the key "incident" in the story.[8] After her initial escape and flight to her grandmother's attic, Linda drills a hole in the wall so that she may observe the world below, becoming in some ways the omniscient narrator who views the story from above rather than remaining a character within it, as she details Dr. Flint's increasing rage at her absence. The novel ends with her eventual flight to the North, where she is able to reunite with some family, though even after Flint's death she lives in fear of capture.

From these four texts, then, we have the task of understanding how what Laura Doyle has noted are the twin traumas of oceanic crossing and rape contribute to the aesthetic work of ruin[9]—to, that is, a notion of subjectivity that inhabits a space somewhere between the dyad of the self/other binary, a subjectivity that resists the violation of rape by resisting certain ideas about individuality and indeed about interiority itself.

Rape in the Seduction Novel

The rape-as-ruin narrative often seems to anticipate what we might term the scene of consent, the moment in which the words "I do" or "I do not" would determine what happens next. But in the rape-as-ruin tale, of course, no such scene is possible because the contractual utterance is entirely unavailable to bodies subject to force. Crucially, however, in the texts under consideration here, the rape scene is never represented. And the substitutions that take its place account for some of the most radical thought in the early Atlantic novel. After offering a theoretical overview about the aesthetic work of rape in the eighteenth- and nineteenth-century novel, then, I wish to discuss those substitutions and the rhetorical strategies used by Richardson, Rowson, and Jacobs to create them. Tropes of containment, passage, and omission, alongside an astonishing array of textual anomalies, are deployed by these narratives in their interrogation of rape's power and their presentation of radical resistance to the ideological goals that acts of rape attempt to achieve.

Those alternatives do not deny the violence at stake in the rape narrative; the fact of the violence itself remains uncontested. Each story regards rape as an act of terror, and in the case of the slave novel, the particular horrors of slave rape are explored in full. Indeed, in its critique of the white rape-as-ruin narrative, Jacobs's slave narrative interrogates the fiction of choice that a society based on the ideals of the social contract supposedly offers, an especially vicious fiction given that sexual refusal is utterly unavailable to slave women. In fact, in their own unique ways, all of these works reveal consent's unavailability to their heroines, then embark on a study of the consenting individual as a model that is ultimately used against bodies subject to the violence of a white supremacist patriarchy. Their work depicts the binary between consent and refusal as a political structuring of agency that for white women always retains the possibility of consent's violation, and for slave women guarantees that violation, or rather guarantees the master's sadistic pleasure in committing a violation he may simultaneously dismiss as impossible for black bodies. The critique of consent in this work is especially critical in the slave novel, if we understand that the enslaved body is before all else and by definition of the state a body that cannot withhold consent. The novels that explore the politics of rape expose the horrors of sexual and racial violence experienced by real bodies as they expose the nature of rape's violence, its originary violation, which, as we will soon see, is to interpellate the raced and sexed body as a container that must be broken into in order to call forth—in order to gain access to and thus violate—the "self" residing within. The novels by Richardson, Rowson, and Jacobs refuse that scene entirely, and they do so through their investigation into exactly how and why a patriarchal slaveholding culture relies on the ideology of consent.

At work in these rape-as-ruin narratives is a profound skepticism about consent and the merits of the social contract. The idea that citizenship denotes an agreement among a consenting people is a political fiction that produces great benefits for propertied white men. For everyone else, however, the principle of consent produces a peculiar kind of subjugation. These novels are interested in defining that subjugation and the ways in which the idea of consent, when it is used as a foundation for social relations, constitutes a political fraudulence because so very few people actually have the power to refuse. To define that subjugation, then, the rape-as-ruin narrative lingers upon the absurdity of the idea that the one who need not *ask*—for access to bodies over whom he holds absolute legal power—would nevertheless take "no" for an answer.

Several tropes reveal the architecture of that fraudulence, including containment, omission, and the presence of print irregularities. Containment is certainly one of the most powerful of the tropes. These texts are riddled with inescapable spaces in which the heroine is imprisoned and yet remains elusive. These novels also want to understand bodies differently, and as a result the spaces that bodies inhabit, and the space of the body itself, become imbricated by an unstable relationship between the sexed body and its absences. In concert with these missing bodies, then, the next trope these novels use is the act of textual omission. Perhaps it bears repeating: the rape scene is entirely omitted from novels that are explicitly and centrally about rape. This is no matter of historical prudery; the texts refer to sexual content and sexual violence often enough. Rather, it is a matter of managing startling and glaring omissions that call attention to themselves. This is a radical rhetorical move, an animated insistence on absence managed through a host of strategies, including the nimble administration of tropes they reclaim for that purpose. In light of these absences, perhaps what is most intriguing and most radical about these novels is the final trope, that of textual and print irregularities. They use white space, pronoun play, scrambled pages, missing pages, plot omissions, abridgements—even words visually falling off of the page—in order to make the generic instability of the text a metonym for the ontological instability of the body. Radical books, they suggest, signify radical bodies. By rejecting interiority as the prerequisite for subjectivity, these novels reject patriarchal understandings of the self as the body's captive. These texts resist rape by insisting that the raced, sexed body is something other than a fortress to be taken; in part they achieve that resistance by rejecting the materiality of embodiment as stable. What I mean to suggest is that through the textual irregularities I will be discussing, these novels rethink the terms of embodiment. In some ways, the material book from which words seem to be escaping represents the body that does not fulfill the corporeal promise of containment. These stories have no fidelity to genre or to print culture, and holding them in your hands can feel itself like a kind of fraud, since what appears to be a "book" is also something else. Indeed, the irregularity of the texts comes to stand in for the irregularity of embodiment itself.

The stories under consideration here deftly manage the rape scene through its omission. Rape is the ultimate act of consent's denial, and yet these texts refuse to engage with it under those terms. Again, this is not to suggest that these texts deny the violence of rape or the horrors of such violation. Rather, these novels regard the ideal of consent as a political lie that permits specific forms of violence. What these novels reveal is that the ultimate expressions of contract culture—the phrase "I do," and especially the phrase "I do not"—are entirely unutterable for sexed and raced bodies; for them, the scene of consent, if it can be said to occur at all, can occur only as a vicious and terribly ironic parody. "Will you?" is not a politically innocent question, because for the heroines of these novels it is an unanswerable one. The slavers and libertines in the novels we are about to encounter do not have to ask, and when they do, their words act as menacing imitations.

What I mean to say is that in the rape-as-ruin narrative, the very question, "Will you?" is a *hail* that calls forth an iteration of the embodied individual in the form of the subaltern subject. By omitting the rape scene—by refusing, in Butlerian terms, to repeat it loyally—the texts recognize the scene of consent as a hail, one that might be—that must be—refused. This hail is an attempt to call the violable subject into being. It insists on the existence of an interiority, a self that must then be policed through sexual and racial violence. Its goal is to trespass the boundary it creates. The refusal of this scene comes through what Butler calls the "range of *disobedience*" that is possible in response to the Althusserian hail, those repetitions "which fail to repeat loyally and, in their failure, open possibilities for resignifying the terms of violation against their violating aims."[10] If consent is the political capital that women lack—if the political utterances of "I do" or "I do not" are unavailable to them—then what might such disobedience look like?

In order to answer that question, a theory of rape is in order. Before we examine the ways in which these four texts rhetorically manage the rape scene in order to contest contract culture's reliance on consent and the individual as the twin principles of political agency in a democracy, we must understand the political goals that rape is used to achieve. The use of rape in the novels under consideration here does and means many things, too many to account for fully in this work. Scholars of the eighteenth- and nineteenth-century Atlantic novel have accounted for the political work of white rape and slave rape and have carefully interrogated the supremacist and patriarchal privilege sexual injury accomplishes.[11] To add to this important historical and theoretical work, we might begin by noting what the novels in this chapter insist is rape's most fundamental injury, the attempt to impose a Cartesian nightmare of corporeal confinement through sexual violence. Rape enforces as it imagines a mind/body split that contains a violable interiority inside the material body of the female other. *This imagining itself* constitutes the originary act of violence in the rape-as-ruin novel. Yet the novels discussed in this chapter, about seductions that turn into rapes, disrupt the attempt to construct an inside/outside dichotomy of embodiment, an ontology in which a self is housed in a body. This dichotomy often presents itself as a staging of the walls that guard female chastity. Indeed, the aesthetic work of rape is in part the brutalizing attempt to build those walls *in order to* scale them, to mark the body as a set of boundaries in order to cross them, even arguably the invention of such boundaries as sites of crossing or violation. Resistance against such a brutalizing attempt resembles what Butler calls the way "bodies tend to indicate a world beyond themselves" and how in the "movement beyond their own boundaries" they come to constitute "a movement of boundary itself."[12]

So when Charlotte Temple sails to the colonies, when Harriet Jacobs turns her survival inside a crawlspace into a metonymic Middle Passage and ends her novel with the image of "a dark and troubled sea" (208), when Clarissa Harlowe processes her rape with a hallucination that places her in a slave galley: these are the crossings that define a radical embodiment that resists, even elides, the kind of violation imagined by the rape wish.[13] And while Clarissa does not cross the Atlantic, *Clarissa* does, a meta-journey that, alongside its English original and read in concert with its literary heirs *Charlotte Temple* and *Incidents,* helps readers to see how rape ultimately fails to construct, in order to access (and to access, in this context, is to obliterate), a private interiority. They contest all the premises of jurisdictional embodiment even as their heroines suffer from the worst kind of bodily violation. In their sly management of the rape scene, then, these texts reveal the failure of rape to call that embodied, violable interiority into being.

Rape-as-ruin texts reveal that for women, the status of "individual" is ideologically a promise of self *and simultaneously* the promise of the self's violation. The aesthetic work of ruin, then, becomes using the consent drama typical of eighteenth-century seduction novels, or rather the drama of consent's absence, to stage the imagining of an interiority that is essential to the idea of the possessive individual. This staging reveals the horror of its intentions, which are the violation and obliteration of that interiority. To repeat: the very ideal of containment, of a bounded embodiment, is revealed as a violent imagining. In this way, the ideal of the individual self is weaponized against women. The captivity of the woman under attack, whether it is in a gothic manor, a carriage, or a plantation, serves metonymically to reveal the distinctly gendered horror of bodily containment as a condition of violability. Her captivity is redundant. The argument of rape that these authors contend with, then, is that a contained self is made to be broken into. In other words, these novels observe that the mythology of the individual works differently for women. And then they refuse to participate in that mythology.

Through tropes of omission and containment, the works considered in this chapter show how rape (again, in addition to all the other meanings and arguments it achieves) might be said to execute a scene of semiotic error, the vagina mistaken as a passage into an interiority that is imagined as contained, accessible, and violable.[14] Indeed, these novels often show the female body being misread as a site of crossing. The attempt to violate a woman's body by forcing one's way into it insists she is *in there*. This insistence likewise asserts a separateness between self and other that is enforced by the material body. In the attempt to manufacture such distances and such spaces, which occur literally as well as metaphorically in the texts I discuss, is a performance of containment's construction. What ensues is the subsequent *failure* of rape in each text to achieve a "crossing" or "passage" into the imagined interiority of a singular female self, the crossing that defines the rape wish. In *The Rape of Clarissa*, Terry Eagleton notes that the rapist Lovelace is frustrated in his attempts to reach this interiority through sexual violence.[15] As Eagleton says, "the 'inviolable' is also that which slips through the net of signification." In other words, Lovelace can never arrest "the immaculate mystery beneath the skin" through rape because the totality he imagines as identity does not exist.[16] The first attempted act of violence, then, is one of containment. Put another way, novelists from Richardson to Jacobs dramatize the failure of rape as the failure to assert, through violence, the distance between self and other. And they point to the consequent failure of that dichotomy's premise, namely that the feminine inhabits an "inside" to which there is access, a construction that then allows for an embodied male interiority that is imagined as abstract, inviolable, and inaccessible.[17]

This resistance models an alternative way of imagining bodies, in part through the ways these books present oceanic space as textual space. They present an argument for the oceanic boundarilessness of embodiment, the lack of boundary between self and other. Instead of a violable self contained inside the body, the libertine rapists in these stories encounter identities that are too fluid to be contained, and, more radically, bodies that cannot always be surveilled or bounded and that are not even always materially stable. They find in their folly that they have not taken what they sought, that in their wish to capture the ocean, their violence has merely been like the cutting of water.

In its occurrence within the seduction novel, rape might usefully be read as the interpellation that refuses the response it elicits. Rape acts as a hail whose utterance must imagine a silencing, a hail that insists no one is *in there* to respond even as that interior self is the target of its violating aims. Indeed, rape is a policing of that absence, though this policing is suspect from the very beginning, since it lacks the logic of absence: if no one is (in) there, no violence, no violation, is possible. In the Enlightenment novel's investment in self and consent, then, instances of rape reveal a man's attempt to obliterate a person he insists is not there, for he at once denies a woman her personhood and asserts it through his very attempt to violate it. The Everyman in this age of revolution needs to secure his sovereignty by materializing and then terrorizing "self" in the female other to assure its inviolable abstraction as a distinctly *male* right. In this sense, the ruin narrative presents rape as issuing a terrorizing, ironic hail. Its violence is in part its attempt to finesse a totalizing subjectivity, to call into being the self of a woman as fully contained within, but not protected by, the body. The violence of rape thus denies, as a means of calling into being, the person, which is of course what all interpellation in some sense *does*.

It is also what contract theory does. It asserts that every white man is a person, who in a state of nature "carries his entire self" with him. Eighteenth- and nineteenth-century narratives of rape show how white women are set apart from this idea of self-possession. White women exist under the tenuous protection of the men to whom they are related by marriage or blood. Contract theory promises that a man can say "no," but that a white woman can never access the full power of that utterance. Of course, the enslaved woman is defined by its absolute impossibility. In both cases, the body of the other supposedly issues utterances of its own that belie any verbal denial. As Rousseau writes in *Emile* (1762), the erotics of the "no" that means "yes" define the power he says a woman is meant to wield. Describing sex as a provocation by refusal, he continues, "The surest way of arousing this strength is to make it necessary by resistance." As Gillian Brown succinctly summarizes the politics of such gender norms, "Far from female consent being a contradiction in terms, then, female consent epitomizes individual subjection in a liberal society." Arguing that consent is simply a ruse designed to actualize male power, Brown concludes, "women's adroitness compels even violence against themselves. Rousseau locates in woman's natural constitution—that is, in her given coquettishness—the ontological state of not just a false accuser but a provocateur. In this imagination, rape can scarcely be said ever to occur."[18]

The notion that rape might be mistaken for seduction, and that it might lead to the same end—sexual ruin—is particularly offensive to modern readers. Yet some of the most popular novels of the Enlightenment Atlantic explore the rape/seduction dynamic, not, or not only, to sensationalize it, but also in pursuit of subjectivity's understanding. As the frustrated admissions of failure spoken by the sexual predators in the novels under consideration here attest to, the emotional violence of rape is the site of an investment in patriarchal power that exposes an intolerable *someone-ness* in a woman that is uncontainable. After drugging Clarissa into a near unconscious state and then raping her, for example, Lovelace admits he has not "completed" his true goal: "And yet why say I, *completed?* when the *will,* the *consent,* is wanting—and I have still views before me of obtaining that?"[19] He wishes to alter who she is and what she wants, but because he misreads the conditions of embodiment, that, too, will end in failure. In novels like *Clarissa,* rape is the liberal possessivist pursuit (both predatory and ideological) of selfhood in another, in *the* other, rendered as the social death of a woman.

Time and time again, the story of rape-as-ruin represents it as a failed pursuit. The failure of rape in these ruin narratives is of particular significance. And it is this failure upon which Jacobs signifies (and against which she protests) in *Incidents*.[20] Though Jacobs's text occurs decades after the others, it is central to understanding the aesthetic work of rape in eighteenth-century white novels about ruin. As critics have firmly established, *Incidents* includes the staples of the seduction genre to both perform and critique that genre's cultural work in defining white femininity.[21] While enslavement changes the context of rape in ways so fundamental as to make a comparison to rape in the white-authored seduction novel seem specious, Jacobs's work overtly refers to the genre of the white seduction novel, at first to elude, and then to lambast that context. Jacobs's generic samplings therefore offer a new and important take on the aesthetic work of rape-as-ruin texts worth investigating.

Though Linda's relocation to her grandmother's attic provides distance from the foul aims of Dr. Flint, it brings few of the freedoms readers of the classic slave narrative genre might reasonably expect. Representing her safety as an imprisonment inside quarters that resemble a slave ship galley, Linda is not characterized as a female Frederick Douglass. This is not a book about the quest to be recognized as an individual whose rights are as self-evident as any white man's. It is a journey inward, a radicalization of interiority that refuses the notion of embodiment as containment. For, like the seduction novels *Incidents* uses as generic referents, Jacobs's work is not a plea for American individualism and the identity it implies, but a challenge to them. Through these differences, *Incidents* manages the aesthetic work of the master's rape in surprising ways. Jacobs explores the powers of censorship and omission to signify upon the use of rape in the white seduction novel.

But like the other stories considered here, two elements of the story are missing. As is the case in *Clarissa* and *Charlotte Temple*, *Incidents* does not present us with a coherent rape scene. Charlotte faints before she is taken into Montraville's carriage; Clarissa is drugged before Lovelace attacks her. As we shall see, in *Incidents*, Jacobs replaces the rape of the female slave girl with other scenes. None of these characters can be said to be cognitively present when men rape them. In neither the English nor the American versions of Richardson's novel, in neither *Charlotte Temple* nor in *Incidents in the Life of a Slave Girl*, do we find a victim who is either present or even *awake* during the moment of sexual assault.[22]

Incidents teaches us how to read these omissions. To deny what her readers would have assumed, namely the story of her own rape as the representational "incident" dominating the life of all female slaves, she retells her own sexual history as a seduction novel, and then does what the white heroine has not had to do: in full command of her faculties, she ruins herself. Yet the layers of storytelling do not end here. Jacobs *then* uses *Incidents* to "ruin" the very seduction novel genre that she has used, a genre that she employs to *not* tell her story. Thus she uses generic ruin as a metonym for sexual ruin even as she calls into question the merits of that genre. And the fact that she stages the self-ruin, rather than entirely removing the troubling constellation of sex, seduction, and rape from the story, abets Jacobs's insistence upon the failure of rape to work its violation. Finally, *Incidents* does something more shocking—it reverses the race and sex of victim and rapist, depicting a white woman raping an enslaved man—an outrageous act of writing that radicalizes the ruin narrative as it reveals the ways in which the politics of consent incorporate the promise of violation.

Ultimately, the aesthetic work of ruin in *Incidents* is to explore the agency that is not vulnerable to sexual violation because in part it denies the predatory imagining of a violable female interiority. It is no wonder that *Incidents* revisits, interrogates, and revises Richardson's *Clarissa,* the most famous rape narrative of its time. The story of the slave woman almost certainly invokes the specter of the master's rape, making Richardson's fifteen-hundred-page failed rape fantasy the perfect text to appropriate; *Incidents* refigures *Clarissa*'s failure in multiple, multiform ways. Richardson's, and Lovelace's, failures to invent and then to invade a contained female interiority depict what Jacobs later uses as her narrator's hiding space, called the "loophole of retreat." Unlike other spaces of rape (the whorehouse in *Clarissa* and the carriage in *Charlotte Temple*), Linda Brent both chooses and marks this space as her own, a place to deal with the traumas of female enslavement and a place where the rape hail cannot reach and a place where other, more radical utterances become possible. It is in such radical spaces—spaces at once confining and boundariless—that the failure of rape occurs, when the disunified subject of ruin cannot be contained.

Containment and the Atlantic

The metonymic chain of carriage, slave galley, locked room, and finally the body itself helps us to explore the containment motif. For as we are about see, there is no space of containment, not even the material page of the text or the material fact of the body, that successfully holds anything *in.* Symbolically, as Clarissa is running away from home, riding in Lovelace's carriage, she asks, "Can it be that I am here?" (388). Clarissa's uncertainty at the moment of her departure is a legitimate question. For all three heroines, the spaces that they encounter at key moments are unstable. What it means to be either "I" or "here" is truly a matter of significant confusion that destabilizes the terms by which "consent" might be possible.

Such confusion is nowhere in more evidence than in the carriage in which Charlotte Temple is kidnapped and raped. It is described through a parallel carriage ride by her grandfather, a narrative trick Rowson may have used to identify Montraville's rape without depicting a scene of overt sexual violence.[23] Charlotte despairs over the impossible choice between her parents and Montraville, crying, "my torn heart!" (48) Chapter 12 of *Charlotte*

Temple ends with the line that indicates her sexual ruin: "The chaise drove off. She shrieked, and fainted into the arms of her betrayer." The very next line in the text is the first sentence of chapter thirteen, separated only by the white space of a chapter break, a space standing in, I would argue, for both the Atlantic voyage Charlotte is taking and the omission of Montraville's rape, a curtain drawn conspicuously by Rowson. It is also a stand-in for the ruptures defining the ruin narrative's disunified subject.

Chapter 13's title, "Cruel Disappointment," indicates that what happens in the white space between those chapters of *Charlotte Temple* is the substance of tragedy, a reading which is confirmed by what follows. That next line begins with the pseudo-sexual metonymic representation of her journey that quickly breaks down into violence: "'What pleasure,' cried Mr. Eldridge, as he stepped into the chaise to go for his grand-daughter" (49). Such a line begins with the implication that Charlotte has experienced some kind of sexual pleasure, yet soon the scene grows much darker. As her grandfather discovers Charlotte has been taken by Montraville, Rowson notes, "Slow and heavy passed the time while the carriage was conveying Mr. Eldridge home" (53). His carriage ride stands in for hers. The promise of pleasure turns to tragedy, and the scene becomes a nuanced representation of the ways in which a seduction novel can become a tale about rape. The chapter's depiction of his lethargic, tragic posture after he receives news of Charlotte's disappearance, then, stands in for the raped body of his granddaughter:

> The old man returned to the chaise, but the light step and chearful [*sic*] countenance were no more; sorrow filled his heart, and guided his motions; he seated himself in the chaise, his venerable head reclined upon his bosom, his hands were folded, his eye fixed on vacancy, and the large drops of sorrow rolled silently down his cheeks. There was a mixture of anguish and resignation depicted in his countenance, as if he would say, henceforth who shall dare to boast his happiness, or even in idea contemplate his treasure, lest, in the very moment his heart is exulting in its own felicity, the object which constitutes that felicity should be torn from him. (52)

The chaise ride becomes the scene of Charlotte's rape, told through the metonymic body of the grandfather. Standing in for Charlotte, the grandfather unsexes the rape and figures Charlotte in a paternalistic coverture that can only reenact the trauma, not prevent it. Yet the displacement of her body with his, and of her suffering with his, creates a scene of ontological confusion. The repeated imagery of the torn heart, the torpid body, the character resigned to tragedy: all echo, or rather duplicate, descriptions of Charlotte, and depict her in moment of post-rape defeat. The symbol of the heart has long stood in for the presumed anatomical invitation of the labial spread, here "torn" by Montraville. The torn heart figures as a symbol of vaginal violence, the "treasure" Charlotte's stolen virginity. Yet what is most important rhetorically in this textually disruptive moment is Charlotte's absence, which resists her containment. The standing in of the grandfather at once places Charlotte inside the carriage and removes her entirely from it. The carriage becomes an unstable space, one we cannot be sure contains anything. The carriage first carrying Charlotte and then her grandfather thus stands in for the rupture of subjectivity and the material body that can be occupied by another, not in a moment of violation but in a moment of sympathy.

Like the space of the carriage and its radical ontological possibilities, in Jacobs's work, the loophole shows how that containment fails. In a layered performance that reclaims the imagery of rape, Linda drills a hole in the crawlspace wall with the phallic gimlet. The drilling of the hole represents the aesthetic work of ruin in *Incidents,* as it shows the feminine space to be penetrated *and* safe, inviolable because it is permeable. Jacobs uses the hidden interior in which Linda Brent protects herself from her master's rape as a site of escape that is an exposed and porous space, heavy with visual traffic—a space without structural integrity that is nevertheless safe.[24] Through this and other such moments, *Incidents* recalculates the ruin genre, resisting the rape scene after building up to it. It's a challenge against the genre, using its conventions against itself.

Critics have done inspiring work on the Middle Passage imagery within *Incidents* and its negotiation of issues relating to sex, race, power, and confinement. Robin Miskcokze argues for example that much of the text is devoted to Middle Passage imagery, including Linda hiding under the floorboards during the early part of her escape as "comparable to a slave below deck." "The dimensions and experiences in the attic allude to slaves' experiences aboard slave ships," including extreme heat and cold, a cramped space, and an insect infestation, so that "these images recall the horrors of the Middle Passage." In this case, Miskcokze notes, the gimlet transforms the sea into an island when Linda compares herself to Robinson Crusoe. Like him, she cleverly uses found objects as tools to make the space of her confinement her own.[25]

In her excellent discussion of *Clarissa,* Laura Doyle also sees an attempt by Richardson to use Middle Passage imagery and the trope of containment in his management of the rape scene. Doyle notes that he uses metaphorical references to the trauma of kidnapping, enslavement, and the misery of the Middle Passage experienced by African slaves in *Clarissa*'s "mad papers"— the fragmented notes and bits of poetry Clarissa scribbles after Lovelace rapes her and she is slowly recovering from being drugged.[26] Paper X is

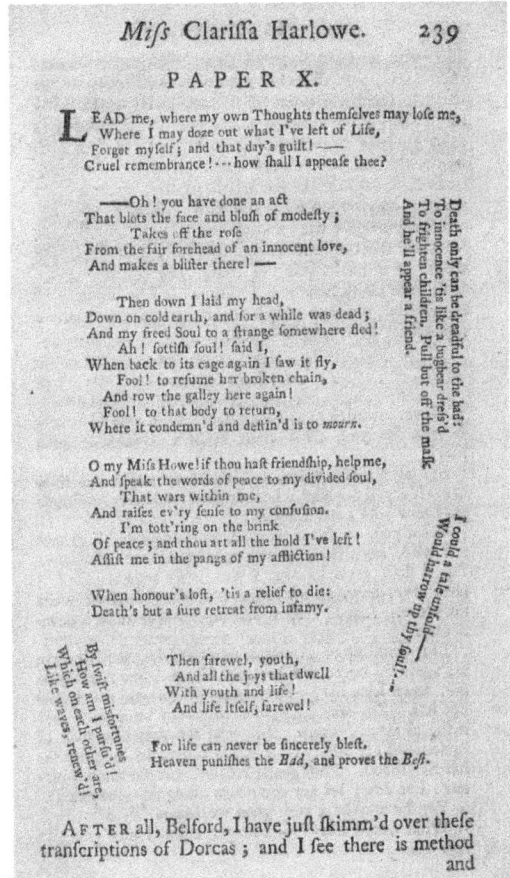

Figure 4. "Paper X" from Samuel Richardson's *Clarissa,* 1748. (Princeton University Library)

a series of poetic stanzas, some appearing at crazy angles in the margins, others with uneven justification. (See figure 4.) In one stanza, Clarissa writes,

> Then down I laid my head,
> Down on cold earth, and for a while was dead;
> And my freed soul to a strange somewhere fled!
> Ah! sottish soul! said I,
> When back to its cage again I saw it fly,
> Fool! to resume her broken chain,
> And row the galley here again!
> Fool! to that body to return,
> Where it condemn'd and destin'd is to *mourn*.

On the margin outside the text, she includes a floating stanza that symbolizes her "misfortunes" that pursue her "Like waves" (893). Doyle notes that this language "resonate[s] exactly within the ruinous, unanchoring experience of blacks on the Atlantic, here subsumed within the story of a pure, Anglo-Atlantic martyr" that links to "the sexual matrix of . . . possessive Atlantic ontology" that defines enslavement.[27]

Additionally, the notion of a soul that returns to its cage and resumes a broken chain acts as a powerful symbol of the subject whose "consent" is ontologically separate from that "I." The speaker in these bits of poetry is Clarissa, but a disembodied, fractured, "sottish" version of herself. Comparing this body to a galley slave's portrays the raped body as a physical prison, a space that is, in the imagery of Paper X, both a "cage" and a "strange somewhere." The space of the page itself, like the white space standing in for the rape scene in *Charlotte Temple*, might also be understood to represent that "strange somewhere." With its marginal anarchy and disparate passages, Paper X seems to be moving. *Clarissa* is a story about imprisonment, but the mad papers explore the ruin narrative's ironic visions of the uncontainable through images of captivity. Clarissa's madness exists in opposition to the libertine's individualist subjectivity—hers is instead a radical subjectivity engaged at a site of crossing, an Atlantic seascape, a borderless place. The novel itself resembles the oceanic vastness of that which cannot be contained, the fifteen hundred pages constituting a space inhabited by a woman whose interiority is never, and can never, be "found."

The mad papers remind us that *Clarissa,* the material book, is a space that invites "penetration" yet also a space whose margins might already be open.[28] The mad papers show a seascape—wavelike stanzas rolling off center, headed off the page—in which Clarissa might be escaping *Clarissa,* a rhetorical move that problematizes the body as a fixed precinct of selfhood. The character "Clarissa" defies the man Richardson, denies the very type of subjectivity all those pages have been trying so desperately to insist is (in) there. The rape in Richardson's *Clarissa* is about staging a subjectivity that the villain attempts to injure by penetration, about his pursuit of a body he believes he can colonize, but in every instance, the scene of that violence, that break *in,* is denied.

Paper X reveals that rogue waves of self may, however, break out. While the novel acknowledges the horrors of sexual violation, it also questions what a body is, and whether a body is violable. As Eagleton notes, *Clarissa* insists on "the unspeakable truth that Clarissa is not to be possessed. She is absolutely impenetrable, least of all by rape."[29] Though there is no denying the violent sexual attack against Clarissa, still, something has *not* been accessed, a failure the omission of the rape scene underscores. The violating aims acted out by the politics of consent are simply unenforceable. As a space, then, Paper X is not so much a site of brokenness as it is a site of radical subjectivity, a reminder that even as Richardson seems to wish to write the interiority of self (and then contain it in the body of the novel), it slips away from him, revealing the attempt to be the pursuit of a failed construct. Instead, *Clarissa* becomes a map of what is outside the ideological range of the contract, evidence of extramarginal space inhabited by extramarital bodies.

"Let Me Cut Short the Rest": The Omissions of Rape

Like the containment motif, textual omissions do the work of resisting the consent ideal of contract theory that marriage represents. The problem of omission is a consistent one in the rape-as-ruin text. In *Clarissa,* for example, readers can go fifty pages past the rape scene without knowing it has happened. Richardson manages an oblique line from Lovelace, whose admission of rape reads, "I can go no farther. The affair is over. Clarissa lives" (883). In *Charlotte Temple,* all that readers learn is told through the classically opaque line, "She shrieked, and fainted into the arms of her betrayer" (48). And in *Incidents,* the expected rape of the slave girl never happens at all, but is deftly managed through episodes of deferral and substitution. As readers, we encounter several instruments of omission in these texts, even when we know a rape has occurred. There is the failure to remember the rape, there is the use of metonyms and metaphors for rape, and there is the substitution of one victim for another, so that the rape happens to someone else, someone offstage. All of these literary devices and more contribute to the problem of omission in novels about rape. In searching for the scene of sexual violation, the reader, too, becomes inscribed by the attempt to break into this textual interiority, to unearth its untold secret. The search parallels a search for the violable self of the other. In some ways, through these omissions the novels deny at the metanarrative level the power of rape to achieve its goals, but of course the novels also explore the horrors of rape. How does the omission of rape figure into the aesthetic work of ruin within the rape-as-ruin genre and its resistance to the fiction of consent as a means of oppression? And how do the omissions of rape scenes contribute to the aesthetic work of articulating non-individual models of agency? What do we make of the sexed, suffering body's absence at the moment of its greatest peril?

Again, it is Jacobs's novel that provides answers to these questions through its exposure of consent as a politically fraudulent promise that holds the power of its violation. *Incidents* contributes to the argument that despite its horrific violence, rape fails to achieve its goal of contained, individual subjectivity. In other words, Jacobs forces white readers to acknowledge the horrors of slave rape even as she refuses to present them with a rape scene, and she argues that the slave woman who does not have consent to give or refuse reveals the deeply flawed ideology informing consent as a political ideal. Jacobs's work also critiques the idea that only stories about free white women can reveal rape's ideological failures. The generic play in *Incidents* contributes to both of these tasks. Critics have spent decades establishing that *Incidents* uses, in order to interrogate, the generic rules of the seduction novel. It is important, however, to see just *how* Jacobs uses the generic staples found in a novel like *Clarissa*. One of the most important critiques comes through Jacobs's handling of the omission of the rape scene, and the way that *Incidents* signifies on that omission is worth extended comparison.

The difference between how those omissions are represented in *Clarissa* and *Incidents* is startling. First we have Clarissa's description of rape:

> Let me cut short the rest. I grew worse and worse in my head; now stupid, now raving, now senseless. . . . I remember, I pleaded for mercy—I remember that I said *I would be his—indeed, I would be his*—to obtain his mercy—But no mercy found I!. . . . And then such scenes followed—Oh my dear, such dreadful scenes!—fits upon fits (faintly indeed, and imperfectly remembered) procuring me no compassion. (1011)

And then we encounter Linda's radical departure from that act of forgetting. Instead of offering the story of the master's rape that readers have come to expect, she presents a story of a sexual affair with a white man not her master:

> And now, reader, I come to a period in my unhappy life, which I would gladly forget if I could. The remembrance fills me with sorrow and shame. It pains me to tell you of it; but I have promised to tell you the truth, and I will do it honestly, let it cost me what it may. I will not try to screen myself behind the plea of compulsion from a master; for it was not so. (54)

In its engagement with the politics of consent, Jacobs's text presents a scathing refusal to mimic *Clarissa*'s most famous moment. In referring to her inability to forget, and her refusal to screen herself, Linda shows how the story of the enslaved woman has no access to a vile plot to drug her, to "fits" of hazy, episodic consciousness marring her memory. Instead, she identifies forgetting as a tool that is available only to the white woman. Thus she suggests that the claim of forgetting rape is itself dishonest. She further signifies upon this dishonesty by denying the rape itself, not through forgetting, but through this act of self-ruin. To mimic the dishonesty of forgetting—to repeat it disloyally—is *Incidents*'s rhetorical move, perhaps the only one left for the slave woman, whose pornographic rendering in the white imaginary all but permanently defines her as a subject circumscribed by sexual violence. Through this substitution of rape for seduction, the reader cannot force a way *in* to Linda's rape experience. Indeed, the invention of "Linda," a semi-autobiographical literary character, and the insistence that no violation occurred against this Linda, blocks the reader's own attempt to repeat that violation by discovering it among the pages of Jacobs's novel. *Incidents* thus confronts the reader's own troubled relationship with consent—the reader's desire to penetrate the slave girl, to see into her through the scene of sexual violence against her. If *Clarissa* at times presents its center as a vaginal interiority protecting that which cannot be known except by violence, the reader's gaze into that interiority of the text is blocked in *Incidents* with Linda's refusal to forget, a refusal compounded by the ironic insistence (itself a mimicry of the white women's dishonesty) that there is nothing, no violation, to remember.

In these ways, Jacobs's work overdetermines the omission of rape in order to critique the power of that omission in white seduction-as-rape narratives. In a signifying reproduction of the kind of white forgetting present in novels like *Clarissa*, *Incidents* is devoted to a study of the omissions and elisions of rape. It signifies on the presence/absence binary explored above in the white accounts of rape-as-ruin. Indeed, *Incidents* is loaded with antagonism for the ideal of a self-possessed individual and rich with alternatives to this subjectivity. For while the white use of seduction rhetoric to obscure the rape of the master, or what Saidaiya Hartman calls "the discourse of seduction in slave law," makes the rape of the slave "unimaginable," in *Incidents*, the rhetoric of seduction actually *unmasks* the predatory sexual intent of slavery.[30]

Jacobs portrays Linda turning to self-ruin at the exact moment when in *Clarissa* and *Charlotte Temple* an omission of rape occurs. That is, Linda elects to have a sexual affair with the white man Mr. Sands. This affair is not motivated by the kind of desire operating in novels like *The Power of Sympathy* or *The Coquette*. It is a "deliberate calculation," a move that, as we saw earlier, is echoed by her use of the phallic gimlet to make a hole in her crawlspace (54). In essence, she takes her own virginity, removing it from the master-rapist's grasp and from the traditional scene of consent. So while other texts make it their business to explain why the rape is not remembered, or to obscure its presence altogether except through suggestive metaphor, Linda prefaces her open admission of self-ruin with a different kind of refusal, the refusal to forget.

When it is her turn to explain how her tryst with a white lover led to her ruin, she gives no carriage scene, no chase. "I will not try to *screen* myself behind the plea of compulsion from a master," she writes (54, emphasis added).³¹ Significantly, a few chapters later, the familiar language of "screening" moves from a metaphorical screen to a literal one. When meeting in a decidedly unromantic scene to plead for Mr. Sands to buy her children before he moves out of town, she must wait for him in hiding. "I crawled on my hands and knees to the window," she writes, "and, *screened* behind a barrel, I waited" (128, emphasis added). The obsequious posture, the storeroom floor—these material details describe a cognizant debasement—and later, she notes, "I had slunk down behind a barrel, which entirely *screened* me" (128, emphasis added). Jacobs redirects the "screen" of compulsion to the exigencies of slavery, the hiding of Linda's body doubly announcing her presence. For in this passage as in others following it, Linda's body is not passively hidden so much as it is actively hiding, a rhetorical move that points to the presence of the body's shrewdly managed unavailability to the sexual predator.

The "screening" and its critique of the white rape narrative's omissions continue in *Incidents*. In Jacobs's treatment of female slavery, the text offers everything except a fifteen-year-old girl raped by her master. Several critics have explored the significance of this particular omission. P. Gabrielle Foreman calls these evasions the "field of undertell," whereby Jacobs is able to "systematically come short of the truth" in order to tell it.³² Jacobs packs the passage with as many genres as possible to highlight what is not there: her rape by her master.³³ Geneva Cobb Moore argues that in this context, Linda Brent "is nothing more than an instrument for Jacobs's remembered agony as a slave girl." Georgia Kreiger agrees that Jacobs's problem is "the task of presenting one's present writing self as a radical remove from the self of the past." In other words, Jacobs uses Linda Brent as an unraped slave whose story white readers would not censor. Jacqueline Goldsby agrees—the fact of rape must be "fictionalized" to pave the way for its telling. "Linda" can make claims that, taken as "stories" rather than memories of actual events, are easier to read. When Jacobs wrote *Incidents*, few writers had yet dared discuss the master's rape of the slave in a mainstream publication.³⁴ "Linda," a narrativized, fictional cover, tells the story by not telling it as conspicuously as possible, thus reversing the semiotic message of the "screen" of forgetting in the white seduction narrative.

The omission of rape is what *Incidents* represents most powerfully, as it shows a former slave deploying the seduction novel's generic trait of absent female will, a trait that of course identifies the logic of the seduction tale as following the logic of slavery. The purpose of omitting the rape scene in *Incidents* is to repeat, ironically and disloyally, the rape hail in the white seduction novel. To deploy that omission of the rape scene is to announce it. The omission does the aesthetic work of ruin by revealing as unsuccessful the pursuit of what is *in there,* the failure of rape to construct an interiority it can contain in order to invade. Linda Brent, as we have seen, uses the attic crawl space as her own constructed interiority, a space she violates herself in a disloyal repetition of her own rape that underscores rape's failure to contain her.

It also reveals the failures of the rape hail in *Clarissa* and *Charlotte Temple* all the more powerfully. Several moments of *Incidents* depict Linda in her hideout, secretly observing her master Dr. Flint as he exhibits an enraged frustration over not being able to find her. Read through *Incidents,* Richardson's whole book appears as a testament to that failure to reach inside, the predecessor to Flint's fruitless hunt for the fugitive who is *right there.* The same is true in *Clarissa:* she is *right there,* held in captivity for hundreds and hundreds of pages, yet still "pursued" by Lovelace. As we have seen, Clarissa's telling of her rape is important here in that she says outright she will censor what her imperfect memory from being drugged cannot censor for her. "Let me cut short the rest," she says, just before her incomplete assessment of what happened (1011). Similarly, we find Rowson's narrator, normally so loquacious, saying just before Montraville puts the unconscious Charlotte in the carriage, "It would be useless to repeat the conversation that here ensued" (48). Indeed, the major abridgement itself of the US version of *Clarissa* acts out a "cutting short" of the rape by omitting almost all of the original novel's nuanced exploration of Lovelace's predatory strategies.

In *Incidents,* a similar editorial comment "cuts short" the story of rape. In an anecdotal discussion of a plantation she uses to illustrate the horrors of slavery, Linda briefly remarks, "If they are girls, I have indicated plainly enough what will be their inevitable destiny" (52). In both the omission of conscious personhood and in the omissions of rape scenes, we find the white fantasy of absence exposed. Linda's word "indicated" reveals the trick of the seduction/rape genre. She identifies the master's rape as that which inhabits the white imagination and thus does not need telling but only "indicating." No censorship is necessary, since the rape is already unfolding in the reader's mind, and the narrator's "indication" is enough to point to the origin of that imagining. Linda's remark "plainly enough" points to the predatory imagination of a slaveholding populace. Yet as we are about to see, even with this bold rhetorical move, what comes *before* it is the subject of one of the most compelling and difficult passages in *Incidents*.

From Omission to Substitution

In some ways, *Incidents in the Life of a Slave Girl* still follows the traditional narrative arc of the slave autobiography. It leads with the "I was born" rhetoric of the child who does not know she is a slave, but soon discovers it; this fact moves through the expected phases of innocent childhood, troubled adolescence, master–slave conflict, and finally escape. But the heart of the book is really the moment readers are waiting for, though they never quite get it. Now as then, readers' minds instantly conjure the one "incident" sure to befall a female slave: rape by the master. Jacobs exploits such expectations, beginning with her title, specifically that vexed, suggestive word "incidents."[35] In a life that entailed *seven years* of life in a room the size of a small closet, instead of a title that highlights this astonishing and unique aspect of her life, we get "incidents," and one can hardly conjure a more banal autobiographical stance, except that in this case the word "incidents" is a barely concealed stand-in for rape.

Called "A Perilous Passage in a Slave Girl's Life," chapter 10, in both title and context, refers to the master's rape a bit more directly. Initially, the text presents this assault as an inevitability. The narrator lingers on the meaning of a slave girl's adolescence, "a sad epoch in the life of a slave girl" who "will be compelled to realize she is no longer a child" (26, 27). Jacobs casts Dr. Flint as a sexual predator who whispers repugnant and abusive sexual threats in Linda's ear, telling her of the cabin in which he will keep her. Rape is his explicit goal, here and throughout the narrative. Its description, rhetorically anticipated in this way, speaks to the white female reader's admission into—and admission of—the particular horror of female enslavement, the final avowal of a manifest but unspoken truth, that built into the laws of slavery is the master's rape. Nobody can pick up this book and not expect the telling of this inexorable outrage.

Yet Jacobs's inclusion of the unexpected, unimaginable rape of *someone else* allows for the omission of the slave girl's rape. The failure to deliver what readers expect functions to scrutinize the white woman reader's posturing as a compassionate, sentimental presence witnessing the slave woman's suffering. This part of *Incidents* also "fails to repeat loyally" as Butler would have it, using and then abandoning the genre of the sentimental novel to show that no genre, and no singular protagonist, can tell her story. The word "incidents" seems to promise the reader the pleasure of schadenfreude disguised as charity, but that reader finds herself as the object of a critical gaze instead. Linda mentions the stunning fact of her seven years in the crawl space much later and despite its remarkable shock value, somehow those years manage not to dominate her tale. If the rape of the slave girl is not the dominant fact of Linda's life, why doesn't the book showcase instead this amazing near decade of imprisonment, not as one in a series of incidents, but as the central reality of her life story?

The answer to this question lies at the end of *Incidents*'s previous chapter where that other rape occurs. In quick succession, Jacobs invokes her white reader's mix of excitement and horror at the notion of the female slave's rape, then replaces, or rather in Butlerian terms fails to repeat loyally, that violence with something perhaps more astonishing than those seven years lived in a crawl space. Mimicking a sentimental abolitionist appeal, the narrator begins a discussion about the devastating effects of slavery upon the white community, especially white women who are corrupted by its influences.[36] As she says, "The white daughters early hear their parents quarrelling about some female slave. Their curiosity is excited, and they soon learn the cause" (52). The narrator follows the prurient "excited" with what is perhaps the single most shocking and salacious passage of the entire text: the story of a white daughter *who rapes a male slave* in order to satisfy the excitement by her parents' talk, and, as if that is not enough, the daughter becomes pregnant by the slave, and then frees him before her father can murder him.[37] There's more: "She selected the most brutalized, over whom her authority could be exercised with less fear of exposure" (52). Knowing that her readers await the rape of the female slave, Jacobs instead satisfies their "excitement" with the rape of the slave man, an act that follows the logic of slavery but not the logic of the seduction-as-rape genre. The passage in part becomes an allegory of the white female reader's titillation, followed by an exposure of her desire to read about sexual violation (from which her deepest sympathy can presumably be gleaned).

Only then does Jacobs refer to the master's rape of slave girls with that remark we saw earlier, "If they are girls, I have indicated plainly enough what will be their inevitable destiny" (52). Jacobs thus scrambles the sociology of the moment, as the "incident" figures the white woman not as the victim but as the sexual predator. This move redirects the hail toward the white woman as the *transgressor,* a move in which the hail goes haywire, repositioning the white woman and the male slave so that it is she who performs the role of Dr. Flint, not Linda Brent. Such a redirect of the hail establishes it as an instrument of culture rather than an inherent apparatus of power. The hail no longer constitutes the "inevitable destiny" of social agents, but instead has become that which might be deliberately employed. Once the hail is established as a tool, anyone might wield it, and there is no "inevitable destiny" determined by social norms, most importantly the rape of the slave girl the title of the book so ironically suggests.

In fact, *Incidents* argues that there is nothing "inevitable" about the master's rape except in the cultural imagination. The chapter begins with the odious notion that Dr. Flint has built a "secluded" and "small house" where he will keep the narrator imprisoned. The idea that she will be his sexual slave is explicit. When she learns of this house, she says, "I shuddered; but I was constrained to listen, while he talked of his intention to give me a home of my own, and to make a lady of me" (53). Notably, he delivers this news "[i]n the blandest tones." It is a site of failed repetition indeed, a bitterly ironic revision of domesticity, for what the sentimental story of becoming a "lady" means for the narrator is clear enough; a "home" is a prison; the "lady" is the sexual slave. She shudders but listens all the same, mimicking the white daughters listening to their parents fight over a slave woman.

Redirect the hail, then answer it disloyally: in Jacobs's new rhetoric, no one is legible, and no one has a stable role. Casting the white woman reader as the rapist in part unsettles the self via the unutterable undercurrent of the white reader's desire. To locate the unspeakable within the reader fractures that reader's sense of self. In other words, together, chapters 9 and 10 question the stability of identity, starting with the reader's own. That reader might think she is the maiden but Jacobs casts her as the rake; she thinks she is the victim but she is the rapist. Jacobs seems to be asking: If those roles can be destabilized, who then do readers suppose *she* is?

Indeed, the screen of forgetting gives rise to a new way of thinking about subjectivity. This new perspective attempts to see third terms residing within the ontological dichotomies presented in narratives of ruin: awake/asleep; alive/dead, and that most powerful dichotomy that dominates representations of self in eighteenth- and nineteenth-century literature: consent/resistance. If the foundational concept of liberty—defined as a freedom from compulsion, which is the central justifying motive behind the revolutions in the seventeenth and eighteenth centuries in England, America, Haiti, and France—requires a rational, consenting subjectivity, then to break away from that concept is made to seem like a mistake, a move away from "freedom" being automatically designated as an irredeemable "choice." Such a concept is blind to alternative subjectivities. To refuse to answer "yes" or "no" to the ultimate question informing all contractual relations, namely, "Will you?" is to remove from consent its ideological thrall. The Enlightenment rational mind cannot conceive of a society outside the jurisdiction of the consenting subject as anything other than the Hobbesian nightmare of lawless barbarism. For these narratives, though, the only way to resist force is to exit the sphere of consent altogether. The alternative to the consenting subject must somehow avoid the anarchy and violence of the world without contract, which is to avoid the trap of constant vulnerability to force as a retributive site for those who refuse to *agree* to anything, a trap that enacts a hail to the individual as the self who "signs." Yet this imagined scene of exchange—signature for safety—is a white male fantasy of containment, power, and patriarchal right, privileges that are predicated upon their denial to the enslaved and to white women. In these narratives, that alternative comes in the form of ambivalence, or rather a multivalent state of simultaneous, contradictory desires.

As I have been arguing, the rape wish is defined by the desire to obliterate an individual self, a wish that needs first to imagine an individual, contained in a body, accessible via sexual violence. But the *ruin* of self is defined by a fragmented ontology, the self not located in a single site and imagined instead as a porous and eminently contactable identity, a relational beingness that in the novels discussed in earlier chapters is modeled by desire. The agency question of novels of ruin—if the individual is a limited model of identity in eighteenth- and nineteenth-century seduction novels, what alternative models exist?—is answered through the radical management of embodiment. For when rape fails in its attempt to formulate a contained and containable subjectivity, it is the ontological work of identity we encounter as a response. Though rape has failed in this goal, the women nevertheless remain traumatized as well as sexually ruined. What these texts do with that ruin and its attendant trauma in rape, and how they use it to represent radical agency, is to use omission as a trope that makes the body unavailable to assault, and, more radically, unavailable as a mode of containment.

That rape does actual, immeasurable harm is never in question in these texts, despite the fact that its intended injury does not hit its mark. Rather, we encounter the aesthetic work of undoing binaries, of disentangling force from consent, to show how the individual(ized) subject is limited. This is the work that desire does in the novels discussed in earlier chapters; novels about incest, seduction, and adultery establish the way that agency becomes something that can exist between emotional and physical bodies, a current of feeling that constitutes shared desires forming shared identities. The aesthetic work of ruin in rape-as-ruin stories also interrogates the idea of consent as definitive of individual, contractual subjectivity. For Clarissa and Charlotte, their entries into the carriages driven by Lovelace and Montraville are neither forced nor intentional. Linda's stay in a tiny crawl space is both compulsory and voluntary. Clarissa both freely enters and is held captive in a whorehouse. In other words, it is the intersection between consent and force upon which stories of rape-as-ruin linger.

In Toni Bowers's excellent study of rape and seduction, *Force or Fraud,* she notes that these stories "dethrone the liberal fantasy of consent-or-resistance in order to experiment with other relational rubrics." As rape shifted historically in meaning from theft to sexual force, "the Enlightenment's ideas about individual subjectivity and consensual government" redefined rape. Indeed, "by exercising submission and refusal simultaneously, a newly nuanced model for virtuous subjecthood . . . emerged in a time of severe constraint." In the "force or fraud" dichotomy, Bowers astutely notes that the "or" is the "disturbing remainder" that "at once creates distinction and suggests synonymy." As the hinge of the dichotomy, the word "or" expresses a "sly tendency to complicate attempts to define a stable difference between seduction's consent and rape's resistance" that is difficult to negotiate for novelist and reader alike. Without questioning the "abomination" of rape, the instability of this "or" "inhabits a space between action and passivity, a third way that partakes of the other two but that cannot be reduced to either."[38]

Ambivalence, not refusal, is thus posited as the opposite of consent, and that opposition furthers the depiction of contract culture's understanding of consent as a political fraudulence. In the famous kidnapping scene, for example, Clarissa runs *toward* Lovelace's carriage while simultaneously refusing to go with him. Describing this ambivalence, she says, "my voice, however, contradicting my action; crying, No, no, no, all the while" (380); in the American version, this is, notably, one of the scenes in which the omniscient narrator does not divert significantly from the original, saying "her voice contradicted her actions, for while she was running she continually kept crying, No, no, no" (67). Emphatically, this is not an exemplification of Rousseau's misogynist chivalry that defines "no" as a woman's demure reluctance to utter a straightforward "yes." Something much more radical is happening during this moment, something nearly illegible and indeed a kind of political paradox: Clarissa's actions stage yes *and* no at the same moment, constituting *the same response*. That response is a multivalent utterance that speaks to an alternative to the individual.

Charlotte's expostulation about her torn heart at the moment of her kidnapping is similarly marked by a powerful ambivalence. We will remember that at the moment where she would otherwise have been said to make a "choice," she says, "'Alas! My torn heart!'" adding "'how shall I act?'" (48) The labial semiotic power of the heart represents it as an organ of sentiment and sex, alongside its depiction as both the symbol of ambivalence and a site of genital violence. Rowson writes, "Alas! when once a woman has forgot the respect due to herself, by yielding to the solicitations of illicit love," then "in the eyes of the man whose art has betrayed them" she has lost her claim to respect. Rowson continues, "every libertine will think he has a right to insult her with his licentious passion; and should the unhappy creature shrink from the insolent overture, he will sneeringly taunt her with pretence of modesty" (62–63). In other words, Charlotte has ceded her right to say "no," and the passage suggests as directly as it can that Montraville has raped her, and may do so again at any time.[39]

Indeed, this ambivalence speaks to what Marion Rust describes as "a female populace with increasingly limited capacity to experience themselves as independent, coherent beings," a notion of self that was "at best [an] unwieldy fit with the mechanisms of agency in the new republic."[40] In other words, the patriarchal rule in the new republic prevented women from obtaining status as individuals. In some cases, this leads not to a more aggressive pursuit of such subjectivity, but to the pursuit of much more radical "mechanisms of agency." Such mechanisms may make room for the simultaneity of "no" and "yes" that does not justify rape but forms a subjectivity immune to its totalizing goals. Thus Bowers notes "the disturbing truth" that Lovelace knows just as well as Clarissa does "that Clarissa went off against her consent *and* as a result of her own collusion."[41] This radical observation is equally applicable to Charlotte. Rowson offers a passage that exemplifies space apart from the consent/refusal binary when Montraville puts Charlotte into the carriage. "'No,' said she, withdrawing from his embrace, 'I am come to take an everlasting farewell,'" a refusal she articulates just at the moment when her "resolution began to waver, and he drew her almost imperceptibly toward the chaise" (48).

The strata of refusals and collusions, the confusion of bodies both present and absent, all work toward a nonjurisdictional embodiment that insists on an erratic corporeality and a vacillating, precarious characterization of will. Although it may seem at first that feminist politics ought to repudiate any argument that denies consent to women, especially within the context of sexual violence, it is important to note what is at stake in the seduction-as-rape narrative. The conversation these narratives are having is about subjectivity itself and is a very different conversation than the one feminists are having about rape centuries later. In these eighteenth- and nineteenth-century texts, feminism occupies the space that refuses yes and no as separate or distinct, since "no" is not an available, sincere utterance according to the logic of a supremacist patriarchy. Ambivalence articulates a refusal to become the violable subject, a refusal to inhabit one's body as a container that is always already violable. It prohibits the body from being read as an invitation to that which the subject does not want. Ambivalence insists that relationships are networked and relational. To suggest that this ambivalence is a justification for sexual attack misunderstands the aesthetic work with which these novels engage.

And in fact none of these novels exhibits any ambivalence whatsoever about the terrorizing injustice of sex by force. *Clarissa* especially lingers on the destructive aftermath of rape, and the entire premise of *Incidents* is flight from the master's rape, a prospect filled with such horror that it prompts Linda to make the most tremendous sacrifices to prevent it. Yet invested as they are in depicting rape as a horror, the novels still include these passages about ambivalence and agency. Just before Lovelace's rape, we might recall, Clarissa says, "I remember that I said I would be his—indeed I would be his—to obtain his mercy" (1011). Of course it is entirely unclear what this might mean. Is she saying she will marry him if he refrains from raping her? That she will consent to sex if he will remove the element of force?

Willingness and unwillingness are indiscernible. The main point of the scene is to elude the yes/no binary. She does not reject Lovelace so much as she rejects the dishonest rhetoric of refusal. Her *refusal to be clear* denies the gendered codes of contract culture that will hear her "no" as a Rousseauian "yes."

Similarly, Jacobs shows Linda to both choose and not choose Mr. Sands, for hers is a "calculation" rather than an affair of the heart. As Hartman notes, slavery ensures that "the captive female was both will-less and always already willing," such that the female slave's body is "inhabited by sexuality" rather than expressive of experience or desire. The "discourse of seduction in slave law" makes the rape of the slave "unimaginable."[42] To combat the hail that teaches the subject to hear her name spoken in the accusatory "Hey, you," the aesthetic work of the rape-as-ruin text is to deny the hail its power by answering twice, by answering yes *and* no. This is to run toward the very thing one refuses, to offer a polyvocal response to the hail that attempts to reduce the respondent to an "I." To answer twice refutes the hail much more powerfully than an unheard utterance of the word "no" ever could.

The "Ruin" of Authorship

One of the most stunning commonalities among Richardson's *Clarissa*, its American abridgement, Jacobs's *Incidents*, and Rowson's *Charlotte Temple* is how utterly strange they all are. *Clarissa*'s very voluminousness announces its uniqueness, pointing to Richardson the author in pursuit of a subjectivity he cannot ever quite reach. The American edition counters with its own announcement of what makes it different, confronting readers with the missing fourteen hundred pages and the change to an omniscient narrator. Jacobs's narrative, too, relies on constant generic instability and pronoun play, work with authorship that obfuscates the author as such (readers often forget to refer to "Linda," as the story seems so much to be Jacobs's own). And Rowson's many authorial intrusions, with the emotive outbursts of the motherly narrator, show how even the most conservatively wrought storytelling can reflect back on the storyteller in metafictional ways.[43] The challenge is in reading these texts at all without getting entirely lost in them.

Again, *Incidents* teaches us how to work through this challenge. Understanding the more unusual characteristics of *Incidents* helps us to do so. We ought to begin by examining its lack of a single identifiable genre, or even an identifiable protagonist. That is, while Jacobs's text is about identity, it is not exactly an autobiography; while it uses the seduction tale as a rhetorical model, it could not work if it allowed itself to be indistinguishable from the stories we would associate with that genre. There are two current schools of thought about the genre instability in *Incidents*. The first holds that Jacobs's text is an overtly anti-individualist endeavor. Critics argue that Jacobs's tale promotes interdependence, rather than independence, as the superior principle that ought to govern social relations, and that this move constitutes a radical rejection of the ostensibly prevailing American value of individualism in the nineteenth century.[44] According to this reading of *Incidents*, there are simply too many layers of self in Jacobs's work for the individual to take up significant narrative space—pseudonyms, disguises, performances, and the like exist instead—and Jacobs uses these narrative devices to sustain an instability of identity from the first page to the last.[45] The other school of critical thought considers the impact of the book's "oft-noted schizophrenic quality."[46] Jacobs incorporates several genres into a single narrative, critics contend, manipulating genres that traditionally belong to black men and white women, in order to tell her story in ways that subvert the racial and gendered oppressions of her day and to "accommodate her particular experience."[47] Such interpretations further maintain that the mixing of genres allows Jacobs to tell, between the lines, the story of the slave woman's rape, a story that could not be told in explicit terms. According to this reading, Jacobs's text should not be classified generically. *Incidents* belongs to none of them because it belongs to all of them.

In addition to these two readings, we might say that in Butlerian terms, *Incidents* repeats, disloyally, the traits of multiple genres. One particularly telling example of just such a failed repetition in *Incidents* occurs during Linda's recounting of her first sexual encounter with Mr. Sands. During this complex passage, Jacobs uses her narrator to explore the possibilities of agency in a world that denies personhood. Her narrative is full of slippery pronouns that resist a singular self. They suggest an agency at work that exists well outside the bounds of Enlightenment personhood: as we are about to see, even in a single paragraph, Jacobs refers to herself as "I," "we," "they," "she," and "you," and this navigation among first and second person, singular and plural, argues for a redefinition of ruin as the site of a polyontological identity. Such a rhetorical strategy entirely dissociates self from singularity. The grammatical and ontological illegibility of this stance contraindicates corporeal containment. She is not *in there* but is instead everywhere and nowhere. *She* is none of them because she is all of them.

As the moment arrives when readers expect Dr. Flint's sexual assault on Linda, instead, we encounter a seduction tale about the narrator as a ruined woman having an illicit affair with a different white man, one not her master. The narrator offers a strange mixture of agency and absence when she recounts this liaison, which, weirdly, she uses as a ploy to escape the unwanted advances of Dr. Flint, the idea being that because she has given herself to another man, he has been denied the pleasure of "ruining" her himself. Recounting her illicit affair with Mr. Sands, she begins the passage in the first person singular, and in the first three and a half paragraphs of this so-called "confession," the narrator uses the word "I" twenty-seven times. But then this "I" disappears, and the shift into multiple pronouns that ensues causes the text to rupture. Within the space of a paragraph, we move from this:

> I have promised to tell you the truth, and I will do it honestly . . . I will not try to screen myself. . . . Neither can I plead ignorance or thoughtlessness . . . I knew what I did, and I did it with deliberate calculation.

To this:

> It seems less degrading to give *one's self*, than to submit to compulsion. There is something akin to freedom in having a lover who has no control over *you*. . . . A master may treat *you* as rudely as he pleases, and *you* dare not speak. . . . There may be sophistry in all this; but the condition of *a slave* confuses all principles of morality, and, in fact, renders the practice of them impossible. (54–55, emphases added)

Several questions arise from such a shift. Why does the narrator insist that she will not screen herself, and then seem to do exactly that as the text slides into the pronoun play of "you," "one's self," and "a slave"? Why does she use "I" so often and then abandon it entirely? Who is ultimately the speaker here—is this Linda Brent the character, Linda Brent the pseudonymous

Jacobs, or Jacobs herself intervening as a sort of omniscient narrator? And what genre of text is this, when we move so quickly from the blunt first-person singular confessional of a criminal plot to the "sophistry" of multiple pronouns to the sentimental lament, "O, ye happy women, whose purity has been sheltered from childhood!" (54)?[48] In this desertion of the first person singular, Jacobs's narrative disputes the notion that freedom necessitates the self-possession of personhood. Such a position rejects the authority of the singular individual, what Stephanie A. Smith refers to as "Mr. Self Reliance," the white heterosexual man who is the exclusive heir to the rights of sovereignty and citizenship. Smith takes this notion one step further, by adding that "what Jacobs throws open to revision is the whole framework of individuality that has supported the value of 'liberty' in nineteenth-century American culture." In its place, Jacobs supplies "an alternative definition of identity" that offers "an alternative version of national identity," one based on interdependence and one that eschews a masculine, solipsistic singularity.[49]

Jacobs's passage above certainly resonates with Hannah Webster Foster's *The Coquette*. We might recall from chapter 4 the passage in which Eliza characterizes her agency as that which is irretrievably relational and therefore something she cannot control:

> The heart of your friend is again besieged. Whether it will surrender to the assailants or not, I am unable at present to determine. Sometimes I think of becoming a predestinarian, and submitting implicitly to fate, without any exercise of free will; but, as mine seems to be a wayward one, I would counteract the operations of it, if possible. (122)

It is almost as if Eliza is a participant-observer in her own volition, an ontological curiosity that suggests she both is and is not "herself." The pronoun play of Linda's "confession" above, alongside the role of pseudonym in *Incidents,* is an equally curious example of ontological uncertainty, since the "I" of slave autobiography is such a central characteristic of the genre. "I was born" constitutes the immediacy of a real self, a real person in the here and now: I am here, hear me, I am a man. Yet the pseudonym (if that's what it is), this vexing figure of "Linda Brent," often goes unremarked, especially because modern editions identify "Harriet Jacobs" as the author on the book's cover. As I noted earlier, some critics simply refer to "Jacobs" as the autobiographical protagonist of this text. But then readers may assume an absence of irony in a story about how to hide—about how to utter, ironically, the paradox of slave presence: "I am not (in) here." This narrator's identity is in part a double-voiced figure speaking truth.[50] But the idea that one might be an author with two names offers another interpretation of how identity operates in this book. "Linda Brent" is a narrative device and an author and a pseudonym, a cloaking device and an alias and a disguise. The layers without center suggest the *ruin* of self but not its violation.

They also offer an argument about authorship, the notion that in order "[t]o write a realistic account" of slavery, "one must rewrite his or her own appearance and fictionalize his or her own identity."[51] Interrogating what it means to fictionalize in this way is central to our understanding of Jacobs's text. To fictionalize is to call what is true a story, and to call the person to whom it happens a character. "Linda," as the named protagonist, turns Jacobs the person into Linda the character, what Michael Bennett calls "her greatest creation, herself."[52] A character has an amplified humanity, but also a representational dimension, no matter how realistic the portrayal. A character is malleable, interpretable, not a person who is, but a representation, a figure who exists *as* a person. The power of the character thus lies in part in the fact that he or she is the reader's intellectual property, a repository of the reader's wishes as directed by the author. Within the world of the text, a character can have an additional layering of identities. We might compare Jacobs's use of character in this way to moments like, for example, Clarissa saying after her rape, "my name is—I don't know what my name is!" (890). She becomes radicalized as a figure of ever-increasing pluralities, her amnesia making her in some ways the perfect American, one ready to invent herself as many ways as possible. "I am no longer what I was in any one thing," she asserts (890). If anything is omitted in such a moment, it is the possibility of containing such a multitudinous identity. And *Incidents* may be said to be entirely about such a plurality.

The pronoun play of Jacobs's text achieves the same goal of evading a totalizing and thus objectifying gaze. If in her rape scene's inversion of race and gender, Jacobs has established that her reader is reading with the gaze of a white female rapist—if the act of reading is recast as an attempt to "break in"—the ensuing pronoun play won't let that attempt be successful. The text will not let readers "in" because it shows there is no self/other, in/out dichotomy in the first place. When Jacobs depicts the rapist as a white woman, white female readers must encounter their own imagined intent, a violating gaze that Jacobs simply directs to the male slave to reveal what Marcus Wood calls the sadistic pornographic intent of the slaver's gaze.[53] The reader has sought Jacobs's interiority, only to be confronted by the pronoun play and generic mixture that denies the reader a hidden "self" to be exposed.

This confrontation recalls the strange battle Richardson seems to be waging, or more generously, the one he seems to be staging, in *Clarissa*. If the character Clarissa defies the man Richardson, denies the very subjectivity the novel insists is "in" there, then the character Linda parallels that of Clarissa, as a character who unleashes the tremendous possibility of a multivocal response to the authorship that brought her into being, the promise of telling your story with as many voices as are speaking within you, a Bakhtinian identity formation.

The US edition[54] of *Clarissa* reflects such multiplications, as well as the fragmentations, elisions, and omissions that occur in the rape-as-ruin narrative. In that 1773 abridgement of Richardson's novel, a vast ocean of text has gone missing. Together, the omniscient narrator of the American edition (who has replaced the epistolary multivocality of Richardson's original and who is clearly not telling the whole story) and this omission of nearly fifteen hundred pages assist the cagey narrative play at stake in the literary production of the self's ruin. In her extensive study of the many editions Richardson's novel underwent in the 150 years after its initial publication, Leah Palmer Price notes that the US abridgement speaks to issues much more complex than an American readership that did not want to slog through a very long book. Says Price, "The impossibility of fitting all eight volumes of *Clarissa* . . . into the human mind at once turns readers into editors."[55] A reader's interaction with the text necessarily involves memory's editorial function. The act of editing itself, of cutting and splicing a text, can be said to be part and parcel of any act of reading but especially an act of reading so much. In addition, Price notes that the use of the third-person in the abridgement's switch to omniscient narrator cannot be said to serve the editorial cutting short of a text. "Brevity," she reminds us, "has no intrinsic connection with narrative distance: a sentence phrased in the past tense and the third person is no shorter than one in the present and the first."[56]

The relationship between authors and texts is thus at stake in the abridgement. Intriguingly, Richardson could not stop with the mere telling of his story; the text of *Clarissa* includes strange post-textual matter, including a long postscript and efforts to make *Clarissa* appear to be a collection of actual letters written by living people. In its original form, *Clarissa*'s weird paratextual elements fussily insist there is an author at work among all these letters, while nevertheless presenting that author's coy gestures toward anonymity. (Richardson appears then as the person who "found" and published these letters, not the writer who created them.) The quotations, footnotes, and summaries included in the original *Clarissa* show how Richardson was concerned with whether an author can contain a text. Yet the massiveness of *Clarissa* is not resolved via omniscient narration; instead, it seems to reject epistolarity itself. The same may be going on in Richardson's own work, for, as Price notes, "By paraphrasing the letters that it refrains from reproducing, [Richardson's] post script draws attention to the novel's eleventh-hour repudiation of the epistolary mode."[57] Price continues, "Within the covers of the first edition as much as over the course of its publication history, *Clarissa* set into motion the shift towards a single impersonal voice that abridgements would eventually complete."[58]

Richardson's prolixity, and the subsequent abridgements it invited publishers to make, offer models of authorship and editing as attempts to contain—to contain a story, a text, an interiority. The abridgement omits the epistolary promise of individual self formation, the first-person singular recording its own existence. What the shift to omniscient narrator means in this context is difficult to determine. There is an irresolvable tension in the abridged *Clarissa* between the omniscient narrator (as an isolating, containing force, the "I" that cannot be refuted or refused) and the rejection of the epistolary "I" that establishes the interiority of the individual. Ultimately, though, the omniscient narrator, who cannot possibly know or plumb the interior depths of the subject, offers an intriguing rejection of epistolarity's attempt to do so.

The question of why the abridgement was preferred by American readers is taken up by Leonard Tennenhouse's *The Importance of Feeling English*. The abridgements are less about lazy American readers, Tennenhouse argues, than about highlighting elements of plot that represent how to sustain, while editing, the Englishness of the family as an institution serving the exchange of women as property.[59] Through its omissions, however, the "bare bones" plot of the abridgement loses its literary value. The original novel's extended mapping of self constitutes a literariness that the abridgement abandons. For Tennenhouse, in the unabridged *Clarissa* preferred by readers in England, Richardson "gave . . . Clarissa a form of interiority whose verbal prowess challenged the libertine's powers of sexual enticement and intellectual mastery." The abridgement offers instead a completely "replaceable" Clarissa, one whose sacred peculiarity as a character—as an individual—matters little.⁶⁰ In other words, Richardson used the combination of epistolarity and length to explore what an individual is by having Clarissa unveil her innermost thoughts and feelings through written words, which suggests that our most intimate selves are contained inside us, and can be let out only with deliberate expression.

Though Tennenhouse's overall purpose is to explain that the literature available in British colonial and post-revolutionary America tells us something of the cultural needs of readers and writers trying to sustain their English identity, his analysis of the role of individuality in the two editions is worth extended discussion. There is clearly, as he notes, a "lack of literary interiority" at work in the abridged version of the novel so popular in America. The use of an omniscient narrator, in lieu of long letters written in the first-person singular of the characters themselves, omits the possibility of an extended interest in designing that interiority of character. Yet that which we call literary can also be read as the ideological investment in individual identity. He adds that "[s]tripped" of its artful quality, the US abridgement lacks Clarissa's "exquisite awareness of sexual propriety."⁶¹ According to such terms, a text is "literary" in part because it values self, and expresses that value as superior in its use of nuanced and figurative language about that self; the unabridged *Clarissa* has aesthetic merit because of its almost inexhaustible verbal investment in self-construction. Whether readers of both texts will find Richardson's original work more aesthetically pleasing may depend on how this literariness acts as an embrace of the individual, which necessitates a kind of gregariousness from characters in an epistolary novel as they go on about how they feel.

Tennenhouse says of the original Clarissa, "The putative author—though a woman—was the model for 'the individual,' and her discourse presumed that virtually anyone with sufficient literacy could emulate a brand of interiority that denoted a superior quality of Englishness."⁶² The problem with this reading is that it goes on to ignore that putative authorship; the fact remains that Clarissa's voice is not a woman's voice—it is the voice of a man ventriloquizing a woman's exposure of what he imagines is her distinctly female interiority. Indeed, if Richardson is to be credited with contributing to the formation of the individual as such, then his model for the individual is not Clarissa but a gendered mode of authorship, the male gaze seeking to penetrate the contained self of a woman. It is thus that Tennenhouse can add that "Richardson made passive aggression—withholding of the self—into a sublime testament to selfhood."[63] Yet the story is also, as Tennenhouse notes, about keeping one's body safe from sexual violation. This seems less a testament to selfhood than evidence that selfhood can be a liability to any woman imagined to possess it. Self-possession is a perilous state for the female subject, since if she possesses a self, it is read by the libertine—and indeed perhaps the author (or by this kind of authorship)—as a Rousseauian invitation, as the promise of access.

The abridgement may have a different sort of agenda. It keeps all the major conflicts of the story intact: Clarissa's refusal to marry a man she does not love despite extreme familial pressure, her flight from her father's house with Lovelace, her captivity in the hands of Lovelace, the fire he stages to get into her bedroom, and of course her drugging, rape, and death. Notably, in these key scenes, the story is retold nearly word for word. Yet these fidelities to the original text are surely overshadowed by the massive amount of text that has gone missing, the metatextual erasure of *Clarissa's* journey from England to the United States. The abridgement is a book you hold in your hands knowing that most of it is gone. It speaks of its own absence, its new, lighter form functioning as a constant reminder of what it once was. And this absence calls forth the ghost of those other pages. Indeed, now as then, instead of a simple omission, the abridgement invites readers to fill in the blanks—to imagine those letters, to give voice to those characters themselves—and in so doing readers accomplish the work of each epistolary "I" that has been edited out. The text asks readers to create a sympathetic encounter between themselves and this *Clarissa,* to find its many voices speaking within themselves. Understood this way, the omission of fourteen hundred pages does not so much offer evidence of an inviolable interior subjectivity, a sublime self reveling in its interiority, as it invites the intriguing possibility of readers inventing *all* of those (distinctly multiple) interiorities for and within themselves.

We might look at the way that the rape scene appears in both editions to more fully explore the roles of narrative perspective and interiority in each. As we saw earlier, in the original *Clarissa,* Clarissa writes:

> I remember, I pleaded for mercy—I remember that I said *I would be his—indeed I would be his—*to obtain his mercy—But no mercy found I! My strength, my intellects, failed me!—And then such scenes followed—Oh my dear, such dreadful scenes!—fits upon fits (faintly, indeed, and imperfectly remembered) procuring me no compassion—but death was withheld from me. That would have been too great a mercy! (1011)

In the abridged version, we read:

> What followed was the most base and inhuman acts of violence. The poor *Clarissa*, roused from the dreadful lethargy into which she was sinking, pleaded for mercy, and cried, I will be yours—Indeed I will be yours to obtain your mercy. But no mercy could she find. Her strength, her intellects failed her. Fits upon fits followed, which procured her no compassion. And death was withheld from her, which she would have received as the greatest mercy. (US ed., 100–101)

What stands out the most is perhaps the clarity of what has happened. In the abridged edition, the prefatory line, "What followed was the most base and inhuman acts of violence," clarifies that Lovelace rapes Clarissa. But the narrative voice is, in scenes so full of drama and emotion, a powerful reminder that Clarissa does not speak for herself in this text; apart from short instances of dialogue, readers must supply her voice, and the voices of all the other characters in the novel, elsewhere. I do not mean to suggest that the epistolary "I" is a pronoun walled in from a reader's sympathy. But what would readers have done with that "she," knowing as they did that most of the book was missing?

President Adams's famous remark about *Clarissa* that we saw at work in chapter 3 reminds us that what is so central to this question is the role of consent, or rather its refusal, in the story. How Adams saw Richardson's libertine as a model for a corrupt democracy is worth a second look in this light: "When the people once admit his courtship, and permit him the least familiarity, they soon find themselves in the condition of the poor girl, who told her story in this affecting style. . . . Democracy is Lovelace, and the people are Clarissa. The artful villain will pursue the innocent lovely girl to her ruin and her death."[64] What I mean to suggest is that when *Clarissa* arrives in America, readers of the abridgement are admitting a kind of courtship. They are, in essence, answering an invitation, answering what we might even call a hail. In Adams's remark, Clarissa's consent initiates the patriarchy's rape narrative ("*admit* his courtship"). But it may be that in their relationship to the lacunae of all of those missing pages, readers "admit" a multivocality. To permit such familiarity is to be ruined; for readers of the abridgement, this may mean experiencing the feelings and thoughts of others through an act of sympathetic authorship.

In this chapter, I have tried to show how part of the aesthetic work of the rape-as-ruin narrative is the heroine's refusal to experience embodiment as containment. Her refusal is part of a larger rejection of the ideology of self-possession. Neither the marriage plot nor the rape plot (the two sides of the consent narrative) works to represent the kind of sympathetic subjectivity that the novels under consideration here offer as an alternative to the self-possessed individual. Indeed, in both the original and the abridged versions of *Clarissa,* the heroine staunchly refuses the imperative to marry Lovelace, though he tries in a kind of despotic fury to force her to do that as well. Her refusal is clear. "I am not married—ruined, as I am, by your assistance, I bless God, I am *not* married to this miscreant," cries Clarissa in both versions. If there is one truth both editions of *Clarissa* agree upon, it is that marriage is a prison that reduces consent to a mere fiction.[65]

If democracy is a rake, and, as Clarissa suggests, tyranny is a husband, then it must be asked: What is the monarchy that the new nation has just rejected? It is time to consider the figure of the monarch and his role in Enlightenment understandings of ruin. As we shall soon see, the monarch is a figure that speaks to the fraught interrelations of consent, sovereignty, and the sexed, suffering body. Examining this figure will bring us back to Hobbes and Shaftesbury, back to the questions about what constitutes a political body. Does that body consent to rule? To representation? Or do the political body's natural, if grotesque, attractions form a different kind of civil society altogether? What sort of nation do ruined bodies build?

CONCLUSION

The Anatomy of Ruin

(I am large, I contain multitudes.)
—Walt Whitman, *Leaves of Grass*, 1855

Throughout all the iterations of the ruin narrative thus far considered, one characteristic remains consistent: the aesthetic work that the sexed, ruined body does to forge communities. This work leaves no room for the individual and indeed contests that figure's right to be imagined as a mainstay of Enlightenment sovereignty in the antebellum Atlantic. But a pressing political question underlying this aesthetic work opens the genre to a new field of inquiry. The ruin narrative represents the sexual fall as a political ideal, yet the ruined body is also necessarily a suffering one. An unwavering staple of the genre is the body in crisis. This genre requires torment: bodies ruled by lust, harangued by angry mobs, broken by the labor of birth, violated by the horrors of rape. Ruined bodies are not merely suffering from a loss of sexual chastity. They are poisoned, drowned, and forced into suicide; they are beaten, enslaved, and imprisoned. These are tales of bodies in peril—of bodies ruined not just sexually but vitally and anatomically. Why?

A brief review of the iconography of the age reveals the answer. For alongside the prose texts of ruin, sometimes even among their pages, a visual representation of the body politic was also being circulated, in frontispieces, political cartoons, engravings, and portraits, to name but a few sources. These images explore, graphically, the notion that nation building requires a nonjurisdictional subjectivity, and in doing so they explore the political logic of ruin. Not surprisingly, perhaps, early instances of such images accompanied the philosophical and political writings of the Atlantic

Enlightenment that posited increasingly democratic formulations of sovereignty. They were produced and circulated throughout the Atlantic world in the seventeenth and eighteenth centuries, finally taking on a new life in the forging of the American republic. And like novels about incest, seduction, martyrdom, and rape, they imagine an Enlightenment subjectivity through the dual lenses of sex and violence.

It is the final claim of this book that a political body is necessarily a ruined body. In these visual representations of post-revolutionary Atlantic nation building, bodies are ruined, sexually and anatomically, in the forging of shared political power. The images sketch out what a democratic or parliamentary state might mean, showing how political bodies experience a kind of intimacy when they come together, through force or social attraction, to form a civic body. The intimacy of *e pluribus unum* (and the *e pluribus unum* of sex) invests a peculiar kind of political capital in the Enlightenment subject, and it is violence that achieves this intimacy. What the erotic underlife of such political intimacy tells us about these joinings is that sexed, broken bodies achieve the democratic values the ruin genre seeks to define.

Indeed, the more commonplace Enlightenment images of sovereignty constitute a study of the era's indecent and sometimes bloodthirsty imagination, of its tendency to use sex and violence in tandem to represent civic spaces and political associations. In these images, the political body so often misread as the site of self-possession, mastery, and industry—in other words, as an individual—is in fact illustrated as an erotically charged, and sometimes violently maimed, grotesque mass of bodies,[1] a crowd forged by principles of democracy run amok. We can see the ruinous aesthetic work of this grotesquerie in the illustrations designed and commissioned by two figures already considered at some length in this study, Thomas Hobbes[2] and Anthony Ashley Cooper, the Third Earl of Shaftesbury, alongside the famous political cartoons of Benjamin Franklin.[3] In addition to writing important historical, philosophical, and political texts that made them three of the most famous figures of the Atlantic Enlightenment, each of them personally created or commissioned images that depict the experience of shared political power as a strangely erotic, yet darkly violent, moment of embodiment. Taken collectively, their graphic work provides a visual logic for the antebellum ruin narrative's claim that the democratic body as the Enlightenment imagined it must by its very nature also be a ruined one.

In conversation with competing notions of Enlightenment subjectivity, the images created by Hobbes, Shaftesbury, and Franklin work to deny the supremacy of the individual. Like illicit sex, the acts of violence required to construct the grotesque political bodies of their works stage a rupturing of the body's boundaries. The examples of violence considered below serve as a reminder that the body is not (and never was) inviolate. In these images, sexed and broken bodies are figured as permeable, disassembled artifacts of the modern nation. Both sex and violence represent modes of opening the body, of triggering its receptiveness to joinings with the (political) other. They represent the body in intimate collectivity. Ruin, in both the bed and the public square, stages the scene of that collectivity, which nullifies the fantasy of the body as a mode of isolated containment. In other words, these images provide a visual language that, like the rhetoric of the ruin novel, uses sex and violence to accomplish the same aesthetic work, and this work gauges the Enlightenment as an age in which political bodies are not just broken into but understood to be porous, assembled of parts that constitute a disunified subjectivity that democratic unions require.

The images designed by Hobbes, Shaftesbury, and Franklin represent a much more radical political ontology than the one that posits the self-possessed individual as the centerpiece of the people's sovereignty. Their images are composed of bits and pieces from disassembled and reassembled bodies that en masse suggest a public totality where the inviolate individual subject might have been. They are positively fixated on the erotic incongruities of the grotesque body and its somatic history of detachments and reattachments. Bodies are forced together, then torn apart and rearranged in frightening configurations. The joints of these grotesque bodies—where sex and violence define the unseemly seams of these mergers—testify to the power of the radical civic hail at the center of Enlightenment political formations. And, crucially, they illustrate the idea that it takes a disunified subject to refuse the monarchical hail.

These images illustrate the ontology of ruin on the scale of the nation. The shared embodiments they depict—a sharing accomplished through violence—deny the Enlightenment fantasy of embodiment as a condition of isolated containment. They depict a grotesque multitude: masses of people forming a mutilated assembly. In image after image, the sovereign body is composed of parts that are amassed only to be sliced and butchered, then refastened and rebonded. These ruined bodies are often quite sexual in nature; they are interosculatory hybrids inhabiting a distinctly polyontological quarter. Indeed, the cycles of separation and unification, of amputations and fusions, often of phallic or otherwise sexualized "parts" that are forced, or that fit, together, lead to some profoundly freakish models of liberal subjectivity. They are bodies that must be ruined to do the work of nation building that the Enlightenment age requires. Such depictions assert a political relationship between severance and hybridity. They show a condition of disjointedness that on the one hand speaks to anxiety about union and on the other speaks to a nearly fetishistic impulse toward sexed, illicit joinings. And in doing so, they work through what they mark as the ontological trauma of citizenship.

The literary ruin narrative and the iconography of political formation do the same aesthetic work of wrecking the integrity of bodies in order to explain how nations work. They devote themselves to observing the hinge of the grotesque, the precise juncture at which these disfigured, disjointed bodies join together into a mass. This grotesque hinging is, in some of the most famous images of Enlightenment political bodies, depicted as the site of a shared or democratic sovereignty. Where bodies meet is the site of sovereignty in the ruin narrative as well as in the grotesque multitude. In both tales of sexual ruin and images of Enlightenment community, it is in the nature of union to ruin bodies. In the wake of that ruin lies the fantasy of self-possession and the jurisdictional mode of embodiment it implies.

Hobbes's Sexed Sovereign

Critical study of that fantasy necessarily begins by returning to the image of Hobbes's sovereign giant. The mode of ruin at stake in the cover of *Leviathan* (1651), a text immeasurably important to the American founders and indeed throughout Enlightenment Europe, features a dramatic mode of bodily ruin.[4] Though there is some debate about the artist responsible for the engraving, there is little doubt that Hobbes himself was deeply involved in its design. There is reason to believe that the original sketch Hobbes invested so much time in, and that he eventually sent to the restored King Charles II, was commissioned from the well-known artist Wenceslaus Hollar, and that the image that appears on the frontispiece was a simplified revision of Hollar's work done by the engraver Abraham Bosse.[5] As we saw in chapter 2, Bosse's version tells a powerful visual story about both the civic body's capacity for disassembly and about the monstrous construction of this body out of constituent "parts." The original, and infinitely creepier, sketch by Hollar illuminates the point quite effectively. (See figure 5.) The image hovers somewhere between a medieval, mystic understanding of the king's two bodies ("the body natural" and "the body civil," about which more in a moment) and a reference to the beheading of Charles I in 1649. An image designed to illuminate the sovereign unity of a monarch and his people, it perversely insists on depicting the kind of political unrest and antimonarchical sentiment that led to civil war and regicide, a historical moment that, it is important to note, helped to make the American Revolution's repudiation of King George III imaginable. The head of the Leviathan would almost have to have seemed to readers a reminder of its potential for violent detachment. Contained within the image is also a more collective sense of the sovereign as such. It offers a grotesque but succinct image of Hobbes's political vision through the living "parts" of the civic body.

Figure 5. Wenceslaus Hollar, sketch for the frontispiece to Thomas Hobbes's *Leviathan*, 1651. (British Library)

In the very beginning of his work, Hobbes argues that government is man's greatest artifice, for man "can make an Artificiall Animal" like an "*Automata* . . . with artificiall life" (1). Seen in this light, the sovereign is a kind of Frankenstein's monster: a manmade machine, a built thing that (yet) has life. Perhaps counterintuitively, the description Hobbes gives, and the original sketch for the frontispiece, remind us that an artificial body is not the antithesis of an organic one; this is a figure made of *living* parts. As Hobbes saw him, the sovereign is less a "theophantic incarnation"[6] and more a monstrous birth, a body teeming with diverse sources of a nevertheless shared life full of democratic promise living under monarchical power.[7] The smaller heads of Hollar's sketch appear veritably plucked off and reassembled to form a torso; the softness of the lines suggests facial expressions that are disturbingly indistinct and yet distinguishable. The whole image points to an unsettling sharing of agency, a corporeal throng that animates but does not quite recede into the comfortable anonymity of the People. In the text, Hobbes enumerates the pieces making up this artificial man as sovereign. He assigns each organ of the state its corresponding body "part" (the nation's magistrates, for example, are the "artificiall *Joynts*") and explains that the social contract is the life-giving force that brings everything together. As Hobbes says, "Lastly, the *Pacts* and *Covenants,* by which the parts of this Body Politique were at first made, set together, and united, resemble that *Fiat,* or the *Let us make man,* pronounced by God in the Creation" (1).

The most striking feature of Hobbes's Leviathan is not the sum of its parts, but the parts themselves, the sheer multitudinousness of the body politic that remains disturbingly discernible in the image of the unified "whole." Thus while the Leviathan might show "the sovereign person who represents the commonwealth [as] a corporeal self writ large,"[8] in many ways the matter of embodied citizenship inhabits the more mystical sphere of the king's two bodies. The grotesque nature of this creature is explicit. Indeed, the grotesque *e pluribus unum* of the figure is the very force that animates it. Only out of the many can there be this one. The civitas, in other words, requires not just many bodies but broken bodies. The political union among them voids their totality as separate, contained individuals. They are now organs of the colossus. This grotesque union reveals the need to ruin bodies in order to constitute a community, and it hacks away at the ideal of the individual in order to create something more capacious.[9]

Bosse's engraving is a figure not only of ruined bodies that form the civic whole, but also of distinctly *sexually* ruined bodies. In addition to expressing anxiety about the English Civil War and the beheading of a king, the image unmasks the sexual heat that joins political bodies together. (See figure 6.) The image contains a somewhat lurid vision of the coupling between the people and their monarch. The king looks to be, metonymically at least, in sexual congress with his people: his lower half, hidden by the foregrounded countryside, is clearly also entering the landscape that stands in for the body politic. Yet those tiny bodies must of necessity also make up that lower half that hides below the horizon; though it is blocked from view, the logic of the image suggests that the people themselves constitute the sexed undercarriage of the sovereign body. (See figure 7.) The countoured mound of land at the midsection, just above where the phallus of the sovereign would be, is suggestive of just such a relation. This hillock, shaded on both sides for the full effect, finds the monarch in sexual congress with his people; the sceptre in his left hand, also penetrating the landscape, acts as a reminder of the kind of union at stake in what is essentially a graphic political

Figure 6. Detail from the frontispiece to *Leviathan*, 1651.

Figure 7. Detail from the frontispiece to *Leviathan*, 1651.

allegory of ruin. The frisson among political bodies in this image thus signifies a sort of sexed colossus that points to the erotic quality of political unions. For Hobbes, this might have seemed more a marriage than a scene of ruin, *Leviathan* after all being a book about the merit of contracts. But the troubling addition of the drawn sword in his right hand, while doubling the phallic presence, also adds a sinister, coercive edge to the scene. This union may be borne of the sympathetic bond between a king and his people, but their consent to this intimacy is utterly dispensable.[10]

The controversy over *Leviathan*'s understanding of this intimacy raged for nearly a century. One of the most intriguing rebukes to Hobbes's vision was Aylett Sammes's *Britannia Antiqua Illustrata* (1676). Published just twenty-five years after *Leviathan*, Sammes's work is meant to be a report on the Roman period in British antiquity. Though its innovations in iconography have received some critical attention, it is mostly dismissed by scholars as a work of dubious historical significance. But the text contains an iconography that at times speaks to a more contemporary political scene. Included among its pages is one of Sammes's most famous images, the picture of the wicker man, which depicts the same horror with which some regarded Hobbes's vision. (See figure 8.) Sammes's illustration refers to the historical practices of early British peoples as described by Julius Caesar in *The Gallic War*, in which he notes that at "state sacrifices," the Gallic nation would erect "huge images of the gods, and fill their limbs, which are woven from wicker, with living people. When these images are set on fire the people inside are engulfed in flames and killed."[11] The burning of criminals jammed into a colossal public body serves as a sly satire of Hobbes's

Figure 8. Aylett Sammes, The Wicker Man, *Britannia Antiqua Illustrata*, 1676. (Master and Fellows of St. John's College, Cambridge University)

argument about the social contract, pointing to Hobbes's Leviathan as it suggests what the civic body does to the individual: it consumes, imprisons, and destroys. The image in *Britannia Antiqua Illustrata* thus dramatizes the absence of consent through the caging of criminals (decidedly a "nasty, brutish" sort). For Sammes, this is the violence of ideological sacrifice. But for Hobbes, it is the anatomy of ruin, the assembly of the civic body and its parts, which always points back to a disunified subject, the ruined body of civitas. For Hobbes, the violence is collateral damage.

The Earl's Two Bodies

In chapter 2, we saw the way in which Shaftesbury's *Characteristicks of Men, Manners, Opinions, Times* (1711) was his own more direct rejection of Thomas Hobbes.[12] The engravings accompanying *Characteristicks*, which Shaftesbury himself designed in painstaking detail, were critical to explicating his most radical ideas about self and sovereignty. It took no fewer than four artists, plus Shaftesbury's own sketches and a mountain of correspondence alongside careful written directions, for him to complete the project of the illustrations from his deathbed in Naples. These illustrations, what Shaftesbury referred to as the "'underplot'" of his work, had become for him an obsession.[13] The plate illustrating Shaftesbury's "Doctrine of Two Persons" discussed in chapter 2—the theory of multitudinous identity that he explains through his use of a story of sexual ruin—is a veritable itemization of the polyontological subject.[14] (See figure 9.)

The plate depicts an ontologically curious moment. The harpies flying above the two figures are outward embodiments of their own selves—plural—illustrating what we might more accurately call the doctrine of *many* persons. But the image suggests even more than this radical idea of multiple selfhood. These embodiments represent an internecine hail that

Figure 9. Illustration of "The Doctrine of Two Persons," designed by Shaftesbury and engraved by Simon Gribelin from *Characteristicks*, 1711.

recalls the populated torso of Hobbes's grotesque sovereign. Certainly both images are removed from the idea of singularity. In Shaftesbury's image, the harpies represent an ontological multitude that becomes a leviathan of self. Here are multiple embodiments, an assembly that earlier we saw Shaftesbury artfully describe as the seductive women living in one's head. They represent the subject's multiple selves and ultimately describe the human experience as free of the corporeal prison of singularity. Those "temptresses," "correctrices," and "sorceresses" we saw at work in *Characteristicks* in fact initiate the seduction, or rather the *ruin*, of self to which their influence leads. In other words, just as Shaftesbury describes them in his "Doctrine of Two Persons," his drawing of the temptresses shows them at work populating the Enlightenment subject, seducing him into a state of multitudinous embodiment. The illustration's expressive characterization of these "seductresses" tells their story with an intriguing triptych. The engraving includes three main panels, two figures in opposing relation with an empty room featuring a great mirror in between. Of especial interest here is the design of the harpies, made to look like grotesque representations of self. These tiny monstrosities represent, for Shaftesbury, the ontological confusion described by the "Doctrine of Two Persons." Though one of the people in the illustration fares better than the other because he practices the art of soliloquy, neither human figure represents the possibility of singularity. Rather, there is merely the ability to create peace among the beings peopling one's "self," or the possibility of confusion, of being ruled by a monarchical (note the crown and staff) and decidedly feminine set of demons, their hybrid little bodies representing a very fragmented self.[15] The image represents the Enlightenment self as a grotesquerie and reveals the fear of shared political power in the civic body. The source of that fear is a denial of self-possession and in its place an insistence on the grotesque ontology of the liberal subject.

Indeed, the illustration implies that self-possession is always already a plural condition, since it implies an original "possessor" and a remainder that is "owned." A brief detour into the medieval underpinnings of these ontological mysteries may be useful here. The depiction of conflict with the harpies echoes the aforementioned principle of "the king's two bodies," a notion that helps explain the roots of selfhood imagined as anything but a hermetic totality. This principle encapsulates what Ernst H. Kantorowicz calls the "political mysticism" that affords the monarch a rarified ontology (and indeed the term "political mysticism" might be applied just as usefully to the conjuring power of *e pluribus unum*). The king's two bodies are, first, the "superbody or body politic," and then of course the natural or biological body: "'For the King has in him two Bodies, viz., a Body natural and a Body politic'" and "'to this Body is conjoined his Body politic.'" Crown lawyers used a distinct glossary of the grotesque to define this condition of the "persona mixta." They employed terms including *indivisible, consolidated, incorporated, annexed, conjoined*. One nineteenth-century lawyer even uses the word *hermaphrodite* to explain how one person can in fact be two.[16]

This monarchical *persona mixta* resembles nothing so much as Shaftesbury's "Doctrine of Two Persons"—the ordinary man with multiple selves that preclude self-possession and its attendant singular embodiment. With their suggestively protruding breasts and phallic tails, the most prominent of the three outfitted with a crown and scepter, the harpies represent the power of the sexed, ruined body as a set of internal, warring monarchs that unsettle the idea of self-possession. Describing the condition of humanity rather than of the monarchy, Shaftesbury has simply democratized the ontology of what we might call the omnicorporeal monarch.

Shaftesbury's portrait makes just such a case. (See figure 10.) Commissioned from John Closterman by Shaftesbury in 1704, the original portrait shows Shaftesbury in the foreground, and in a style typical of the period, he is surrounded by images of classical antiquity as he meets the viewer's gaze; what is so strange about the original portrait, however, is that it includes an unnamed *second* figure. This second man is slightly older, and the viewer finds him walking into the frame in the background of the painting as he directs his gaze backward. In her brilliant analysis of the Closterman painting, Lori Branch presents the astonishing thesis that Shaftesbury commissioned the portrait so that he could direct Closterman to paint him *twice* in the same painting (once at his current age and then again imagining him as an older man); in this way he could illuminate the "plate tectonics of the split Enlightenment self."[17] Indeed, the doubled Shaftesbury represents not only the two figures of the "Soliloquy" engraving, but also the harpies themselves—the uncannily shared embodiment of the self/other figure. Viewed this way, the painting captures the woozy impossibility of something like omnipresence. Building on Branch's hypothesis, then, we might say that the Closterman portrait was Shaftesbury's way of pointing to the monstrous hybrid of self, a dizzying incorporation of the many signaling a sense of

Figure 10. John Closterman, *Portrait Shaftesbury*, 1704. (National Portrait Gallery, London; reproduced by permission of the Twelfth Earl of Shaftesbury, Wimborn, St. Giles)

identity that radicalizes embodiment. The portrait stages the discovery that one's "self" is a multitude, and in this way it is a portrait of the Enlightenment. By having himself painted twice in the same portrait, Shaftesbury democratizes the idea of monarchical omnipresence into the polyontological subject.

In a fascinating turn, Shaftesbury had his engraver *omit* this second figure from the copy of his portrait that he included seven years later in the original edition of *Characteristics*. It is a conspicuous absence. This prominent revision offers yet another reminder of the disunified subject's potential for disassembly. (See figure 11.) Such doublings and omissions underlie the grotesquerie of the Enlightenment subject, a figure at once reproducing and vanishing. The contrast between the two portraits certainly asks us to rethink the terms of Enlightenment identity and to replace the self/other

Figure 11. Simon Gribelin, frontispiece to Shaftesbury's *Characteristicks of Men, Manners, Opinions, Times*, 1711. Engraving based on the portrait by John Closterman.

dichotomy with a poly/mono-ontological one. For the argument these images make is that despite what we might wish to say about the material limits of bone and skin, Enlightenment thinkers did not always understand the body as a singularity. In these images, embodiment signals a bi-locality, perhaps even a multivocality, that prodigalizes the body's political meaning.

America in Ruins

American thinkers took up these images in their own iconography of nation building. In their metaphorical envisioning of the body politic, the violence inflicted on the individual in the forging of unions proved central to the visual narrative of the new republic. Like Hobbes's Leviathan and Shaftesbury's harpies, Franklin's political cartoons, "JOIN, or DIE" (1754) and "MAGNA *Britannia; her Colonies* REDUC'D" (1767) also speak to matters of self-reproduction and self-splitting, for the body of the people and the body of the liberal individual, whose singular personhood is marked as a fracturing and a trauma. Franklin's images present instability and injury as the site of community. Franklin, the founding father perhaps most often associated with the mythology of the self-made American, saw the utility and the political potential of that instability in the task of building a nation. In his *Observations Concerning the Increase of Mankind, Peopling of Countries, Etc.* (1751) Franklin writes,

> In fine, A Nation well regulated is like a Polypus; take away a Limb, its Place is soon supply'd; cut it in two, and each deficient Part shall speedily grow out of the Part remaining. Thus if you have Room and Subsistence enough, as you may by dividing, make ten Polypes out of one, you may of one make ten Nations, equally populous and powerful; or rather, increase a Nation ten fold in Numbers and Strength.[18]

The implications of Shaftesbury's editorial play with his portrait may lie in the division of which Franklin speaks. In the self-dissection of Enlightenment practice, one risks becoming two—or perhaps tenfold—and the peopling of self and nation mimics the regenerative capacity of violence.

Franklin's cartoons depict political unions in danger of being broken up. Those unions are also, however, in danger of reattachment into a monstrous civic body that recalls Hobbes's Leviathan. (See figures 12 and 13.) On one level, "MAGNA *Britannia*" speaks to the threat of using military power against the colonies to enforce an unwanted tax; the image warns that Great Britain will pay for its abandonment of the colonies, will be literally "reduced" in power, like the once great warrior Bellisario who was abandoned by his monarch.[19] But it is the reattachment implied by the

Figure 12. Benjamin Franklin, "MAGNA *Britannia; her Colonies* REDUC'D," 1766. (Library of Congress, Prints and Photographs Division)

cleanly sliced limbs, inviting a kind of monstrous reassembly of the body, that is of especial interest here. The synecdochal life of the people relies on a grotesque joint, not an originary or totalizing wholeness. The limbs look as if they might be snapped back into place; the parts of a political body, in other words, might be put back together again. If the body of Britain is ruined, this image also suggests the uncanny possibility of reassembly, a move that refuses totality but embraces reunification. The image insinuates that no whole body can represent a people or a nation. A nation's body must be imagined as dismembered and reattached, but never an organic totality. The same jointedness appears in Franklin's earlier political cartoon, the famous "JOIN, or DIE" emblem of a snake that was originally designed as a warning to the colonies that they must unite in order to survive the French and Indian War, though of course over time it took on much more revolutionary, antimonarchical meanings.[20] On the one hand, images like Franklin's cartoons seem to "conjoin a libidinal attachment to a political position with the violent inscribing of that political position on sexualized bodies."[21] On the other hand, Enlightenment images of the state must depict violence against bodies, their unions wounding them—*ruining* them—in ways that articulate the anatomy of nation building. These images thus diagram the modern state as an ontological problem. The alchemy of national identity exists in the absences between the severed sections of the serpent

Figure 13. Benjamin Franklin, "JOIN, or DIE," 1754. (Library of Congress, Prints and Photographs Division)

and the mutilated female torso, tidily contained but for the blank sites of injury that seem to reach with geometrical precision back toward each other to restore the whole (relating to the folklore that a severed snake could be put back together if reassembled before nightfall).[22] The image issues a direct response to Hobbes, with the head of the snake a distinctly collective "part" in its combination of the New England colonies. The fracturing of the states represented by these butchered bodies implies great anxiety about the role of the individual, a "body part" that resembles, in "JOIN, or DIE," nothing so much as the tragedy of the broken phallus, the potency of the union compromised through an anatomically suggestive injury.

The illustration that resolves this injury and that seems to restore that phallus through political unification is the seal illustrated on a publication of the First Continental Congress, *Journal of the Proceedings of the Congress* (1774). (See figure 14.) The image is at once phallic and monstrous, the twelve hands holding onto the ultimate Atlantic Enlightenment symbol of shared political power, the Magna Carta.[23] Yet this image of the incomplete bodies emerging from the margins, the severed collection of insectile arms reaching toward the Magna Carta, is certainly an overdetermined icon of what it means to form a union. With its long shaft and the liberty cap at its tip, it is difficult to look at the image and see anything other than a phallic tower. The onanism of the multitude—twelve hands seemingly part of a monstrous body grasping a shared phallus—indicates an illicit sexual impulse at work in the sharing of political power. One might well ask: Where is the individual in such an image? Those indistinct, bulky shapes in the margins of the seal hardly represent the individual will as the centerpiece of a republic. Indeed, they resemble the similarly indistinguishable masses of bodies that constitute the arms and torso of Hobbes's Leviathan.

Conclusion

Figure 14. Seal illustrated on the title page of *Journal of the Proceedings of the Congress*, 1774. (Library of Congress, Prints and Photographs Division)

The Anatomy of the Nation

As a collection, these images question the teleology of the individual. They ask: If the Enlightenment is principally about this figure, this *individual*, then why are representations of political power so often about sexed bodies, maimed bodies, bodies that look like participants in an orgy of sex and violence, bodies that cannot be said, through any abuse of the word "possession," to be in possession of themselves? Why do these images sex that body as they slash away at the fantasy of the singular, contained self? The answer lies in the ruin genre, in which the unity implied by sexual congress, and the disunity implied by dismemberment, offer a grotesque vision of identity that challenges the dualism of the Lockean self. As Elizabeth Grosz argues, feminism reveals that dualism sees the body as "a vessel occupied by an animating, willful subjectivity. For Locke and the liberal political tradition more generally, the body is seen as a possession, a property of a subject, who is thereby disassociated from carnality."[24] The images considered here, however, reassociate the subject with carnality, and refute the ideal of corporeal containment, the idea of the body as a "vessel occupied."

The images are, in fact, iterations of the ruin narrative in graphic form. As such they configure civic agency as a site of monstrous unions composed of the masses. Such political unions seek to disassemble basic ontological barriers; in this way sodality risks the grotesque, revealing the sexed pleasures and the somatic horrors of shared political power. Thus images of ruin present us with bodies that are wrecked in peculiarly erotic ways. Possessed or dismembered, a colossus or a miniature: these instances of embodiment point to the kind of radical civic ontology that we see at work in the novel of sexual ruin.

Sexual ruin radicalizes the democratic subject, turning the ruined body into the site of a darkly enchanted vox populi, the monstrous hybrid of the one out of the many, the very thing the founders pursued with such determination. Critics have pilloried and problematized the individual as an incomplete artifact of Enlightenment thought that only partially informs definitions of self. They identify, as *Erotic Citizens* does, iterations of "self" in the Atlantic Enlightenment world of letters that most emphatically do not fit into the model of the rights-bearing individual. This is a conversation about aesthetics, and also in part one that participates in the continuing study of what the Revolution was—what it was for and against, and what it meant for the literature of the time that so distinctly explores the subjectivities possible in an era that was both liberatory and oppressive. It was a time in which what it meant to be a citizen individual of the republic—a free white man—was not nearly the only question on the minds of writers. For instead of producing novels about this hero and what he might be capable of with his rights and his freedoms, novels published at this historical moment ask instead: Besides the end of the monarchical subject, what other subjectivities do revolutions authorize? What else might a democratic body be? In answering these questions, *Erotic Citizens* explores why the texts wrestling with the notion of nation building continued to turn to sexual ruin as the best trope for this aesthetic and cultural moment.

The Commons Body

The stuff of nations is the stuff of bodies: this is the guiding principle of the ruin genre. The aesthetic work of the illicitly sexed body functions as a prevalent model for nation-building unions in the Atlantic Enlightenment; the novels of ruin that proliferated as the new American republic was taking shape demonstrate that the authors who wrestled with what it means to form a democratic union saw the sexually ruined body as the best means of imagining one. It must be said, however, that this model was something of a loser in the long-term battle of ideas and national imaginaries. If the ruin narrative is something of a call to reckon with the id of the nation, the United States—and indeed the West—has largely progressed down the path of repression. Eclipsing the ruin genre, there has always been a dominant aesthetic at work that pathologizes the sexed nature of the nation as such, one that demonizes as it obscures the civic contributions of the politically sexed body. Understanding this pathology reveals that the virtuous abstinent body and the solipsistic male are profoundly linked figures. In other words, this dominant narrative, which is none other than the story of the self-possessed individual, figures as a story of mastery over the self through mastery over the other. It is the story of mastery over the ruined self, and the ubiquity of this story can easily—tragically—be mistaken for something like truth.

In both its narrative and visual forms, however, the ruin genre argues against this vision. Belonging, not consent, functions as the principal sensibility advocated by these texts. It is an important difference, one that the ruin genre defines as what it means to join a nation: it means to be a *part* of it, a piece that is incomplete outside the ideological reach of political joinings. The self-possessed individual cannot be a "part" of anything. As Jean-Luc Nancy observes, the individual is rather "merely the residue of the experience of the dissolution of community."[25] What the sexed body of the ruin narrative offers as an alternative is the experience of community's formation. To be a part of that formation, these texts insist, is to understand the simultaneity of self and other as a condition of embodiment. Imagining sex as the mechanism for nation building removes the morally damning connotations of what we ought to think of as the commons body. These texts insist upon dissociating the body's sexual traffic from contract's idealization of self-possession. In the ruin narrative, the body is not an object bartered by the self in the formation of rational agreement. Rather, embodiment is always already in a state of corporeal belonging.

One image in particular helps encapsulate the tensions between these two traditions. "The Able Doctor; or, America Swallowing the Bitter Draught" shows the leading forces involved with what became known as the Intolerable Acts (including the infamous tax on tea that incited the Boston Tea Party in 1773), which led to a major upswing in revolutionary sentiment. (See figure 15.) The image shows the sexual assault of a Native American woman who represents the British colonies; Britannia averts her eyes as America suffers the violation.[26] British politicians force a tea spout into America's mouth and begin to disrobe her, with Boston's coast under an ominous cloud in the background. It was first produced in England for the *London Magazine* in 1774 but copied by Paul Revere for the *Royal American Magazine* later that year. The print was prolifically reproduced and widely circulated in several forms throughout the British Atlantic.[27]

Figure 15. "The Able Doctor; or, America Swallowing the Bitter Draught," 1774. (Library of Congress, Prints and Photographs Division)

If we read the image in a more traditional mode, we can learn about the divisive differences among bodies that lead to a hierarchy defined by mastery, a story of punishing racial and gendered violations that speak to the individual's power. That is, if we read the image traditionally, what we see is an announcement of the perniciously racialized dualism at work in the gendered representation of America as an accessible female subject (Native American, fleshly, violable) who must endure the burdens of the material body, while Britannia (white, abstract, inviolate) is exempted from the male gaze and granted the privilege of disembodiment. Often mistaken by scholars for an emblem of Liberty, in this reading Britannia appears as an abstraction removed from the material violence of the scene.[28] America's status as a Native American renders her a violable, materially contained subaltern. Britannia's whiteness renders her an inviolate idea—a man's ideal—a cerebral manifestation of the nation that is completely separate from the body of America. Britannia is just another bystander, and America's isolation becomes the central term of her violation.

Reading the image through the lens of the ruin genre, however, reveals whole new layers of meaning that point us toward an ontological joining among ruined bodies that form a community where only the aforementioned instances of mastery and division might have been. That lens reveals America and Britannia working together as a doubly embodied personification of the sexed, ruined subject. The eye toggles back and forth between America and Britannia, the only two female figures in the image. They mirror one another's appearance in several ways: Britannia's breasts are nearly revealed with a loose, draping fabric like the one revealing America's breasts; the phallic spear slants against her shoulders and almost appears to slice through her; she is covering her face and literally shielding herself below the waist. Britannia is, in effect, experiencing the sexual violations of the tea spout and the grope. Such a doubling posture problematizes the notion that Britannia is an abstraction exempt from the violable peril of the material body. Britannia is not inviolate because hers is not a fully discrete body. The attempt to read her as a female emblem fails in the face of her doubling of America, a doubling that insists on a sexed body, a sympathetic *flesh* that she shares with another sexed body. America and Britannia's bodies enact a material doubling, a bicorporeal attachment signaling a shared distress. In other words, the logic of the image insists that because both figures represent the nation qua nation, they must both have sexed, ruined bodies, and in their shared ruin they become something quite distinct from "individuals." Thus unfolding at the very shores of the Atlantic is the uncanny duplication of the Enlightenment subject understood through a scene of racial violence and sexual ruin that insists upon material embodiment even as it questions the ontological limits of that embodiment.

If the ruin narrative issues a warning, then within that warning is also a promise of a peculiarly alchemical ideal of unity, of community that is not a Hobbesian "warre of every man against every man" but a commons body. The sympathy of this commons body issues its call throughout the genre. The first American novel, *The Power of Sympathy* (1789), perhaps best articulates this call. Describing the traits of his lover that enthrall him the most, the incestuous hero of William Hill Brown's novel opines,

> But to the question—What is love? Unless it is answered now, perhaps it never will be. Is it not an infinitude of graces that accompany every thing said by *Harriot?* That adorn all she does? They must not be taken severally—they cannot be contemplated in the abstract.—If you proceed to a chymical analysis, their tenuous essence will evaporate—they are in themselves nothing, but the aggregate is love.
>
> When an army composed of a great number of men, moves slowly on at a distance, nobody thinks of considering a single soldier. (31-32)

It is in the refusal of the singular that the promise of ruin begins to take shape; only the aggregate can embody the ontological uncertainty of what Harrington calls "love" but which might just as easily be read on the scale of the nation. The ruin genre insists that political bodies "must not be taken severally." It argues instead that the way to build a nation is to embrace the ontological uncertainty that experiences of embodiment create. It rejects the division of the democratic subject into abstinent (male) and sexed (female) bodies as it suggests that the forming of a nation does not require a promiscuous body so much as a polyamorous one. These texts represent the fall into community as the precinct of bodies, and they see sexual ruin as the clearest portrayal of that fall, which they understand to be an admission into democratic identity. Reading the early American novel as an expression of such Enlightenment values shows that its quintessential protagonist is not a rebel but a lover. For it is the profanity of the ruined body that comes to define community as an authentically American ideal.

Notes

Introduction

1. From, respectively, Susanna Rowson's *Charlotte Temple*, 36; Nathaniel Hawthorne's *The Blithedale Romance*, 218; Samuel Richardson's *Clarissa*, UK Edition, 974. Subsequent page citations to these works will appear in the text parenthetically.

2. Using the phrase "the body of the other," I am thinking of the figure imagined by Luce Irigaray as the subjugated copy of the "self." As she says, "Others were only copies of the idea of man . . . not defined in and of themselves." Instead, they were "defined in terms of an ideal subjectivity and as a function of their inadequacies with respect to that ideal: age, reason, race, culture, and so on. The model of the subject thus remained singular and the 'others' represented less ideal examples, hierarchized with respect to the singular subject." Irigaray and Guynn, "The Question of the Other," 7.

3. William Hill Brown, *The Power of Sympathy*, 9–10. Subsequent page citations to this work will appear in the text parenthetically.

4. Certainly the literary criticism and historical analysis of the past two decades would support such a claim. As early as 1997, in *States of Sympathy*, Elizabeth Barnes takes issue with "the notion that American individualism represents the hallmark of the American novel and American identity" and suggests using "a model of affinity" that reveals identity to be flexible and porous. As Barnes says, "The myth of classic American literature—the idea that an autonomous individualism (and a specifically *male* individualism) represents the hallmark of the American novel and American identity—breaks down in the face of early American culture's prevailing concern for promoting sympathetic relations between individuals. In the sentimental scheme of sympathy, the boundaries of identity . . . are shown as distinctly flexible" (xi, xii, 13–14). And as recently as 2014, Siân Silyn Roberts's *Gothic Subjects* includes nearly the same argument: "I question the long-held critical assumption that early Americans conceived civil society almost exclusively in terms of the sovereign individual" (18). That nearly twenty years later such statements are still being made attests to the continued need to explore alternatives to the individual. The list of other excellent

works that challenge the primacy of the individual in early American thought is too long to include here, though certainly no such list would be complete without mention of books like Julia Stern's *This Plight of Feeling*, Sarah Knott's *Sensibility and the American Revolution*, and William Hunting Howell's *Against Self-Reliance*.

5. This might explain why instead of consent, "[c]haracters experience emotions beyond their control or understanding, directed toward figures that their communities find inappropriate—that they themselves find inappropriate . . . and yet [they] cannot free themselves." Erica Burleigh, *Intimacy and Family in Early American Writing*, 7.

6. From, respectively, Rowson's *Charlotte Temple*, Brown's *Ira and Isabella*, Foster's *The Coquette*, Hawthorne's *The Blithedale Romance*, and Irving's *The Sketch Book of Geoffrey Crayon, Gent*.

7. As Jane Tompkins says in the still-influential book *Sensational Designs* (1985), "rather than asking how a given text handled the questions which have recently concerned modern critics—questions about the self, the body, the possibilities of knowledge, the limits of language—I have discussed [these works] in relation to religious beliefs, social practices, and economic and political circumstances that produced them" (xii). A text's relation to these last four defines its "cultural work."

8. Terry Eagleton's definition of the aesthetic is noteworthy: for him, it is "a discourse of the body" that speaks of "the whole of our sensate life together—the business of affections and aversions, of how the world strikes the body on its sensory surfaces, of that which takes root in the gaze and the guts and all that arises from our most our banal, biological insertion into the world." *The Ideology of the Aesthetic*, 13.

9. In terms of the former understanding of aesthetics, one thinks of William Hogarth's *The Analysis of Beauty* (1753) and Alexander Gottlieb Baumgarten's *Aesthetica* (1750), both of which are more about matters of taste and the class values imbued within them. The study of the aesthetic as the study of bodily perception precedes them by a few decades, especially through the work of Anthony Ashley Cooper, the Third Earl of Shaftesbury, and the moral sense school that grew up around his work, which are considered at length in chapter 2. For a more nuanced history of aesthetic philosophy and especially of the difference between aesthetics as the study of beauty and the study of bodily perception, see Eagleton's *Ideology of the Aesthetic*.

10. There is important scholarship that sees sex for unmarried women as only ever harmful to their social status. For example, in "Daughters of the American Revolution," Holly Blackford provocatively describes the semiotic complexities surrounding the punitive nature of sex for women in the post-revolutionary American seduction novel when she writes, "The new-world girl is stalked by sensational European villains, her awakening sensations and blushes opening her up to old-world penetration" (46). In terms of the semiotic role of unmarried sex in the colonial imagination, Leonard Tennenhouse adds to this case when he writes in *The Importance of Feeling English*, "If Anglo-Americans imagined their culture as a woman—that is, as a Mary Rowlandson, a Charlotte Temple, or even a Clarissa Harlowe—then the perpetuity of

that identity would depend on her remaining faithful to her origins. Seduction would threaten that bond, and rape would declare it had been forcibly broken" (64).

11. Jan Lewis's ground-breaking work on the role of women and marriage in the new nation in "The Republican Wife" still holds true, namely that "citizens were to be bound together not by patriarchy's duty or liberalism's self-interest, but by affection, and it was, they believed, marriage, more than any other institution, that trained citizens in virtue.... Marriage was the very pattern from which the cloth of the republic was to be cut" (689).

12. Certainly such assertions have not gone without discussion of what makes the contract problematic in ways that are fundamentally gendered. Foremost among these discussions is Carole Pateman's *The Sexual Contract*.

13. Downes, *Democracy, Revolution, and Monarchism in Early American Literature*, x.

14. Jacobs, *Incidents in the Life of a Slave Girl*, 207. Subsequent page references to this work will appear in the text parenthetically. I also quote here from the abridged US edition of *Clarissa* (though Clarissa makes the same assertion in both the UK and US versions of the novel).

15. Readers have long supposed that the attractions of novels about seduction and adultery are not, as their title pages and prefaces often suggest, didactic in nature. Hawthorne certainly never suggests that his novel is a text to be used for the moral instruction of girls. Indeed, his work seems to anticipate Winfried Fluck's observation in "Reading Early American Fiction" regarding "the suspicion that the sentimental novel's striking popularity should perhaps not be attributed to its didactic goals but to the fact that it represented 'unspeakable acts' under the guise of moral instruction" (574).

16. There is some excellent criticism attempting to answer this question about alternative models, criticism that is forging what I think of as agency studies in early American literature. Peter Coviello's *Tomorrow's Parties* and Roberts's *Gothic Subjects* are remarkable examples of where this conversation can go. Roberts argues, for example, that the gothic genre was used by early US novelists to explore alternatives to the individual, alternatives that ranked "ontological mobility" and the "adaptable subject" as priorities for the new nation, in which the flow and relational nature of identity was an asset (12, 19). Coviello introduces the idea of "not yet coordinated vectors of being"—of identities that had not yet begun to settle into sexually punitive, static categories. In *Dislocating Race and Nation*, Robert Levine too describes works of American literature "in which identities—national, gender, and even racial—seem anything but stable, and in which stability (or the ability to 'recognize' identity) can appear to be the biggest fiction of all" (25). Knott, in *Sensibility and the American Revolution*, usefully calls this unstable identity the "socially turned self" formed by a sensibility that "eschewed traditional dichotomies of reason and feeling, mind and body" and instead authorized "multiple modes of self" based on "social interdependency and mutual malleability" (12, 5, 22).

17. Coviello, *Tomorrow's Parties*, ebook.

18. Pateman, *The Sexual Contract*, 1.

19. Nancy, *The Inoperative Community*.

20. An example of such work is Milette Shamir's *Inexpressible Privacy*, which offers a study of cultural ambivalence regarding the meaning of privacy, especially as it is represented in nineteenth-century American law and architecture. Though I am arguing that the ruin narrative offers an alternative to the private individual, critics like Shamir argue instead that privacy was a means to political power. In this regard, "subaltern literature . . . seeks to extend the right of privacy to those to whom it has been historically denied, realizing that the claim to full humanity involves the privilege to disappear from, not just to appear in, public" (16).

ONE. The Aesthetic Work of the Ruin Narrative

1. In addition to the terms *sensation* and *sentiment*, scholarly discussion has also hinged upon the terms *sympathy* and *sensibility*. (Though I will discuss the meanings of most of these terms at somewhat greater length later in this chapter, *sympathy* is a concept so central to the ruin narrative that the entire second chapter of this book is devoted to its definition as well as its origins in eighteenth-century political and philosophical works.) Certainly there is an abundance of excellent scholarship that offers careful historical and literary analysis of all these terms. The list of critical works is too long for anything but a brief selection here. While just about all of the following authors present in-depth analysis of sympathy, sentiment, sensibility, and sensation, each has a focus on one that may be particularly useful. For an invaluable overview of the power of feeling in this era, see Julie Ellison's *Cato's Tears and the Making of Anglo-American Emotion*. For work on defining the role of sympathy, see, for example, Kristin Boudreau's *Sympathy in American Literature* and Rachel Ablow's *The Marriage of Minds*; for work on defining sentiment, see Cindy Weinstein's *Family, Kinship, and Sympathy in Nineteenth-Century American Literature*, Christine Levecq's *Slavery and Sentiment*, and James D. Lilley's *Common Things*. For work on sensibility, see Knott's *Sensibility and the American Revolution*, and for work on the sensational, see Roberts's *Gothic Subjects* and Paul Kelleher's *Making Love*.

2. I am here thinking specifically of Tompkins's *Sensational Designs* and her innovative notion of literature's "cultural work" as a measure of its merit.

3. The most impressive of such genre-bending studies is Marianne Noble's *The Masochistic Pleasures of Sentimental Literature*. As Noble argues, sentimentalism does not simply offer a "powerless critique of patriarchal brutality" and to claim that it does is to "create a false picture of the trajectory of American literary history" (5).

4. In *Men beyond Desire*, David Greven offers an important counterpoint to the ruined woman in this regard, the "inviolate male" who, as a "hermetically sealed vessel of chastity and purity" is a perfectly "self-governing vessel of hygienic, moral purity" (1, 13). As Greven notes, this figure's "sexual identity remains an elusive, socially maddening blank" (29).

5. Hobbes, *Leviathan*, 70. Subsequent page citations to this work will appear in the text parenthetically.

6. It was also the subject of much political thought, and certainly occupied the interest of the founding fathers. As Richard B. Sher notes in *Scottish Authors and Their Publishers*, Thomas Jefferson's library, for example, contained the works of David Hume, Adam Smith, and Sir Francis Hutcheson. John Adams's library too included works by Hutcheson, Smith, and Hume (*Catalogue of the John Adams Library in the Public Library of the City of Boston*).

7. Arguments about sympathy and its ideological impact on early American thought have proliferated in American studies since the 1980s at least. These arguments posit that sympathy is the foundational vehicle for democratic feeling. The first wave of sympathy studies comes from works like Cathy Davidson's *Revolution and the Word*. Later on in *States of Sympathy*, Barnes brilliantly refers to the "blurring of ego boundaries" (33) in early American literature and adds that sympathy "was to be the building block of a democratic nation" (x).

8. William Hill Brown, *Ira and Isabella*, 22; *Clarissa*, UK edition, 890; Foster, *The Coquette*, 165. Subsequent page citations to these works will appear in the text parenthetically.

9. My use of "masculinity" is deliberate, since the individual's characteristics are distinctly patriarchal. I am thinking here specifically of Pateman's arguments about the social contract as a "sexual-social pact" that secures patriarchal right in *The Sexual Contract*. For Pateman, the marriage contract is "half the original contract" and guarantees for men that "[c]ivil freedom depends on patriarchal right" (1, 4). Like Pateman, I am not ruling out the possibility of female individuals but, following the mindset of contract philosophers like Hobbes and Rousseau, I am considering the association between power and property in the self as a gendered one.

10. R.W.B. Lewis, *The American Adam*, 91. Such understandings of American individualism have since been the subject of much critical disapproval. Lewis's *The American Adam*, Leslie Fiedler's *Love and Death in the American Novel*, and D. H. Lawrence's *Studies in Classic American Literature* all argued that American exceptionalism could be defined by what troubles the masculine, a perspective that has long since been rejected as an unhelpful and misogynist dismissal of sentiment. In *Sensational Designs*, Tompkins changed the course of the conversation by arguing for the definitive principle of new historicism, that the "sub-literary" works by and about white women and people of color in American literature performed the important "cultural work" of sentiment, work that led scholars to interrogate the nation-building powers of emotion as the political province of women. Questions about agency, race, and gender are of course still informing critics' understandings of early American literature. As Shirley Samuels argues in *Reading the American Novel*, "[W]hile celebrating what twentieth-century critics have variously called the hero in space, the American Adam, or the virgin land, . . . plots of early novels frequently focus on women's bodies" (ebook).

11. Scholarly works that analyze the individual as the principal model of identity in the Anglo-Atlantic fiction of the eighteenth and nineteenth centuries show the way in which critics have come to see the individual as a source of oppressive power. For example, in "Engendering American Fictions," Martha J. Cutter and Caroline F. Levander argue that "what he [the individual] does have is the United States itself: a blank slate, a *tabula rasa*, on which, and in which, he can inscribe his identity," an understanding that seeks to understand a separate, willed agency in the making of one's self. This version of the American Adam sees in the New World a "New Eden of America, his chance to cast off the tainting influence" of European corruption to "make himself anew" (41). Yet while they may interrogate this figure, many critics do not challenge the imagined ideological supremacy of the individual. For example, in his astute study of the "aesthetics of belonging," in *Common Things*, Lilley sets the stakes of his work on how this aesthetics helped to bring about "the mysterious figure at the heart of Western political communities: the liberal, rights-bearing subject" (3). In *How Novels Think*, Nancy Armstrong also argues that the central work of the novel is to sustain the ideology of the individual, the "universalizing of the individual subject" (10). Geoff Hamilton similarly posits the rise of the individual and the ideal of separation as a site of freedom in *The Life and Undeath of Autonomy in American Literature*.

12. As Laura Doyle provocatively asserts in *Freedom's Empire* (in her discussion of Rowson's *Charlotte Temple*), "the American Adam arrives on stage as an Eve, a ruined wanderer of humble yet virtuous origin" and the "French-named seducer has done Satan's new-world work—and the expanse of the Atlantic aids him" (161). Sexual ruin, in other words, transfigures the American Adam into an Eve, still an individual, though perhaps a much more intriguing one. For a more detailed discussion of Doyle's interpretation of the Adam-to-Eve transformation in *Charlotte Temple*, see especially *Freedom's Empire*, 118–44.

13. Coviello, *Tomorrow's Parties*.

14. Locke, *Two Treatises of Government*, 134.

15. McMillan, *Embodied Avatars*, 53.

16. Though I will go into more detail regarding Judith Butler's analysis of the relational body in chapter 2, her notion of "plural forms of agency" is illustrative here. In her discussion of acts of assembly, she says in *Notes toward a Performative Theory of Assembly* that it "is neither my act nor yours, but something that happens by virtue of the relation between us, arising from that relation, equivocating between the I and the we, seeking at once to preserve and disseminate the generative value of that equivocation, an active and deliberately sustained relation, a collaboration distinct from hallucinatory merging or confusion" (9).

17. The first term comes from Mimi Sheller's *Citizenship from Below* (9). The call for breaking down such a dichotomy comes from McMillan's *Embodied Avatars* (9).

18. Grosz, *Volatile Bodies*. Grosz's feminist vision of the body replaces mind/body dualism with the symbolic image of the Möbius strip, which helps us to see the "somatophobia" at work in mind/body dualism (5). As she argues, "Bodies and

minds are not two distinct substances or two kinds of attributes of a single substance but somewhere in between" (xii). The shape of the Möbius strip invites us to see the subject as a "corporeal being" whose "psychical interior" and "corporeal exterior" exist in a "torsion of the one into the other, the passage, vector, or uncontrollable drift of the inside into the outside and the outside into the inside" (ix, xii). Theorists of the body and especially the queer body are still making this argument. In *Assuming a Body*, for example, Gayle Salamon notes phenomenology's continuing "insistence that the body is crucial for understanding subjectivity, rather than incidental to or a distraction from it."

19. Berlant and Edelman, *Sex, or the Unbearable*. As they write in their introduction, "To encounter ourselves as nonsovereign, we suggest, is to encounter relationality itself."

20. Laqueur, *Making Sex*, viii. As Laqueur notes, "[N]o particular understanding of sexual difference historically follows from undisputed facts about bodies," and, in fact, "before the seventeenth century," sex "was still a sociological and not an ontological category" (viii, 8). As Grosz puts it, "Biology is somehow regarded as the subject minus culture" (*Volatile Bodies*, 191).

21. I am thinking here of Doyle's *Freedom's Empire*, which forcefully argues that the individual is born out of scenes of racial and sexual violence. Such scholarship represents the birth of the modern subject as a violating, racialized loss and reemergence of self as a contained interiority. (Whereas Doyle sees rape as a moment in which the individual emerges, I see rape as a moment that intends, but fails, to assert the ascendance of the individual, in the figure of the master/rapist, over the other.) That violence can take additional forms; for more on the ways in which the category of "the individual" is sequestered from white women and people of color as "an unequally available resource" in which the "rhetorics of disincorporation" are idealized, see Michael Warner, "The Mass Public and the Mass Subject," 250.

22. Diedrich, Gates, and Pedersen, "The Middle Passage between History and Fiction." As they put it, "[T]he modern era . . . arguably began with the encounter between Europe, Africa, and the Americas—and thus also with the beginning of the slave trade in the sixteenth century" (5). It also began with "the hierarchical concepts of culture" that make the institution of slavery imaginable. In other words, this encounter occurs in, as it gives rise to, a culture in which one is always subject *to*—to a master, a monarch, or even, in the case of the sovereign individual, to oneself. Eurocentrism therefore "relegated Africa to the subordinate position of the Dark Continent, which represented the fallen image of Europe's past, and the Americas to the Virgin Land, which contained the hope for Europe's future" (5). In racial and gendered terms, then, Europe, Africa, and the Americas represent the whore, the enslaved concubine, and the virgin—all possessed, ruined, or ruinable bodies, all potential properties of the sovereign individual.

23. The novel is often attributed to William Pittis, a drunkard who spent significant time in debtor's prison, and who also published quite a bit of scandalous material, mostly of a political bent. The official authorship of the text is still anonymous,

though it is worth noting that much of Pittis's work was published anonymously. For more on Pittis, see Newton, "William Pittis and Queen Anne Journalism."

24. In his analysis of Isaac Teale's poem "The Sable Venus: An Ode" as an example of such literature (and in his analysis of the illustration of it painted by Thomas Stothard, both of which will be discussed later on), Marcus Wood notes, "The rape of the slave woman is presented not as the direct result of white male depravity" but as an example of the "hideous irony" of black female sexuality dominating white men. "Celebrating the Middle Passage," 131, 130.

25. Ibid., 130.

26. In fact, among Stothard's most well known works were those he produced for an illustrated edition of Samuel Richardson's *Clarissa*. www.royalacademy.org.uk/art-artists/work-of-art/charity-1.

27. Teale, "Ode," 28. Teale's poem was originally written in Jamaica in 1765, and was then published and widely circulated in a collection by Bryan Edwards called *Poems, Written Chiefly in the West-Indies*. A reproduction of Edwards's work is available from Bodleian Library.

28. For more on Wood's analysis of the pornographizing gaze, see *Slavery, Empathy, and Pornography*, especially his analysis of the engravings William Blake did for John Gabriel Stedman's *Narrative of a Five Years Expedition against the Revolted Negroes of Surinam*, 98–103. See also Greg Thomas, *The Sexual Demon of Colonial Power*.

29. In "Celebrating the Middle Passage," Wood offers a brilliant analysis of what he sees as the unresolvable tensions that haunt the engraving. On the one hand, he says, *The Voyage of the Sable Venus* is "an unproblematic piece of pro-slavery propaganda." On the other hand, given the "extreme musculature" and angry gaze of the Sable Venus, it is at least possible to interpret the image as "a critique of the sexual abuse of female slaves" or even "a celebration of black female agency" (134, 129). Wood thus offers a different reading of the image, emphasizing its potentially ambivalent political stance on slavery and its contrast to Teale's "essentially plantocratic" poem; he discusses the ways in which Stothard's image, produced thirty years after Teale's poem, might have been influenced by the rising abolitionist presence in the United Kingdom and his friendships with powerful abolitionists like William Blake (for more see especially pages 129–35).

30. Hartman, *Scenes of Subjection*, 19.

31. Ibid., 21, 51, 93.

TWO. Ruin's Subject in Shaftesbury's *Characteristicks*

1. The scholarship on the antebellum American novel over the past twenty years or so has established this link between democratic feeling and the cultural work of sympathy. There are too many sources to cite here, but no list would be complete without Barnes's *States of Sympathy*, Knott's *Sensibility and the American Revolution*, and Boudreau's *Sympathy in American Literature*.

2. Fleischacker, "The Impact on America."

3. Again, there are too many resources establishing the link between moral sense theory (often associated with the Scottish Enlightenment) and colonial and post-revolutionary American political thought to include them all here, but a list of a few key sources would include William R. Brock's *Scotus Americanus*, Andrew Hook's *Scotland and America*, and Jane Judge's encyclopedic overview, "The Scottish American Enlightenment."

4. In his foreword to Shaftesbury's work, Douglas Den Uyl notes that it was the second-most published book written in English in the eighteenth century.

5. Shaftesbury, *Characteristicks*, 71, 58, 86. Subsequent page citations to this work will appear in the text parenthetically.

6. Uyl, foreword, vii. As Den Uyl notes, "The 'Inquiry' is deductive and reads like a formal treatise," whereas "[m]ost of the other works" in *Characteristicks* are "discursive and literary in character."

7. As G.A.J. Rogers notes, "Hobbes generated more hostile literature than any other thinker in the seventeenth century. Indeed, if judged by the number of hostile books and pamphlets he generated, he may well be the most maligned philosopher of all time." "Hobbes and His Contemporaries," 412.

8. The moral sense is often erroneously attributed to Francis Hutcheson.

9. Downes offers important insights into why this misreading occurs—and a reading of Hobbes's influence in early American literature and politics more generally—in *Hobbes, Sovereignty, and Early American Literature*.

10. As Nancy Yousef so aptly puts it, "[T]he Hobbesian principles of human nature from a view of individuals as isolated protagonists" inform his infamous claim that in a state of nature, human life is "nasty, brutish, and short." "Feeling for Philosophy," 614.

11. Downes's discussion of what he calls supplementary sovereignty offers insight into this idea in *Hobbes, Sovereignty, and Early American Literature*.

12. Again in *Hobbes, Sovereignty, and Early American Literature*, Downes rightly points out, "the conceptual space that separates the Hobbesian sovereign from the Hobbesian people has repeatedly been mistaken for the abyss that separates the tyrannical ruler from his subjects" (3).

13. To warn others of the innate selfishness of man is itself an act of generosity. Shaftesbury goes on: "Is there then such a thing as *natural Affection?* If not; why all this Pain, why all this Danger on our account? Why not keep this Secret to Your-self? Of what advantage is it to You, to deliver us from the Cheat? The more are taken in it, the better," he quips, adding, "'Tis not fit we shou'd know that *by Nature* we are all *Wolves*. Is it possible that one who has really discover'd himself such, shou'd take pains to communicate such a Discovery?" (58–59) As Kelleher puts it in his discussion of this passage in *Characteristicks*, such an argument is "self-rebutting" (*Making Love*, 32).

14. Certainly Shaftesbury is not alone in his rejection of Hobbes. Sir Francis Hutcheson's *An Essay on the Nature and Conduct of the Passions and Affections, with*

Illustrations on the Moral Sense (1728), for example, takes Shaftesbury's ideas about the moral sense and develops them as a second refutation of *Leviathan*. Undoubtedly it was Hobbes whom Hutcheson had in mind when, in the very first page of his work, he icily refers to "some previous Notions" that have distorted human nature so egregiously that what ought to be obvious to anyone—our natural inclination to sociability and goodness—has become an unfashionable idea. Hutcheson offers his own haughty response to Hobbes, which according to him simply requires a little self-reflection: "[N]othing [is] more necessary than a little Attention to what passes in our own Hearts" to see how entirely off the mark Hobbes's understanding of human nature really is (3–4, 23). It is worth noting that Hutcheson was extremely popular among colonial US readers. For more on this see Norman S. Fiering's "Irresistible Compassion."

15. Again in *An Essay on the Nature and Conduct of the Passions and Affections*, Hutcheson clarifies the power of this moral sense. He defines the twin forces of the moral sense and *sensus communis* by explaining that there are plenty of senses in addition to the familiar five, if by "sense" we mean perceptions that occur independently of our will—experiences we "receive" but do not control. Among these are the "Publick Sense" (and here he quotes Shaftesbury, noting that he called it *sensus communis* after the Ancients), and the moral sense (17). Hutcheson explains, "*Sympathy* with others is the Effect of the Constitution of our Nature, and not brought upon our selves by any Choice." The fact that fellow feeling is unwilled is an important facet of Hutcheson's support of Shaftesbury's theory, one he emphasizes when he adds, "[E]very one feels that this *publick Sense* will not leave his Heart . . . nor does it depend upon a Man's *Choice*, whether he will be affected with their Fortunes or not" (23). Elsewhere he emphasizes that "Men cannot live without the *Society* of others" (75). For thinkers like Shaftesbury and his ally Hutcheson, our emotions, built into the architecture of the sensate body, rule the "state of nature," not savagery or selfishness.

16. Jacob Bodway notes that Shaftesbury sees the "operation of the moral faculties" as "embodied." "The Matter of Moral Sense," 536–37.

17. Ibid., 547, 536–37.

18. As Yousef rightly notes, for Shaftesbury, the virtues that impel us toward the social good are "tirelessly and exclusively advanced by appeals to what we cannot deny, cannot fail to see, cannot choose but feel" ("Feeling for Philosophy," 614).

19. Ibid., 611, 612. The notion of the "imperative" comes from Susan M. Purviance, "Intersubjectivity and Sociable Relations in the Philosophy of Francis Hutcheson," 23–28.

20. For a reading of Shaftesbury that situates his work within sexuality studies, see Kelleher, *Making Love*. Although Kelleher is more interested in the role of filial love in Shaftesbury's work and sees Shaftesbury's references to natural love and family as pointing to a likely embrace of marriage, he does agree that subjectivity for Shaftesbury is about sympathy's power. As Kelleher argues, love and desire in Shaftesbury are "imagined to open an intersubjective window" (20).

21. Not all readers of *Characteristicks* agree on this point. Many see Shaftesbury's work as ultimately about safeguarding the core individual self from the dangers of too much influence at work in the sociable self. As Rebecca Tierney-Hynes asserts in "Shaftesbury's Soliloquy," for example, soliloquy is then an act of "solipsism" and "deep narcissism" that interiorizes the subject (618). "The purpose, in the end, of the 'self-discoursing practice' seems to be a kind of therapeutic mental masturbation—a way of purging sexual self-indulgence in order to purvey a philosophical product that is free, in the end, of seductive possibilities" (613). In fact, some critics see the moral sense as a mechanism designed to protect the individual self. For more on this, see the September 2014 issue (37.3) of the *Journal for Eighteenth-Century Studies*, especially Patrick Müller, "Hobbes, Locke, and the Consequences" and Joanne E. Myers, "'Supernatural Charity.'" As for the notion of the "manager," Kenneth P. Winkler sees this figure as "[t]he real or true self" or "the rational self who rules," which constitutes a "rationally informed will" in "'All Is Revolution in Us,'" 11.

22. Hume, *A Treatise of Human Nature*, 331.

23. Pateman, *The Sexual Contract*.

24. Also a huge contribution to current understandings of gender, the family, and the new republic is Linda Kerber's well-known analysis of the republican gender roles, *Women of the Republic*, which establishes that the role of the mother in the new nation was to raise patriotic sons—the future of the republic was therefore in her hands. For more about how the companionate ideal in marriage functioned both as a metaphor and as a lived reality of the new egalitarianism, also see Anya Jabour, *Marriage in the Early Republic*.

25. In one of the stranger moments in *Discourse on the Origin and Basis of Inequality among Men*, Rousseau describes a kind of fight-club fantasy of the physical combat between natural man and the civilized gentleman of his own time, a scene which is meant to illustrate the power and virtue of self-possession but which turns on an overdetermined moment of eros and masculine aggressiveness. It is a contest in which the mettle of the gentleman can be measured via his nakedness. Without clothing, the tools of modern warfare, or any other accoutrements of modernity—only then can the contest be a fair one, and then the natural man is sure to win because his self-possession is unfettered by a lower-order reliance on the possession of things. And as Rousseau goes on to say in *Discourse*, the "savage man" or natural man is described as "always carrying one's entire self, so to speak, with one" (147). The brute knows himself because that is all he can be said to *have*. It is this episode that teaches us what it means to invest in self-possession as that which defines self-giving. "For in the first place, since each man gives himself entirely, the condition is equal for all," he says in *The Social Contract*, and to do this right one must be in full possession of oneself to engage in the fiction of that possession's exchange and return (17).

26. He authored extremely popular novels about passion and seduction like *Julie; or, The New Heloise* (1761) and the posthumously published sequel to *Emile* (1762), *Emile and Sophie; or, The Solitaries* (1780).

27. Amy Dru Stanley, qtd. in Morgenstern, "Marriage and Contract," 110.

28. Morgenstern, "Marriage and Contract," 111.

29. Coviello, *Intimacy in America.*

30. Weyler, *Intricate Relations,* 21. There is certainly no dearth of scholarship on the intersections of female sexuality, the home, and contract culture. Some of the best work looks at the ways in which eighteenth-century culture expressed deep ambivalence about expressions of female sexuality that revealed the home to be that unfriendly place. In addition to Weyler's important work, there is, for example, Katherine Kittredge's interesting collection, *Lewd and Notorious.* See especially the chapter in which Julia Shaffer offers a discussion of cultural and literary lenience toward sexually ruined women, "Ruined Women and Illegitimate Daughters: Revolution and Female Sexuality." For a discussion of eighteenth-century pleasure culture and the instability of patriarchal power within that realm, see Clare A. Lyons, *Sex among the Rabble.* For a discussion of the "scandal memoir" as a genre interested in female sexuality, voice, and agency, see Knott's "Female Liberty?"

31. Some of the most familiar passages in these novels erupt in pronoun confusion, as when in Harriet Jacobs's slave narrative, the protagonist Linda Brent refers to herself at the moment of seduction as "one's self," "you," and "a slave" in a passage I will discuss at greater length in chapter 6.

32. Butler, *Senses of the Subject,* 36. Subsequent page citations to this text will appear in the text parenthetically.

33. Eagleton, *The Ideology of the Aesthetic,* 13.

34. Adam Smith, *The Theory of Moral Sentiments,* 15–16. Subsequent page citations to this work will appear in the text parenthetically.

35. Ibid., 16.

36. Coviello, *Intimacy in America.*

37. Nancy, *The Inoperative Community,* 29.

THREE. Incest and the Nature of Ruin in the Novels of William Hill Brown

1. *The Correspondence between the Honorable John Adams, Late President of the United States, and the Late William Cunningham, Esq.*, 18–19. From https://archive.org/details/correspondencebe01adam.

2. Several scholars have established that *The Power of Sympathy* is the first novel written by someone born in colonial America and published by an American printer. Davidson discusses the publication history of the novel in *Revolution and the Word.* Earlier accounts of Brown as America's first novelist include Tremain McDowell's "The First American Novel," and Phillip Young's "'First American Novel.'"

3. For example, Barnes notes in *States of Sympathy* that to be "*truly* American," men had to learn how to emulate women, to be "suggestible" and "seducible" (xi).

4. *The Power of Sympathy* is based in part on what was known as the Apthorp-Morton scandal, in which Perez Morton seduced his sister-in-law, Fanny Apthorp; after giving birth to Morton's child, Fanny committed suicide. Her sister, Sarah Wentworth Apthorp, was a well-known poet and friend to William Hill Brown. For a

comprehensive discussion of the historical facts related to the "true" story of the Apthorp/Morton seduction scandal on which *The Power of Sympathy* is in small part based, see Bryan Waterman, "'Heaven Defend Us from Such Fathers.'"

5. For more on the tension between "the ideal of all humans' intrinsic freedom and the nightmare of unrestrained passion," as well as the contradictions inherent in the "self-possession" (90) of contract theory, see Barbara M. Benedict, "Radcliffe, Godwin, and Self-Possession in the 1790s."

6. Fluck calls this "the multivocal potential of the epistolary novel" in "Reading Early American Fiction" (572). And of course the reference to heteroglossia comes from Mikhail Bakhtin's *The Dialogic Imagination.*

7. Davidson, *Revolution and the Word,* 99. As Davidson goes on to say, "[N]o one clear note or melodic line sounds in the novel" so that "at times it almost seems as if we have two distinct and even contradictory discourses, a didactic essay and a novel, shuffled together and bound as one book" (101, 99). A similar take on this argument comes from James Chandler, who argues that the "tonal lability" of the novel establishes it as a transatlantic text marked by "epistemological ambiguity" and an "ethical ambivalence" about the power of sympathy (134, 148) in "Placing *The Power of Sympathy.*"

8. Terence Martin, one of the only critics to have written on *Ira and Isabella,* dismisses it as "clumsy" and full of "overwrought sentimentalized narrative" ("William Hill Brown's *Ira and Isabella,*" 238). While the posthumous publication suggests at least the possibility that Brown would have revised the manuscript, the aesthetics of the novel seem less a sign of awkward prose than of a text exploding with the energy of contradictions within a treatise on the "natural" body.

9. Richard Walser reports on the reception of *The Power of Sympathy* and the cultural moment that anticipated it: "On the basis of what was appearing in the Boston press during 1788 and 1789, the city's writers, editors, and readers were downright neurotically fascinated by the themes of adultery, suicide, and seduction" ("Boston's Reception of the First American Novel," 66).

10. In fact, argues Walser, audiences were disappointed that the Apthorp scandal occupies so little of the novel. Given the frontispiece and its promise of seduction tales, Walser notes, readers were understandably miffed (ibid., 69). For an in-depth account of the novel's initial advertising and publication, see Davidson, *Revolution and the Word,* 89–90.

11. Anne Dalke notes that the incest theme was quite popular in novels printed in the United States, up to at least the 1830s; such texts generally use incest, Dalke argues, as a punishment for upward class mobility—seduction represents marrying outside of one's own social class as a cultural crime. Dalke, "Original Vice."

12. An interesting take on this incest-once-removed familial structure comes from Erica Burleigh's *Intimacy and Family in Early American Writing.* Burleigh suggests that such practices kept women located within the family in a perversion of chivalry that protects the virtues of the young female by incorporating her into "a sort of appropriate incest" (54).

13. Critics have argued that in Brown's novels, the incest-as-ruin narrative presents a metaphor for sympathetic identification as the reigning political model in early US relations, both fictional and real. This is because the blood relation dictates that siblings will respond involuntarily to the call of blood, and when they do not know of the familial relation, that call will translate as sexual desire. Barnes's close reading of *The Power of Sympathy* is of great use here. In *States of Sympathy*, she argues that the power of sympathy is the "dangerous capacity to undermine the democratic principles it ostensibly means to reinforce" (4). Barnes notes that in Brown's novel, incest "represents the logical outcome" of the rhetoric of sympathy that tries to use the family as the model for public life by turning others into affective, familiar attachments (3). Barnes's astute analysis is invested in discovering the nuanced cultural work of Brown's text, which is to characterize the incestuous family as a metaphor for democratic institutions. Nature is "the author of Harrington and Harriot's misfortune, calling into question the power of human reason and resolution ever to overcome the power of sympathy" because incest stories prove "that feeling cannot be controlled" (146).

14. Barnes, *States of Sympathy*, 20.

15. Young, "'First American Novel,'" 123.

16. Boudreau notes, "Those who speak the language of conventional morality" in the novel "are at best ineffective and at worst corrupt" (*Sympathy in American Literature*, 32). Young says that the supporting cast of the novel can be characterized as "somewhat unfeeling," and even calls one moralizer "a bore" and the other "a pain," concluding, "It is hard to believe, though most assume it, that Brown was really serious with these people" ("'First American Novel,'" 120).

17. Fluck, "Reading Early American Fiction," 577.

18. For an account of the poem's history, authenticity, and meanings, see Waterman, "Elizabeth Whitman's Disappearance and Her 'Disappointment.'"

19. Fluck, "Reading Early American Fiction," 575. On the other side of the critical discussion, Christian Quendler argues that the seduction stories "occur at a remove from the main story line as to provide critical distance," allowing Brown the ability to include the tales without presenting them too salaciously ("Bodies of Letters," 125).

20. As I have argued elsewhere, these rhetorical tensions are not accidental, or proof of Brown's incompetence as a writer (or even proof of the novel as a genre taking its shaky first steps in the new United States). Rather, the rhetorical tensions argue for a particular ideal of romance.

21. Burleigh notes the power of incest to render biological the call to community that becomes exile from it: "Characters experience emotions beyond their control or understanding, directed toward figures that their communities find inappropriate—that they themselves find inappropriate . . . and yet cannot free themselves, in part because the logic that underlies their affections is one predicated on biological connection as a kind of affective relation." Burleigh, *Intimacy and Family in Early American Writing*, 7.

22. As Coviello so insightfully asks in *Intimacy in America,* "Does sympathy, which forever tugs at the body, carry that agitated body over into states of desire?" Brown's novels answer that question emphatically in the affirmative, and they do so by characterizing desire ontologically, presenting the lover who has come undone as a competing model for the modern subject.

23. See Knott, *Sensibility and the American Revolution.* In Knott's work on the sociomedical understanding of feeling, she notes, "The stakes were high, for, as the nervous system and its sensibility were understood as a bridge possessing attributes both of body and mind, this physiology tended to monism, to the denial of the traditional duality of body and mind" (10). Additionally, she notes that "in linking body and mind by sensation, nervous sensibility was a basis of self" and "did not belong exclusively to the physicians but were part of the acquired wisdom of the middling and elite families and social circles" (69, 83).

24. Indeed, the seduced women are presented as not simply innocent but likeably so. Brown describes Elizabeth Whitman as having "a good heart" tempered by "patience and fortitude," a victim of a man's world that found she was "easily deceived" (23). Ophelia is even more of an innocent: Brown describes the fragile nature of "the heart of the unsuspicious Ophelia" who is "doomed" and "hapless" (38). Similarly, Fidelia is referred to as "harmless" and "inoffensive," a "poor maniack" whose sanity has been lost in addition to her virtue. Maria is described as "decoyed" from virtue though "virtue and harmony were blended" in her character, as evidenced in her "tears of penitence" (67, 72, 68). The same likeability factor holds true in *Ira and Isabella.* Even Lucinda, Ira's irrepressible mother, is "affable and simple" though she "had successfully laid a snare" to seduce a man (34).

25. See Davidson, *Revolution and the Word,* especially 90–96. The frontispiece image may have had additional purposes. For instance, Christopher J. Lukasik notes in his description of it that "[t]he vial of poison was a common post-revolutionary metaphor for the negative effects of reading romance novels" (*Discerning Characters,* 273n43).

26. Weyler's discussion of self-discipline in early American fiction suggests that we might read the mirror passage through a pedagogical lens: "[T]he intense emphasis on internalized discipline in . . . epistolary fiction suggests that the responsibility for maintaining—and punishing lapses in—female virtue rested with the individual" and "illustrates . . . whether or not, and how well, young men and women have developed internalized monitors of their own passions and whether they are habituated to control themselves" (*Intricate Relations,* 25, 37).

27. Indeed, the genre instability's aesthetic work articulates outrage over a lack of choices for women as it interrogates "the supposed binary consent/resistance." Toni Bowers and Tita Chico, "Introduction," *Atlantic Worlds in the Long Eighteenth Century.*

28. It is possible that Brown had a transatlantic set of imagery in mind. As Susan Manning and Francis D. Cogliano note in their introduction to *The Atlantic Enlightenment,* "traversing the Atlantic, whether on a boat or in the mind, was an

extraordinarily powerful agent and image of defamiliarization, setting Enlightened minds 'at sea' in the uncertainties of an existence become irredeemably comparative and relative" (6). Doyle offers an extended reading of Atlantic imagery in *The Power of Sympathy* in *Freedom's Empire*. See especially 166–70.

29. As Matthew Stewart argues, the deist founding fathers rejected the notion that there is a god meddling in the petty affairs of humankind, and to think otherwise would constitute a colossal act of hubris. Instead of the human exceptionalism found in so many other religious doctrines, Stewart notes, "the definitive teaching of the radical philosophy that revolutionized the early modern world is that the human being is a part of nature, no less subject to its laws than everything else in the infinite universe" (*Nature's God*, ebook).

30. Downes, "Does the Declaration of Independence Declare a State of Emergency?"

31. The work of sympathy has been assessed prolifically by writers already cited in this study, like Julia Stern, Elizabeth Barnes, June Howard, and Terry Eagleton.

32. Stowe, *Uncle Tom's Cabin*, 385.

33. Adams, *The Political Writings of John Adams*, 176.

34. We might think of this version of nature in the helpful terms outlined by Adela Pinch, whose discussion of "the passions" shows that eighteenth-century British philosophers understood them to be "natural forces tied closely to the body but also the essence of volition," such that "it is passion that allows us to be persons, rather than the other way around." Pinch, *Strange Fits of Passion*, 18, 19.

35. *The Correspondence between the Honorable John Adams, Late President of the United States, and the Late William Cunningham, Esq.*, 18–19.

36. Hugh McIntosh offers a more literary reading, placing Adams's remark in the context of the role of the patriarchy to defend the people: "Like Adams's populace perpetually threatened by Lovelace, the fallen woman reflects the need for patriarchal care" because of "the lack of self-control possessed by social inferiors" like herself who need "patriarchal guidance." McIntosh, "Constituting the End of Feeling," 332.

37. Paul Downes takes this line further when he notes that ending revolutionary fervor would require "limiting access to that very conflation of the natural and the political that gave the Declaration of Independence its felicitous force." "Fiction and Democracy," 27.

38. As Knott puts it, sensibility was interpellated as "most bodily . . . the physical body was brought alive and interconnected with sensibility." Knott, *Sensibility and the American Revolution*, 9.

39. Yet incest can also be read as representing the nation's fears about itself as an enemy worse than any outsider. As Stern notes, "the pervasive figure of incest in the Early American novel [emblematizes] the way in which what are perceived as disturbances from without are themselves always already operative within the nation" (*This Plight of Feeling*, 282n108).

40. Greven, "Incest and Intertextuality," 42.

41. In a fascinating study of growing instances of suicide in post-revolutionary literature, Katherine Gaudet notes that taking one's own life came to represent not a heroic action but "conflicted anxiety" about voluntarism and "the incommensurability of voluntaristic individualism with lived reality." Indeed, the suicides in novels like *The Power of Sympathy* are figured through "an aesthetic of *reaction*" because those who take their own lives "cannot control either the worlds they live in or their own reactions to them." Instead, "suicide emerges as a site of uncontrollable emotion that could threaten the basis of rationalist government" (Gaudet, "Liberty and Death," 610).

42. As Kerber has argued, republican ideology rested on the notion that dispassionate women would discipline the nation out of its unruly and vicious ways. Kerber, *Women of the Republic*, 58–59.

43. In Weyler's excellent overview of desire and self-control in *Intricate Relations*, she notes that "the failure of . . . self-regulation leads to," among other things, seduction, "all to the detriment of the individual, the family, and the Republic" (3). In other words, when Harriot struggles to control her incestuous desires, in part what happens is that her ability to see herself as part of the human institutions around her deteriorates.

44. Indeed, as Burleigh argues, if anything, Harrington would replace one type of incest with another. He further tells Worthy that if he had only known Harriot was his sister, his "love would have been more regular," and he would have sought to protect her beauty from men *not* related to her. He thus "invokes the specter of incest by suggesting that his sister's 'beauty' and 'virtues' need to be kept from external threats by being located safely within the bosom of the protecting family." Burleigh, *Intimacy and Family in Early America*, 54.

45. As Barnes puts it, here is where "the story's true rebellion lies," when Harriot and Harrington do not "return to their previous condition as independent beings." Barnes, *States of Sympathy*, 149.

46. Ibid.

47. Brown's quotation is not entirely accurate according to today's available editions. The nurse's speech in *Romeo and Juliet* includes the lines, "Then hie you hence to Friar Lawrence's cell;/There stays a husband to make you a wife:/Now comes the wanton blood up in your cheeks,/They'll be in scarlet straight at any news" (2.5.61–64).

FOUR. Seduction and the Patriotism of Ruin in Hannah Webster Foster's *The Coquette*

1. The term "coquette" is itself fraught with competing definitions. One of the best comes from Theresa Braunschneider's *Our Coquettes: Capacious Desire in the Eighteenth Century*, in which the word is defined as "Vain young women who defy dominant codes of sexual conduct by encouraging several suitors at once" so that they may "insist upon marrying only whom they want, when they want, and

if they want." Because of its emphasis on free choices made by women rather than for them, "the term eventually comes to refer specifically to disingenuous sexual encouragement." Braunschneider, *Our Coquettes*, 102.

2. For the full story of Elizabeth Whitman and its connection to *The Coquette*, see Davidson, *Revolution and the Word*, 140–50. For a fascinating take on Jonathan Edwards's philosophical antagonism to the founders' understandings of nature, see Stewart, *Nature's God*.

3. Danvers played an important role in the Revolutionary War as well. The most well-known figure from Danvers is General Israel Putnam, whose military accomplishments earned him that fame, and whose parents, perhaps not incidentally, were dead set against the witch trials of Salem. For the full manuscript of Harriet Silvester Tapley's *Chronicle of Danvers: 1632–1923*, published in 1923, see archive.org/details/chroniclesofdanvootapl.

4. For a reading of Eliza as an epistolary character Foster emphasizes as illegible and fragmented and who "never has any sense of coherent selfhood," see Diez Couch, "Eliza Wharton's Scraps of Writing," 695.

5. On the other hand, it is worth noting critics who see Eliza acting as a representative of the individual rather than in defiance of such an identity. In her study of Eliza, Carroll Smith-Rosenberg proposes a reading of the body as a "representation of the civic individual" in eighteenth-century fiction that repositions "the political and the sexual." She continues: "No longer will [the body] appear simply as a repository of the erotic and the reproductive, a psychic entity confined to social margins and domestic space . . . the body's physical integrity constitutes a significant a material vehicle for symbolic representation as the body's evocative sensuality." Her reading recognizes this sensuality as well as the body's "representation of the civic individual." Smith-Rosenberg, "'Domesticating Virtue,'" 161, 171, 175.

6. For more on the significance of "possession" in this passage, see the work of Abram Van Engen, who offers in "Eliza's Disposition" a discussion of how the text plays with notions of free will and agency through the lens of Christian notions of liberty.

7. As Braunschneider says in *Our Coquettes*, "to cure a woman of coquetry is to make her sit still," as a coquette often "registers a concern about placelessness" in the modern age (95, 96).

8. This in direct opposition to other modes of sensationalism, which in other contexts can signify what Bryce Traister calls the libertine's "radical individualism" that is "unfettered by the restraints of institutionalized social mores and dedicated to the freedom paradoxically conferred by the total submission of self to sensualism," and now signifies an entirely sentimental impulse to comfort Eliza ("Libertinism and Authorship in America's Early Republic," 7–8).

9. Adams, *The Political Writings of John Adams*, 176.

10. Gordon S. Wood, *The Idea of America*.

11. Jefferson, *Letters*, 1791.

12. For more on Jefferson and Shaftesbury in this context, see Stewart, *Nature's God*.

13. Jefferson, *Letters*, 1814.

14. Rush, *Essays*, 7.

15. The theme of seduction in this novel thus engages with the debate over which principles really do, and really *should*, bring people together as a nation. As the historian Isaac Kramnick argues, over and against the principles of republican civic humanism that insisted "Man was a political being who realized his telos only when living in a *vivere civile*," the position of possessive individualism gloried "in an individualistic and competitive America, which was preoccupied with private rights and personal autonomy." Kramnick, "The 'Great National Discussion,'" 36–37.

16. Locke, "The Second Treatise of Government," 32.

17. Nancy, *The Inoperative Community*, xxxviii.

18. Mary Wollstonecraft's *A Vindication of the Rights of Woman* offers what reads like a rebuttal to Thomas Selby's characterization, and is worth taking note of here, given that *Vindication* was popular enough in America to go through two printings. Wollstonecraft does not contradict Selby so much as she blames him and others like him for the problem when she demonizes coquetry as the unfortunate but inevitable result of the raising of women to be "hothouse flowers," an artifact of misogynist culture. Davidson details the appearance of *Vindication* in many libraries and its advertisement by publishers on the backs of other novels circulating in America. She argues that its popularity accounts for "the single most important theoretical contribution to the egalitarian cause" (*Revolution and the Word*, 131). Bristling at the perception of women as objects of appetite, Wollstonecraft issues what reads like a reprimand to Thomas Selby: "Women then having necessarily some duty to fulfill, more noble than to adorn their persons, would not contentedly be the slaves of casual lust; which is now the situation of a very considerable number who are, literally speaking, standing dishes to which every glutton may have access." Wollstonecraft, *A Vindication of the Rights of Woman*, 273.

19. For a discussion of how the trope of letter writing is used to explore the ways in which women's agency is compromised, see Kacy Tillman, "Paper Bodies."

20. Grantland S. Rice's innovative argument that "the novel in republican America took on the deportment of a 'coquette' . . . to engage a changing reading public" explores the impact of that kind of circulation. Seen as a trope of women's writing, the coquette participates in "a tradition of public writing in America [that] found its origins in civic rather than economic or artisanal imperatives." Thus the sociability of the coquette, even as it endangers her public virtue, gestures toward a model of civic power for women. Rice, *The Transformation of Authorship in America*, 152.

21. Noting the primacy of female friendships in *The Coquette*, Claire C. Pettengill develops an explanation as to why Eliza uncharacteristically asks Boyer to reconsider marrying her after she has rejected him. Pettengill argues that alongside the seduction plot in Foster's novel exists another plot about the evolution of friendships broken apart by marriage. It is only after Eliza's two best friends evolve from the roles of sisterly friends into those of mother (Mrs. Richman has a baby) and wife (Lucy gets married) that the seduction is possible. "To repair the loss" of the female friendships,

"she must accept the unappealing, unsympathetic Rev. Boyer, who, by presiding over her transformation into a republican wife and mother, would enable her to rejoin their circle." Pettengill, "Sisterhood in a Separate Sphere," 195–96.

22. Instead of seeing her "natural disposition" as that which precludes making rational choices, Gillian Brown argues that "Eliza's insistence on following her 'natural propensity' for enjoyment invokes the natural rights basis for self-determination prevalent in eighteenth-century republican theory" ("Consent, Coquetry, and Consequences," 636).

23. A different reading of Eliza's failure to make choices comes from Laura H. Korobkin, who argues that Eliza is a good-time girl who evades the responsibilities of adult life in an effete and aristocratic model of pleasure-seeking: what "she seeks is not self-sufficiency or even self-realization but self-indulgence and luxury, the banes of the old world rather than the potentials of the new" ("'Can Your Volatile Daughter Ever Acquire Your Wisdom?'" 80).

24. Yet critics continually see Eliza as sexually indifferent to Sanford. For example, while offering the compelling assessment that Eliza "has invested her female independence and liberty of choice with desire," Smith-Rosenberg also insists that "the sexual fall comes unaccompanied by either pleasure or passion" ("'Domesticating Virtue,'" 160). Similarly, Davidson says that Eliza's consent to Sanford signifies "sexual acquiescence, accomplished with an appalling lack of desire" (*Revolution and the Word*, 149). Davidson also argues that "the spectre of spinsterhood" drove Eliza to have sex with Sanford, not physical desire or love. Smith-Rosenberg builds on Davidson's reading when she says that Eliza's "downfall . . . was not lust but the desire for independence coupled with the wish to rise socially" ("'Domesticating Virtue,'" 169). Korobkin says Eliza "enters the sexual liaison with Sanford because she associates him with her lost dream of material gratification. . . . The 'delusive dream of sensual gratification' she briefly enjoys functions as a synecdochal fragment of the life of sensual material gratification she had fantasized would be hers if they married"—a love of luxury, not sex, that is "un-American" (Korobkin, "'Can Your Volatile Daughter Ever Acquire Your Wisdom?'" 91). Gillian Brown reads *The Coquette* as a novel not about personal desire but rather personal consent as a problematic issue for women. According to Gillian Brown, "Far from expressing her own desire, Eliza's consent represents the subordination of personal desire" ("Consent, Coquetry, Consequences," 638). The most extreme denial of Eliza's desire comes from Christopher Lukasik, who says, "Eliza's choice of intimacy with Sanford is notoriously difficult to understand" ("Breeding and Reading," 163).

25. Traister, "Libertinism and Authorship in America's Early Republic," 7–8.

26. Indeed, the assumption of her lack of desire indicates a larger political problem in play. Cora Kaplan observes, for example, that the problem with much Anglo-American philosophy, starting with Wollstonecraft, is that it has "too often accepted the paradigm which insists that desire is a regressive force in women's lives, and [has] called for a sublimation of women's sexual pleasure to meet a passionless and rational ideal" ("Wild Nights," in *Sea Changes*, 35).

27. Gillian Brown, "Consent, Coquetry, Consequences," 630.

28. The notion that Eliza must make a choice at all is one critics have taken up. Intriguingly, part of the role of the coquette may be to question the assumption of monogamous desire. As Braunschneider argues in *Our Coquettes,* the coquette's lack of a single choice of gallant "calls our attention to the operations of axes *other* than homo/hetero—for instance, plural/singular—in the discursive construction of sexual possibilities"; instead of finding satisfaction in the one choice a single woman must make—whom to marry—the coquette is portrayed as "finding pleasure *in the act of choosing*," not in a finite moment of choice but in insisting that to live is to always be choosing. Braunschneider, *Our Coquettes,* 17.

29. Such a remark suggests that Foster may have meant for Sanford to be a more natural, and a more radical, figure than critics have tended to see him as. As Peter Nagy argues, the libertine of the eighteenth century pursued "the establishment of a natural morality founded on the expansion of man's vital instincts," ones like "liberty and the pursuit of happiness" (383). Quoted in Elena Russo, "Sociability, Cartesianism, and Nostalgia in Libertine Discourse," 383.

30. Indeed, with remarks like this one, Eliza sounds like what Jennifer Harris calls "the justified pariah," the banished martyr to a higher cause ("Wax Coquettes," 385).

31. Hoffert, *A Politics of Tensions,* 115.

32. Kramnick, "The 'Great National Discussion,'" 47.

33. Not all readers agree that Eliza's misanthropy is so tragic. McIntosh argues that stories of ratification era seduction can sometimes "reveal a politically engaged fantasy of feeling's disappearance" and "the tranquil withdrawal from life with others"—something Shaftesbury clearly couldn't imagine. McIntosh, "Constituting the End of Feeling."

34. Davidson, *Revolution and the Word,* 149.

35. For more on the role of female friendship in the novel, see Ivy Schweitzer, *Perfecting Friendship.* As Schweitzer astutely observes, "the threat female friendships pose for heteronormative social order" is, in *The Coquette,* "a social alternative to unequal and privatizing Federalist marriage" against which "women of the emerging middle class took up the elaborate rituals of homosocial friendship with enthusiasm" (*Perfecting Friendship,* 105, 222, 227). See also Pettengill, "Sisterhood in a Separate Sphere."

36. Bateman, "Queer Coquetry," 6, 8.

37. Ibid., 7.

38. Bersani, "Is the Rectum a Grave?" 222.

39. Most critics disagree. Gillian Brown argues that "female consent epitomizes individual subjection in a liberal society" in the novel ("Consent, Coquetry, Consequences," 633). As Braunschneider argues, the coquette's liberty "denies men sexual access to and dominion over her, but her *choice*—which she would presumably be able to exercise only in a state of freedom—is essential to ensuring that dominion" (*Our Coquettes,* 15). In other words, the coquette's main dramatic purpose is to interrogate the presence or absence of her consent; when she withholds the choice,

she also anticipates its eventuality, and the fact that she *will* make a choice sustains male power over her. Complicating any idealization of "choice" as it is presented to the unmarried white woman is the idea that a woman's virtue could save the corrupting realms of social engagement, except of course that they must be shielded from them (Harris, "Wax Coquettes," 363).

40. Wollstonecraft, *A Vindication of the Rights of Woman*, 246.

41. Rousseau, *Discourse on the Origin and Basis of Inequality among Men*, 167–68.

FIVE. Ruin, Martyrdom, and the Spectacle of Sympathy from *Clotel* to *The Scarlet Letter*

1. Nancy, *The Inoperative Community*, xxxvii.

2. In his thorough study of *Clotel*'s source material history, Geoffrey Sanborn points out that seventy-three passages or more are plagiarized in Brown's novel. "There are, in fact, at least seventy-three passages, ranging in length from ten to 1,335 consecutive words, that are lifted from other texts. In those passages, Brown copies 13,002 words, nearly twenty-three percent of the novel, from fifty different sources. And if one groups those passages together with all of the epigraphs, poems, songs, newspaper clippings, and miscellaneous quotations in *Clotel*, the proportion of the novel written by people other than Brown jumps to thirty-five percent" ("'People Will Pay to Hear the Drama,'" 67).

3. Rousseau, *The Essential Rousseau*, 147.

4. Locke, *Two Treatises of Government*, 134.

5. Abdur-Rahman, "'This Horrible Exhibition,'" 235.

6. The most cited work in this critical conversation continues to be Hartman's *Scenes of Subjection*. See also Wood's *Slavery, Empathy, and Pornography* and McMillan's *Embodied Avatars*.

7. As Ivy G. Wilson notes, "African Americans manipulated visuality in art that depicted images of national belonging not only as a mode of critique but as an iteration of democratic representation itself." Wilson, *Specters of Democracy*, ebook.

8. For an extensive discussion of the role of those source materials in *Clotel*, see Sanborn, *Plagiarama!* As Sanborn argues, "The more we learn about the plagiarism in *Clotel*, the more it begins to appear that the only fixity in the novel is in fact the lack of fixity to which it repeatedly returns us, both through its reminders of the contradiction at the heart of American democracy and through its unpredictable movement from idiom to idiom. By exposing us, via his narrative persona, to an incessant re-beginning, Brown invites us to associate blackness with a migrating instability that is, for him, the most pleasurable—and hence the most promising—basis of abolitionist consciousness" (68).

9. Wilson defines *Clotel*'s generic weirdness as "bricolage" in *Specters of Democracy*.

10. Bhabha, *The Location of Culture*.

11. Roberts, *Gothic Subjects*, 141–43.

12. It is worth noting that William Wells Brown characterizes the nonlegal "marriages" among slaves as more reflective of romantic love than any contract, as an agent of enforcement, ever could; such marriages represent a more natural union, nature here understood as William Hill Brown characterizes it in *The Power of Sympathy*. As Tess Chakkalakal notes, novels in the period of *Clotel* "position slave-marriage as . . . a more intimate form of marriage than those bound by the law," so that we observe what might be called "a new story of marriage" in Brown's novels that "crossed the line between private and public life in surprising ways." Chakkalakal, *Novel Bondage*, 3, 17, 16. Wilson calls the sphere in which such rebellion is possible the "counterpublic where African Americans created both ethereal and material forms of political agency to contest the meanings of citizenship and democracy in the United States" in *Specters of Democracy*.

13. Sherrard-Johnson, "Delicate Boundaries," 205.

14. Stupp, "Slavery and the Theatre of History," 61.

15. Ibid., 62.

16. Elliott, *Robert Emmet*.

17. Robert Emmet's speech on the witness stand before his death sentence was announced was quite famous among oratorical instances of rebellion against the crown in the eighteenth century. It may be that Brown chose Irving's story about Robert Emmet and Sarah Curran because of Emmet's overt reference to George Washington. In part of Emmet's speech, he refers to himself as a martyr for his country, and his language echoes the themes of *Clotel* quite remarkably in his focus on martyrdom and oppression, as he says "I wished to procure for my country the guarantee which Washington procured for America. . . . What, my lord, shall you tell me, on the passage to that scaffold. That I am accountable for all the blood that has and will be shed in this struggle of the oppressed against the oppressor?—shall you tell me this—and must I be so very a slave as not to repel it?" "Speeches from the Dock, Part I."

18. Hawthorne, *The Scarlet Letter*, 50. Subsequent page citations to this work will appear in the text parenthetically.

19. In *Gothic Subjects*, Roberts makes the even stronger claim that, "made into a letter of the alphabet, Hester loses her status as an individual and becomes known for small deviances from abstract norms" (125). Roberts also offers an illuminating interpretation to link Hester's status as an outcast and a deviant to Michel Foucault's notion of "the population."

20. Jan-Melissa Smith, *Atonement and Self-Sacrifice in Nineteenth-Century Narrative*, 16. Smith further notes that "the civic sphere at mid-century was underpinned by the hope that individual appropriations of the pain of another, when acted upon, would generate a wider social concord" (15). Thus we might say that Hester's suffering provides an occasion for a community in harmony—her martyrdom realizes that hope for an emotional conscience that creates a civic interdependence.

21. Csengei, *Sympathy, Sensibility, and the Literature of Feeling in the Eighteenth Century*, 31.

22. Hawthorne, *The Blithedale Romance*, 12, 13. Subsequent page citations to this work will appear in the text parenthetically.

23. In their more sinister reading of Zenobia's death, John Harmon McElroy and Edward L. McDonald suggest that it is not a suicide at all, but a murder at the hands of the men at Blithedale. McElroy and McDonald, "The Coverdale Romance."

24. For some critics of the novel, Zenobia's sexuality further problematizes her status as a sentimental figure. Greven uses the phrase "Medusan harlot" to describe how Zenobia's status is perceived within the world of the novel; she is an antagonistic figure with a "threateningly vivid, voracious sexuality" ("In a Pig's Eye," 138). John N. Miller likewise identifies that status as the "love-crazed Ophelia" ("Eros and Ideology," 15). According to Robert Milder, the novel presents her power is gendered in unflattering ways, so that she appears as "shopworn goods" and a force of disorder, both a Pandora and a Galatea ("Beautiful Illusions," 10).

25. In critical readings of Zenobia as a feminist, scholars often conclude that she is a figure of anti-sentimental defeat. Her show of female power undermined by her love for the ultimate patriarch, Hollingsworth, she becomes a character who despite "all her feminist rhetoric . . . proves to be another dependent woman" (Millicent Bell, "Hawthorne and the Real," 33). As Noble puts it, after all her speeches about women's rights, she ultimately reveals herself to be a "masochist" who is "attracted to abusive men" and, what is perhaps worse, "the feminist [who] betrays her sister" (*The Masochistic Pleasures of Sentimental Literature*, 195–97).

26. Many critics of *The Blithedale Romance* present interpretations of Zenobia that either omit discussions of her sentimentality or suggest that Hawthorne designed her as a distinctly anti-sentimental figure. Some critics even suggest that associations between Zenobia and sentimentalism are incongruous with her feminist power. As Frank Christianson argues, her suicide, presumed to be the result of Hollingsworth's rejection of her, "reduces her to a sentimental convention that is hard to reconcile with her development up to that point in the novel" ("'Trading Places in Fancy,'" 256). For other critics, her suicide disqualifies her as a sentimental figure and even marks Hawthorne's dismissal of sentimentalism. As Laura Tanner argues, by ending her life, Zenobia makes "a mockery of herself as a sentimental heroine" ("Speaking with 'Hands at Our Throats,'" 12). In "Hawthorne's Anti-Romance," for example, Ken Egan Jr. reads Zenobia as a figure of realism, an explicitly anti-sentimental figure designed to lampoon sentimental stereotypes; *Blithedale* is according to Egan "a pastiche of parodized sentimental conventions" centering on Zenobia, who "breaks the mold of sentimental stereotyping" ("Hawthorne's Anti-Romance," 45, 48).

27. As Levine suggests, we might rate Hawthorne's novel along with "the more explicitly reformist sentimental novels of the period." Indeed, Levine notes that Blithedale is not necessarily a total failure, but a suggestion of what sentimentalism might be capable of in terms of social reform. Thus Blithedale represents "a potentially promising reform culture" (210), and Hawthorne uses his novel to present a radicalized view of sentimentality in which feeling can perform cultural work in ways

it had heretofore failed to do. Levine, "Sympathy and Reform in *The Blithedale Romance*," 208, 225.

28. Miles lets us in on the fact that its philosophy inspires a group of people to flee the cold sophistication of urban life and to embrace egalitarian communal living. But it is worth noting that what Blithedale stands for is not a subject upon which many critics can agree. Because there are no open manifestos or stump speeches elaborating on this theme, "[t]he result appears to be a novel about a man writing a novel about things he does not sufficiently understand" (Colacurcio, "Nobody's Protest Novel," 4). Many critics insist that the "moral center" of Blithedale is, as Boudreau puts it, "tantalizingly elusive," a vague ideal best understood as simply a gathering of those who feel "an attraction to philanthropy" (*Sympathy in American Literature*, 144, 143).

29. Mills, "'The Sweet Word, Sister,'" 98. Blithedale is, first and foremost, what Stacy Margolis sees as a culture of affiliation that values intimacy over competition (*The Public Life of Privacy in Nineteenth-Century American Literature*, 24). Margolis calls *Blithedale* "a thought experiment on the nature of affiliation . . . designed to explore the mysterious effects of group life on those who join," this time to a society that models itself on the family and aims "to replace competition with intimacy" (22). According to Margolis, this "contagiousness of communal living" exercises a deeply shared experience of intimacy on a public level. One could say this assessment provides an apt definition of the cultural workings of sentimentalism. Miles's narrative demonstrates as much; even with all that physical labor, the lives he describes are characterized as lives principally defined by emotion.

30. As Miller argues, in *The Blithedale Romance* the heart is the social organ that makes utopian fellow-feeling possible. Miller additionally contends that the fundamental ideology of *Blithedale* clearly involves "the concepts of *brotherhood* and *sisterhood*, *familiar* (or *familial*) *love*, and *mutual bond*" ("Eros and Ideology," 2).

31. Not all readers of *The Blithedale Romance* agree that sympathy holds this community together. Many insist instead that the novel seeks to chastise reformers. If it is a philanthropic project, in that the upper class relieves laborers of the work that sustains them, it is either a satire or a failure, a "utopian delusion" (Bell, "Hawthorne and the Real," 2). Boudreau furthers this idea of failure by suggesting that Hawthorne used *Blithedale* to reveal the "bourgeois squeamishness" that reinforces the gap between the classes (*Sympathy in American Literature*, 146). Similarly, Egan sees Blithedale as a "parody" of the pastoral setting and its associations with the "morality, piety, and domestic harmony" of sentimentalism ("Hawthorne's Anti-Romance," 49). As Roberta Weldon argues, their efforts at equality in categories of both class and gender constitute a dismal failure, since while Blithedale is a group of "radical communitarians" that "signified the possibility of a social order conceived on the principles of justice and equality for all," it ultimately retreats to "the old script of accusation and betrayal of women." Weldon, *Hawthorne, Gender, and Death*, 101, 85. According to Weldon, Zenobia's death signifies that the patriarchy has won and that any effort at an egalitarian community will eventually suffer a vicious backlash.

32. On the other hand, in *Necro Citizenship,* Russ Castronovo argues that Miles's "nonintercourse with [Zenobia's] corpse ensures that her unbecoming resistance will make no tangible impression on any member of utopia" (147).

33. Wilson, *Specters of Democracy,* 55.

34. Indeed, that release may be all the more necessary since, as Castronovo puts it, the novel represents "the overembodied form of Clotel" as a failed application to citizen status because she "futilely appeals to a disembodied white male legacy" (*Necro Citizenship,* 259n31).

35. Sherrard-Johnson, "Delicate Boundaries," 205. Sherrard-Johnson presents this idea as one of the highlights of Dwight McBride's book *Impossible Witness.*

36. Roberts, *Gothic Subjects,* 127.

37. Michael Davitt Bell perhaps says it best when he refers to the "obscene double entendre" of this scene. *The Development of American Romance,* 190.

SIX. Ruin, Rape, and the Aesthetic Work of *Clarissa* in England and America

1. As Pateman notes in *The Disorder of Women,* consent is necessarily illegible in both contract theory and sexual relations, for, "as in Locke's civil society, there are no obvious expressions of it at all" in Rousseau's characterization of heterosexual sex (76).

2. In fact, in *Rousseau in America,* Paul Merrill Spurlin argues that the impact of Rousseau's fiction in early America was stronger than that of his political writings.

3. Rousseau, *Politics and the Arts,* 85.

4. In Sharon Block's study, *Rape and Sexual Power in Early America,* she notes that rape culture insists on defining consent through force. "Elite white masculinity," she argues, "helped such men reshape coercion into the appearance of consent before, during, and after a sexual attack" (4).

5. *Charlotte Temple* was first published in England in 1791 to little commercial success. Ann Douglass, "Introduction," *Charlotte Temple and Lucy Temple.*

6. In *The Importance of Feeling English,* Tennenhouse has done a great deal to bring the issue of *Clarissa* as it was published in America to critical attention. See especially chapter 3, "The Sentimental Libertine," 43–73.

7. Ibid., 54. Tennenhouse notes that this edition was immensely popular in the United States, though not in England.

8. Though some readers of *Incidents* may argue that there simply is no rape in Jacobs's text, as we shall soon see, several critics suggest that *Incidents* in fact includes rhetorical hints to rape, in part because Jacobs was limited in what as she could expect white publishers to print.

9. Doyle describes the "associations between rape and the founding of republics" in that Atlantic voyages to the New World or the new republic "merge the notion of 'entry' as transatlantic arrival in a new society with 'entry' as coercive physical or sexual violence" (*Freedom's Empire,* 7). While Doyle sees rape particularly as a story that reveals the rise of the individual modern subject, or what she calls "the inward

turn," I argue that the use of rape in seduction narratives is to posit a resistance to this modern subjectivity.

10. Butler, *Bodies That Matter*, 122, 124. My earlier line is meant to echo Butler's: "This 'one' who appears not to be in a condition of trespass prior to the call, for whom the call establishes a given practice as a trespass, is not fully a social subject" (121).

11. Toni Bowers's *Force or Fraud* offers a nuanced understanding of the role of rape in the seduction novel that is of use here. She notes the difficult (but impossible to ignore) ambiguity that at times in eighteenth-century seduction novels precludes the ability to distinguish between force and consent. "That faltering, that moment when it is difficult for a narrative to sustain a clearly discernible, stable difference *of a kind* between seduction and rape" describes an ambivalence that does not deny the horror of sexual attack but still examines the radicalization of agency as both subversive and subordinate in such texts. Bowers sees at such unreadable moments a "model for subordinate agency" that defines women who, "when presented with 'force or fraud' respond in excess of resistance *or* consent" (4). Bowers's reading ought to be understood, however, in the larger context of Atlantic slaving culture, for, as Hartman contends, "The incessant reiteration of the necessity of submission—the slave must be subject to the master's will in all things—upheld it as the guiding principle of slave relations, if not the central element in the trinity of savagery, sentiment, and submission" (*Scenes of Subjection*, 90). Kimberly Juanita Brown emphasizes this important point when she notes that the female slave body signifies "the ineffable impression of forced volition" no matter what the scene of white observation might be ("Black Rapture," 45).

12. Butler, *Bodies That Matter*, ix.

13. I am indebted to Doyle's excellent reading of Clarissa for identifying the slave galley symbolism in Richardson's novel. See *Freedom's Empire*, especially 139–44.

14. This idea recalls Eagleton's *The Rape of Clarissa*, in which he offers a troubling interpretation of the letter in *Clarissa*, which he says "comes to signify nothing quite so much as female sexuality itself, that folded, secret place which is always open to violent intrusion" (54). The bulk of Eagleton's case is a powerful feminist argument against rape and against literary critics who romanticize the rapist Lovelace. He describes Lovelace's "misogyny and infantile sadism" as that which find "expression in the virulently anti-sexual act of rape" (63). But when he notes that "writing, like sexuality, is a private, always violable space, a secret enterprise fraught with deadly risk" (49) he assumes that violence always gets what it wants—that the attempt at violation is always its accomplishment, a reading that relies on the sure knowledge that the private individual's body acts as the guardian of that which is sacred and destructible, the pure and delicate human soul (itself characterized as violable and thus feminine in such an assumption). Clarissa's triumph of character after Lovelace's rape suggests there are more possibilities.

15. Stacks of criticism on the rape of Clarissa and its engagement with issues of consent and subjectivity exist, too many to cite here. Certainly no list of such work

would be complete without mention of Bowers's *Force or Fraud*. Additional feminist readings of *Clarissa* take discussion of sex and subjectivity to new understandings of Richardson's potentially feminist politics. For instance, Kathleen Lubey notes the growing number of critics who "argue that Richardson strategically elides his heroine's interiority in order to prove the insufficiency of a depth model of psychology, and its mimetic partner the liberal subject, for demanding something like social justice" and goes on insightfully to note that for Richardson, sex may have meant "the systematic instrumentalization of women's bodies to support the sociopolitical institutions that both disenfranchise them and delimit their ontological possibilities" ("Sexual Remembrance in *Clarissa*," 160, 164).

16. Eagleton, *The Rape of Clarissa*, 87.

17. Mortgenstern, "Marriage and Contract," 108–15. In this context, the aesthetic work of rape is to materialize the female body and to dematerialize the male body. It is the invention of violability through sexual violence. As Morgenstern so insightfully notes, rapists and feminists both want contractual consent to exist—the first to violate it, the second to assert it. In order for feminists to work through this problem, Morgenstern insists we need to ask, "Is the problem, in the aftermath of the democratic revolutions, that women are not allowed access to the (fantasy of a) disembodied subject position (the contractual subject with property in his own person), or is it precisely this fantastic and contractual account of the subject that feminism ought to disrupt?" (115) Similarly, Lauren Berlant notes "how white male privilege has been veiled by the rhetoric of the bodiless citizen, the generic 'person' whose political identity is a priori precisely because it is, in theory, noncorporeal" in "the American male body" (*The Female Complaint*, 110).

18. Gillian Brown, *The Consent of the Governed*, 128.

19. Richardson, *Clarissa*, UK edition, 888. Subsequent page citations to this work will appear in the text parenthetically. For the sake of simplicity, for in-text citations, I will specify when the citation comes from the US edition but not when it comes from Richardson's original UK edition.

20. Anita Goldman notes that Jacobs's text participates in "rhetorics of protest in nineteenth-century American culture" such that the attic, like Thoreau's prison cell, "reveal[s] distinctive utopian possibilities for political community in America." "Harriet Jacobs, Henry Thoreau, and the Character of Disobedience," 234, 238.

21. Indeed, Andrea Stone argues, Jacobs's novel radically critiques the racism inherent in the seduction genre's omission of black women when it confronts "master-slave sexual violence at a time when such an abuse was theoretically impossible"; that is, only a person can experience violation, a legal status not afforded to slave women ("Interracial Sexual Abuse and Legal Subjectivity in Antebellum Law and Literature," 69). Further, Xiomara Santa Marina writes that to expose the sexual vulnerabilities of slave women "also exposed these women in ways that were antithetical to nineteenth-century formulations of womanhood" ("Black Womanhood in North American Women's Slave Narratives," 232–33).

22. This unconscious state recalls *The Power of Sympathy*'s deployment of a similar tale of kidnapping and/as rape discussed in chapter 3. Fidelia's story, like most other stories of rape to be discussed in this chapter, has more than one version, and carries with it an obfuscating ambivalence about Fidelia's state of mind. The language of her story is this: "'the poor distracted girl was carried off by a ruffian'" (48). That word "distracted" is central to the story, for it is impossible to know how Fidelia herself experiences the scene. "Distracted" may of course refer to her as she is in the novel's present moment—she has been driven mad by what was either a seduction or a rape and the ensuing suicide of her fiancé—or it may refer to the idea that at the time, she lacked the cognitive wherewithal to understand what was happening when the "ruffian" Williams takes her away. The ambivalence and ambiguity about consent alongside the omission of actual rape scenes in these texts, stories that cannot be recounted since the heroines were unconscious or otherwise absent, is a constant feature, in other words, of the seduction-as-rape story.

23. The carriage ride and the Atlantic crossing in *Charlotte Temple* may, as Doyle provocatively asserts, also represent a grand narrative about the promise of America and the power of sexual "sin." Indeed, as noted earlier, Doyle suggests that we might read this moment as one of transatlantic transformation: "[T]he American Adam arrives on stage as an Eve, a ruined wanderer of humble yet virtuous origin" and the "French-named seducer has done Satan's new-world work—and the expanse of the Atlantic aids him." Sexual ruin, in other words, transfigures the American Adam into an Eve, still an individual, though perhaps a much more intriguing one. *Freedom's Empire*, 159, 161.

24. Importantly, the crawl space can be read as an original insistence of an interior self as a necessary part of personhood and the pursuit of freedom. As Joycelyn Moody says, "The slave narrative genre" itself "challenges the myth of the African's basic lack of interiority" ("African American Women and the United States Slave Narrative," 114).

25. Miskcokze, "The Middle Passages of Nancy Prince and Harriet Jacobs," 288, 289.

26. Additionally in *Freedom's Empire*, Doyle offers some important insights into the links among the traumas of the Middle Passage and rape. She notes that rape is often linked to revolution and new republics. Doyle offers a theory of what she calls the "Atlantic swoon," a moment of entry into modernity that often doubles as sexual violence (7–9).

27. Doyle, *Freedom's Empire*, 142, 255.

28. Certainly the irregularity of the mad papers suggests a destabilization of the very idea of interiority, and the openness of the text is further suggested by the notion that Richardson himself might be in pursuit of his own character's interiority. In other words, Lovelace and Richardson want, and fail to achieve, an occupation of female interiority. As Eagleton says in *The Rape of Clarissa*, "Lovelace requires from Clarissa the very autonomy he finds unbearable" since he "will never . . . lay bare the springs of her subjectivity" (83, 61). More recently, Doyle has written that the form of

the novel is "promising revelations of hidden interiors" that "[cultivate] a desire for psychological access" and Foucauldian surveillance, though Richardson "also teases us with the possibility that we never do penetrate the deepest layers of self" a move that I would argue uses the failure of prose to reveal the failure of rape, though Doyle ultimately sees that through Lovelace, Richardson has successfully achieved "entry into her interiority." *Freedom's Empire*, 139–40.

29. Eagleton, *The Rape of Clarissa*, 60. The sense of Clarissa's power against the Lovelace/Richardson attempt to get "inside" of her is characterized in more misogynist terms by Eagleton in *The Rape of Clarissa*, who goes on to note that the rape "goes wholly unrepresented, as the hole at the centre of the novel towards which this huge mass of writing is sucked only to sheer off again" (61). The imagery, of the vagina dentata castrating the text/author, here represented as a huge phallic mass, clarifies what is so threatening about Clarissa's "impenetrability."

30. Hartman, "Seduction and the Ruses of Power."

31. Though of course out of all these texts one would think her claim to compulsion is unquestionably valid, it may be that Jacobs refuses this course because it relies on the white reader as the arbiter of what really happened. In *Slavery, Empathy, and Pornography* Wood makes the case that many portrayals of black suffering constituted a kind of empathy pornography that eroticized slave torture and rape; it may be that Jacobs's refusal to incorporate a particular kind of suffering is a way to obstruct the white reader's attempts to colonize her story in this odious way. In her analysis of the white seduction novel, Donna R. Bontatibus notes the voyeuristic infrastructure of sentimental identification when she says, "The seduction novel of the early nation voices and represents fears of rape" in order to "explore the lives of characters who have suffered from those atrocities while providing readers with an imaginative space in which to suffer along with the heroine" (*The Seduction of the Early Nation*, 11).

32. Similarly, Bowers notes that the rape in *Incidents*, both told and untold, is "not an aberration, but an inexpressibly vile embodiment of the structures of dominance and subordination that order the novel's world, a manifestation at once so rank and so inevitable that it defies representation" (*Force or Fraud*, 282). Cynthia S. Hamilton adds to the problem of representation in her discussion of *Incidents* when she writes, "[A] few suggestive details are supplied as indicative" of rape, "leaving the conventional expectations of the Gothic to supply the suspense while shielding Jacobs to a certain extent from the need for fuller revelations" ("Dislocation, Violence, and the Language of Sentiment," 112).

33. One of the definitions of "signifyin'" proposed by Henry Louis Gates Jr. is instructive on this point: "[W]hen one writer repeats another's structure by one of several means including a fairly exact repetition of a given narrative"—for instance, Jacobs's use of sentimental and sensational genres—they are yet "filled incongruously with a ludicrous or incongruent content"—in *Incidents*, for instance, the rape of the slave. *The Signifying Monkey*, 103.

34. For more discussion about Jacobs's daring seen in its historical and literary context, the following texts are central: P. Gabrielle Foreman, "Manifest in Signs";

Geneva Cobb Moore, *Maternal Metaphors of Power in African American Women's Literature*; Georgia Kreiger, "Playing Dead"; and Jacqueline Goldsby, "Through Her Brother's Eyes."

35. As Anna Stewart notes, Jacobs's text was marketed by publishers who focused on its scandalous material. The first edition had "a seductive spine exclaiming 'LINDA' in gilt letters and a title page emphasizing the alluring 'incidents' of a 'slave girl.'" A pirated edition in London a year later "focused still more on the narrative's salacious qualities, tempting readers through its packaging with the promise of sexual intrigue" ("Revising 'Harriet Jacobs' for 1865," 719).

36. Critics like Andrea Powell Wolfe discuss the white female reader's role in Jacobs's text, arguing that "she purposefully uses the sentimental approach as her primary narrative paradigm in order to enlist the sympathies and support of the Northern white women who were readers of such narratives, and who represented for Jacobs a receptive audience for her story" ("Double-Voicedness in *Incidents in the Life of a Slave Girl*," 523).

37. Moody provides a context for such a move when she notes that "many Anglo-American readers from the late eighteenth century through the Civil War exoticized blackness and black people as sources of fascination, titillation, and entertainment" ("African American Women and the United States Slave Narratives," 111).

38. Bowers, *Force or Fraud*, 23, 16, 20, 3, 287, 268.

39. For Marion Rust, the omission of a rape scene might mean something else for Charlotte. Argues Rust, "Charlotte does not so much surrender her chastity—in the sense of giving up under duress something she values—as lose track of it altogether, along with every other aspect of her being" (102). In other words, Charlotte's hold on her "self" stands in for her ability, or rather her inability, to protect herself from Montraville. Rust, "What's Wrong with 'Charlotte Temple'?" 99–118.

40. Ibid., 107.

41. Bowers, *Force or Fraud*, 275.

42. Hartman, *Scenes of Subjection,* 81. Hartman goes on to ask the question quite succinctly: "[H]ow does one grapple with issues of consent and will, when the negation or restricted recognition of these terms determine the meaning of enslavement?" Indeed, as Hartman notes, "the violence 'necessary' to the maintenance of slave relations, that is, black submission, unmoors the notion of 'force'" (539).

43. Blackford characterizes Rowson's narrator as "a hovering, maternal" figure who "emerges to put forth a theory of 'the talking book' as a democratic parent, protector, and teacher" representing a "univocal chorus" that is stronger than Charlotte herself ("Daughters of the American Revolution," 42, 45). Interestingly, Hamilton makes a similar case about the narrator in Jacobs's work. She describes the narrator as a different version of the character Linda Brent than the one she describes: "[T]he older writer who relates the events of her past life exhibits the gestures and postures that mark her as a refined woman of sensibility, while the younger self she presents to the reader as the object of empathetic involvement has violated one of the most basic tenets of sexual propriety under the domestic ideology," a rhetorical move

that creates the impossible, "a 'fallen women' of 'refined sensibilities'" ("Dislocation, Violence, and the Language of Sentiment," 111).

44. See Levine, "The Slave Narrative and the Revolutionary Tradition of American Autobiography."

45. Anne Bradford Warner notes, for example, that *Incidents* presents "a multiple and many-voiced figure . . . that moves among masks, breaking barriers, and working always toward regeneration and away from definition" ("Carnival Laughter," 221). Indeed, "the narrator's changeability" creates a "revolutionary impulse through a plenitude of disguises" (223). Such analysis suggests that in *Incidents* there is an absence of individual self that "invites revisionist responses and challenges all natural authority that has become arbitrary or authoritarian" (229). Similarly, Angelyn Mitchell argues that "in African American culture, feminist individuality has little in common with the Anglo-American concept of rugged individualism. For mainstream Anglo-America, individuals refer to the efforts by which the isolated individual advances. In African American female culture, the individual's efforts are part of and supported by the community" (*The Freedom to Remember*, 38, qtd. in Braxton, "Autobiography and African Women's Literature," 131).

46. The critical discussion about genre use in *Incidents in the Life of a Slave Girl* is a universe unto itself. What follows is merely a representation of some of the key figures and claims in this discussion, rather than an exhaustive survey. Michael Bennett asserts that *Incidents* "drew on, infiltrated, and transformed traditional genres" (*Democratic Discourses*, 15). Bennett argues that Jacobs's text, along with other abolitionist works like *Uncle Tom's Cabin*, presents an "experimentation with genre" that "blended fact and fiction in a generic mélange (mixing, to various degrees, elements of the picaresque, romance, slave narrative, and sentimental novel). . . . If genres are essentially received forms through which an author fulfills audience expectations, then the abolitionists needed to destabilize traditional generic expectations and so rewrite the contract between author and reader" (15, 119–20). Likewise, Foreman notes that black female authors employ "multiple imbricated agendas" that produce a "simultextuality," an intersection of Bakhtinian languages (*Activist Sentiments*, 4, 6). Kerry Sinanan adds that "Slave narratives were . . . hybrid writings that evolved within a range of diverse dialogues, debates, and arguments" ("The Slave Narrative and the Literature of Abolition," 61). Yolanda Pierce further states that "using conventional Anglo-American literary genres" allowed writers like Jacobs "to tell unconventional African-American stories" ("Redeeming Bondage," 83). Robert Reid-Pharr calls this the "messy, parodic, over-determined, promiscuous, multiform . . . tradition" of the slave narrative ("The Slave Narrative and Early Black American Literature," 149). Donald B. Gibson concurs: Jacobs's text "reflect[s] not the unwillingness or inability of the author to fit her story into the existing forms, but . . . reflect[s] her desire to stretch the boundaries of the genres of slave narrative and novel of sentiment to whatever extent necessary to accommodate her particular experience" ("Harriet Jacobs, Frederick Douglass, and the Slavery Debate," 170). Stephanie A. Smith argues that we ought to read *Incidents* as a text that is "questioning the gendered and

racial assumptions made about those narrative patterns," when Jacobs employs, in order to challenge, genres like the seduction narrative or the sentimental novel. Smith adds that "her evocation of diverse authorities and texts, and her undermining of the sanctity of authoritarian texts are conducted not only through 'dialogization' of the narrative but through intertextual 'narrative parody' and an 'internal polemic' famously described by Henry Louis Gates as 'signifyin(g)'" while "Jacobs reworks the genres she inherited, writing under the weight of discourses not her own" (*Conceived by Liberty*, 139, 217, 220).

47. Gibson, "Harriet Jacobs, Frederick Douglass, and the Slavery Debate," 170.

48. While here Linda's stance gains power both through a direct address to the sentimental white female reader and the ability to shift from "I" to "you" as a deferral and even an erosion of individual self, it is worth noting that as Daneen Wardrop says, "In the final chapters of the narrative Jacobs shows confidence in her writing strategies by way of using personal pronouns," moving from an empowered "I" to "the black community" that "speaks its insistent 'we.'" Wardrop, "'What Tangled Skeins Are the Genealogies of Slavery!'" 224.

49. Smith bases her analysis on the "semiotics of agency" in the power of motherhood and mothering in *Incidents*, as opposed to the masculine rhetoric of individualism. Smith, *Conceived by Liberty*, 150, 257.

50. Critics describe the narration of *Incidents* as, for example, a "masquerade" (Goldsby, "'I Disguised My Hand,'" 12) and a "mask" (Garfield, "Earwitness," 108); Warner notes the "ventriloquism" in "Brent's female appropriation of an African American trickster figure" who "represents a fluidity and a playful version of metamorphosis . . . to change form, to avoid stasis" ("Carnival Laughter," 220, 217, 218).

51. Garfield, "Earwitness," 12. Garfield also underscores this when she argues that "[d]isplaced from 'Heroine' and 'Woman,' the author often stands peculiarly outside even the more explicit role of 'slave woman,' for she must manipulate its very comprehensiveness as a generalized mask for her own transgressive female 'I'" ("'I Disguised My Hand,'" 108). Jean Fagin Yellin agrees, noting that "Harriet Jacobs had become 'Linda Brent,' but not to hide behind a pseudonym. . . . As 'Linda,' she had empowered herself to write about a life that as 'Harriet,' she could neither speak nor write" (Yellin, *Harriet Jacobs*, 144).

52. Bennett, *Democratic Discourses*, 139.

53. Wood, *Slavery, Empathy, and Pornography*.

54. There is a veritable library of research and sources available on the publication and abridgement history of *Clarissa* in England and America. Multiple editions of *Clarissa* were available in the eighteenth and nineteenth centuries in both countries. Indeed, as Leonard Tennenhouse notes in his important study of this history in *The Importance of Feeling English*, there were several US abridgements—an "intense explosion" of them—circulating in America in the decades following the Revolution (55). As Tennenhouse notes, they were based on abridgements that originally appeared in London. In other words, the abridged versions of *Clarissa*

circulating in the late eighteenth century were truly transatlantic texts: the versions Americans were reading were copied from, or based on, abridgements that were originally printed in England. The abridged edition I work with here comes from *The Paths of Virtue Delineated; or, the History in Miniature of the Celebrated Pamela, Clarissa Harlowe, and Sir Charles Grandinson*. It was originally produced in London in 1773 by Oliver Goldsmith, and as Barbara E. Lacey notes in *From Sacred to Secular*, it was reprinted in America along with several other works from the same printer (59).

55. Price, *Anthology and the Rise of the Novel*, 13.

56. Ibid., 16. The popularity of abridged editions of *Clarissa* that kept the epistolarity of the novel but edited out most of the letters deemed nonessential also shows that brevity is not the goal of a switch from an epistolary novel to one with an omniscient narrator.

57. Ibid., 26–27.

58. Ibid., 28.

59. Tennenhouse notes that the abridged versions of both of Richardson's novels, *Pamela* and *Clarissa*, underwent publication booms in the 1780s and 1790s, though even as early as the 1740s the original versions were available (but much less popular) in the United States. See *The Importance of Feeling English*, 53–54.

60. Ibid., 43–44.

61. Ibid., 44.

62. Ibid., 57.

63. Ibid., 56.

64. Adams, *The Correspondence between the Honorable John Adams, Late President of the United States, and the Late William Cunningham, Esq.*, 18–19.

65. As Bowers notes in *Force or Fraud*, *Clarissa*'s refusal to marry Lovelace after he rapes her equals a refusal "to distinguish the narratives on offer. She declines to protect the hidden term—*rape*—behind its recuperative recasting, *seduction* and *courtship*. As long as Clarissa so refuses, no amount of spin can change the abomination at the heart of her story" (287). The matter of consent in marriage is particularly fraught: "It is as if marriage is what happens to women—virtuous women, at least—while they're busy doing other things. The heroine need not concern herself with finding a husband, b/c she will end up married, such novels blithely assume, *whether she wants to or not*" (Valery Rohy, "Sexualities," 83).

Conclusion

1. I am using Emily Russell's insightful definition of the four categories of the grotesque: material reality, dissolution of boundaries, the folk, and spectacle. *Reading Embodied Citizenship*, 61.

2. I have already discussed Shaftesbury's impact in America in chapter 2; for Hobbes's influence, especially on the founders, see "Hobbes in America," in Downes's *Hobbes, Sovereignty, and Early American Literature*, 69–85.

3. For a full review of Shaftesbury's influence upon Benjamin Franklin, see Douglas Anderson's *The Radical Enlightenment of Benjamin Franklin,* especially 9–11, 41–46, 102–5.

4. A letter from Thomas Jefferson to John Adams in October of 1816 is one succinct representation of how the founders reacted to Hobbes's work. Jefferson writes that according to "the principle of Hobbes, . . . justice is founded in contract solely, and does not result from the construction of man. I believe, on the contrary, that it is instinct, and innate, that the moral sense is as much a part of our constitution as that of feeling, seeing, or hearing; as a wise creator must have seen to be necessary in an animal destined to live in society." *Letters,* www.founders.archives.gov/documents/Jefferson.

5. In "The Artist of the *Leviathan* Title-Page," Keith Brown argues that the "'deadness'" of the engraving is atypical of Hollar's work, whereas the "'soft'" quality of the sketch is much more typical of Hollar's work (26, 28). Brown argues convincingly that Hobbes must have worked closely with Hollar to produce the sketch (30). He also traces the sketch's delivery from Holland, where Hobbes was living, to Charles II in 1651, and it was this original manuscript sketch by Hollar that the king received (26). Brown also offers convincing arguments regarding Hobbes's personal investment in the design of this image.

6. Stillman, "Hobbes's *Leviathan,*" 815.

7. As Russell puts it, the image calls into focus the "contradictory realities of becoming a political subject, with its inclusion of the tools of coercion," the staff and sword, "and the tension between the successful containment of the social body and its visual suggestion of a teeming, noisy crowd" (*Reading Embodied Citizenship,* 6).

8. Kow, "Corporeal Interiority and the Body Politic in Hobbes's *Leviathan,*" 240.

9. It is, as Downes writes, Hobbes "imagining the deconstruction of the opposition between the individual and the social. . . . The Hobbesian sovereign is thus, inevitably, a peculiar and almost fantastic, if not frightening, hybrid or monstrosity." In other words, Hobbes accomplishes "what twentieth-century political vocabulary might call a willingness to think the subject's opening onto the other without panic." *Hobbes, Sovereignty, and Early American Literature,* 59, 99.

10. Some Hobbes critics disagree. For example, Hannah Dawson argues that Hobbes "sees the brute reality in the same breath as consent and agency," such that "[w]e all consent; it's just that there is a vast attitudinal spectrum of permission" (*Hobbes: Great Thinkers on Modern Life,* 4).

11. Julius Caesar, *Seven Commentaries on the Gallic War,* 128.

12. In fact, one of the illustrations that Shaftesbury designed for *Characteristicks* actually depicts the conflict between himself and Hobbes. Called "The Triumph of Liberty," it places Hobbes "'ungraceful and stooping'" at an easel, in which he is painting the war god Mars stepping on a vanquished enemy. A wolf sits atop the image. The image of Shaftesbury in the opposite panel shows him with a liberty cap, painting the peaceful Orpheus beside olive branches, with a lamb sketched on top.

This description and its analysis come from Felix Paknadel, "Shaftesbury's Illustrations of *Characteristicks*."

13. Ibid. The word "underplot" comes from Shaftesbury's letter to the friend he entrusted the most with the completion of the illustrations, Thomas Micklethwayte, and is quoted in Paknadel's article "Shaftesbury's Illustrations of *Characteristicks*" (290).

14. As I go into at some length in chapter 2, Shaftesbury's *Characteristicks* (1711) is about how we need none of Hobbes's contract theory because human nature includes a benevolent social sense that compels us to form communities. But this principle has a distinctly radical side in Shaftesbury's work, what he called the "Doctrine of Two Persons," and it understands the self to be a hybrid monster. This illustration appears at the beginning of the section of *Characteristicks* called "Soliloquy: Or Advice to an Author."

15. Paknadel ("Shaftesbury's Illustrations of *Characteristicks*") argues that the image represents the contrast between ancients and moderns, the latter being besieged by the consequences of a lack of self-reflection.

16. Kantorowicz, *The King's Two Bodies*, 3–16. Kantorowicz's main source is Edmund Plowden, a sixteenth-century lawyer for the crown who collected legal precedents for a land dispute involving the nonage of King Edward I in his *Les Commentaries ou Reports de Edmund Plowden*, 1571. The report was published in the 1816 by S. Brooke and is now available via open resource at www.archive.org.

17. Lori Branch elsewhere calls this "tectonic shift" the "self-splitting produced in the quest for [the] fantasy of totality" (*Rituals of Spontaneity*, 122). I am deeply indebted here to Branch's work on Shaftesbury's portrait and her splendid analysis of its doubling; her analysis of the portrait's mystery emerges out of her study of religion and sensibility in the period. Regarding the portrait, Branch notes that the elder figure in it has for hundreds of years been a mysterious addition. Unlikely to be a servant or an unknown associate, Branch concludes that it is Shaftesbury himself, painted "literally with a dark cloud over his head, not unlike the dark boy or unnatural self in the emblem for 'Soliloquy'" (123–24, 129). In this way, the portrait is a double of Shaftesbury's illustration of the "Doctrine of Two Persons." (Not all viewers agree with this interpretation, and it is worth noting that the Twelfth Earl of Shaftesbury himself believes the second figure is Shaftesbury's brother Maurice.)

18. Franklin, "Ordeals Concerning the Increase of Mankind, Peopling of Countries, & Etc."

19. The popularity of the 1767 French novel *Bellisario* by Jean-François Marmontel reflects the notoriety of this figure.

20. Olsen, *Benjamin Franklin's Vision of American Community*. Olsen offers a thorough history of both images; for an in-depth look at "MAGNA *Britannia*," see chapter 2 (77–111); for the same on "JOIN, or DIE" see chapter 3 (28–76).

21. Samuels, *Romances of the Republic*, 6.

22. Or, as Bernd Herzogenrath alternatively argues, Franklin's image "shows unity as a phantasmatic *starting point* to be reestablished—wholeness and unity are

here regarded as the *natural* state of being, envisioned as a mythical origin to which America must return, if it wants to survive" (*An American Body/Politic*, 9–10).

23. The twelve hands represent twelve rather than thirteen colonies because Georgia's representatives did not attend this session.

24. Grosz, *Volatile Bodies*, 8.

25. Nancy, *The Inoperative Community*, 3.

26. Samuels's description of the image is useful here. In her assessment of the gendered and racial ideologies at work in the image, Samuels notes, "The scene resembles a gang rape" and the sexual violence of the scene shows that "America is here literally a fallen woman" (*Romances of the Republic*, 6).

27. Olsen, "Pictorial Representations of British America Resisting Rape." Olsen traces the many iterations of the print in colonial America, England, and Ireland, and demonstrates how the seemingly minor differences among the reproductions show how such images could signify different revolutionary meanings.

28. Ibid., 5.

Bibliography

Abdur-Rahman, Aliyyah I. "'This Horrible Exhibition': Sexuality in Slave Narratives." In *The Oxford Handbook of the African American Slave Narrative*, edited by John Ernest. New York: Oxford University Press, 2014.

Ablow, Rachel. *The Marriage of Minds: Reading Sympathy in the Victorian Marriage Plot*. Stanford, CA: Stanford University Press, 2007.

Adams, John. *The Correspondence between the Honorable John Adams, Late President of the United States, and the Late William Cunningham, Esq.: Beginning in 1803, and Ending in 1812*. Boston: True and Green Printers, 1823.

———. *The Political Writings of John Adams*. New York: Liberal Arts Press, 1954.

Anderson, Douglas. *The Radical Enlightenment of Benjamin Franklin*. Baltimore: Johns Hopkins University Press, 1997.

Armstrong, Nancy. *How Novels Think: The Limits of Individualism from 1719–1900*. New York: Columbia University Press, 2005.

Bakhtin, Mikhail. *The Dialogic Imagination: Four Essays*. Translated by Michael Holquist and Caryl Emerson. Austin: University of Texas Press, 1981.

Barnes, Elizabeth. *States of Sympathy: Seduction and Democracy in the American Novel*. New York: Columbia University Press, 1997.

Bateman, Benjamin. "Queer Coquetry: Communalizing the Death Drive in Hannah Foster's *The Coquette*." *Studies in American Culture* 35.1 (2013): 5–28.

Bell, Michael Davitt. *The Development of American Romance: The Sacrifice of Relation*. Chicago: University of Chicago Press, 1980.

Bell, Millicent. "Hawthorne and the Real." In *Hawthorne and the Real: Bicentennial Essays*, edited by Millicent Bell, 1–21. Columbus: Ohio State University Press, 2005.

Benedict, Barbara M. "Radcliffe, Godwin, and Self-Possession in the 1790s." In *Women, Revolution, and the Novels of the 1790s*, edited by Linda Lang-Peralta, 89–110. East Lansing: Michigan State University Press, 1999.

Bennett, Michael. *Democratic Discourses: The Radical Abolition Movement and Antebellum American Literature*. New Brunswick, NJ: Rutgers University Press, 2005.

Berlant, Lauren. *The Female Complaint: The Unfinished Business of Sentimentality in American Culture*. Durham, NC: Duke University Press, 2008.

Berlant, Lauren, and Lee Edelman. *Sex, or the Unbearable*. Durham, NC: Duke University Press, 2014.

Bersani, Leo. "Is the Rectum a Grave?" *October* 43, AIDS: Cultural Analysis/Cultural Activism (Winter 1987): 197–222.

Bhabha, Homi K. *The Location of Culture*. London: Routledge, 1994.

Blackford, Holly. "Daughters of the American Revolution: Sensational Pedagogy in Susanna Rowson's *Charlotte Temple*." In *Transatlantic Sensations*, edited by Jennifer Phegley, John Cyril Barton, and Kristin N. Huston, 41–58. New York: Ashgate Publishing, 2013.

Block, Sharon. *Rape and Sexual Power in Early America*. Chapel Hill: University of North Carolina Press, 2006.

Bodway, Jacob. "The Matter of Moral Sense: Shaftesbury and the Rhetoric of Tact." *Modern Philology* 111.3 (February 2014): 533–48.

Bontatibus, Donna R. *The Seduction of the Early Nation: A Call for Socio-Political Reform*. East Lansing: Michigan State University Press, 1999.

Boudreau, Kristin. *Sympathy in American Literature: American Sentiments from Jefferson to the Jameses*. Gainesville: University Press of Florida, 2002.

Bowers, Toni. *Force or Fraud: British Seduction Stories and the Problem of Resistance*. New York: Oxford University Press, 2011.

Bowers, Toni, and Tita Chico, "Introduction." In *Atlantic Worlds in the Long Eighteenth Century: Seduction and Sentiment*. New York: Palgrave Macmillan, 2012.

Branch, Lori. *Rituals of Spontaneity: Sentiment and Secularism from Free Prayer to Wordsworth*. Waco, TX: Baylor University Press, 2006.

Braunshneider, Theresa. *Our Coquettes: Capacious Desire in the Eighteenth Century*. Charlottesville: University of Virginia Press, 2009.

Braxton, Joanne M. "Autobiography and African Women's Literature." In *The Cambridge Companion to African American Women's Literature*, edited by Angelyn Mitchell and Danille K. Taylor, 128–49. New York: Cambridge University Press, 2009.

Brock, William R. *Scotus Americanus: A Survey of the Sources for the Links between Scotland and America in the Eighteenth Century*. Edinburgh: University of Edinburgh Press, 1982.

Brown, Gillian. "Consent, Coquetry, and Consequences." *American Literary History* 9.4 (1997): 625–52.

———. *The Consent of the Governed: The Lockean Legacy in Early American Culture*. Cambridge, MA: Harvard University Press, 2001.

Brown, Keith. "The Artist of the *Leviathan* Title-Page." *British Library Journal* 4.1 (Spring 1978): 24–36.

Brown, Kimberly Juanita. "Black Rapture: Sally Hemings, Chica da Silva, and the Slave Body of Sexual Supremacy." *Women's Studies Quarterly* 1–2 (Spring–Summer 2007): 45–66.

Brown, William Hill. *Ira and Isabella; or, The Natural Children*. 1809. Reprint, Whitefish, MT: Kessinger Publishing, 2000.

———. *The Power of Sympathy; or, The Triumph of Nature*. 1789. Reprint, New York: Penguin Books, 1996.

Brown, William Wells. *Clotel; or, the President's Daughter*. 1853. Reprint, New York: Penguin Books, 2003.

Burke, Edmund. *A Philosophical Enquiry into the Origin of Our Ideas of the Sublime and Beautiful*. 1757. Reprint, Oxford: Oxford University Press, 2015.

Burleigh, Erica. *Intimacy and Family in Early American Writing*. New York: Palgrave Macmillan, 2014.

Butler, Judith. *Bodies That Matter: On the Discursive Limits of "Sex."* New York: Routledge, 1993.

———. *Notes toward a Performative Theory of Assembly*. Cambridge, MA: Harvard University Press, 2015.

———. *Senses of the Subject*. New York: Fordham University Press, 2015.

Castronovo, Russ. *Necro Citizenship: Death, Eroticism, and the Public Sphere in the Nineteenth-Century United States*. Durham, NC: Duke University Press, 2001.

Catalogue of the John Adams Library in the Public Library of the City of Boston. Boston: Trustees Publication, 1917.

Chakkalakal, Tess. *Novel Bondage: Slavery, Marriage, and Freedom in Nineteenth-Century America*. Urbana: University of Illinois Press, 2011.

Chandler, James. "Placing *The Power of Sympathy*: Transatlantic Sentiments in the 'First American Novel.'" In *The Atlantic Enlightenment*, edited by Susan Manning and Francis D. Cogliano, 131–48. Burlington, VT: Ashgate Publishing, 2008.

Christianson, Frank. "'Trading Places in Fancy': Hawthorne's Critique of Sympathetic Identification in *The Blithedale Romance*." *Novel: A Forum on Fiction* 36.2 (2003): 244–62.

Colacurcio, Michael J. "Nobody's Protest Novel: Art and Politics in *The Blithedale Romance*." *Nathaniel Hawthorne Review* 34.1-2 (2008): 1–39.

Cooper, Anthony Ashley, Third Earl of Shaftesbury. *Characteristicks of Men, Manners, Opinions, Times*. Indianapolis, IN: Liberty Fund, 2001.

Coviello, Peter. *Intimacy in America: Dreams of Affiliation in Antebellum Literature*. Minneapolis: University of Minnesota Press, 2005.

———. *Tomorrow's Parties: Sex and the Untimely in Nineteenth-Century America*. New York: New York University Press, 2013. Ebook.

Csengei, Ildiko. *Sympathy, Sensibility, and the Literature of Feeling in the Eighteenth Century*. New York: Palgrave Macmillan, 2012.

Cutter, Martha J., and Caroline F. Levander. "Engendering American Fictions." In *A Companion to American Fiction, 1780–1865*, edited by Shirley Samuels, 40–51. New York: Blackwell Publishing, 2007.

Dalke, Anne. "Original Vice: The Political Implications of Incest in the Early American Novel." *Early American Literature* 23.2 (1988): 188–201.

Davidson, Cathy. *Revolution and the Word: The Rise of the Novel in America*. New York: Oxford University Press, 1986.

Dawson, Hannah. *Hobbes: Great Thinkers on Modern Life*. New York: Pegasus Books, 2015.

Den Uyl, Douglas. Foreword to *Characteristicks of Men, Manners, Opinions, Times*, by Anthony Ashley Cooper, Third Earl of Shaftesbury. Indianapolis, IN: Liberty Fund, 2001.

Diedrich, Maria, Henry Louis Gates Jr., and Carl Pedersen. "The Middle Passage between History and Fiction: Introductory Remarks." In *Black Imagination and the Middle Passage*, edited by Diedrich, Gates, and Pedersen, 5–13. New York: Oxford University Press, 1999.

Diez Couch, Daniel. "Eliza Wharton's Scraps of Writing: Dissipation and Fragmentation in *The Coquette*." *Early American Literature* 49.3 (2014): 683–705.

Douglass, Ann. "Introduction." In *Charlotte Temple and Lucy Temple*, vii–xliii. New York: Penguin Books, 1991.

Downes, Paul. *Democracy, Revolution, and Monarchism in Early American Literature*. New York: Cambridge University Press, 2002.

———. "Does the Declaration of Independence Declare a State of Emergency?" *Canadian Review of American Studies* 42.1 (2012): 7–20.

———. "Fiction and Democracy." In *A Companion to American Fiction, 1780–1865*, edited by Shirley Samuels, 20–30. Malden, MA: Blackwell Publishing, 2007.

———. *Hobbes, Sovereignty, and Early American Literature*. New York: Cambridge University Press, 2015.

Doyle, Laura. *Freedom's Empire: Race and the Rise of the Novel in Atlantic Modernity, 1640–1940*. Durham, NC: Duke University Press, 2008.

Eagleton, Terry. *The Ideology of the Aesthetic*. Malden, MA: Blackwell, 1990.

———. *The Rape of Clarissa*. Minneapolis: University of Minnesota Press, 1982.

Egan, Ken, Jr. "Hawthorne's Anti-Romance." *Journal of American Culture* 11.4 (2004): 45–52.

Elliott, Marianne. *Robert Emmet: The Making of a Legend*. London: Profile Books, 2003.

Ellison, Julie. *Cato's Tears and the Making of Anglo-American Emotion*. Chicago: University of Chicago Press, 1999.

Emmet, Robert. "Speeches from the Dock, Part I." www.gutenberg.org.

Fiedler, Leslie. *Love and Death in the American Novel*. Champaign, IL: Dalkey Archives Press, 1960.

Fiering, Norman S. "Irresistible Compassion: An Aspect of Eighteenth-Century Sympathy and Humanitarianism." *Journal of the History of Ideas* 37.2 (April–June 1976): 195–218.

Fleischacker, Samuel. "The Impact on America: Scottish Philosophy and the American Founding." In *The Cambridge Companion to the Scottish Enlightenment*, edited by Alexander Broadie, 316–37. New York: Cambridge University Press, 2003.

Fluck, Winfried. "Reading Early American Fiction." In *A Companion to the Literatures of Colonial America*, edited by Susan Castillo and Ivy Schweitzer, 566–86. New York: Blackwell Publishing, 2005.

Foreman, P. Gabrielle. *Activist Sentiments: Reading Black Women in the Nineteenth Century*. Urbana: University of Illinois Press, 2009.

———. "Manifest in Signs: The Politics of Sex and Representation in *Incidents in the Life of a Slave Girl*." In *Harriet Jacobs and Incidents in the Life of a Slave Girl: New Critical Essays*, edited by Deborah M. Garfield and Rafia Zafar, 76–99. New York: Cambridge University Press, 1996.

Foster, Hannah Webster. *The Coquette; or, The History of Eliza Wharton; A Novel; Founded on Fact*. 1797. Reprint, New York: Penguin Books, 1996.

Franklin, Benjamin. "Ordeals Concerning the Increase of Mankind, Peopling of Countries, & Etc." www.franklinpapers.org.

Garfield, Deborah M. "Earwitness: Female Abolitionism, Sexuality, and *Incidents in the Life of a Slave Girl*." In *Harriet Jacobs and Incidents in the Life of a Slave Girl: New Critical Essays*, edited by Deborah M. Garfield and Rafia Zafar, 100–130. New York: Cambridge University Press, 1996.

Gates, Henry Louis Jr. *The Signifying Monkey: A Theory of African-American Literary Criticism*. New York: Oxford University Press, 1988.

Gaudet, Katherine. "Liberty and Death: Fictions of Suicide in the New Republic." *Early American Literature* 47.3 (2012): 591–622.

Gibson, Donald B. "Harriet Jacobs, Frederick Douglass, and the Slavery Debate: Bondage, Family, and the Discourse of Domesticity." In *Harriet Jacobs and Incidents in the Life of a Slave Girl: New Critical Essays*, edited by Deborah M. Garfield and Rafia Zafar, 156–78. New York: Cambridge University Press, 1996.

Goldman, Anita. "Harriet Jacobs, Henry Thoreau, and the Character of Disobedience." In *Harriet Jacobs and Incidents in the Life of a Slave Girl: New Critical Essays*, edited by Deborah M. Garfield and Rafia Zafar, 233–50. New York: Cambridge University Press, 1996.

Goldsby, Jacqueline. "'I Disguised My Hand': Writing Versions of the Truth in Harriet Jacobs's *Incidents in the Life of a Slave Girl* and John Jacobs's '*A True Tale of Slavery*.'" In *Harriet Jacobs and Incidents in the Life of a Slave Girl: New Critical Essays*, edited by Deborah M. Garfield and Rafia Zafar, 11–43. New York: Cambridge University Press, 1996.

Greven, David. "In a Pig's Eye: Masculinity, Mastery, and the Returned Gaze of *The Blithedale Romance*." *Studies in American Fiction* 34.2 (2006): 131–59.

———. "Incest and Intertextuality: Female Desire and Milton's Legacy in *The House of the Seven Gables*." *ESQ: A Journal of Nineteenth-Century American Literature and Culture* 62.1 (2016): 39–76.

———. *Men beyond Desire: Manhood, Sex, and Violation in American Literature*. New York: Palgrave Macmillan, 2005.

Grosz, Elizabeth. *Volatile Bodies: Toward a Corporeal Feminism*. Bloomington: Indiana University Press, 1994.

Hamilton, Cynthia S. "Dislocation, Violence, and the Language of Sentiment." In *Black Imagination and the Middle Passage*, edited by Maria Diedrich, Henry Louis Gates Jr., and Carl Pedersen, 103-16. New York: Oxford University Press, 1999.

Hamilton, Geoff. *The Life and Undeath of Autonomy in American Literature*. Charlottesville: University of Virginia Press, 2014.

Harris, Jennifer. "Wax Coquettes: Elizabeth Whitman, Henry Wadsworth Longfellow, and the Nineteenth-Century Travelling Waxwork Exhibition." *Canadian Review of American Studies* 40.3 (2010): 373-89.

Hartman, Saidiya. "Seduction and the Ruses of Power." *Callaloo* 19.2, Emerging Women Writers: A Special Issue (Spring 1996): 537-60.

——. *Scenes of Subjection: Terror, Slavery, and Self-Making in the Nineteenth-Century*. New York: Oxford University Press, 1997.

Hawthorne, Nathaniel. *The Blithedale Romance*. 1852. Reprint, New York: Oxford University Press, 1991.

——. *The Scarlet Letter*. 1850. Reprint, New York: Bantam Books, 1981.

Herzogenrath, Bernd. *An American Body/Politic: A Deleuzian Approach*. Hanover, NH: Dartmouth College Press, 2010.

Hobbes, Thomas. *Leviathan*. Edited by Richard E. Flathman and David Johnston. 1651. Reprint, New York: W. W. Norton & Company, 1997.

Hoffert, Robert W. *A Politics of Tensions: The Articles of Confederation and American Political Ideas*. Niwot: University of Colorado Press, 1992.

Hook, Andrew. *Scotland and America: A Study of Cultural Relations, 1750-1835*. Glasgow: Blackie Press, 1975.

Howell, William Hunting. *Against Self-Reliance: The Arts of Dependence in the Early United States*. Philadelphia: University of Pennsylvania Press, 2015.

Hume, David. *A Treatise of Human Nature*. 1739-40. Reprint, New York: Penguin Books, 1984.

Hutcheson, Sir Francis. *An Essay on the Nature and Conduct of the Passions and Affections, with Illustrations on the Moral Sense*. Edited by Aaron Garrett. 1728. Reprint, Indianapolis, IN: Liberty Fund, 2002.

Irigaray, Luce, and Noah Guynn. "The Question of the Other," *Yale French Studies* 87, Another Look, Another Woman: Retranslations of French Feminism (1995): 7-19.

Irving, Washington. *The Sketch Book of Geoffrey Crayon, Gent.* Edited by Susan Manning. 1820-21. Reprint, New York: Oxford University Press, 1998.

Jabour, Anya. *Marriage in the Early Republic: Elizabeth and William Wirt and the Companionate Ideal*. Baltimore: Johns Hopkins University Press, 1998.

Jacobs, Harriet A. *Incidents in the Life of a Slave Girl*. Edited by L. Maria Child. 1861. Reprint, New York: Harcourt Brace Jovanovich, 1973.

Jefferson, Thomas. *Letters*. www.founders.archives.gov/documents/Jefferson.

——. "To Thomas Law Poplar Forest, June 13, 1814." *Letters of Thomas Jefferson: 1743-1826*. www.let.rug.nl/usa/presidents

Judge, Jane. "The Scottish American Enlightenment." In *Handbook of Transatlantic North American Studies*, edited by Julia Straub, 587–604. Berlin: De Gruyter Press, 2016.

Julius Caesar. *Seven Commentaries on the Gallic War*. Translated by Carolyn Hammond. New York: Oxford University Press, 1996.

Kantorowicz, Ernst H. *The King's Two Bodies: A Study in Medieval Political Theology*. 1957. Reprint, Princeton, NJ: Princeton University Press, 2016.

Kaplan, Cora. *Sea Changes: Essays on Culture and Feminism*. London: Verso Press, 1986.

Kelleher, Paul. *Making Love: Sentiment and Sexuality in Eighteenth-Century British Literature*. Lanham, MD: Bucknell University Press, 2015.

Kerber, Linda. *Women of the Republic: Intellect and Ideology in Revolutionary America*. Chapel Hill: University of North Carolina Press, 1997.

Kittredge, Katherine. *Lewd and Notorious: Female Transgression in the Eighteenth-Century*. Ann Arbor: University of Michigan Press, 2003.

Knott, Sarah. "Female Liberty? Sentimental Gallantry, Republican Womanhood, and Rights Feminism in the Age of Revolutions." *William and Mary Quarterly* 71.3 (2014): 425–56.

———. *Sensibility and the American Revolution*. Chapel Hill: University of North Carolina Press, 2009.

Korobkin, Laura H. "'Can Your Volatile Daughter Ever Acquire Your Wisdom?': Luxury and False Ideas in 'The Coquette.'" *Early American Literature* 41.1 (March 2006): 79–107.

Kow, Simon. "Corporeal Interiority and the Body Politic in Hobbes's *Leviathan*." *Dalhousie Review* 85.2 (2005): 239–48.

Kramnick, Isaac. "The 'Great National Discussion': The Discourse of Politics in 1787." In *What Did the Constitution Mean to Early Americans?* edited by Edward Countryman, 35–67. New York: Bedford St. Martin's Press, 1999.

Kreiger, Georgia. "Playing Dead: Harriet Jacobs's Survival Strategy in 'Incidents in the Life of a Slave Girl.'" *African American Review* 42.3/4 (Fall–Winter 2008): 607–21.

Lacey, Barbara E. *From Sacred to Secular: Visual Images in Early American Publications*. Newark: University of Delaware Press, 2007.

Laqueur, Thomas. *Making Sex: Body and Gender From the Greeks to Freud*. Cambridge, MA: Harvard University Press, 1990.

Lawrence, D. H. *Studies in Classic American Literature*. New York: Penguin Books, 1923.

Levecq, Christine. *Slavery and Sentiment: The Politics of Feeling in Black Atlantic Antislavery Writing, 1770–1850*. Lebanon, NH: University of New Hampshire Press, 2008.

Levine, Robert. *Dislocating Race and Nation: Episodes in Nineteenth-Century American Nationalism*. Durham, NC: University of North Carolina Press, 2008.

———. "The Slave Narrative and the Revolutionary Tradition of American Autobiography." In *The Cambridge Companion to the African Slave Narrative*, edited by Audrey Fisch, 99–114. New York: Cambridge University Press, 2007.

———. "Sympathy and Reform in *The Blithedale Romance*." In *The Cambridge Companion to Nathaniel Hawthorne*, edited by Richard H. Millington, 207–29. Cambridge: Cambridge University Press, 2004.

Lewis, Jan. "The Republican Wife: Virtue and Seduction in the Early Republic." *William and Mary Quarterly* 44 (1987): 689–721.

Lewis, R.W.B. *The American Adam: Innocence, Tragedy, and Tradition in the Nineteenth Century*. Chicago: University of Chicago Press, 1955.

Lilley, James D. *Common Things: Romance and the Aesthetics of Belonging in Atlantic Modernity*. New York: Fordham University Press, 2014.

Locke, John. "The Second Treatise of Government." 1689. In *The Political Theory Reader*, edited by Paul Schumaker, 31–36. New York: Wiley-Blackwell, 2010.

———. *Two Treatises of Government*. 1689. Reprint, New York: Hafner Press, 1947.

Lubey, Kathleen. "Sexual Remembrance in *Clarissa*." *Eighteenth-Century Fiction* 29.2 (Winter 2016–17): 151–78.

Lukasik, Christopher. "Breeding and Reading." In *A Companion to American Fiction 1780–1865*, edited by Shirley Samuels, 158–67. Malden, MA: Blackwell Publishing, 2009.

———. *Discerning Characters: The Culture of Appearance in Early America*. Philadelphia: University of Pennsylvania Press, 2011.

Lyons, Clare A. *Sex among the Rabble: An Intimate History of Gender and Power in the Age of Revolution, Philadelphia, 1730–1830*. Chapel Hill: University of North Carolina Press, 2006.

Manning, Susan, and Francis D. Cogliano. "Introduction." In *The Atlantic Enlightenment*, edited by Manning and Cogliano, 1–18. Burlington, VT: Ashgate Publishing, 2008.

Margolis, Stacy. *The Public Life of Privacy in Nineteenth-Century American Literature*. Durham, NC: Duke University Press, 2005.

Martin, Terence. "William Hill Brown's *Ira and Isabella*." *New England Quarterly* 32.2 (June 1959): 238–42.

McBride, Dwight. *Impossible Witness: Truth, Abolitionism, and Slave Testimony*. New York: New York University Press, 2001.

McDowell, Tremain. "The First American Novel." *American Review* 2 (November 1933): 73–81.

McElroy, John Harmon, and Edward L. McDonald. "The Coverdale Romance." *Studies in the Novel* 14.1 (1982): 1–16.

McIntosh, Hugh. "Constituting the End of Feeling: Interiority in the Seduction Fiction of the Ratification Era." *Early American Literature* 47.2 (Spring 2012): 321–48.

McMillan, Uri. *Embodied Avatars: Genealogies of Black Feminist Art and Performance*. New York: New York University Press, 2015.

Milder, Robert. "Beautiful Illusions: Hawthorne and the Site of Moral Law." *Nathaniel Hawthorne Review* 33.2 (2007): 1–23.

Miller, John N. "Eros and Ideology: At the Heart of Hawthorne's Blithedale." *Nineteenth-Century Literature* 55.1 (2000): 1–22.

Mills, Angela. "'The Sweet Word, Sister': The Transformative Threat of Sisterhood and *The Blithedale Romance*." *American Transcendental Quarterly* 17.2 (2003): 97–121.

Miskcokze, Robin. "The Middle Passages of Nancy Prince and Harriet Jacobs." *Nineteenth-Century Contexts* 29.2 (June–September 2007): 283–93.

Mitchell, Angelyn. *The Freedom to Remember: Narrative, Slavery, and Gender in Contemporary Black Women's Fiction*. New Brunswick, NJ: Rutgers University Press, 2002.

Moody, Joycelyn. "African American Women and the United States Slave Narrative." In *The Cambridge Companion to African American Women's Literature*, edited by Angelyn Mitchell and Danille K. Taylor, 109–27. New York: Cambridge University Press, 2009.

Moore, Geneva Cobb. *Maternal Metaphors of Power in African American Women's Literature: From Phillis Wheatley to Toni Morrison*. Columbia: University of South Carolina Press, 2017.

Morgenstern, Naomi. "Marriage and Contract." In *A Companion to American Fiction, 1780–1865*, edited by Shirley Samuels, 108–18. Malden, MA: Blackwell Publishers, 2007.

Mulford, Mulford. "Introduction." In *The Power of Sympathy* and *The Coquette*. New York: Penguin Classics, 1996.

Müller, Patrick. "Hobbes, Locke, and the Consequences: Shaftesbury's Moral Sense and Political Agitation in Early Eighteenth-Century England." *Journal for Eighteenth-Century Studies* 37.3 (September 2014): 315–30.

Myers, Joanne E. "'Supernatural Charity': Astell, Shaftesbury, and the Problem of Enthusiasm." *Journal for Eighteenth-Century Studies* 37.3 (September 2014): 299–314.

Nancy, Jean-Luc. *The Inoperative Community*. Translated by Peter Connor, Lisa Garbus, Michael Holland, and Simona Sawhey. Minneapolis: University of Minnesota Press, 1991.

Newton, Theodore F. M. "William Pittis and Queen Anne Journalism." *Modern Philology* 33:3 (February 1936): 279–302.

Noble, Marianne. *The Masochistic Pleasures of Sentimental Literature*. Princeton, NJ: Princeton University Press, 2000.

Olsen, Lester C. *Benjamin Franklin's Vision of American Community: A Study in Rhetorical Iconology*. Columbia: University of South Carolina Press, 2004.

———. "Pictorial Representations of British America Resisting Rape: Rhetorical Recirculation of a Print Series Portraying the Boston Port Bill of 1774." *Rhetoric & Public Affairs* 12.1 (2009): 1–36.

Paknadel, Felix. "Shaftesbury's Illustrations of *Characteristicks*," *Journal of the Warburg and Courtauld Institutes* 37 (1974): 290–312.

Pateman, Carole. *The Disorder of Women: Democracy, Feminism, and Political Theory*. Stanford, CA: Stanford University Press, 1990.

———. *The Sexual Contract*. Stanford, CA: Stanford University Press, 1988.

Pettengill, Claire C. "Sisterhood in a Separate Sphere: Female Friendship in Hanna Webster Foster's *The Coquette* and *The Boarding School*." *Early American Literature* 27 (1992): 185–203.

Pierce, Yolanda. "Redeeming Bondage: The Captivity Narrative and the Spiritual Autobiography in the African American Slave Narrative." In *The Cambridge Companion to the African Slave Narrative*, edited by Audrey Fisch, 83–98. Cambridge: Cambridge University Press, 2007.

Pinch, Adela. *Strange Fits of Passion: Epistemologies of Emotion, Hume to Austen*. Stanford, CA: Stanford University Press, 1996.

Price, Leah. *Anthology and the Rise of the Novel: From Richardson to George Eliot*. New York: Cambridge University Press, 2000.

Purviance, Susan M. "Intersubjectivity and Sociable Relations in the Philosophy of Francis Hutcheson." *Eighteenth-Century Life* 15.1–2 (1991): 23–28.

Quendler, Christian. "Bodies of Letters: National, Literary, and Gender Identities in Epistolary Fiction of the Early Republic." In *Making National Bodies: Cultural Identity and the Politics of the Body in (Post-) Revolutionary America*, edited by Stefan L. Brandt and Astrid M. Fellner, 117–32. Bergstrasse, Germany: Wissenschaftlicher Verlag Trier, 2010.

Reid-Pharr, Robert. "The Slave Narrative and Early Black American Literature." In *The Cambridge Companion to the African Slave Narrative*, edited by Audrey Fisch, 137–49. Cambridge: Cambridge University Press, 2007.

Rice, Grantland S. *The Transformation of Authorship in America*. Chicago: University of Chicago Press, 1997.

Richardson, Samuel. *Clarissa; or, The History of a Young Lady*. 1747–48. UK edition. Reprint, New York: Penguin Books, 1985.

———. *The Paths of Virtue Delineated; or, The History in Miniature of the Celebrated Pamela, Clarissa Harlowe, and Sir Charles Grandison*. ECCO Print Editions, London: Oliver Goldsmith; S. Crowder, T. Lowndes, S. Bladon, and R. Baldwin, 1773.

Roberts, Siân Silyn. *Gothic Subjects: The Transformation of Individualism in American Fiction, 1790–1861*. Philadelphia: University of Pennsylvania Press, 2014.

Rogers, G.A.J. "Hobbes and His Contemporaries." In *The Cambridge Companion to Hobbes's Leviathan*, edited by Patricia Springborg, 413–40. Cambridge: Cambridge University Press, 2007.

Rohy, Valerie. "Sexualities." In *A Companion to American Fiction 1780–1865*, edited by Shirley Samuels, 413–40. Malden, MA: Blackwell Publishing, 2009.

Rousseau, Jean-Jacques. *Discourse on the Origin and Basis of Inequality among Men*. In *The Essential Rousseau*, translated by Lowell Bair, 125–201. New York: Meridian Press, 1983.

———. *The Essential Rousseau*. Translated by Lowell Bair. New York: Meridian Press, 1983.
———. *Politics and the Arts: Letter to M. d'Alembert on the Theatre*. Translated by Allen Bloom. Ithaca, NY: Cornell University Press, 1960.
———. *The Social Contract*. In *The Essential Rousseau*, translated by Lowell Bair, 1–124. New York: Meridian Press, 1983.
Rowson, Susanna. *Charlotte Temple: A Tale of Truth*.1794. Reprint, New York: Penguin Books, 1991.
Rush, Benjamin. *Essays: Literary, Moral, and Philosophical*. Schenectady, NY: Union College Press, 1988.
Russell, Emily. *Reading Embodied Citizenship: Disability, Narrative, and the Body Politic*. New Brunswick, NJ: Rutgers University Press, 2011.
Russo, Elena. "Sociability, Cartesianism, and Nostalgia in Libertine Discourse." *Eighteenth-Century Studies* 30.4 (summer 1997): 383–400.
Rust, Marion. "What's Wrong with 'Charlotte Temple'?" *William and Mary Quarterly*, 3rd ser., 60.1, Sexuality in Early America Edition (January 2003): 99–118.
Salamon, Gayle. *Assuming a Body: Transgender Rhetorics of Materiality*. New York: Columbia University Press, 2010.
Samuels, Shirley. *Reading the American Novel: 1780–1865*. Malden, MA: Blackwell Publishing, 2012. Ebook.
———. *Romances of the Republic: Women, the Family, and Violence in the Literature of the Early American Nation*. New York: Oxford University Press, 1996.
Sanborn, Geoffrey. "'People Will Pay to Hear the Drama': Plagiarism in *Clotel*." *African American Review* 45.1–2 (Spring–Summer 2012): 65–82.
———. *Plagiarama! William Wells Brown and the Aesthetic of Attractions*. New York: Columbia University Press, 2016.
Santa Marina, Xiomara. "Black Womanhood in North American Women's Slave Narratives." In *The Cambridge Companion to the African American Slave Narrative*, edited by Audrey Fisch, 232–45. New York: Cambridge University Press, 2007.
Schweitzer, Ivy. *Perfecting Friendship: Politics and Affiliation in Early American Literature*. Durham, NC: University of North Carolina Press, 2006.
Shaftesbury, Third Earl of. *See* Cooper, Anthony Ashley.
Shakespeare, William. *Romeo and Juliet*. New York: Simon and Schuster, 1994.
Shamir, Milette. *Inexpressible Privacy: The Interior Life of Antebellum American Literature*. Philadelphia: University of Pennsylvania Press, 2006.
Sheller, Mimi. *Citizenship from Below: Erotic Agency and Caribbean Freedom*. Durham, NC: Duke University Press, 2012.
Sher, Richard B. *Scottish Authors and Their Publishers in Eighteenth-Century Britain, Ireland, and America*. Chicago: University of Chicago Press, 2006.
Sherrard-Johnson, Cherene. "Delicate Boundaries: Passing and other 'Crossings.' in Fictionalized Slave Narratives." In *A Companion to American Fiction 1780–1865*, edited by Shirley Samuels, 204–15. Malden, MA: Blackwell Publishing, 2009.

Silvester, Harriet. Tapley's *Chronicle of Danvers: 1632–1923*, published in 1923. www.archive.org/details/chroniclesofdanv00tapl.

Sinanan, Kerry. "The Slave Narrative and the Literature of Abolition." In *The Cambridge Companion to the African Slave Narrative*, edited by Audrey Fisch, 61–80. Cambridge: Cambridge University Press, 2007.

Smith, Adam. *The Theory of Moral Sentiments*. 1759. Reprint, London: Excercere Cerebrum Publications, 2014.

Smith, Jan-Melissa. *Atonement and Self-Sacrifice in Nineteenth-Century Narrative*. New York: Cambridge University Press, 2012.

Smith, Stephanie A. *Conceived by Liberty: Maternal Figures and Nineteenth-Century American Literature*. Ithaca, NY: Cornell University Press, 1994.

Smith-Rosenberg, Carrol. "'Domesticating Virtue': Coquettes and Revolutionaries in Young America." In *Literature and the Body: Essays on Populations and Persons*, edited by Elaine Scarry, 160–84. Baltimore: Johns Hopkins University Press, 1988.

Spurlin, Paul Merrill. *Rousseau in America: 1760–1809*. Tuscaloosa: University of Alabama Press, 1969.

Stern, Julia. *This Plight of Feeling: Sympathy and Dissent in the Early American Novel*. Chicago: University of Chicago Press, 1997.

Stewart, Anna. "Revising 'Harriet Jacobs' for 1865." *American Literature* 82.4 (December 2010): 701–24.

Stewart, Matthew. *Nature's God: The Heretical Origins of the American Republic*. New York: W. W. Norton & Company, 2014. Ebook.

Stillman, Robert E. "Hobbes's *Leviathan*: Monsters, Metaphors, and Magic." *ELH* 62 (1995): 791–819.

Stone, Andrea. "Interracial Sexual Abuse and Legal Subjectivity in Antebellum Law and Literature." *American Literature* 81.1 (March 2009): 65–92.

Stowe, Harriet Beecher. *Uncle Tom's Cabin*. 1852. Reprint, New York: W. W. Norton, 1994.

Stupp, Jason. "Slavery and the Theatre of History: Ritual Performance on the Auction Block." *Theatre Journal* 63.1 (March 2011): 61–84.

Tanner, Laura. "Speaking with 'Hands at Our Throats': The Struggle for Artistic Voice in *The Blithedale Romance*." *Studies in American Fiction* 21.1 (1993): 1–19.

Teale, Isaac. "The Sable Venus: An Ode." In *Poems, Written Chiefly in the West-Indies*, edited by Bryan Edwards. 1792. Reprint, Oxford: Gale ECCO Print Edition, 2010.

Tennenhouse, Leonard. *The Importance of Feeling English: American Literature and the British Diaspora, 1750–1850*. Princeton, NJ: Princeton University Press, 2007.

Thomas, Greg. *The Sexual Demon of Colonial Power: Pan-African Embodiment and Erotic Schemes of Empire*. Bloomington: Indiana University Press, 2007.

Tierney-Hynes, Rebecca. "Shaftesbury's Soliloquy: Authorship and the Psychology of Romance." *Eighteenth-Century Studies* 38.4 (September 2005): 605–21.

Tillman, Kacy. "Paper Bodies: Letters and Letter Writing in the Early American Novel." *Tulsa Studies in Women's Literature* 35.1 (Spring 2016): 123–44.

Tompkins, Jane. *Sensational Designs: The Cultural Work of American Fiction: 1790–1860*. New York: Oxford University Press, 1985.

Traister, Bryce. "Libertinism and Authorship in America's Early Republic." *American Literature* 72.1 (2000): 1–30.

Van Engen, Abram. "Eliza's Disposition: Freedom, Pleasure, and Sentimental Fiction." *Early American Literature* 51.2 (2016): 297–331.

Wardrop, Daneen. "'What Tangled Skeins Are the Genealogies of Slavery!': Gothic Families in Harriet Jacobs's *Incidents in the Life of a Slave Girl*." *Literary Griot: International Journal of Black Expressive Cultural Studies* 14.1–2 (2002): 23–43.

Warner, Anne Bradford. "Carnival Laughter: Resistance in *Incidents*." In *Harriet Jacobs and Incidents in the Life of a Slave Girl: New Critical Essays*, edited by Deborah M. Garfield and Rafia Zafar. New York: Cambridge University Press, 1996.

Warner, Michael. "The Mass Public and the Mass Subject." In *American Studies: A Methodological Reader*, edited by Michael A. Elliott and Claudia Stokes, 243–63. New York: New York University Press, 2003.

Wasler, Richard. "Boston's Reception of the First American Novel." *Early American Literature* 17 (1982): 65–74.

Waterman, Bryan. "Elizabeth Whitman's Disappearance and Her 'Disappointment.'" *William and Mary Quarterly* 2 (April 2009): 325–64.

———. "'Heaven Defend Us from Such Fathers': Perez Morton and the Politics of Seduction." In *Atlantic Worlds in the Long Eighteenth Century: Seduction and Sentiment*, edited by Toni Bowers and Tita Chico. New York: Palgrave Macmillan, 2012.

Weinstein, Cindy. *Family, Kinship, and Sympathy in Nineteenth-Century American Literature*. New York: Cambridge University Press, 2004.

Weldon, Roberta. *Hawthorne, Gender, and Death: Christianity and Its Discontents*. New York: Palgrave, 2008.

Weyler, Karen A. *Intricate Relations: Sexual and Economic Desire in American Fiction, 1780–1814*. Iowa City: University of Iowa Press, 2004.

Wilson, Ivy G. *Specters of Democracy: Blackness and the Aesthetics of Politics in the Antebellum United States*. New York: Oxford University Press, 2011. Ebook.

Winkler, Kenneth P. "'All Is Revolution in Us': Personal Identity in Shaftesbury and Hume." *Hume Studies* 26.1 (April 2000): 3–40.

Wolfe, Andrea Powell. "Double-Voicedness in *Incidents in the Life of a Slave Girl*: 'Loud Talking' to a Northern Black Readership." *Atlantic Transcendental Quarterly* 22.3 (Spring 2008): 517–25.

Wollstonecraft, Mary. *A Vindication of the Rights of Woman; The Vindications: The Rights of Men, The Rights of Woman*. Edited by D. L. Macdonald and Kathleen Scherf. 1792. Reprint, Peterbrough, ON: Broadview Press, 1997.

Wood, Gordon S. *The Idea of America: Reflections on the Birth of the United States*. New York: Penguin Books, 2011.

Wood, Marcus. "Celebrating the Middle Passage: Atlantic Slavery, Barbie, and the Birth of the Sable Venus." *Atlantic Studies* 1.2 (October 2004): 123–44.

——. *Slavery, Empathy, and Pornography*. New York: Oxford University Press, 2002.

Yellin, Jean Fagin. *Harriet Jacobs, A Life*. New York: Basic Civitas Books, 2004.

Young, Phillip. "'First American Novel': *The Power of Sympathy*, in Place." *College Literature* 11.2 (Spring 1984): 115–24.

Yousef, Nancy. "Feeling for Philosophy: Shaftesbury and the Limits of Sentimental Certainty." *ELH* 78.3 (Fall 2011): 609–32.

Index

Page numbers in *italics* indicate illustrations. Titles of works mentioned in the text will be found under the author's name, except for ruin narratives, which are also listed by title.

"Able Doctor, The; or, America Swallowing the Bitter Draught" (1774), *217,* 217–19, 257nn26–27
Adams, John: *Correspondence* (1804), 1, 7; on democracy, 1, 77–78, 89, 90, 195–96, 236n36; Jefferson on Hobbes to, 255n4; on sociability, 89, 109; writers on sympathy read by, 43, 225n6
aesthetic work, 11–13, 23–41; the body in, 33–36; on citizenship and nation-forming, 26–28; defining aesthetic, 11, 222n8; democratic feeling and, 78; feeling, rooted in notions of, 24–26; in Foster's *Coquette,* 104, 105, 107, 108–9, 111, 117, 118, 120, 125; genre, ruin narratives as, 2, 18, 23–26; in images of ruined political body, 197–200, 215–16; in incest novels of William Hill Brown, 78, 81, 83, 84, 85, 88–89, 95, 96, 99, 235n27; the individual/individualism in, 32–33; philosophical underpinnings of, 43–44, 50, 55, 59–61, 64, 66, 71–72; rape-as-ruin narratives, 36–41, 156, 157, 159, 163, 166–68, 170, 174, 178, 183, 185, 186, 193, 196; sex, portrayal of, 16–17, 28–29; slave women, rape of, 36–41; in spectacle of ruin and female martyrdom, 127, 130, 133, 140, 145, 150, 153; sympathy, defined and described, 29–32

agency. *See* identity and agency
Althusser, Louis, 58, 100, 162
"American Adam," 32, 226nn11–12
American Enlightenment, 4, 9–10. *See also* Atlantic Enlightenment
American Revolution, 17, 22, 27, 31, 93, 158, 201, 215, 217, 238n3, 253n54
antebellum ruin narratives. *See* ruin narratives
Apthorp, Fanny, and Apthorp/Morton scandal, 83, 232–33n4, 233n10
Armstrong, Nancy, 226n11
Atlantic, crossing. *See* transatlantic imagery
Atlantic Enlightenment, 3, 33, 35, 77, 89, 99, 148, 155, 198, 213, 215, 216

Barnes, Elizabeth, 221n4, 225n7, 234n13, 237n45
Bateman, Benjamin, 121
Baumgarten, Alexander Gottlieb, *Aesthetica* (1750), 222n9
Beard, John Reilly, *The Life of Toussaint L'Ouverture* (1853), 132
Bell, Michael Davitt, 246n37
Bennett, Michael, 190, 252n46
Berlant, Lauren, 35, 227n19, 248n17
Bersani, Leo, 121–22
Bhabha, Homi K., 132

Blackford, Holly, 222n10, 251n43
Blake, William, 228n29
Blithedale Romance, The (Hawthorne, 1852), 19, 126, 142–54; community of Blithedale in, 146–49, 244–45n27, 245nn28–31; death of Zenobia, 149–54, 245n31, 246n32; feminism of Zenobia in, 144, 145, 244nn25–26; ruin and self-sacrifice in, 142–46, 244n24; self-possession, treatment of, 2; sentimentalism in, 145–46; setting of, 130–32, 144; storyline of, 128, 129, 142–43; suicide in, 143, 145, 149–51, 244n23, 244n26; sympathy in, 142, 144, 145, 147–49
Block, Sharon, 246n4
bodies, ruined. *See* embodiment and the ruined body
Bodway, Jack, 230n16
Bontatibus, Donna R., 250n31
Bosse, Abraham, 200–201
Boudreau, Kristin, 234n16, 245n28, 245n31
Bowers, Toni, *Force or Fraud* (2011), 183, 184–85, 247n11, 250n32, 254n65
Branch, Lori, 208, 256n17
Braunschneider, Theresa, 237–38n1, 238n7, 241n28, 241n39
"Broken Heart, The" (Irving, 1819–20), 19, 126, 128, 137–39
Brown, Gillian, 115, 165–66, 240nn22–23, 241n39
Brown, Keith, 255n5
Brown, Kimberly Juanita, 247n11
Brown, William Hill, 10, 76, 232n2. *See also* incest novels of William Hill Brown; *Ira and Isabella; or, The Natural Children* (William Hill Brown); *Power of Sympathy, The; or, The Triumph of Nature* (William Hill Brown)
Brown, William Wells. *See Clotel; or, The President's Daughter* (William Wells Brown)
Burke, Edmund, *Philosophical Enquiry into the Origin of Our Ideas of the Sublime and the Beautiful* (1757), 126

Burleigh, Erica, 222n5, 233n12, 234n21, 237n44
Butler, Judith, 71–72, 75, 162, 163, 180, 187, 226n16, 247n10; *Senses of the Subject* (2015), 18, 71

captivity: intimacy experienced as type of, 1, 8, 9, 93, 99, 117–18; in rape-as-ruin narratives, 160–61, 163, 166–67, 168–73
Cartesian body/mind dualism, 4, 20, 35, 71, 93, 162
Castronovo, Russ, 246n32, 246n34
Chakkalakal, Tess, 243n12
Chandler, James, 233n7
Characteristicks of Men, Manners, Opinions, Times (Shaftesbury, 1711), 18, 41, 44–61; on "Doctrine of Two Persons," 54, 57, 60–61, *206,* 206–8, 256n14, 256n17; on free will, 102; Hobbes's social contract theory, rejecting, 44, 46–52, 206, 255–56n12, 256n14; images of ruined political body in, 198–99, *206,* 206–10, *210;* "An Inquiry Concerning Virtue and Merit" in, 45, 229n6; on nature/natural moral sense, 44–47, 49–52, 76, 77, 88, 229n13; on *sensus communis,* 44, 46, 53, 76, 103, 141, 230n15; sociability in, 45, 46, 51, 52, 63, 71, 75, 103, 230n14; on soliloquy/talking to oneself, 57–61, 69–70, 231n21; "The Story of an Amour" in, 18, 46, 53–57, 59–60, 65, 75
Charles I (king of England), 201, 203
Charles II (king of England), 200, 255n5
Charlotte Temple (Rowson, 1791), 20, 157–58; alternative view of agency/consent in, 15; author and text, relationship between, 186; containment/confinement in, 168–70; omission of rape scene in, 158, 167, 169–70, 172, 173–74, 176, 178, 251n39; self-possession, treatment of, 2; sleeping maiden motif in, 87; transatlantic imagery in, 163, 249n23; treatment of consent-or-resistance trope in, 184, 185. *See also* rape-as-ruin narratives

Child, Lydia Maria: preface to *Incidents in the Life of a Slave Girl*, 158; "The Quadroons" (1842), in *Clotel*, 132

Christianson, Frank, 244n26

citizenship and nation-forming. *See* democracy, citizenship, and nation-forming

Clarissa; or, The History of a Young Lady (Richardson, 1748), 20, 156–57; abridged colonial American edition (1773), 20, 155, 157, 183, 186, 191–96, 253–54n54, 254n56, 254n59; Adams on democracy and, 90, 195–96, 236n36; author and text, relationship between, 186, 190–92, 249–50n28; containment/confinement in, 168, 171–73; failure, rape portrayed as, 164, 166, 178, 249–50n28; identity/agency in, 190–91; *Incidents in the Life of a Slave Girl* and, 168, 174–76, 178, 190–91; marriage contract in, 196, 254n65; omission of rape scene in, 157, 167, 173, 175, 176, 194–95; Paper X in, *171*, 171–73; self-possession, on idealization of, 2–3; sleeping maiden motif in, 87; Stothard's illustrations for, 228n26; transatlantic meta-journey of, 163, 194; treatment of consent-or-resistance trope in, 183–84, 185–86. *See also* rape-as-ruin narratives

Closterman, John, 208–10; portraits by, *209, 210*

Clotel; or, The President's Daughter (William Wells Brown, 1853), 19, 126, 127–28, 130–39, 144, 150–52. *See also* spectacle of ruin and female martyrdom

Cogliano, Francis D., 235–36n28

consent: abandonment of social contract as surrendering of notion of, 65; alternative account provided by ruin narratives, 10–17; coverture law both requiring and removing, 67, 68–69; Foster's *Coquette* and, 124, 241–42n39; lack of conscious decision, in ruin narratives, 16–17, 23–24; race/slavery problematizing, 248n21, 251n42; in rape-as-ruin narratives, 9–10, 155–56, 159–60, 161–62, 165–66, 172, 176, 182–86, 246n4; Rousseau on rape and, 155–56, 165–66, 184, 246n1; in Shaftesbury's "The Story of an Amour," 53–54; as signature of democratic sovereignty, ruin narratives problematizing, 5, 6, 8, 9, 28

contract culture: philosophical questioning of, 63–67; rape-as-ruin narratives critiquing, 161–62; slavery and, 67–68. *See also* consent; marriage contract; social contract

Cooper, Anthony Ashley. *See* Shaftesbury, Anthony Ashley Cooper, Earl of

coquette, the, and coquetry: choice and, 241n28, 241–42n39; defined, 237–38n1; as expression of female power, 69; Rousseau on "silent consent" and, 155–56, 165–66, 184; as stock character in antebellum literature, 103, 121, 239n20; Wollstonecraft on, 239n18

Coquette, The; or, The History of Eliza Wharton (Foster, 1797), 19, 102–25; aesthetic work of, 104, 105, 107, 108–9, 111, 117, 118, 120, 125; alternative view of agency/consent in, 15; based on Elizabeth Whitman story, 82–83, 104; consent and, 124, 241–42n39; contractual culture, critiquing, 69; Danvers, Massachusetts (Salem), setting in, 104–5, 238n3; democracy, citizenship, and nation-forming in, 103, 105, 107, 108–13, 239n15; embodiment/the body in, 104, 105, 107, 118; female friendship in, 120–21, 239–40n21, 241n35; free will in, 102, 107, 115, 116, 238n6; gothic imagery in, 88, 104, 110; grave of Eliza in, 120–23; identity/agency in, 108–13, 115–16, 189, 238n5; incest novels of William Hill Brown compared, 82–83, 101, 102, 103, 104, 107, 108, 112, 115, 117, 124; *Incidents in the Life of a Slave Girl* compared, 189; on love, 124–25; "magic arts" and bewitchment in, 104–5, 106, 108, 114–18, 124; marriage contract in, 105–7, 112–13; public property, identity

Coquette, The (*continued*)
   as, 108–13; self-possession and, 111, 116; sex in, 114–18, 240n24, 240n26; sleeping maiden motif in, 87; sociability in, 103–12, 114, 117–20, 122, 123, 239n20; social death in, 118–20; subjectivity in, 106, 115, 116, 122, 124
coverture law, 67, 68–69, 169–70
Coviello, Peter, 74–75, 235n22; *Tomorrow's Parties* (2013), 16, 223n16
Curran, Sarah, 137–39, 243n17
Cutter, Martha J., 226n11

Dalke, Anne, 233n11
Danvers, Massachusetts (Salem), setting of Foster's *Coquette* in, 104–5, 238n3
Davidson, Cathy, 120, 225n7, 233n7, 239n18, 240n24; *Revolution and the Word* (1986), 79
Dawson, Hannah, 255n10
Declaration of Independence, 18, 61, 77, 78, 88, 90, 94, 110, 135, 236n37
deism, 236n29
democracy, citizenship, and nation-forming, 216–19; Adams on, 1, 77–78, 89, 90, 195–96, 236n36; aesthetic work on, 26–28; community of Blithedale in Hawthorne's *Blithedale Romance*, 146–49; consent as signature of democratic sovereignty, ruin narratives problematizing, 5, 6, 8, 9, 28; *e pluribus unum*, 13–14, 26, 48, 111, 133, 198, 202, 208; as erotic fall into social state, 1–6, 10–11, 14–15, 16–17, 21–22, 74–75; in Foster's *Coquette*, 103, 105, 107, 108–13, 239n15; gender roles in American republic, 231n24; Hume, on self as republic or commonwealth, 61–63; incest novels of William Hill Brown and, 77–78, 89–96, 99, 234n13; spectacle of ruin/female martyrdom and, 130, 134–35, 141, 146–49, 152, 243n20; subjectivity of sexed, ruined body, democratic nature of, 6; sympathy viewed as ground of democratic feeling, 31, 42–43, 78, 225n7. *See also* images of the ruined political body
Den Uyl, Douglas, 229n4, 229n6

didacticism and ruin narratives, 25, 223n15
"Doctrine of Two Persons," 54, 57, 60–61, 206, 206–8, 256n14, 256n17
Douglass, Frederick, 133, 166
Downes, Paul, 13, 88, 229n9, 229nn11–12, 236n37, 255n9
Doyle, Laura, 159, 171, 226n12, 227n21, 246–47n9, 249n23, 249n26, 249–50n28

Eagleton, Terry, 164, 173, 222n8, 247n14, 249n28, 250n29
Edelman, Lee, 35, 227n19
Edwards, Jonathan, 104, 238n2
Edwards, Pierpont, 104
Egan, Ken, Jr., 244n26, 245n31
embodiment and the ruined body: Cartesian body/mind dualism, 4, 20, 35, 71, 93, 162; citizenship, sexed body as portrait of, 27; dead body of female martyr, 149–54; defined and described, 33–36; in Foster's *Coquette*, 104, 105, 107, 118; Hobbes's social contract as civil body, 48, *49;* identity/agency of embodied individual, 71–73, 84–85; in incest novels of William Hill Brown, 83–84, 89; martyred body, 126–27; Möbius strip, Cartesian mind/body dualism replaced by, 226–27n18; nature, body as servant of, 65; philosophical underpinnings of concept of, 42–43; in rape-as-ruin narratives, 161, 162–64; Shaftesbury's conception of, 83; subjectivity of, 34, 35, 42–43; two sexes, "discovery" of, 35–36. *See also* images of the ruined political body
Emmet, Robert, 137–39, 243n17
e pluribus unum, 13–14, 26, 48, 111, 133, 198, 202, 208
Equiano, Olauda, 133
Eve and Garden of Eden, 92, 143–44, 226n12, 249n23

feeling: love, nature of, 124–25; possessing nature of, 108, 117; ruin narratives rooted in notions of, 24–26. *See also* sympathy

feminist theory: Foster's *Coquette* and, 124; on rape-as-ruin narratives, 185, 215, 247n14, 248n15, 248n17, 252n45; Shaftesbury's *Characteristicks* and, 54, 56, 67, 226n18; spectacle of ruin/female martyrdom and, 129, 142
Fiedler, Leslie, 225n10
First Continental Congress, *Journal of the Proceedings of the Congress* (1774), 213, 214, 257n23
Fluck, Winfried, 82, 223n15, 233n6
Foreman, P. Gabrielle, 177, 252n46
Foster, Hannah Webster, 10. See also *Coquette, The; or, The History of Eliza Wharton* (Foster)
Foucault, Michel, 243n19
Franklin, Benjamin: *Observations Concerning the Increase of Mankind* (1751), 211; political cartoons by, 20, 198–99, 211–13, *212, 213*, 256–57n22; works on sympathy read by, 43
free will: in Foster's *The Coquette*, 102, 107, 115, 116, 238n6; in incest novels of William Hill Brown, 91–93, 233n5; philosophical underpinnings of concept of, 50, 55–56, 64, 65, 68; in Richards's *Clarissa*, 182, 189; in ruin narratives generally, 7, 17

Garfield, Deborah M., 253n51
Gates, Henry Louis, Jr., 250n33, 253n46
Gaudet, Katherine, 237n41
gender: American republican gender roles, 231n24; authorship, gendered mode of, 193–94; Danvers, Massachusetts (Salem), setting of Foster's *Coquette* in, 104–5; female friendship in Foster's *Coquette*, 120–21, 123, 239–40n21, 241n35; grave of Eliza in Foster's *Coquette*, 120–23; home/family and, 69, 192, 232n30, 233n12; ideologies of, 36–41, 228n24; the individual and, 32, 225nn9–10, 227n21; inner selves configured as women, in Shaftesbury's *Characteristicks*, 58–59; letters, and

female sexuality, 112, 121, 247n14; marriage contract as proxy for social contract and, 68–69; sexuality of images of the ruined political body, 199–200, 203–4, 212, 213, 214, 218–19; sociability and, 111–12, 120, 239n18, 239n20; two sexes, "discovery" of, 35–36. *See also* coquette, the, and coquetry; marriage contract; rape-as-ruin narratives; spectacle of ruin and female martyrdom
genre: *Incidents in the Life of a Slave Girl*, genre instability in, 187–89, 252–53n46; ruin narrative as, 2, 18, 23–26
George III (king of England), 201
Goldman, Anita, 248n20
Goldsby, Jacqueline, 177
Goldsmith, Oliver, *The Paths of Virtue Delineated* (1773), 254n54
gothic imagery, 88, 104, 110, 152, 163, 223n16, 250n32
Grainger, William, 38–41; engraving by, *39*
Greven, David, 96, 244n24
Gribelin, Simon, frontispiece by, *210*
Grosz, Elizabeth, 35, 215, 226–27n18, 227n20

Hamilton, Cynthia S., 250n32, 251–52n43
Hamilton, Geoff, 226n11
Harris, Jennifer, 241n30
Hartman, Saidiya, 40, 176, 186, 247n11, 251n42
Hawthorne, Nathaniel: on erotic junction of sympathy and democratic feeling, 10; *The Scarlet Letter* (1850), 15, 19, 126, 128–32, 139–42, 143, 144, 150, 152, 153. *See also Blithedale Romance, The* (Hawthorne)
Hemings, Sally, 127, 134
Hobbes, Thomas: on embodiment, 20; Franklin's political cartoons and, 211, 213; gendered nature of the individual for, 225n9; images of ruined political body and, *49*, 198–99, 200–205, *201, 203, 204*, 207, 211, 213, 255n9; on the individual, 32; Jefferson on, 255n4; *Leviathan* (1651),

Index 277

Hobbes, Thomas (*continued*)
30, 46–50, *49*, 60, 155, 200–205, *201, 203, 204,* 229–30n14; as "monster of Malmesbury," 49; Shaftesbury's rejection of ideas of, 44, 46–52, 206, 255–56n12, 256n14; sociability, concept of, versus, 103; on social contract, 47–50, 65; on state of nature, 47, 59, 88, 182, 229n10

Hogarth, William, *The Analysis of Beauty* (1753), 222n9

Hollar, Wenceslaus, 200–201, 202, 255n5

homosociality, 55, 111–12, 120–21, 123, 241n35

Hume, David, 30, 44, 61–63, 72–74, 108, 138, 225n6; *A Treatise of Human Nature* (1739), 42, 61–63, 94

Hutcheson, Sir Francis, 30, 225n6, 229n8; *An Essay on the Nature and Conduct of the Passions and Affections* (1728), 102, 229–30n14, 230n15

identity and agency, 4, 7–11; alternative view offered by ruin narratives, 10–17, 223n16; in citizenship and nation-forming, 26–28; embodied individual and, 71–73, 84–85; in Foster's *Coquette,* 108–13, 115–16, 189, 238n5; Hume, on self as republic or commonwealth, 61–63; in images of the ruined political body, 215; in incest novels of William Hill Brown, 81–82, 84–85, 93; interdependence with community, 12, 13, 66, 226n16; nature as author of agency, Shaftesbury on, 45, 46–47, 49–52; in rape-as-ruin narratives, 182–83, 187–91; in Shaftesbury's "The Story of an Amour," 53–57, 60; soliloquy/talking to oneself, Shaftesbury on, 57–61; spectacle of ruin/female martyrdom and, 127–28, 131; sympathy affecting, 31–32

images of the ruined political body, 20, 197–219; "The Able Doctor; or, America Swallowing the Bitter Draught" (1774), *217,* 217–19, 257nn26–27; as aesthetic work, 197–200, 215–16; First Continental Congress seal, 213, *214,* 257n23; in Franklin's political cartoons, 198–99, 211–13, *212, 213,* 256–57n22; Hobbes's *Leviathan, 49,* 198–99, 200–205, *201, 203, 204,* 207, 211, 213, 255n9; identity/agency in, 215; individual/individualism and, 199, 205–7, 213, 214; "the king's two bodies," 201, 202, 207–8; political bodies as ruined bodies, 197–200; portraits of Shaftesbury, 208–10, *209, 210,* 211, 256n17; self-possession and, 207–8, 214, 215; sexuality of, 199–200, 203–4, *212, 213, 214,* 218–19; sexual ruin narrative and, 215–19; in Shaftesbury's *Characteristicks,* 198–99, *206,* 206–10, *210;* subjectivity and, 196–200, 215; Wicker Man, in Sammes's *Britannia Antiqua Illustrata* (1676), 204–5, *205*

incest novels of William Hill Brown, 77–101; aesthetic work in, 78, 81, 83, 84, 85, 88–89, 95, 96, 99, 235n27; Apthorp/Morton scandal and, 232–33n4, 233n10; *Clotel* compared, 137, 243n12; democracy, citizenship, and nation-forming in, 77–78, 89–96, 99, 234n13; disruption in, 79, 81, 83, 84, 85, 87; embodiment/the body in, 83–84, 89; Foster's *Coquette* compared, 82–83, 101, 102, 103, 104, 107, 108, 112, 115, 117, 124; free will in, 91–93, 233n5; frontispiece drawing of Ophelia in *The Power of Sympathy,* 85–88, *86,* 235nn24–25; heteroglossia of, 78–79, 233nn7–8, 234n20; homophonic names in, 84, 87; identity/agency in, 81–82, 84–85, 93; marginal seduction stories in, 82–85, 234n19, 235n24; nature/natural moral sense in, 77–80, 84, 88–91, 93–97, 98, 100, 234n13; popularity of incest theme, 233nn9–11; self-possession and, 81–82, 92, 99, 235n26, 237n43; sleeping maiden motif in, 84, 87–88, 115; subjectivity in, 81, 83; suicide in, 79, 80, 85, 87, 91, 96, 233n9, 237n41, 249n22; sympathy in, 89, 94–95, 234n13; transatlantic imagery in, 235–36n28; treatment of incest in, 79–80,

96–101, 237n44; treatment of seduction and ruin in, 80–81. See also *Ira and Isabella; or, The Natural Children* (William Hill Brown); *Power of Sympathy, The; or, The Triumph of Nature* (William Hill Brown)
Incidents in the Life of a Slave Girl (Jacobs, 1861), 20, 157, 158–59; alternative view of agency/consent in, 15–16; author/narrator and text, relationship between, 186–91, 251–52n43, 252n45, 252–53n46, 253n48, 253nn50–51; *Clarissa* and, 168, 174–76, 178, 190–91; containment/confinement in, 166–67, 168, 170–71, 181, 248n20, 249n24; Foster's *Coquette* compared, 189; genre instability in, 187–89, 252–53n46; identity/agency in, 187–89, 252n45; omission of rape scene in, 158, 167, 174–79, 246n8, 250nn31–32; pronoun confusion in, 15–16, 232n31; publication history, 158, 251n35; rape of enslaved man by white woman in, 167, 180–81, 250nn31–33; seduction/rape dynamic in, 166–68, 176–78, 186, 248n21; sexual affair with white man in, 175–77, 186, 187–88; substitutions for rape scene in, 179–81; transatlantic imagery in, 163, 170–71; white female readers of, 181, 251n36, 253n48. *See also* rape-as-ruin narratives
individual/individualism: alternative view offered by ruin narratives, 10–17; American Adam, concept of, 32, 226nn11–12; complication of unproblematized reference to, 4–5, 6–9, 21; defined and described, 32–33; embodied individual, identity/agency of, 71–73; images of ruined political body and, 199, 205–7, 213, 214; male gender/white race, identification with, 32, 225nn9–10, 227n21; in rape-as-ruin narratives, 155, 159, 160, 162, 163–64, 165, 167, 172, 174, 176, 182–84, 187, 189, 192–94, 196, 252n45; rape of slave women reinforcing legitimacy/power of, 36–37; spectacle of ruin/female martyrdom and, 126–29, 131, 133, 139–41, 145–48, 150, 152, 154, 243n19; sympathy questioning concept of, 71
intersubjectivity, 18, 27, 29, 51, 70–72, 96, 230n20
Ira and Isabella; or, The Natural Children (William Hill Brown, 1807), 18–19, 77–101; democracy, citizenship, and nation-forming in, 90–91, 92, 94, 95; extramarital sex, language for indicating, 29; heteroglossia of, 79, 233n8; marginal seduction stories in, 82–84; nature/natural moral sense in, 78, 79–80, 89; on novels based on passion, 23; Shakespeare's *Romeo and Juliet* in, 100, 237n47; treatment of incest in, 80, 97, 99–100, 101; treatment of seduction and ruin in, 81. *See also* incest novels of William Hill Brown
Irigaray, Luce, 221n2
Irish rebellion (1803), 128, 137–39
Irving, Washington: "The Broken Heart" (1819–20), 19, 126, 128, 137–39, 243n17; on erotic junction of sympathy and democratic feeling, 11

Jabour, Anya, 231n24
Jacobs, Harriet, 17. See also *Incidents in the Life of a Slave Girl* (Jacobs)
Jamaica Lady, The; or, The Life of Bavia (Pittis, 1720), 37, 227–28n23
Jefferson, Thomas, 43, 109–10, 127, 134, 135, 225n6, 255n4; *Letters* (1814), 42
"JOIN, or DIE" (Franklin cartoon, 1754), 211, 212–13, *213*
Julius Caesar, *The Gallic War*, 204

Kantorowicz, Ernst H., 207–8, 256n16
Kaplan, Cora, 240n26
Kelleher, Paul, 229n13, 230n20
Kerber, Linda, 231n24, 237n42
"king's two bodies, the" 201, 202, 207–8
Knott, Sarah, 223n16, 235n23, 236n38
Korobkin, Laura H., 240nn23–24
Kramnick, Isaac, 239n15

Lacey, Barbara E., 254n54
Laqueur, Thomas, *Making Sex* (1990), 35–36, 227n20
Lawrence, D. H., 225n10
Levander, Caroline F., 226n11
Levine, Robert, 223n16, 244–45n27
Lewis, Jan, 223n11
Lewis, R. W. B., 225n10
libertines and libertinage, 20, 23, 25, 29, 114, 164–65, 172, 195, 238n8, 241n29
Lilley, James D., 226n11
Locke, John, 8, 33, 70, 111, 130, 215, 246n1
Lubey, Kathleen, 248n15
Lukasik, Christopher, 235n25, 240n24

Madison, James, 43
"MAGNA *Britannia; her Colonies* REDUC'D" (Franklin cartoon, 1766), 211–13, *212*
Manning, Susan, 235–36n28
Margolis, Stacy, 245n29
Marmontel, Jean-François, *Bellisario* (1767), 211, 256n19
marriage contract: in *Clarissa*, 196, 254n65; companionate ideal of marriage, 231n24; coverture law and, 67, 68–69, 169–70; fault lines of social contract revealed by, 68; in Foster's *Coquette*, 105–7, 112–13; as proxy for social contract, 8, 12, 27, 63–64, 68–69; ruin narratives as critique of, 8, 12–14, 27, 52, 67–78; Shaftesbury's *Characteristicks* not using, 52; slave-marriage, 136–37, 243n12
Martin, Terence, 233n8
martyrdom. *See* spectacle of ruin and female martyrdom
McIntosh, Hugh, 236n36, 241n33
Meade, William, *Sermons Addressed to Masters and Servants,* 132–33
Middle Passage, evocations of, 38, 58, 163, 170–71, 227n22, 249n26
Milder, Robert, 244n24
Miller, John N., 244n24, 245n30
Mitchell, Angelyn, 252n45

Moody, Jocelyn, 249n24, 251n37
Moore, Geneva Cobb, 177
moral sense philosophy, 34–35, 44, 70, 73, 229n3, 229n8. *See also* Shaftesbury, Anthony Ashley Cooper, Earl of
Morgenstern, Naomi, 248n17
Morton, Perez, 232–33n4

Nagy, Peter, 241n29
Nancy, Jean-Luc, 19, 128, 216; *The Inoperative Community* (1991), 75, 111
Nat Turner rebellion, 128, 137
nature/natural moral sense: the body as servant of, 65; in Declaration of Independence, 77; in deism, 236n29; Hobbes's state of nature, 47, 59, 88, 182, 229n10; Hutcheson on, 230n15; in incest novels of William Hill Brown, 77–80, 84, 88–91, 93–97, 98, 100, 234n13; Rousseau on natural (naked) man versus civilized (clothed) gentleman, 65; Shaftesbury's *Characteristicks* on, 44–47, 49–52, 76, 77, 88, 229n13; in Shaftesbury's "The Story of an Amour," 54–55, 56
Noble, Marianne, 224n3, 244n25

Olsen, Lester C., 256n20, 257n27

Paknadel, Felix, 256n15
partus sequitur ventrem law (1662), 133
Pateman, Carole, 64, 223n12, 225n9, 246n1
Pettengill, Claire C., 239–40n21
philosophical underpinnings, 18, 42–76; of aesthetic work, 43–44, 50, 55, 59–61, 64, 66, 71–72; contract culture, questioning, 63–67; Hume, on self as republic or commonwealth, 61–63; moral sense school, 34–35, 44, 70, 73, 229n3, 229n8; self-possession ideology, resistance to, 67–76; of subjectivity of the body, 42–43; of sympathy, 43–44, 73–76. *See also Characteristicks of Men, Manners, Opinions, Times* (Shaftesbury); nature/natural moral sense

Pierce, Yolanda, 252n46
Pinch, Adela, 236n34
Pittis, William, *The Jamaica Lady; or, The Life of Bavia* (1720), 37, 227–28n23
Plowden, Edmund, 256n16
Pope, Alexander, 111
Power of Sympathy, The; or, The Triumph of Nature (William Hill Brown, 1789), 18–19, 77–101, 219; Apthorp/Morton scandal and, 232–33n4, 233n10; democracy, citizenship, and nation-forming in, 90–96; as first American novel, 6–10, 232n2; footnote on Elizabeth Whitman, 82–83, 88; frontispiece drawing of Ophelia in, 85–88, *86,* 235nn24–25; heteroglossia of, 79, 233n7; marginal seduction/rape stories in, 82–84, 249n22; nature/natural moral sense in, 78, 79–80, 89; philosophical underpinnings of, 76; self-possession in, 237n43; suicide in, 79, 80, 85, 87, 91, 96, 233n9, 237n41; treatment of incest in, 79–80, 96–101, 237n44; treatment of seduction and ruin in, 81. *See also* incest novels of William Hill Brown
Price, Leah Palmer, 191–92
private and public, cultural ambivalence regarding, 21, 131, 224n20
pronoun confusion in ruin narratives, 15–16, 69–70, 161, 186–91, 232n31, 253n48
Putnam, Israel, 238n3

queer theory, 121–23, 227n18
Quendler, Christian, 234n19

race and slavery: in *Clotel,* 19, 126, 127–28, 130–39, 150–52; consent, problematization of, 248n21, 251n42; contract culture and, 67–68; the individual, racialized notion of, 32, 227n21; marriage contract and slave-marriage, 136–37, 243n12; Middle Passage, evocations of, 38, 58, 163, 170–71, 227n22, 249n26; *partus sequitur ventrem* law (1662), 133; rape of slave women, 36–41, *39,* 133–37, 158–59, 227n22, 247n11, 248n21; spectacle of ruin/female martyrdom and, 131, 132–39, 150–52; tragic mulatta motif, 127–28, 133, 134. *See also Incidents in the Life of a Slave Girl* (Jacobs)
rape-as-ruin narratives, 19–20, 155–96; aesthetic work of, 36–41, 156, 157, 159, 163, 166–68, 170, 174, 178, 183, 185, 186, 193, 196; authors and texts, relationship between, 186–94, 249–50n28; consent, treatment of, 9–10, 155–56, 159–60, 161–62, 165–66, 172, 176, 182–86, 246n4; containment/confinement in, 160–61, 163, 166–67, 168–73; embodiment and the body in, 161, 162–64, 180; failure, rape portrayed as, 164–65, 166, 173, 174, 177, 249–50n28; feminist theory on, 185, 215, 247n14, 248n15, 248n17, 252n45; identity/agency in, 182–83, 187–91; individual/individualism in, 155, 159, 160, 162, 163–64, 165, 167, 172, 174, 176, 182–84, 187, 189, 192–94, 196, 252n45; novels typifying, 157–59; omission of rape scene, 157, 158, 161, 162, 167, 169, 172, 173–79, 249n22, 250n29; replacing consent-or-resistance trope with ambivalence, 182–86; Rousseau on rape and consent, 155–56, 165–66, 184, 246n1; seduction/rape dynamic, 165–68, 176–78, 247n11, 248n21; self-possession and, 165–66, 194; sex as defined/described in, 29; Shaftesbury's "The Story of an Amour" as, 53–57; slave women, rape of, 36–41, *39,* 133–37, 158–59, 227n22, 247n11; social contract critiqued in, 160; subjectivity in, 20, 159, 161, 165, 166, 170, 172–74, 176, 181–86, 191, 194, 196, 246–47n9; textual and print irregularities in, 161, 169, *171,* 171–73; theory of rape, 162–64; transatlantic imagery in, 158–59, 163, 164, 170–72, 246–47n9, 249n23; violence of rape in, 155–56, 159–60, 161, 165, 185. *See also Charlotte Temple* (Rowson);

rape-as-ruin narratives (*continued*)
Clarissa; or, The History of a Young Lady (Richardson); *Incidents in the Life of a Slave Girl* (Jacobs)
Reid-Pharr, Robert, 252n46
Revere, Paul, 217
Revolutionary War, 17, 22, 27, 31, 93, 158, 201, 215, 217, 238n3, 253n54
Rice, Grantland S., 239n20
Richardson, Samuel: *Pamela*, abridged versions of, 254n59. See also *Clarissa; or, The History of a Young Lady* (Richardson)
Roberts, Siân Silyn, 152, 221n4, 223n16, 243n19
Rogers, G. A. J., 229n7
Rohy, Valerie, 254n65
Rousseau, Jean-Jacques: *Discourse on the Origin and Basis of Inequality among Men* (1754), 1, 7, 129–30, 231n25; *Emile* (1762), 165, 231n26; *Emile and Sophie; or, The Solitaries* (1780), 231n26; gendered nature of the individual for, 225n9; on the individual, 32; *Julie; or, The New Heloise* (1761), 155–56, 231n26; on love, 124; on rape and consent, 155–56, 165–66, 184, 246n1; on self-possession, 66, 68, 129–30; *Of the Social Contract* (1762), 30, 65–66, 155; on sympathy and surrender, 73–74, 93
Rowson, Susanna. See *Charlotte Temple* (Rowson)
ruin narratives, 1–22, 216–19; as alternative account of identity, sympathy, and consent, 10–17; binaries, generative energy in space between, 21; defined, 23–24; democracy as sexual fall into social state, 1–6, 10–11, 14–15, 16–17, 21–22; as genre, 2, 18, 23–26; images of the ruined political body and sexual ruin narratives, 215–19; intimacy experienced as type of captivity in, 1, 8, 9, 93, 99; non-didactic nature of, 25, 223n15; pronoun confusion in, 15–16, 69–70, 161, 186–91, 232n31, 253n48; woman's sexed body as subject of, 5. *See also* aesthetic work; embodiment and the ruined body; identity and agency; individual/individualism; philosophical underpinnings; rape-as-ruin narratives; self-possession; spectacle of ruin and female martyrdom; sympathy; *and specific authors and texts by name/title*

Rush, Benjamin, 43, 110–13, 140; "Of the Mode of Education Proper in a Republic" (1798), 110
Russell, Emily, 254n1, 255n7
Rust, Marion, 184, 251n39

Salomon, Gayle, 227n18
Sammes, Aylett, *Britannia Antiqua Illustrata* (1676), 204–5, 205
Samuels, Shirley, 225n10, 257n26
Sanborn, Geoffrey, 242n2, 242n8
Sand, George, 146
Santa Marina, Xiomara, 248n21
Scarlet Letter, The (Hawthorne, 1850), 15, 19, 126, 128–32, 139–42, 143, 144, 150, 152, 153. *See also* spectacle of ruin and female martyrdom
Schweitzer, Ivy, 241n35
Scottish Enlightenment, 44, 229n3
self-possession: Foster's *Coquette* and, 111, 116; images of the ruined political body and, 207–8, 214, 215; incest novels of William Hill Brown and, 81–82, 92, 99, 235n26, 237n43; lack of, in ruin narratives, 2–3, 23–24, 67–76; rape-as-ruin narratives and, 165–66, 194; Shaftesbury's *Characteristicks* rejecting idea of, 46; social contract theory and, 65; spectacle of ruin/female martyrdom and, 129–32; surrender, social/sexual, trope of, 66–67
sensationalism and sensational novels, 18, 24–26, 238n8
sensus communis, Shaftesbury on, 44, 46, 53, 76, 103, 141, 230n15
sentimentalism and sentimental novels, 18, 24–26, 130, 145–46, 158, 224n3, 244nn24–26, 244–45n27, 245n29, 245n31

sex: as alternative model for social relations, 65; in Foster's *Coquette*, 114–18, 240n24, 240n26; portrayal of, in ruin narrative novels, 16–17, 28–29; social state, democracy as erotic fall into, 1–6, 10–11, 14–15, 16–17, 21–22, 74–75
sexuality of images of the ruined political body, 199–200, 203–4, 212, 213, 214, 218–19
Shaffer, Julia, 232n30
Shaftesbury, Anthony Ashley Cooper, Earl of: on aesthetics, 222n9; on embodiment, 83; on "inward eye," 94; as key figure for Enlightenment philosophers, 44; on love and lovers, 124; portraits of, 208–10, *209, 210*, 211, 256n17; on ruin as operation of sympathy, 17; on sociability, 109; on sympathy, 30, 140–41, 147. See also *Characteristicks of Men, Manners, Opinions, Times* (Shaftesbury)
Shakespeare, William, *Romeo and Juliet*, 100, 237n47
Shamir, Milette, 224n20
Sinanan, Kerry, 252n46
Sketch Book of Geoffrey Crayon, Gent., The (Irving, 1819–20). See "Broken Heart, The" (Irving)
slavery. See captivity; race and slavery
sleeping maiden motif, 84, 87–88, 115
Smith, Adam, 30, 44, 74, 89, 151, 225n6; *The Theory of Moral Sentiments* (1759), 72–73
Smith, Jan-Melissa, 243n20
Smith, Stephanie A., 189, 252–53n46, 253n49
Smith-Rosenberg, Carroll, 238n5, 240n24
sociability: concept of, 19, 45, 46, 51, 52, 63, 71, 75, 230n14; in Foster's *Coquette*, 103–12, 114, 117–20, 122, 123, 239n20; gender and, 111–12, 120, 239n18, 239n20; incest novels of William Hill Brown and, 89
social contract: consent, abandonment of social contract as surrendering of, 65; marriage contract as proxy for, 8, 12, 27, 63–64, 68–69; philosophical questioning of culture of, 63–67; rape-as-ruin narratives critiquing, 160; Shaftesbury's *Characteristicks* rejecting, 44, 46–52; sympathy and, 30–31, 68
social state, democracy as erotic fall into, 1–6, 10–11, 14–15, 16–17, 21–22, 74–75
soliloquy/talking to oneself, 57–61, 69–70, 231n21
spectacle of ruin and female martyrdom, 19, 126–54; aesthetic work of, 127, 130, 133, 140, 145, 150, 153; in *Clotel*, 19, 126, 127–28, 130–39, 144, 150–52; death/the dead body, 149–54; democracy, citizenship, and nation-forming, 130, 134–35, 141, 146–49, 152, 243n20; in Hawthorne's *Scarlet Letter*, 15, 19, 126, 128–32, 139–42, 143, 144, 150, 152, 153; identity/agency and, 127–28, 131; individual/individualism and, 126–29, 131, 133, 139–41, 145–48, 150, 152, 154, 243n19; Irving's "The Broken Heart" and *Clotel*, 19, 126, 128, 137–39, 243n17; multiple source materials for *Clotel*, significance of, 132–33, 136, 137, 242n2, 242n8; novels and stories evincing, 126, 127–29; public figures, male lovers as, 129; reclamation of heroine's virtue through, 128, 134, 140; self-possession and, 129–32; settings of, 130–32, 135–36, 139, 152; sex as defined/described in, 29; subversive nature of, 129; sympathy and, 140–42, 144, 145, 147–48, 151. See also *Blithedale Romance, The* (Hawthorne)
Stedman, John Gabriel, *Narrative of a Five Years Expedition against the Revolted Negroes of Surinam* (1790), 37
Stern, Julia, 236n39
Stewart, Anna, 251n35
Stewart, Matthew, 236n29
Stone, Andrea, 248n21
"Story of an Amour, The" in Shaftesbury's *Characteristicks* (1711), 18, 46, 53–57, 59–60, 65, 75
Stothard, Thomas: Richardson's *Clarissa*, illustrations for, 228n26; *The Voyage of the Sable Venus, from Angola to the West Indies* (1794), 38–41, *39*, 228n24, 228n29

Stowe, Harriet Beecher, 89, 145; *Uncle Tom's Cabin* (1852), 252n46
subjectivity, 8; coverture law and, 67; democratic subjectivity of sexed, ruined body, 6; of embodiment, 34, 35, 42–43; in Foster's *Coquette,* 106, 115, 116, 122, 124; images of the ruined political body and, 196–200, 215; in incest novels of William Hill Brown, 81, 83; intersubjectivity, 18, 27, 29, 51, 70–72, 96, 230n20; problematization in ruin narratives, 4; in rape-as-ruin narratives, 20, 159, 161, 165, 166, 170, 172–74, 176, 181–86, 191, 194, 196, 246–47n9; slave women, rape of, 36, 37, 227n22; spectacle of ruin/female martyrdom and, 133
suicide: in incest novels of William Hill Brown, 79, 80, 85, 87, 91, 96, 233n9, 237n41, 249n22; in post-revolutionary literature generally, 19, 25, 197, 233n9, 237n41; social suicide, in Foster's *Coquette,* 118; spectacle of ruin/female martyrdom and, 129, 136, 143, 145, 149–51, 244n23, 244n26; of Zenobia, in *Blithedale Romance,* 143, 145, 149–51, 244n23, 244n26
surrender, social/sexual, trope of, 66–67, 73–76
sympathy: contract culture undermined by, 67–76; defined and described, 29–32, 224n1; democratic feeling, as ground of, 31, 42–43, 78, 225n7; in Hawthorne's *Blithedale Romance,* 142, 144, 145, 147–49; identity and agency affected by, 31–32; importance of concept of, 3–4; in incest novels of William Hill Brown, 89, 94–95, 234n13; individual, questioning concept of, 71; philosophical underpinnings of, 43–44, 73–76; ruin narratives offering alternative view of, 10–17; social contract and, 30–31, 68; social/sexual surrender and, 67–76; spectacle of ruin/female martyrdom and, 140–42, 144, 145, 147–48, 151

talking to oneself/soliloquy, 57–61, 69–70, 231n21

Tanner, Laura, 244n26
Teale, Isaac, "The Sable Venus: An Ode" (1765), 37, 38, 228n24, 228n27
Tennenhouse, Leonard, *The Importance of Feeling English,* 192–94, 222–23n10, 246nn6–7, 253n54, 254n59
Thoreau, Henry David, 248n20
Tierney-Hynes, Rebecca, 231n21
Tocqueville, Alexis de, 32
Tompkins, Jane, 11, 222n7, 224n2
tragic mulatta motif, 127–28, 133, 134
Traister, Bryce, 238n8
transatlantic imagery: in incest novels of William Hill Brown, 235–36n28; Middle Passage, evocations of, 38, 58, 163, 170–71, 227n22, 249n26; in rape-as-ruin narratives, 158–59, 163, 164, 170–72, 246–47n9, 249n23

Van Engen, Abram, 238n6

Walser, Richard, 233nn9–10
Wardrop, Daneen, 253n48
Warner, Anne Bradford, 252n45, 253n50
Warner, Susan, 145
Washington, George, 243n17
Weldon, Roberta, 245n31
Weyler, Karen A., 235n26, 237n43
Whitman, Elizabeth, 82–83, 88, 104, 119, 120, 235n24
Whitman, Walt, *Leaves of Grass* (1855), 197
Wicker Man, 204–5, 205
Wilson, Ivy G., 152, 242n7
Winkler, Kenneth P., 231n21
Wolfe, Andrea Powell, 251n36
Wollstonecraft, Mary, *A Vindication of the Rights of Women* (1792), 124, 239n18, 240n26
Wood, Gordon S., 109
Wood, Marcus, 37–38, 228n24, 228n29

Yellin, Jean Fagin, 253n51
Young, Philip, 234n16
Yousef, Nancy, 229n10, 230n18

CPSIA information can be obtained
at www.ICGtesting.com
Printed in the USA
LVHW041808011119
636089LV00001B/84/P

9 780813 943398